CIVIL SOCIETY IN THE INFORMATION AGE

Civil Society in the Information Age

Edited by

PETER I. HAJNAL
University of Toronto

LONDON AND NEW YORK

First published 2002 by Ashgate Publishing

Reissued 2018 by Routledge
2 Park Square, Milton Park, Abingdon, Oxon OX14 4RN
711 Third Avenue, New York, NY 10017, USA

Routledge is an imprint of the Taylor & Francis Group, an informa business

Copyright © Peter I. Hajnal 2002

The Editor hereby asserts his moral right to be identified as the editor of the Work in accordance with the Copyright, Designs and Patents Act, 1988.

All rights reserved. No part of this book may be reprinted or reproduced or utilised in any form or by any electronic, mechanical, or other means, now known or hereafter invented, including photocopying and recording, or in any information storage or retrieval system, without permission in writing from the publishers.

Notice:
Product or corporate names may be trademarks or registered trademarks, and are used only for identification and explanation without intent to infringe.

Publisher's Note
The publisher has gone to great lengths to ensure the quality of this reprint but points out that some imperfections in the original copies may be apparent.

Disclaimer
The publisher has made every effort to trace copyright holders and welcomes correspondence from those they have been unable to contact.

A Library of Congress record exists under LC control number: 2002074453

ISBN 13: 978-1-138-73423-4 (hbk)
ISBN 13: 978-1-138-73420-3 (pbk)
ISBN 13: 978-1-315-18692-4 (ebk)

Contents

List of Tables	*vii*
List of Contributors	*viii*
Acknowledgments	*x*
List of Abbreviations and Acronyms	*xi*

1 Introduction
   Peter I. Hajnal   1

PART I: NGOS AND CIVIL SOCIETY COALITIONS

2 Information and Communication Technologies and Human
   Rights Advocacy: The Case of Amnesty International   19
   Joanne Lebert

3 Scientists and Missile Defence: Organizing Against a
   Dangerous Plan   37
   John Spykerman

4 Oxfam International   57
   Peter I. Hajnal

5 The Working Life of Southern NGOs: Juggling the Promise
   of Information and Communications Technologies and the
   Perils of Relationships with International NGOs   67
   Juris Dilevko

6 Essential Partners: Landmines-Related NGOs and
   Information Technologies   95
   Kenneth R. Rutherford

7 The Power of Global Activist Networks: The Campaign
   for an International Criminal Court   109
   William R. Pace and Rik Panganiban

8 AIDS, Médecins Sans Frontières, and Access to Essential Medicines   127
   James Orbinski

PART II: CIVIL SOCIETY IN RELATIONSHIP WITH INTERGOVERNMENTAL INSTITUTIONS

9 The United Nations and Civil Society   141
   Barbara Adams

10 Thoughts on Religious NGOs at the UN: A Component of Global Civil Society   155
   Benjamin Rivlin

11 Expanding the Trade Debate: The Role of Information in WTO and Civil Society Interaction   175
   Heidi K. Ullrich

12 Citizen Involvement in Canadian Foreign Policy: The Summit of the Americas Experience, Québec City, April 2001   201
   Marc Lortie and Sylvie Bédard

13 Civil Society Encounters the G7/G8   215
   Peter I. Hajnal

14 Conclusion   243
   Peter I. Hajnal

Electronic Sources   249
   Peter I. Hajnal and Gillian R. Clinton

Bibliography   257
   Peter I. Hajnal and Gillian R. Clinton

Index   279

List of Tables

Table 5.1	ICT Infrastructure and Annual Spending on ICT in 2000-2001 by Southern NGOs	72
Table 5.2	Views on the Social and Cultural Consequences of ICT Use	74
Table 5.3	Effect of Frequency of Contact Between Southern NGOs and International NGOs on the Type of Relationship Between Southern NGOs and International NGOs	83
Table 5.4	Effect of Southern NGO Size As Measured by "Paid Workers" on the Type of Relationship Between Southern NGOs and International NGOs	84
Table 5.5	Overall Characterization of International NGOs by Southern NGOs and the Types of Help They Received from International NGOs	89

List of Contributors

Barbara Adams works for the United Nations Non-Governmental Liaison Service. She trained as an economist. Before joining the UN, she was Associate Director of the Quaker United Nations Office from 1981-1988 working on issues of economic and social justice, women, peace and human rights. She has also served as a consultant to UNICEF, and on the board of directors for the Canadian Council for International Cooperation (CCIC). Her career includes development work in Latin America. She has authored and co-authored many articles, reports and book chapters on the United Nations, was keynote speaker and resource person at numerous UN, NGO and academic events, and has attended many UN world conferences.

Sylvie Bédard joined the Canadian foreign service in 1995. She was coordinator for liaison with civil society for the Summit of the Americas. She is currently Deputy Director of the Inter-American Affairs Division of the Department of Foreign Affairs and International Trade.

Juris Dilevko teaches at the Faculty of Information Studies, University of Toronto, Canada.

Peter I. Hajnal is Research Associate, Munk Centre for International Studies, University of Toronto and Adjunct Professor, Faculty of Information Studies, University of Toronto. He is Counsellor of the G8 Research Group and co-investigator of the EnviReform (Strengthening Canada's Environmental Community through International Regime Reform: Exploring Social Cohesion in a Globalizing Era) project. His most recent books are *The G7/G8 System: Evolution, Role and Documentation* (1999) and (ed.) *International Information: Documents, Publications and Electronic Information of International Organizations*, 2nd ed., Vol. 2 (2001).

Joanne Lebert is an Urgent Action Coordinator for Amnesty International's Canadian (English-speaking) Section, based in Toronto. She is also a doctoral student of social anthropology at York University, Toronto. Her research interests include human rights discourse, conflict, migration and identity negotiation as these pertain to Namibia and Angola.

Marc Lortie joined the Canadian foreign service in 1971. He was appointed Prime Minister Jean Chrétien's Personal Representative for the Summit of the Americas in January 2000 and coordinated the overall organization and substance of the event. He is currently Assistant Deputy Minister for the Americas at the Department of Foreign Affairs and International Trade.

List of Contributors ix

James Orbinski is a physician and past president of Médecins Sans Frontières International Council. He is currently a senior fellow at the Munk Center for International Studies at the University of Toronto. His career and current academic work have focused on humanitarianism and global health issues.

William R. Pace is the convenor of the NGO Coalition for an International Criminal Court and the Executive Director of the World Federalist Movement.

Rik Panganiban is the former technical and administrative coordinator for the Coalition for an International Criminal Court and currently serves as the membership director of the World Federalist Movement.

Benjamin Rivlin is Director Emeritus of the Ralph Bunche Institute for International Studies of the City University of New York's Graduate Center where he is also Professor Emeritus of Political Science. His publications include *Ralph Bunche, The Man and His Times* (1990), *The Challenging Role of the UN Secretary-General* (ed. with Leon Gordenker, 1993), and *The Contemporary Middle East: Tradition and Innovation* (ed. with Joseph Szyliowicz, 1965). He is a founding member of the Academic Council on the United Nations.

Kenneth R. Rutherford is Assistant Professor of Political Science and Landmine Studies Coordinator at Southwest Missouri State University and Co-Founder of the Landmine Survivors Network. He was injured by a landmine in 1993 while conducting humanitarian relief work in Somalia.

John Spykerman was the Outreach Coordinator for UCS's Global Security Program. Currently he is the program coordinator for the Program on General Disarmament at the University of Maryland. He received his MA in international security policy from George Washington University.

Heidi K. Ullrich has recently completed her doctorate at the London School of Economics and Political Science, where she has also lectured. She has previously lectured at the University of Southampton and served as a research assistant to the US Mission to the World Trade Organization and to a member of the European Parliament. She is the author of "Stimulating Trade Liberalization after Seattle: G7/8 Leadership in Global Governance" in *New Directions in Global Economic Governance: Managing Globalisation in the Twenty-First Century*, edited by John Kirton and George von Furstenberg (Ashgate, 2001). Her writings have appeared in journals such as *Journal of European Public Policy* and *G8 Governance*.

Acknowledgments

Many people and several organizations have encouraged and helped me in preparing this book. I would like to express my particular appreciation to the Munk Centre for International Studies, University of Toronto, for granting me office space and many other forms of support, and offer special thanks to my colleagues Dr Sylvia Ostry, Dr James Orbinski, and Professors Louis Pauly and John Kirton for their support and insights, readily shared.

My gratitude goes to all the contributors for enriching this volume and for taking a keen interest in the entire book beyond their own chapters. My special thanks go to Professor Benjamin Rivlin for hosting a most interesting and productive roundtable discussion with the contributors, held at his institution, the Graduate Center of the City University of New York, on 20 April 2001. He and Dr Heidi Ullrich deserve additional acknowledgement for their analysis of the nature of civil society.

I thank the University of Toronto Centre for International Studies' project on 'Strengthening Canada's Environmental Community through International Regime Reform' (EnviReform), for allowing this book to appear within its framework. For her very able and dedicated research and editorial assistance, and for her research into the concept of information, I wish to thank Gillian Clinton. For equally conscientious editorial assistance – and for her patience throughout this project – I express my gratitude to my wife Edna Hajnal. I am grateful to Madeline Koch for her many helpful suggestions. Last but certainly not least, I thank Kirstin Howgate, Sarah Horsley and their other colleagues at Ashgate for encouraging and helping along the preparation of the manuscript for publication. All of them contributed significantly to making this a better book. Any omissions or inaccuracies are my sole responsibility.

Peter I. Hajnal
Toronto, February 2002

List of Abbreviations and Acronyms

ABM	Anti-Ballistic Missile (from the 1972 Treaty)
AI	Amnesty International
APEC	Asia-Pacific Economic Co-operation
APS	American Physical Society
ArmsNet	Union of Concerned Scientists' e-mail network
ARV	Anti-retroviral
ATTAC	Association pour une Taxation des Transactions financières pour l'Aide aux Citoyens, (or Association for the Taxation of financial Transactions and the Aid of Citizens)
BINGO	Business (profit-oriented) international nongovernmental organization
BMD	Ballistic Missile Defense System
BMDO	Ballistic Missile Defense Organization
CAA	Community Aid Abroad (Oxfam Australia)
CALDH	Centro de Acción Legal en Derechos Humanos
CBC	Canadian Broadcasting Corporation
CCFPD	Canadian Centre for Foreign Policy Development
CCIC	Canadian Council for International Cooperation
CCW	Convention on Conventional Weapons
CCWG	Computer Communications Working Group (AI)
CFHRI	Catholic Family and Human Rights Institute
CICC	Coalition for an International Criminal Court
CIJ	Coalition for International Justice
CPT	Consumer Project on Technology
CRNGO	Committee of Religious NGOs at the United Nations
CSD	Commission on Sustainable Development
CSO	Civil Society Organization
CTBT	Comprehensive Test Ban Treaty
DESA	Department of Economic and Social Affairs (UN)
DFAIT	Department of Foreign Affairs and International Trade (Canada)
DONGO	Donor-organized NGO
DOT&E	Director of Operational Testing and Evaluation (Pentagon, US)
DPI	Department of Public Information (UN)
DSO	Dispute Settlement Procedure
ECA	Economic Commission for Africa (UN)
ECA	Export Credit Agencies
ECOSOC	Economic and Social Council (UN)
E-mail	Electronic mail
EU	European Union

xii *Civil Society in the Information Age*

FAO	Food and Agriculture Organization of the United Nations
FAS	Federation of American Scientists
FOCAL	Fondation canadienne pour les Amériques (Canadian Foundation for the Americas)
FTAA	Free Trade Area of the Americas
ftp	File transfer protocol
G7/G8	Group of Seven/Group of Eight industrialized countries (Great Britain, France, Italy, Germany, Japan, Canada, United States plus Russia)
GA	General Assembly (UN)
GATT	General Agreement on Tariffs and Trade
GONGO	Government-sponsored NGO; Government-organized NGO
GRO	Grassroots organization
GSF	Genoa Social Forum
GSM	Global social movements
GTW	Public Citizen's Global Trade Watch
Habitat II	United Nations Conference on Human Settlements
HAI	Health Action International
HIPC	Heavily Indebted Poor Countries
HIV/AIDS	Human Immunodeficiency Virus/Acquired Immune Deficiency Syndrome
HTML	Hypertext markup language
ICBL	International Campaign to Ban Landmines
ICBM	Intercontinental Ballistic Missile
ICC	International Chamber of Commerce
ICC	International Criminal Court
ICPD	International Conference on Population and Development
ICRC	International Committee of the Red Cross
ICT(s)	Information and communication technology (technologies); Information/communication technology
ICTSD	International Centre for Trade and Sustainable Development
IGC	Institute for Global Communications
IGO	International governmental organization; Intergovernmental organization
IISD	International Institute of Sustainable Development
IMF	International Monetary Fund
INGO	International nongovernmental organization
IPS	Inter-Press Service
IS	International Secretariat (AI)
ISP	Internet Service Provider
IT	Information Technology
JMI	Jubilee Movement International for Economic and Social Justice
LEAD	Leadership for Environment and Development
LGBT	Lesbian, Gay, Bisexual and Transgender

List of Abbreviations and Acronyms xiii

Like Minded Group	Loose group of government delegations generally supporting more progressive views toward the International Criminal Court
LSN	Landmine Survivors Network
MAD	Mutually assured destruction
MAG	Mines Advisory Group
MAI	Multilateral Agreement on Investment
MBT	Mine Ban Treaty
MDB	Multilateral Development Banks
MEI	Multilateral economic institutions
MIT	Massachusetts Institute of Technology
MNC	Multinational corporations
MP	Member of Parliament (Canada)
MSF	Médecins Sans Frontières
NAFTA	North American Free Trade Agreement
NAM	Non-Aligned Movement
NGLS	United Nations Non-Governmental Liaison Service
NGO	Nongovernmental organization
NMD	National Missile Defense (Clinton administration, US)
OAS	Organization of American States
ODS	Optical Disk System (UN)
OECD	Organisation for Economic Co-operation and Development
OI	Oxfam International
OSI	Open Society Institute
Oxfam GB	Oxfam Great Britain
PC	Personal computer
PDF	Portable document format
PGA	Peoples' Global Action
PINGO	Public-interest-oriented nongovernmental organization
PrepCom	Preparatory Commission for the International Criminal Court (UN)
QUANGO	Quasi-nongovernmental organization
R&D	Research and Development
RDI	Réseau de l'information (Radio Canada)
RQIC	Réseau québécois sur l'intégration continentale
SAFE	Safeguarding America for Everyone organization
SCFAIT	Standing Committee on Foreign Affairs and International Trade (Canada)
SDI	Strategic Defense Initiative aka Star Wars (Reagan administration, US)
SIDS	Global Conference on Small Island Developing States
SIRG	Summit Implementation Review Group
SSI	Sound Science Initiative
TAC	Treatment Access Campaign
TMD	Theatre Missile Defenses (for areas smaller than a nation)
TNC	Transnational corporation

TOES	The Other Economic Summit (also known as: the people's summit; the alternative summit; contre-sommet)
TRIPS	Trade-related Aspects of Intellectual Property Rights
TWN	Third World Network
UA	Urgent Action (AI)
UAN	Urgent Action Network (AI)
UCS	Union of Concerned Scientists
UK	United Kingdom
UN	United Nations
UNAIDS	Joint United Nations Programme on HIV/AIDS
UNCED	United Nations Conference on Environment and Development
UNDP	United Nations Development Programme
UNGA	United Nations General Assembly
UNHCR	United Nations High Commissioner for Refugees
UNICEF	United Nations International Children's Fund
UNOHCR	United Nations Office for the Coordination of Humanitarian Assistance
US	United States
USCBL	United States Campaign to Ban Landmines
VVAF	Vietnam Veterans of American Foundation
WCC	World Council of Churches
WCRP	World Conference on Religion and Peace
WDM	World Development Movement
WFM	World Federalist Movement
WFP	World Food Programme
WHO	World Health Organization
WSSD	World Summit for Social Development
WTO	World Trade Organization
WWF	World Wide Fund for Nature, formerly World Wildlife Fund

Chapter 1

Introduction

Peter I. Hajnal[*]

Background and Definitions

Civil society has been around for hundreds of years, ever since voluntary associations, mutual-help groups and interest groups were first formed.[1] But since World War II, and especially with the end of the cold war following the disintegration of repressive regimes in the Soviet Union, eastern and central Europe, Latin America and in parts of Africa, nongovernmental organizations (NGOs) have proliferated at an unprecedented rate. Thousands of nongovernmental actors concerned with public issues and policy range from voluntary associations, trade unions, religious groups, human rights advocates, environmental groups, economic development proponents, the women's movement, social reformers, and various kinds of anti-globalization protesters.

The vast majority of NGOs operate within countries throughout the world, focusing on domestic interests. Those groups that address global issues are often called 'international nongovernmental organizations' [INGOs]; they constitute the core of 'international civil society' or 'transnational civil society' or 'global civil society'. But the distinction between 'civil society' and 'international civil society' is often unclear: are human rights, development, population, and environment domestic or global matters? While INGOs form the core of international civil society, they are not its exclusive players. Depending on the issue and the circumstances, local NGOs work with INGOs and form a coalition of forces seeking to influence the international community, thus constituting an international civil society network specific to the subject at hand. Benjamin Rivlin, in his chapter on religious NGOs at the United Nations (UN), develops this theme further, and discusses the 'new diplomacy', a topic also touched upon below.

The 2001/2002 edition of the *Yearbook of International Organizations*, a directory that lists international organizations but generally excludes local and national organizations, counts 6,357 'conventional' international NGOs and 28,775 international NGOs of all types (Union of International Associations 2001/2002, 2598). These organizations have extended their concerns and activities into every area of human endeavour ranging from development, trade, labour conditions,

---

[*] I gratefully acknowledge the insights into the nature of civil society kindly shared by Professor Benjamin Rivlin, Dr Sylvia Ostry, Dr James Orbinski and Dr Heidi K. Ullrich, and I wish to thank Gillian Clinton for her research into the concept of information.

human rights, humanitarian action, the impact of globalization, and the environment to peace and security, scientific and technical co-operation, and ethical and moral life. Their diversity, role and influence have seen a corresponding increase. Thanks to their efficient use of information and communications technology (ICT) and of the news media, civil society movements and NGOs are now widely recognized, studied and reported on, yet insufficiently understood in all their complexity.

It is this very complexity that calls for conceptual clarity (or at least a striving for clarity). This is a difficult task; civil society has been described as a "conceptual portmanteau which indiscriminately lumps together everything from households and voluntary associations to the economic system of capitalism" and which "confuses and disguises as much as it reveals" (Wood 1991, 65).

Despite significant growth in the scholarly literature about NGOs and civil society, there is no widely agreed single definition of these entities. Suffice it here to highlight attempts to move that process forward.

The *Yearbook of International Organizations* relies on a rather technical and legalistic definition of NGOs first formulated and later updated by the UN Economic and Social Council (ECOSOC). ECOSOC resolution 288 (X) of 27 February 1950 states that "[a]ny international organization which is not established by intergovernmental agreement shall be considered as a non-governmental organization". (UN 1950) In resolution 1296 (XLIV) of 25 June 1968 ECOSOC adds that NGOs "includ[e] organizations which accept members designated by government authorities, provided that such membership does not interfere with the free expression of views of the organizations" (UN 1968). (As a practical matter, the *Yearbook* accepts as NGOs all organizations that declare themselves to be nongovernmental.) Anthony Judge notes that "[a] clear and unambiguous theoretically acceptable definition of international NGOs remains to be formulated" (Judge, Section 2.2).

A number of useful formulations have, however, appeared. Leon Gordenker and Thomas G. Weiss state that NGOs and civil society organizations "include officials, independent sector, volunteer sector, civic society, grassroots organizations, private voluntary organizations, transnational social movement organizations, grassroots social change organizations and non-state actors. ... [T]hese organizations consist of durable, bounded, voluntary relationships among individuals to produce a particular product, using specific techniques" (Gordenker and Weiss 1996, 18).

Addressing a broader array of concepts, policies and strategies involving global public goods, Inge Kaul, Isabelle Grunberg and Marc A. Stern explore discrepancies in jurisdictions, in participation and in incentives, and conclude that the structure of international co-operation must be reformed to embrace all actors (government, business and civil society) in all countries.[2] And Robert O'Brien, Anne Marie Goetz, Jan Aart Scholte and Marc Williams argue that "there is a transformation in the nature of global economic governance as a result of the MEI [multilateral economic institutions]-GSM [global social movements] encounter" (O'Brien et al 2000, 3).

Categorizing the universe of non-state actors, Bob Reinalda distinguishes three major groups: public-interest-oriented nongovernmental (non-profit) organizations (PINGOs), business (profit-oriented) international nongovernmental organizations (BINGOs), and public intergovernmental organizations (IGOs). He then subdivides PINGOs into:

- transnational actors, some with ingenious acronyms: 'proper' NGOs, government-organized NGOs (GONGOs), quasi nongovernmental organizations (QUANGOs), donor-organized NGOs (DONGOs), grassroots organizations (GROs), and citizen networks; and
- international NGOs or INGOs.

BINGOs, in Reinalda's scheme, can also be:

- transnational actors: transnational corporations (TNCs); and criminal organizations; or
- multinational corporations (MNCs) (Reinalda 2001).

In 1995, the Commission on Global Governance explained the increasing importance of civil society in general and NGOs in particular. These groups "can offer knowledge, skills, enthusiasm, a non-bureaucratic approach, and grassroots perspectives. ... Many ... also raise significant sums for development and humanitarian work, in which their dedication, administrative efficiency, and flexibility are valuable additional assets" (Commission on Global Governance 1995, 33). A more recent paper issued by the Commission notes that 'civil society' is a broader concept than 'NGOs' and adds that "[t]he core of civil society includes those citizen-based associations devoted to advancing any of a wide range of civic, cultural, humanitarian, technical, educational or social purposes, whether at a local, national, regional or global level. These groups are the embodiment of citizen activism, from which they draw their vitality and their legitimacy" (Commission on Global Governance 1999, 22-23).

John W. Foster and his collaborators tackled the concept as they prepared for the World Civil Society Conference held in Montreal, Canada in December 1999. They defined civil society as a "slice of collective life that takes place above the individual yet below the state ... [,] the sphere of economic, cultural and social interaction ... [that] includes the 'broad collectivity of nonofficial, non commercial and more or less formally organized groups that seek in one way or another to reinforce or alter existing rules, norms, and deeper social structures'"[3] (Foster and Anand 1999, 11).

Further elaborating on this theme, Jan Aart Scholte traces the changing meanings of 'civil society' over time and place, from the sixteenth-century English use of the term then referring to the state, through Hegel's nineteenth-century concept of civil society that included the market, and Gramsci's 1930s view of civil society "as an arena where class hegemony forges consent". Scholte contrasts this with the contemporary understanding of civil society "as a site of disruption and dissent" as well as "a political space where voluntary associations explicitly seek to shape the rules (in terms of specific policies, wider norms and deeper social structures) that govern one or the other aspect of social life" (Scholte 2001, 4-5).

Robert W. Cox examines the evolution of the term 'civil society' from the eighteenth-century European Enlightenment onward, and presents a variety of prospects for civil society in circumstances of: evolved capitalism in Europe and North America; Asian capitalism with its particular social and cultural context; state breakdown (in the former Soviet bloc and elsewhere) and predatory capitalism; and Africa. He concludes that "[c]ivil society has become the crucial battleground for recovering citizen control of public life" (Cox 1999, 27).

Jane Jensen sees civil society not as an actor but as a place, a space in which "political discussion and political debate [can happen] and certain sets of rules of the game can be agreed upon". Along similar lines, Manning Marable considers civil society "a site where citizens can participate in decision-making without becoming bureaucrats, without thinking about democratic procedures as a substitute for the reality" (CBC 2001, 5,10).

Other terms found in the literature on civil society include 'transnational social movements', and the 'third force' or 'third sector', to name but a few.[4] Finally, brief mention should be made of what has been termed 'uncivil society' – transnational organized crime, terrorist groups, extreme fundamentalist sects, internet-based or tangible hate groups and the like. The most extreme example of 'uncivil society' in the world of the September 11, 2001 terror attacks and their aftermath is Osama bin Laden's transnational terrorist network, al-Qaeda.

This book builds on the understanding of civil society on the basis of the formulations, outlined above, of Gordenker and Weiss, the Commission on Global Governance, and Scholte's view of civil society in contemporary governance. Several contributors, especially Benjamin Rivlin and Heidi K. Ullrich, discuss and analyse the nature and typology of civil society and NGOs.

'Information' is no less nebulous a concept than 'civil society'. The term is used very widely by the whole gamut of disciplines and by the general public. A popular dictionary provides this definition of 'information': "knowledge obtained from investigation, study, or instruction ... [;] facts or data ... pertaining to a particular subject or regarded as significant ... [;] news [;] a signal or sequence of symbols ... [;] the communication or reception of facts or ideas" (Allen 2000, 720). Somewhat more enlightening is the characterization of information as "something learned, facts that are gathered or a measure of the content of a message. It can be argued whether ... [information] is a product, commodity, resource or process ... [consisting of a] ... statement, opinion, fact, concept or idea" relating to the content of a communication or message (Keenan and Johnston 2000a, 133). According to another formulation, information is data in a communicable and useable form, that is, facts with meaning attached (Feather and Sturges 1997, 184).

Most of those grappling with the concepts of data, information or knowledge build on Shannon and Weaver's 1949 definitions involving the communication of data, its meaning (that is, data transformed into information) and its effect (in the form of knowledge) on the recipient.[5] These definitions refer to the process by which data becomes knowledge at the point that information is "assimilated, correlated and understood" (Keenan and Johnston 2000a, 133). It is generally assumed that information has the qualities of being 'new', 'true' and 'about something' (Losee 1997, 255). Using somewhat circular logic, the concept of information is perceived as a product of communication which, in turn, is essentially understood as an interaction with another for the purpose of exchanging information (Bhattacharyya 1997, 71,80).

Charles T. Meadow and Weijing Yuan survey the literature on this complex subject and proceed to establish with greater precision the distinction among 'data', 'information' and 'knowledge': 'data' are sets of symbols that carry potential for meaning but are not necessarily understood or accepted by a particular recipient; 'information' takes place when the data are understood and are meaningful or useful to the recipient; and 'knowledge' is "the cumulation and integration of information received". Carrying the discussion yet another step further, to the concept of 'wisdom', Meadow and Yuan quote T.S. Eliot: "Where is the wisdom we have lost in knowledge? Where is the knowledge we have lost in information?"[6]

However one defines or understands 'information', it is clear that we have witnessed an exponential growth of computer and communication technology, and a corresponding increase in the volume and influence of messages disseminated and exchanged thanks to that technology. In particular, the internet has become a ubiquitous presence in virtually every discipline and every arena of public discourse. We are well into the information age.

According to the *Concise Dictionary of Library and Information Science*, the information age began at the point when computers and telecommunications converged in the early 1980s (Keenan and Johnston 2000b, 133). E-mail first became available in 1981 and spread throughout the academic and military world. This was followed by the introduction of file transfer protocols (ftp) in 1983 that allowed the sharing of information in much greater quantities. The various electronic FreeNets, the first of which appeared in Santa Monica, California in the 1970s, are an excellent example of the growth of virtual communities which provided electronic conferences of local interest. A primary focus of these electronic communities was the provision of access for the greatest number of constituents (Chambat 2000, 271). Finally, the internet and World Wide Web became available in the early 1990s, connecting people around the world (Gelernter 2001, 67).

Information, and especially modern information technology, is an essential component of the work and strategy of civil society organizations. In many ways, the growth of civil society and its potential global impact on governments has been made possible by, and depends upon, the sharing of knowledge: "[we take] information and we codify it, analyze it, interpret it, and we use it to learn something new and, ideally, we then share what we know with others who can use it" (St. Clair 2001, 7). The globalization of civil society itself is facilitated and enhanced through the "growth of connections between people across the planet" (Scholte 2001, 7). Conversely, the power of the state is weakened by the ability of ICT to transcend national borders by involving pressure groups from outside a nation in issues of significant interest to that nation as well as global groups pursuing their own cultural predispositions (Chambat 2000, 268).

Classification of NGOs and Civil Society Organizations

Scholte distinguishes conformist, reformist, and radical elements within civil society. The radicals "seek to shape the rules ... that govern one or the other aspect of social life ... [; reformists] seek only modest revisions of existing governance arrangements and conformist elements ... seek to reinforce established rules". Many civil society groups are not purely of one or another of these categories but use a combination of these tendencies[7] (Scholte 2001, 5). In her chapter in the present volume, Heidi Ullrich, in the context of trade-related NGOs, offers a critical, more nuanced view of Scholte's three-way division.

Nicholas Bayne characterizes some groups as "constructive and well-informed" while others are "destructive and anarchistic" (Bayne 2000a, 215). Writing elsewhere about the approximately 30,000 demonstrators at the Seattle ministerial meeting of the World Trade Organization (WTO), Bayne classifies them, on the basis of their behaviour in the street, as orderly (20,000-25,000), obstructive (5,000-10,000) and destructive (200-300) (Bayne 2000b, 136). Media coverage, unfortunately if not unexpectedly, tends to focus on the small minority in the latter two categories, especially on the last kind, thereby creating an inaccurate and unbalanced impression of civil society.

Marina Ottaway identifies three patterns of engagement of NGOs and NGO networks with governments and international organizations. These are confrontation (as in Seattle), continued and intensified lobbying, and formal inclusion of NGOs as participants in decision-making. She, too, notes that these categories are not always mutually exclusive but are used variously by NGOs as particular situations require (Ottaway 2001, 273).

Addressing the question of functional classification, Sylvia Ostry – in a refinement of an earlier grouping of civil society into operational and advocacy organizations – distinguishes three categories of civil society coalitions: "'mobilization networks' whose chief objective is to rally support for a specific set of activities; 'technical networks' designed to facilitate and provide specific information; and networks dedicated to servicing developing countries [and constituting] a 'virtual secretariat'" (Ostry 2000, 12-13). And Stanley Fischer, former deputy managing director of the IMF, warns: "We have to be very careful to distinguish between what the critics are saying. ... Some of the critics are isolationists who are opposed to globalization. But others ... just want a better globalization" (Rebello 2000, B5).

Two further dimensions should be added to this already-complex picture. First, many civil society organizations, however classified in functional terms, are not purely of one or another type but belong in more than one category, as is the case of Scholte's behavioural/ideological classification cited earlier; for example, Oxfam International (OI) is both an operational (or service-delivery) and an advocacy organization; so is another major NGO, Médecins Sans Frontières.[8] NGOs that can combine service-delivery and advocacy have the potential to be much more effective in their work.

Second, when distinguishing components of civil society, it is useful to keep in mind the North-South divide that is as evident in the NGO world as it is among states. Observers point out that in Seattle, for example, the overwhelming majority of street demonstrators came from the developed North – which was at least partly a function of the lack of funds to travel – and did not represent the interests of developing countries. But, in the changed world of globalization, the long-established international primacy of Northern NGOs must be shared with NGOs and civil society networks from the South. One observer states that "the strongest civil society groups in the South have rejected the term ['civil society' as] ... an alien term" that originated in the West.[9] More important than the nuances of terminology is the fact that Northern and Southern NGOs and other non-state actors have come together on issues of vital mutual concern; for example, in the campaign for access to essential medicines, the subject of James Orbinski's chapter in this book.

These and other – sometimes overlapping – classifications will undoubtedly help shape and develop the debate about the nature and role of civil society.

Civil Society, and Information and Communication Technology

This book examines, through twelve case studies, the principal goals, programmes, aspects of governance and working methods of selected major NGOs and civil society coalitions, and analyses the relationship of civil society and intergovernmental institutions and, in one case, civil society and a national government. Throughout, issues of ICT are discussed as appropriate to the focus of specific chapters. In particular, the book asks: How has ICT helped civil society in advocacy, service delivery, and networking; and under what circumstances is the use of modern technologies inappropriate? How has ICT furthered civil society's aims and in some instances influenced government and IGO policy and behaviour? How has ICT, especially the internet, shaped and altered NGOs and civil society coalitions? What role has ICT played in enhancing the legitimacy of civil society groups? All chapters, in their diverse ways, address these issues.

The first part of the book studies selected NGO and other civil society organizations in several policy areas: security, development, international law, human rights, and humanitarian assistance. Joanne Lebert explores Amnesty International's (AI's) relationship to ICTs. She examines information production and dissemination; reviews grassroots action involving communication, co-ordination and mobilization; considers issues of access and representation in connection with online activism; and discusses the implications of ICT for AI's organizational and managerial culture. She notes that communication and information technologies have vastly improved the speed with which AI can collect and circulate data both internally and publicly. In turn, this has facilitated the co-ordination of action and the mobilization and delivery of organizational support to AI activists. She argues that AI faces two seemingly contradictory challenges: it must make itself easily accessible and take concrete steps to bridge the digital divide, but at the same time it must protect itself against technological abuse such as misinformation, misinterpretation and manipulation. Because AI has experienced both the benefits and limitations of ICT, it has opted for a utilitarian, pragmatic approach, using technology in conjunction with more traditional forms of communication, including face-to-face interaction. Thus, AI uses ICT strategically in its campaign and other activities.

John Spykerman begins his chapter on the Union of Concerned Scientists' (UCS's) work against the proposed US National Missile Defense (NMD) system, and other forms of ballistic missile defence deployment, with an historical overview of scientists versus missile defences. He then discusses the events leading up to President Bill Clinton's September 2000 ruling to defer to the next administration the decision whether or not to deploy NMD, reviews the role of civil society and scientists in this decades-old debate, and considers lessons to be learned for future debates in this crucial policy area. Throughout the chapter, he shows how ICT has allowed the UCS and other arms-control NGOs to build and develop their campaigns on various levels: communication, research, organization and activism. Beyond information technology, the complexity of this sector has necessitated the use of scientific arguments as an integral element in UCS's campaigns. He observes that even the September 11, 2001 terrorist attacks against the US had little effect on the ideological arguments driving the missile defence debate. Spykerman is under no illusion that opposition to deployment of a missile shield would lead to an easy victory; he notes that "the public's faith in American ingenuity often surpasses the technical realities scientists have used to forge their arguments". This, plus the national security establishment's proclivity to deployment makes it all the more essential for scientists to remain involved in the debate and to expose the technical vulnerabilities of such missile systems. He concludes that information technology will play an increasingly important role in this process.

Peter I. Hajnal, tracing the work of Oxfam International, outlines the origins, history, mandate, governance and structure of this development-oriented NGO group; discusses and illustrates with examples OI's range of activities in development, emergency response, and global advocacy; and touches on its financing. He then assesses OI's use of ICT, particularly regarding the internet. He concludes that OI itself, and the confederation of Oxfams, have achieved some impressive results in co-ordinating the multifaceted work of the group in the areas of development, emergency response and especially advocacy, and have been able to respond to challenges in a speedy and flexible manner. Information technology has played a major role in OI's internal work and public outreach, but questions remain as to how much concrete public support for the organization is attributable to the information it disseminates and how has the information contributed to policy or programme changes by target governments and intergovernmental organizations. OI needs further strategic innovations as well as technical improvements to enhance the effectiveness of its use of ICT.

Juris Dilevko bases his chapter about the NGOs of the South on responses to a questionnaire-based survey of 37 organizations. Survey responses were received from Africa, South America and the Caribbean, East and Southeast Asia, and the Trans-Caucasian area. The chapter explores two themes: the way in which Southern NGOs perceive and use ICTs; and the relationship of Southern NGOs with large international NGOs. As a sub-theme of the former, Dilevko addresses social and cultural consequences of ICT use. He finds that in the competition of Southern NGOs to attract the intellectual attention and financial resources of international NGOs, ICT is the tool of choice to aid fundraising, advocacy and networking activities. Although many NGOs of the South report negative or frustrating experiences with international civil society organizations, few dispute the overall benefits of local-global linkages. The Southern NGOs' enthusiastic embrace of ICT has improved decision-making processes and contributed to the emergence of local networks of expertise. Dilevko suggests that a broad-based alliance of Southern NGOs, aided by ICT, could enhance the capacity and influence of those NGOs and thus bring about more meaningful collaboration with international civil society.

Kenneth R. Rutherford, an analyst as well as victim of landmines, discusses the International Campaign To Ban Landmines (ICBL) and a related NGO that he co-founded, the Landmine Survivors Network (LSN). He provides a brief history of the role of NGOs in promoting the landmine banning issue; addresses the ICBL coalition and the role of ICT (media technologies, e-mail, and websites) in efforts to achieve the Mine Ban Treaty in the face of opposition by the major world powers; and examines how the LSN has used information technologies to increase resources for victim assistance. He concludes that the ICBL and the LSN have used information technologies in new and creative ways to influence the making of foreign policy. In addition, civil society, by using ICT, was able to reduce the cost of coalition-building and of communication. The rapid development of ICT and the fact that the state could no longer have a monopoly on information have contributed to the transformation of NGOs into important international actors able to influence international politics in issue areas that used to be the exclusive domain of states.

William R. Pace and Rik Panganiban of the World Federalist Movement (WFM) focus on the NGO Coalition for an International Criminal Court. They argue that ICT, used in conjunction with broad-based and federative (rather than hierarchical) models of operation, greatly increases the political influence of civil society on international policy-making. Pace and Panganiban trace the beginnings of the international network favouring establishment of the Court and the evolution of that network into an effective coalition. They then discuss the role of ICT during the 1998 Rome conference on the treaty establishing the Court, and the multi-polar advocacy work of civil society in Rome. They continue with an analysis of the devolution of the coalition after Rome into active regional and national networks; and end with comments on lessons to be learned from the experience of the coalition. They conclude that the evolution of the coalition has shown that ICT is an increasingly integral aspect of the functioning and effectiveness of civil society in international decision-making. They caution, however, that the case for ICT should not be overstated; effective global civil society campaigns were mounted before the advent of the information age. Moreover, traditional means of communication, including printed publications, will remain necessary components of campaigning. That said, the wide availability of ICT allowed both the scope and the speed of civil society activity to become much greater. In a postscript dealing with the September 11, 2001 terrorist attacks, the authors warn that apparently benign technologies can be used by criminal and terrorist organizations for their own ends.

In the closing chapter of the first part of the book, James Orbinski highlights the humanitarian work as well as the 'witnessing' – insistence to bring human suffering to public knowledge by speaking out – of Médecins Sans Frontières (MSF), the two pillars of MSF's achievements that led the Norwegian Nobel Committee to award it the 1999 Nobel Peace Prize. He goes on to discuss the role of MSF in the campaign to combat the global HIV/AIDS epidemic by promoting access to essential medicines in developing countries. He affirms the immorality of the lack of access to available treatment for HIV/AIDS and other infectious diseases; traces the emergence and evolution of the civil society coalition that mounted the campaign; and analyzes the goals, strategies and tactics used. He then considers the role of ICT, pinpointing the tremendous impact of the internet, mobile telephones, fax machines and other technologies on the speed and scope of the campaign. He asserts, however, that face-to-face meetings are essential in sharing ideas, building trust and articulating goals. Referring to the effects of September 11, Orbinski concludes that while the political context has changed, the underlying issues of basic justice, dignity and human rights remain.

The second part of this volume focuses on civil society in relationship with intergovernmental institutions. Barbara Adams discusses the evolution of the interaction of civil society and the UN. She compares the long-standing formal relations between NGOs and the UN with the changing patterns that emerged with the major UN world conferences of the 1990s and the accompanying dramatic upsurge of NGO involvement in such traditional UN concerns as development co-operation, human rights, aid to refugees, standard-setting, and information dissemination. Formal procedures governing UN-civil society relations have changed very little despite attempts by the UN to adopt new rules, including proposals to enhance NGO access to and participation in the UN system; the harmonization of UN databases on NGOs to facilitate exchange and compilation of information on NGOs; expansion of information dissemination through the internet; and provision of wider NGO access to the UN's optical disk system (ODS). Regardless of the persistence and increasing irrelevance of old formal procedures, the emerging and proliferating informal practices of the UN's interaction with NGOs have achieved important results. Adams credits NGO coalitions with a major role in achieving the treaty banning anti-personnel landmines and the efforts to establish an international criminal court. She argues that NGO involvement was a significant factor in the ability of major UN conferences to achieve international consensus and commitment of governments on difficult policy challenges; for example, on issues of women's rights and reproductive health. This has larger implications in the broader context of shifting global governance. The participation of civil society has provided the UN not only with technical expertise but has increased public awareness of global issues, and contributed to greater democracy, transparency and accountability on the part of UN member governments.

Benjamin Rivlin examines a special aspect of the UN-civil society relationship, the case of religious groups. He addresses the role of religious NGOs in global civil society, and the effect of information technology on religion. He shows that despite the affinity between the UN and religious groups on the level of ideals of peace, social justice and tolerance, there are major differences and conflicts both between and within religions, and between religious groups and certain member states of the UN. The UN has long provided political space for religious NGOs. Religious or church-based NGOs have used this space to pursue interfaith coalition-building, to serve their own denominational needs, and to provide humanitarian relief in many parts of the world. Religious groups have embraced information technology but are aware and wary of the conflict-creating potential of that technology. Rivlin notes that religious NGOs pursue different strategic goals, but leaves open the question of whether those groups are effective players within the 'new diplomacy'. Although many such groups have distinguished themselves in humanitarian relief work, they have rarely been at the forefront of large global undertakings as in the drafting of the statute of the International Criminal Court, or the treaty banning landmines. He concludes that the effectiveness of the role that religious NGOs play in international society in dealing with the adverse consequences of globalization depends on how those religions live up to their theology and how well they can overcome their complicity in conflicts around the world.

Heidi K. Ullrich's chapter investigates the role of information and, more specifically, ICT, in the interaction between the WTO and civil society. She introduces a typology of trade-related NGOs; surveys recent WTO reforms aimed at increasing and improving the dialogue with civil society; describes the use of ICT both by the WTO and civil society; presents several case studies of NGOs, reflecting the diversity of outlook and approach on the use of ICT; and discusses ways of facilitating communication between the WTO and trade-related NGOs. She also highlights various limitations and challenges inherent in the interaction. She concludes her investigation of the role of information in the relationship between the WTO and civil society – more particularly, trade-related NGOs – with a series of recommendations aimed at making that interaction more effective, thus leading to a knowledgeable two-way dialogue needed to expand the trade debate. The recommendations call for increased transparency and legitimacy on the part of the WTO, greater knowledge of both civil society and the WTO through information exchange, and enhanced civil society guidance for the WTO. All of this should involve more effective use of information both by the WTO and civil society. Ullrich cautions that while information is a most important power resource, it must be transformed into shared knowledge to realize its potential to generate power.

Marc Lortie and Sylvie Bédard look at the nature and implications of the interaction between the Canadian government and civil society at the Québec City Summit of the Americas held in April 2001.[10] They show that globalization has given rise to a multiplicity of social actors (including civil society) and has brought changes in their roles, influence and relationships. ICT has played a major role in the growing influence of civil society in the Western Hemisphere. Lortie and Bédard further argue that all actors must adapt and must find the right balance for the role and influence of the state, the market, and the popular movements. They discuss the integrated and concerted approach that the Canadian host government took to associate civil society groups and other non-state actors with the preparation and conduct of the Summit; analyse the results of this collaboration; and draw the lessons to be learned. Lortie and Bédard assert that the complexity of our globalized world has made the input of various actors – government, business, civil society and others – a necessity, because each actor brings a different expertise and perspective to decision-making. They conclude that a concerted, integrated approach on the part of government leads to increased understanding and co-operation among different sectors of society, leading to an expanded social consensus. They point out that the greater influence that the new actors have acquired – with the significant aid of ICT – places correspondingly greater responsibility on them.

In the final case study, Peter I. Hajnal traces and assesses the G7/G8-civil society nexus. This chapter reviews the progress and highlights the milestones that mark the evolution of that relationship through three phases: mutual non-recognition; recognition of the G7 on the part of civil society; and recognition of civil society by the G7 (and later also by the G8). It continues with a case study of developing-country debt and the civil society coalition Jubilee 2000 and its successors, highlighting that coalition's sophisticated, effective use of ICT. The chapter next discusses the G7/G8-civil society encounters at the summits of Okinawa in 2000 and Genoa in 2001. The author concludes that civil society, at its best, gives voice to the plight and aspirations of the marginalized, and fights for the universal extension of the benefits of globalization. ICT – a relatively inexpensive and powerful tool, used purposefully and efficiently – has been a crucial factor in increasing the influence of civil society. As for civil society relations with the G7/G8, these have been characterized by informal practice rather than by formal rules. There is increasing mutual recognition of the desirability of dialogue and partnership among these actors, along with the inevitable tensions resulting from differing and sometimes conflicting perceptions, objectives and tactics.[11] Carrying this idea further, Hajnal argues that civil society and the G8 (as well as individual G8 governments) need each other; both types of actors are necessary to address meaningfully the injustices of indebtedness of the poorest countries, environmental degradation, lack of access to affordable essential medicines to fight against devastating diseases, and educational deficits. While it is civil society that plays a crucial role in campaigning for solutions, mobilizing people for support of these causes, and lobbying powerful governments and international institutions, in the end it is the governments of rich countries, powerful institutions such as the G7/G8, the International Monetary Fund, the World Bank and the WTO, as well as large pharmaceutical companies, respectively, that must implement debt forgiveness, large-scale health and education measures, and access to essential medicines at affordable prices.

The case studies presented in this book pay particular attention to the role of information in the functioning and impact of civil society. It is the hope of the contributors and the editor that this approach will add a new dimension to the debate on the crucial issues of non-state actors and their interaction with governments and intergovernmental organizations.

Notes

Note on internet addresses (URLs): Websites tend to appear, change or disappear, often without warning. Addresses cited in this bibliography were accurate and active at the time of writing (February 2002) unless otherwise noted.

1 James Madison wrote about interest groups – groups that form the core of the concept of 'civil society' – in *Federalist Paper* No. 10. I thank Professor Benjamin Rivlin for pointing this out.
2 See Kaul, Inge, Grunberg, Isabelle and Stern, Marc A. (1999), *Global Public Goods: International Cooperation in the 21st Century*, Oxford University Press for the United Nations Development Programme, New York, pp. 450-507.
3 See also Scholte, Jan Aart (1998), 'The IMF Meets Civil Society', *Finance and Development*, Vol. 35(3), pp. 42-45.
4 See, for example, Smith, Jackie, Chatfield, Charles and Pagnucco, Ron (eds) (1997), *Transnational Social Movements and Global Politics: Solidarity Beyond the State*, Syracuse University Press, Syracuse, New York; and Florini, Ann M. (2000), *The Third Force: The Rise of Transnational Civil Society*, Japan Center for International Exchange, Tokyo; Carnegie Endowment for International Peace, Washington, DC.
5 See Shannon, Claude E. and Weaver, Warren (1949), *The Mathematical Theory of Communication*, University of Illinois Press, Chicago.
6 See also Charles T. Meadow, "Data, Information, and Knowledge", in *Text Information Retrieval Systems*, 2nd ed., edited by Charles T. Meadow, Bert R. Boyce and Donald H. Kraft (San Diego: Academic Press, 2000): 34-48. The Eliot quote is from his (1936), "Choruses from 'The Rock'", *Collected Poems, 1909-1935*, Faber & Faber, London, p. 157.
7 See also Jan Aart Scholte, Robert O'Brien, and Marc Williams, "The WTO and Civil Society", *Journal of World Trade* 33, No. 1 (1999): 107-23; cited in Heidi Ullrich, "Stimulating Trade Liberalization After Seattle: G7/8 Leadership in Global Governance", paper presented at the Academic Symposium "G8 2000: New Directions in Global Governance? G8's Okinawa Summit", University of the Ryukyus, Okinawa, Japan, 19-20 July 2000.
8 See Peter I. Hajnal (2001), 'International Nongovernmental Organizations and Civil Society', in Peter I. Hajnal (ed), *International Information: Documents, Publications and Electronic Information of International Organizations*, Vol. 2, Libraries Unlimited, Englewood, CO.
9 See John Foster, (CBC 2001, 3); and Kamal Malhotra, (CBC 2001, 19).

10 For an account of the same event from a civil society point of view; see (Friedmann 2001).
11 Preferring the concept of global corporatism rather than of partnership, Marina Ottaway cautions that while "[i]nternational organizations, business, and civil society networks all have much to contribute to the solution of the growing number of problems that transcend national boundaries[,] ... trying to tie the three types of organizations into close cooperative relations may weaken the contributions each can make, while at the same time creating new bureaucratic structures." (Ottaway 2001, 266)

References

Allen, Robert (ed) (2000), 'Information', *The New Penguin English Dictionary*, Penguin Books, London, p. 720.

Bayne, Nicholas (2000a), *Hanging in There: The G7 and G8 Summit in Maturity and Renewal*, Ashgate, Aldershot, The G8 and Global Governance Series.

Bayne, Nicholas (2000b), 'Why Did Seattle Fail? Globalization and the Politics of Trade', *Government and Opposition*, Vol. 35(2), pp. 131-151.

Bhattacharyya, G. (1997), 'Information: Its Definition for its Service Professionals', *Library Science with a Slant to Documentation and Information Studies*, Vol. 34(2), pp. 69-83, Paper C.

Canadian Broadcasting Corporation (2001), 'Civil Society', *Ideas*, 18, 25 June, ID 2395, CBC Ideas Transcripts, Toronto.

Chambat, Pierre (2000), 'Computer-Aided Democracy: The Effects of Information and Communication Technologies on Democracy', in Ken Ducatel, Juliet Webster and Werner Herrmann (eds), *The Information Society in Europe*, Rowman & Littlefield, Oxford, pp. 259-278.

Commission on Global Governance (1995), *Our Global Neighbourhood: The Report of the Commission on Global Governance*, Oxford University Press, Oxford.

Commission on Global Governance (1999), *The Millennium Year and the Reform Process: A Contribution from the Commission on Global Governance*, Commission on Global Governance, London.

Cox, Robert W. (1999), 'Civil Society at the Turn of the Millennium: Prospects for an Alternative World Order', *Review of International Studies*, Vol. 25(1), pp. 3-28.

Feather, John and Sturges, Paul (eds) (1997), 'Information', *International Encyclopedia of Information and Library Science*, Routledge, London, p. 184.

Florini, Ann M. (2000), *The Third Force: The Rise of Transnational Civil Society*, Japan Center for International Exchange, Tokyo; Carnegie Endowment for International Peace, Washington, DC.

Foster, John W. and Anand, Anita (eds) (1999), *Whose World Is It Anyway? Civil Society, the United Nations and the Multilateral Future*, United Nations Association in Canada, Ottawa, quoting Wapner, Paul (1996), *Environmental Activism and World Civic Politic*, State University of New York Press, Albany, p. 158.

Friedmann, Harriet (2001), 'Forum: Considering the Quebec Summit, the World Social Forum at Porto Alegre and the People's Summit at Quebec City: A View from the Ground', *Studies in Political Economy: A Socialist Review*, Vol. 66 (Autumn), pp. 85-105.

Gelernter, Judith (2001), 'The Internet: Yesterday, Today, and Tomorrow', *Information Outlook*, Vol. 5(6), pp. 67-68.

Gordenker, Leon and Weiss, Thomas G. (1996), 'Pluralizing Global Governance: Analytical Approaches and Dimensions', in Thomas G. Weiss and Leon Gordenker (eds), *NGOs, the UN, and Global Governance*, Lynne Rienner Publishers, Boulder, pp. 17-47.

Hajnal, Peter (2001), 'International Nongovernmental Organizations and Civil Society', in Peter I. Hajnal (ed), *International Information: Documents, Publications and Electronic Information of International Organizations*, Vol. 2, Libraries Unlimited, Englewood, CO.

Judge, Anthony (n.d.), *Types of International Organizations*, Section 2.2, Union of International Associations, www.uia.org/uiadocs/orgtypec.htm

Kaul, Inge, Grunberg, Isabelle and Stern, Marc A. (1999), *Global Public Goods: International Cooperation in the 21st Century*, Oxford University Press for the United Nations Development Programme, New York, pp. 450-507.

Keenan, Stella and Johnston, Colin (eds) (2000a), 'Information', *Concise Dictionary of Library and Information Science*, 2nd ed, Bowker Saur, London, p. 133.

Keenan, Stella and Johnston, Colin (eds) (2000b), 'Information Age', *Concise Dictionary of Library and Information Science*, 2nd ed, Bowker Saur, London, p. 133.

Losee, Robert M. (1997), 'A Discipline Independent Definition of Information', *Journal of the American Society for Information Science*, Vol. 48(3), pp. 254-269.

Madison, James (1787), 'The Same Subject Continued: The Union as a Safeguard Against Domestic Faction and Insurrection', *Federalist Papers*, No. 10, memory.loc.gov/const/fed/fed_10.html

Meadow, Charles T. (2000), 'Data, Information, and Knowledge', in Charles T. Meadow, Bert R. Boyce and Donald H. Kraft (eds), *Text Information Retrieval Systems*, 2nd ed, Academic Press, San Diego, pp. 34-48.

Meadow, Charles T. and Yuan, Weijing (1997), 'Measuring the Impact of Information: Defining the Concepts', *Information Processing & Management*, Vol. 33(6), pp. 697-714.

O'Brien, Robert, Goetz, Anne Marie, Scholte, Jan Aart and Williams, Marc (2000), *Contesting Global Governance: Multilateral Economic Institutions and Global Social Movements*, Cambridge University Press, Cambridge.

Ostry, Sylvia (2000), *WTO: Institutional Design for Better Governance*, (Draft), paper presented at the conference *Efficiency, Equity and Legitimacy: The Multilateral Trading System at the Millennium*, Kennedy School of Government, Harvard University, 2-3 June, www.utoronto.ca/cis/WTOID.pdf

Ottaway, Marina (2001), 'Corporatism Goes Global: International Organizations, Nongovernmental Organization Networks, and Transnational Business', *Global Governance: A Review of Multilateralism and International Organizations*, Vol. 7(3), pp. 265-292.

Rebello, Joseph (2000), 'International Economists Fear the Free-Trade Chill', *The Globe and Mail*, 28 August, p. B5, quote by Stanley Fischer at Federal Reserve Bank of Kansas City Symposium on *Global Opportunities and Challenges*, Jackson Hole, Wyoming, 24-26 August 2000.

Reinalda, Bob (2001), 'Private in Form, Public in Purpose: NGOs in International Relations Theory', in Bas Arts, Math Noortmann and Bob Reinalda (eds), *Non-State Actors in International Relations*, Ashgate, Aldershot, pp. 11-40. Non-State Actors in International Law, Politics and Governance Series.

Scholte, Jan Aart (1998), 'The IMF Meets Civil Society', *Finance and Development*, Vol. 35(3), pp. 42-45.

Scholte, Jan Aart (2001), *Civil Society and Democracy in Global Governance*, Department of Politics and International Studies, University of Warwick, CSGR Working Paper No. 65/01; also (forthcoming), 'Civil Society and Democracy in Global Governance' *Global Governance*, Vol. 8(3).

Scholte, Jan Aart, O'Brien, Robert and Williams, Marc (1999), 'The WTO and Civil Society', *Journal of World Trade*, Vol. 33(1), pp. 107-23; cited in Ullrich, Heidi (2000), Stimulating Trade Liberalization After Seattle: G7/8 Leadership in Global Governance', paper presented at the Academic Symposium *G8 2000: New Directions in Global Governance? G8's Okinawa Summit*, University of the Ryukyus, Okinawa, 19-20 July.

Shannon, Claude E. and Weaver, Warren (1949), *The Mathematical Theory of Communication*, University of Illinois Press, Chicago

Smith, Jackie, Chatfield, Charles and Pagnucco, Ron (eds) (1997), *Transnational Social Movements and Global Politics: Solidarity Beyond the State*, Syracuse University Press, Syracuse, New York.

St. Clair, Guy (2001), 'Knowledge Services: Your Company's Key to Performance Excellence', *Information Outlook*, Vol. 5(6), pp. 6-12.

Union of International Associations (2001/2002), *Yearbook of International Organizations: Guide to Global and Civil Society Networks*, 38th ed, Vol. 1B, UIA, Brussels.

United Nations, Economic and Social Council (1950), *Review of Consultative Arrangements with Non-governmental Organizations*, UN, New York, 27 February, E/RES/288(X).

United Nations, Economic and Social Council (1968), *Arrangements for Consultation with Non-governmental Organizations*, UN, New York, 25 June, E/RES/1296(XLIV).

Wood, Ellen Meikins (1991), 'The Uses and Abuses of "Civil Society"', in Ralph Miliband (ed), *The Socialist Register, 1990*, Monthly Review Press, New York, pp. 60-84.

PART I

NGOS AND
CIVIL SOCIETY COALITIONS

Chapter 2

Information and Communication Technologies and Human Rights Advocacy: The Case of Amnesty International

Joanne Lebert

Introduction

Amnesty International (AI), an international human rights organization, works to promote the principles enshrined in the Universal Declaration of Human Rights. It has more than one million members and supporters representing 162 countries and territories. AI acts impartially and independently of any government, political persuasion or religious creed and it is largely financed by subscriptions and donations from its worldwide membership. As a grassroots organization, AI is accountable and responsive to its members, who have voting rights within the organization; they have been the main drivers of its direction and focus over the years. Given the large number of people who are actively affiliated with AI internationally, and given the complexity of attempting to accommodate competing interests and agendas, the introduction of information and communication technologies (ICTs) has proven to be invaluable for most of AI's constituents.

Since its inception in 1961, Amnesty has experienced incredible technological change: from pen and paper, Gestetner machines and conventional mail to short text messaging, satellite news feeds and 'webcasts' all transmitted in real time. However, the adoption of new forms of communication has not necessarily led to the abandonment of more established tools, nor is the adoption of new technologies always a desirable development. Internationally, many AI supporters continue to hand-write appeals and mail these by regular post; telexes and telegrams continue to be used in some countries; and while text messaging may be a popular new medium alerting subscribers to 'calls to action', cyber-activists are still urged to follow-up all e-mailed appeals or electronic petitions with an old-fashioned, personalized 'snail-mailed' or faxed letter. Although speed of action is an important strength of ICTs, the more varied the medium and means of communication, the more accessible the campaign to both members and potential activists. Moreover, a diverse toolkit allows a greater degree of flexibility when the aim is to influence states and non-state actors that have widely divergent technological capacities and equally varied views of ICTs.

ICTs, therefore, have come to be viewed as a leading strategic weapon for Amnesty – something that can no longer be conceived of simply as background infrastructure. E-mail, in particular, has had a profound and largely beneficial impact at all levels of the organization. However, ICTs are not a panacea; they have their share of limitations and, in Amnesty's experience, are best used in conjunction with other more traditional communication tools, such as the fax machine and regular mail.

This chapter seeks to explore AI's relationship to information and communication technologies. Two interrelated branches of Amnesty's work are examined. First, the chapter looks at information production and dissemination, the sound, thorough and highly respected bedrock of Amnesty's reputation and legitimacy. Next, the chapter reviews communication, co-ordination and mobilization, which constitute the nucleus of action at the grassroots level. Subsequently, issues of access and representation with regards to online activism are considered. Finally, the implications for and challenges to AI's organizational and managerial culture will be discussed.

Although Amnesty is an international movement, the views presented here are largely based on the experiences of the International Secretariat (or IS) – Amnesty's international 'head office' based in London – and on those of the Canadian English-speaking section.[1] These have also been heavily influenced by the author's own experiences as an Urgent Action Co-ordinator and as a member of AI, as well as through conversations with colleagues and AI supporters internationally.

The Impact of ICTs on Human Rights Activism

Information Production and Dissemination

Research has always been the backbone of AI. Not only does the organization pride itself on the reliability and relevance of its research, but it also strives to make this information freely accessible to human rights researchers and advocates everywhere. The advent of the internet, though, has greatly facilitated and accelerated the production and dissemination of this information.

Supporting local human rights defenders At the grassroots level, researchers are using e-mail to establish, nurture and maintain their regional networks of trusted contacts. These contacts, consisting of local human rights defenders and Amnesty sympathizers, can instantly communicate the details of local developments to researchers based in London. Depending on the technology available to them, local activists may even relay photos and other scanned evidence to the IS.

Although the security of these informants is clearly a concern, it may be no greater an issue, depending on the degree of electronic monitoring in-country, than when local defenders use more traditional forms of communication. In other words, there is an implicit risk involved for those who commit themselves to defending human rights in countries hostile to such activities.

The electronic medium, however, can lend added protection to local human rights defenders. When contacts or informants are harassed, the IS may be immediately contacted and prompted to issue and distribute a statement and call to action within hours of the act, or even in anticipation of an impending threat. For example, in June 2001, CALDH (*Centro de Acción Legal en Derechos Humanos*), a Guatemalan human rights organization, informed Amnesty that it was planning to launch a lawsuit against officials of the former military government of General Ríos Montt for the massacre of over 1,200 indigenous people in 13 separate incidents in the early 1980s. Because of the advance notice, AI was able to prepare, and circulate by e-mail, an embargoed statement and accompanying urgent letter-writing action in anticipation of threats to the security of CALDH staff. Upon CALDH's news release, sections were given the electronic 'green light' from the IS to release Amnesty's press release and action. Within hours, members from around the world began to flood the offices of Guatemalan authorities with appeal letters urging them to guarantee the security of all those involved in the lawsuit.

Internal access to and sharing of general resources ICTs have also greatly improved Amnesty's ability to collect regional data. Over the years, countless AI volunteers and staff have manually clipped, sorted, filed and distributed news items collected from a host of international sources. Researchers were often frustrated by a lack of access to current, country-specific information. Today, much to the contrary, Amnesty is literally swamped by volumes and volumes of data.

The IS has also recently invested in infrastructure to collect electronic news feeds via satellite, which it sorts and distributes – over 3,000 news stories per day – to IS staff workstations and a systems database, all in real time. This database is in the process of being standardized internationally. Once sections develop the capacity to adopt and support such a system, it is expected that they too will have access to these news feeds. Moreover, other resource and campaign specific databases are increasingly accessible. Sections that have the ability to support such databases have immediate access to the latest campaigning materials, urgent letter-writing actions, AI statements, press releases, member and donor information, and AI images and photos, all of which can be printed and used for campaigning and mobilizing at the grassroots level. Sections may also contribute to the information pool and share their own, locally-produced materials with their international colleagues.

Public access to AI research, campaigning materials and resources The acquisition and circulation of printed reports continue to be difficult and even dangerous for some human rights advocates. Clearly, one of the greatest advantages of the web and e-mail is the ability to distribute information to these individuals and to otherwise closed or isolated communities more cheaply and with less risk to the user.

In many countries, including China, Vietnam and Tunisia, internet traffic is heavily monitored through state-controlled firewalls and internet service providers (ISPs), which prevent access to sites deemed to be offensive, including those of human rights organizations. However, no security system is foolproof. Regardless of which filter is being used or how, avid users of the internet always seem eager both to learn how to circumvent imposed constraints and to convey these system failings to fellow users. Some activists have resorted to using proxy servers and other circumvention methods to get around state security. Uncensored websites may also be used as portals and gateways to the greater virtual world. Therefore, the threat of state monitors may not be insurmountable, at least not for any significant length of time. Nonetheless, state surveillance remains a central and absorbing concern to any discussion of online human rights activism.

Generally speaking, both the web and e-mail offer the public and AI members a wealth of human rights-related information. E-mail subscribers can receive electronic notification of developments in the Amnesty movement, at the local, national and international levels. Once visitors are drawn to a section or IS website, they can access an entire library of documentation. Currently, they can search the IS site by country or by theme to find relevant letter writing actions, reports, news items or press releases, which can be printed out free of charge.

The challenge for Amnesty has been to avoid turning its websites into sinkholes of information – where lengthy documents are stored and essentially forgotten. Archived documents must be interconnected in a relevant, consistent and up-to-date manner. These must be easily called up and searched by site users, whether they be the media looking for a quick statement or position paper, refugee lawyers searching for evidence to support a case, a local activist wanting a print out for an upcoming fundraising event or a group of students working on a school project. In other words, AI materials must not only be available, they must be easily accessible to a wide range of users from human rights professionals to lay persons. Both the IS and AI sections recognize that Amnesty's content must be set within an interactive framework, which anticipates user needs. 'One-stop surfers' should be offered personally tailored means to deepen their commitment to, and understanding of, human rights.

Unprecedented and unfettered international access to AI content raises yet another significant challenge to AI documentalists and strategists. To what extent should Amnesty's work be available electronically, and more importantly, to whom should it be made available? Different levels of commitment and membership to AI require differing levels of access to Amnesty content. For example, country co-ordinators – local volunteers who provide regional expertise to sections – require access to electronic information pertaining to their geographic area of interest. The general public, AI members and other volunteers may be restricted from viewing this same information, because of its sensitivity. Furthermore, it is practically impossible for Amnesty to verify the identity or motives of an individual or member who visits its sites. How does AI ensure the proper handling of reports, documents and campaign materials once a user has downloaded them? How does Amnesty restrict access to some and yet maintain a reliable distribution pattern so that others can be encouraged to use its resources? The risk of manipulation, misinformation and misrepresentation is very real and have all, at some point, tarnished the legitimacy of the organization.

Amnesty is actively working towards minimizing these risks. Among other strategies being considered, passwords may be introduced as a means to differentiate varying levels of membership and access. Also, more than ever, staff are being urged to consider the intended audience, the medium of dissemination and the appropriate security level of a document – confidential, members only or public – prior to its production.

As ICTs continue to facilitate both communication and public access to AI, the organization has been forced to constantly review constantly how to protect itself from abuse and defamation. Greater public interaction, on the one hand, seems to have been met with a redefinition and perhaps even entrenchment of boundaries; on the other, creating lines that delimit 'us', human rights defenders, from 'them', those unfriendly to the cause.

Communication, Co-ordination and Mobilization of Action

E-mail In the 1980s a former Chilean prisoner of conscience, on whose behalf AI had campaigned, developed Amnesty's first e-mail system, donating it to the IS in appreciation of its efforts.

In terms of communication, co-ordination and mobilization, e-mail has had a profound and largely beneficial impact on the internal workings of AI – more so than any other communications tool in the organization's history. Once access to e-mail is acquired, it provides a convenient and inexpensive alternative to the telephone, fax and conventional mail. Contrary to a fax machine, e-mail can be used to contact members of a large mailing list simultaneously and reliably, without the cost of paper, which remains exorbitant in many countries. And, because speed of action is crucial to preventing and stopping human rights abuses, e-mail, although it does have its limitations, has lent itself quite readily to activism.

One of Amnesty's program areas, the Urgent Action Network, has particularly benefited from this medium. Amnesty's 75 active Urgent Action Networks (UANs) comprise a web of letter writing members who respond to urgent cases of human rights violations by firing off letters of appeals to relevant authorities, often within hours of having received their call to action. The results can be impressive. In one-fifth of the 499 Urgent Action (UA) cases in the year 2000, Amnesty was able to document positive developments:[2] torture and/or death threats ceased, the 'disappeared' were found to be alive, investigations into violations of human rights were initiated, medical attention was given to sick prisoners, death sentences were commuted, human rights defenders were protected or the rights of asylum-seekers were respected.

Although Amnesty cannot prove that its letter-writing actions directly or solely influenced these positive outcomes, anecdotal evidence from former prisoners of conscience and victims of human rights violations, in addition to statements made by lawyers and government authorities suggest that these appeal letters have a powerful impact. While a direct positive correlation between e-mail usage and positive developments in UA cases has yet to be proven, e-mail has contributed to this form of activism by significantly increasing the speed and scope of action. It may be that the lack of clear results may be explained by the fact that many UANs or members are just now switching over from conventional mail to e-mail.

In sections where e-mail has been widely used, as in Canada, the UAN has clearly felt its impact. Upon investigation and confirmation of a human rights violation – one which requires immediate and mass mobilization – researchers draft a UA, which is distributed, usually electronically, to UAN co-ordinators around the world so that they, in turn, may render these to their respective members.[3] Because well over 80 per cent of Canada's English-speaking section members' receive their UAs via e-mail, letter writing can begin literally within hours of the IS having received word of a human rights violation.

Speed of action also lends itself to accuracy. As soon as a UA is issued, the facts of the case (such as a person's place of detention or state of health) are all subject to change, particularly when the authorities become aware of international concern. When facts have changed and members are not informed in time, authorities can dismiss their letters as inaccurate and their concern unfounded. Correct, up-to-date, detailed information presented by individuals and groups around the world tends to unnerve and sway authorities. The faster facts are provided, the more likely they are to be accurate. Moreover, as an added benefit, accurate information used in a timely fashion contributes directly to AI's reputation as a reliable source and effective strategist.

UAN members also recognize the importance of speed of action in their human rights work. As a result, those who receive their UAs via e-mail are often frustrated by AI's reluctance to provide them with the electronic addresses of relevant authorities. While UA cases may be drafted and distributed within a number of hours, members are generally forced to use conventional mail – or fax, for those who can absorb the costs of transmission – to deliver their appeals to the appropriate authorities. The use of electronic mail in this final step of letter-writing action – where the AI member contacts the authorities in question – is subject to some controversy within Amnesty.

Many question the effectiveness of e-mail when it comes to influencing abusive governments and non-state actors. The problem stems from the fact that, to date, AI really does not know in any great detail how authorities respond to electronic messages. They may only read the subject line and delete the message. They may simply shut down their e-mail accounts if they are flooded with appeals. Conversely, countries with unreliable telecommunication systems may not be able to support any serious and sudden influx of e-mail or faxes. Also, governments may be suspicious of those who send appeal letters, as their origin may be obscure. They may even suspect that a single person is responsible for a multiplicity of e-mails. Moreover, the tendency to use an informal tone in electronic messages and the playful addresses used by some (for example, satansmonkey@ or goodtimegirl@) may be deemed offensive and may even have a counterproductive effect in the end.

Perhaps most importantly, e-mail may simply not have the physical weight and presence of a hardcopy letter delivered either by fax or conventional mail. Amnesty members have often exercised their ability to fill authorities' offices with bags of mail – with every letter physically demanding action on behalf of an individual. Finally, most governments have a responsibility to sort, document and file these bits of correspondence, which may make dealing with hardcopy letters a comparatively onerous task.

Generally, it has been Amnesty's experience that e-mail, for all its positive attributes, is most effective as an activists' tool when used in combination with more traditional methods such as the fax machine or conventional mail. Again, its impact has been real, profound and extensive – more so than any other communications tool in the organization's history. However, in AI's case, its contribution has remained largely limited to the areas of communication, co-ordination and mobilization of activists – areas that are absolutely crucial to the successful workings of any grassroots movement. The activists' ultimate contact with and influence over those in power, however, continues to be carried out by more traditional means, such as hardcopy correspondence, demonstrations and face-to-face contact, all of which are emotionally charged and involve physical presence.

With regards to its communication and mobilization role, e-mail has been particularly useful to AI activists in large and geographically-dispersed countries. In Canada, for example, members had long complained about feeling isolated from other members. They had complained of a lack of support and direction stemming from lack of access to key staff. E-mail has allowed Canadian members of AI, among others, to work more closely together in-country and transnationally. Members who share a particular thematic or geographic interest have been able to network, brainstorm, consult, plan and mobilize without having to incur the costs and inconveniences of long distance travel. Consequently, events can be organized far more quickly (provided such an online discussion is well mediated) and actions can be broadcast across program areas more easily so that local activism is better co-ordinated and supported. For example, if a local group is staffing an Amnesty information booth at a particular event in their community, the UAN co-ordinators may e-mail the activists the most recently issued UAs for passers-by to act on. At the Gay Pride parade, for example, the UAs on display will pertain to lesbian, gay, bisexual or transgendered individuals who are currently at immediate risk of danger because of their sexuality.

Amnesty staff have generally become more accessible to the membership via e-mail and are thus better able to respond to requests for support. However, as much as the electronic medium has facilitated communication amongst human rights activists, the need for periodic face-to-face contact has not been removed. Virtual discussion groups and forums may be held together by a common interest, but if they are to last in any meaningful way, they will greatly benefit from face-to-face interaction.

Implications of internal web use The web's impact on the internal workings of AI has been far less dramatic than that of e-mail. Without a doubt, the IS, section and local websites have been valuable sources of information for members. However, the web has also proven to be a source of frustration or disappointment for some. Local group members, for example, who have created their own personal AI websites, occasionally speak of lack of support, lack of commitment and confusion with regards to their online initiatives. Many local AI groups and members have eagerly volunteered their time and effort to create their own Amnesty websites. They want to capitalize on the web's potential as a tool for outreach and use it to link up with other groups and to promote both AI and their local activities. The Amnesty Lesbian, Gay, Bisexual and Transgender (LGBT) site, www.ai-lgbt.org, is a case in point.

Like hundreds of other AI sites, it was developed and is maintained by members of a local group, largely at their own personal expense. Www.ai.lgbt.org was created and maintained, on a voluntary basis, by a member of a local AI-LGBT group, based in Toronto, together with a supporter of gay rights. However, unlike other AI group sites, the LGBT site was created with the intention of developing a *transnational* space for defenders of the rights of lesbian, gay, bi and transgendered people to communicate, collaborate and support one another. Ideally, the site was not to be owned by any one local AI group but was to belong to, serve and be maintained by the international gay rights community. As a direct result of the site's development, initial contact with international LGBT human rights defenders has been established and a sense of community has ensued. However, keeping these lines of communication open and active has been time-consuming and frustrated by participants' inability or failure to live up to their initial commitments. Site designers had hoped www.ai-lgbt.org would be truly interactive in its support for the international gay rights community. It was expected, for example, that participants and users would contribute relevant articles and documents to the site where an existing searchable databank would make these easily accessible to the community, thereby generating both discussion and action. However, few, if any, contributions have been made and site designers are despairing – tired of volunteering their own time and effort for naught. Furthermore, the site designers have not been able to convince the IS to actively promote the LGBT site as they had hoped. The IS does provide a directory of links to national section and local group websites but the latter are rarely, if ever, actively promoted.

From the IS's point of view, locally developed AI-group sites are largely beneficial to the organization. They provide yet another avenue via which potential members can get involved at a grassroots level. They also allow for members to communicate with each other across national boundaries. The assortment and mushrooming of local AI group sites reflects Amnesty's broad membership base, its loosely federated organizational structure and its pluralistic, grassroots approach to governance. The result, unfortunately, is a multiplicity of websites with inconsistent presences and different ways of presenting and managing information. Although national sections are expected to have developed their own website policies and guidelines for their respective members, there is little clarity or consistency at the grassroots level. Members are not always aware of what can and cannot be made available to the public; they may not clearly identify their site's relationship to the official international or national section sites; they may not know when actions have become outdated or inappropriate; site styles and wording may be inconsistent with those of official AI sites; and links promoted by the local site may unintentionally reflect poorly on AI's work.

Therefore, in spite of the obvious promotional benefits of locally-developed AI sites, they do occasionally pose a potential threat to AI's credibility, especially since the organization does not have the resources to commit to 'quality control'. Legal action may even be taken against the organization as the result of misinterpretations. Consequently, the IS site, www.amnesty.org, encourages local groups to register with the IS, and offers links to their sites but, also, invites users to comment on these sites so that blatant and harmful misrepresentations can be quickly redressed. This threat of misrepresentation, in addition to the risk of misinformation and manipulation, repeatedly occur whenever web-related activism is seriously considered by the organization. These partly account for Amnesty's slow and reluctant embrace of this electronic medium.

The web and the risks of manipulation, misinterpretation and misinformation No doubt, the web has the potential to lend itself to public calls to action. It is a transnational, public medium that can be both entertaining and educational. However, there are inherent risks in a web-based approach to public mobilization: In order to engage with the public, AI must open itself up to the public. In so doing, Amnesty makes itself vulnerable to its opponents and to the workings of hackers and 'uncivil society'. Hackers can be indiscriminate in their attacks: They may be just as likely to target human rights violators as they are to zero in on human rights defenders. Then again, others who commit themselves to electronically subverting oppressive regimes may be hailed as human rights defenders by Amnesty and considered to be 'hackers' or 'uncivil society' by the government in question. At the end of the day, however, the risks to Amnesty are real and demand some vigilance on its part.

Amnesty documents and campaign materials have always been vulnerable to abuse. However, the web has made it easier than ever to copy and doctor documents so as to reflect a contrary stance. Although online petitions may have a particular strategic relevance in a campaign, they can be easily abused in this way. Likewise, it is believed that providing pre-written letters of appeal on an Amnesty website may pose similar problems. The wording can be easily changed to reflect an oppositional stance. The letter can then be circulated and used contrary to its intended purpose. The IS and many of the national sections are in the process of reviewing and working to improve these techniques so as to capitalize upon their accessibility without compromising effectiveness.

What cannot be avoided or controlled by Amnesty are independent websites that deliberately misrepresent or discredit the organization and/or the human rights movement. However, the same medium may also provide Amnesty with the means to fight back – the means to discredit publicly and undermine attempts at misinformation. A case in point is www.amnesty-tunisia.org. This site, which praised the human rights achievements of the Tunisian government, deliberately misled users by appropriating AI's name. While it did not claim to be an authentic AI website, its creators were obviously trying to gain credibility through the adoption of the word 'Amnesty' (Whaley 2000, 36). When amnesty-tunisia.org was first brought to Amnesty's attention, AI responded by deconstructing publicly the contents of the offending site: its international site, www.amnesty.org, linked to www.amnesty-tunisia.org in one frame and presented AI's critique in a parallel frame. The inaccuracies and contradictions were highlighted and Amnesty's own position was made quite clear: that the Tunisian government's repression of journalists, political activists and human rights defenders, including AI's Tunisian Section, remained widespread, and that torture and ill-treatment in prisons were common.

Yet, AI is slow to commit to online activism. This is reflected in the ongoing debate surrounding the online posting of UAs. The current policy states that active UA cases can be posted to AI websites, at the discretion of the sections' UA Co-ordinators, on condition that no authorities' addresses are provided and no action recommended.[4] Users, who view the case and want to act, are instructed to e-mail the UA Co-ordinator responsible for the UA's posting for further details. This enables Co-ordinators to alert the user should a follow-up or correction to the case be issued. Moreover, the user may also be encouraged to join Amnesty and act on behalf of similar cases on a regular basis.

The prevailing thought had been that by not providing the complete details of the UA case the risk of manipulation would be lessened. However, this risk seems rather unsubstantiated when one considers how little control Amnesty has over the cases it distributes to its members. Members consist of those who contribute to AI in some shape or form. Contributions may be financial and/or they may include some form of commitment such as letter writing or participation in a local group. Anyone can become a member of AI. Presumably, therefore, the possibility exists that a fierce opponent of the human rights movement can receive UAs via e-mail and use the information at will. A less dramatic scenario is how members, in their enthusiasm, tend to share cases with the general public either by distributing these either in hardcopy or electronically, or by posting them to their own personal or group websites without AI's knowledge.

Whatever the means of distribution, Amnesty has little control over the public circulation of UAs (and other documents), and e-mail and the web have greatly increased the extent and speed with which this is done. Amnesty is well aware of the fact that the pro-death penalty lobby in the United States has access to UAs and twists the arguments presented in the UAs in its favour. This largely unimpeded circulation of UAs makes Amnesty more vulnerable to abuse, while increasing its potential outreach. When one considers the power of e-mail, the protection of content on the IS or national sections websites may be more limited and perhaps even more symbolic than real. Amnesty's best line of defence against distortion of information and misrepresentation is good offence: vigilance, at all levels of the organization from the local group webmaster to the IS. Ultimately, a handful of national UA Co-ordinators are now posting, with the blessing of the IS, a select few full text UAs online.

The web and AI's public face Moreover, in addition to being aware of the threat of manipulation and misrepresentation, AI has been reluctant to embrace the web's great potential for public education and outreach. Amnesty's communication has traditionally been directed towards an internal audience – between members, co-ordinators, sections and the IS – and, consequently, e-mail was adopted relatively quickly and has proven to be an invaluable tool. Historically, Amnesty has reached out to the general public almost exclusively via its membership and the media, and with the primary intention of drawing prospective members and donors into the internal stream of communication. Amnesty is now faced with an opportunity (and challenge) to interact directly with the public. The web has made it possible for AI to dialogue with and invest in the broader public that is more casually concerned with human rights – with people who want to be involved with the organization on a sporadic basis or who simply want to educate themselves without necessarily committing to the cause. With over 250 websites worldwide posting information produced by or about AI, and with over 8,400,000 annual visitor sessions to AI's international and umbrella website alone,[5] not only is the potential for public outreach real, but some human rights advocates have come to expect AI to commit to public education in the virtual world.

However, as important as public education and outreach may be, some have cautioned that focusing on these at the expense of AI content, recruitment and calls to action may not be cost effective. In other words, investing in a non-committing public – a public that takes no AI-sponsored action or makes no financial contribution – may be good for the broader cause but financially disastrous for the organization. Some sections of the movement, especially those that have a history of public outreach, believe that this need not be the case and that ignoring the general public may, in fact, prove to be the greatest cost to both Amnesty and the human rights movement. AI is thought to have some degree of responsibility for shaping the opinion of the 'non-committing public' – the greatest users of the Internet – and, without a significant AI web presence, AI is ill-equipped to counter online misinformation. Consequently, these sections are beginning to embrace this Internet-based opportunity. They are experimenting with relatively inexpensive and user-friendly interactive applications: audio files including music downloads, video and short movie clips such as AI-USA's *Conflict Diamonds* flash movie which educates viewers about the link between the diamond trade and the brutal conflict in Sierra Leone.

By and large, however, Amnesty continues to lack an educational focus on how local human rights violations relate to broader historical, socio-economic and political contexts. The IS still does not view the public as its primary audience. Consequently, the co-ordination of electronic campaigns and strategies of sections is, at best, confused, particularly as these have widely varying commitments to web-based activism – commitments which sometime exceed those of the IS. In the end, most AI websites, including the IS's www.amnesty.org, continue to restrict themselves to acting as resource libraries and recruitment agents rather than human rights education portals. In other words, they tend to reflect the pride and bedrock of the organization thorough investigation, documentation and strategic mobilization. Users can join or donate to AI online, act immediately on a particular case, gain access to news releases, reports and documents,[6] learn how to influence legislation in their respective countries, learn how to write an effective appeal letter, or learn of upcoming local events.

Clearly, the web's public face presents a number of opportunities and challenges to AI. Unlike e-mail, which facilitates internal communication and mobilization between committed individuals, the web's broader audience drives AI activists and strategists to think beyond the traditional boundaries of the organization, and arguably at the risk of overshadowing 40 years of highly respected investigative research and action. Moreover, for a human rights organization that has, historically, attempted to maintain its neutrality in partisan politics and limited its commitment to the realm of civil and political rights, an interactive form of public education presents a formidable challenge.

Fundraising online In spite of the challenges raised by the web as an interactive and public medium, its mobilizing potential remains great. Via the web, AI can make its research, documentation and campaign materials available to the public. It can lend itself to the communication and co-ordination of public action, and it provides an important, if intimidating, means for public outreach and education. In addition to these, however, the web also lends itself to yet another form of mobilization – the collection of funds. The fundraising possibilities are promising when one considers that, worldwide, those who have access to the web tend to be aged 21 to 45, relatively well-to-do, urban professionals (Johnson 1999). Also, a survey conducted by Martin Johnson, published in *First Monday,* (Johnson 1999) found that 65 per cent of users would be willing to make an online donation, provided security features were disclosed by site designers. For those users aged between 19 and 45, the more extended their experience with the internet, the more likely they were willing to make such a donation. Even if online security was a concern, a user always has the option of downloading a standard form and using conventional mail to make a donation to a national section or directly to the IS. What appears to be of greater concern to potential online donors – greater than issues of online security in the transfer of funds – is the age-old worry about organizational efficiency – about how their money with be used. If anything, the web can be used to disclose this information to potential donors in a transparent and easily accessible manner.

Up to now, the Web's potential for fundraising has not been fully explored by AI. Among other things, Amnesty is concerned with the web's culture of immediacy; internet users seem to be more obsessed with instant action and one-time giving. The challenge remains to convince these one-stop, drive-through activists to commit themselves for longer periods of time.

To date, few non-profit organizations have been able to raise more than a tiny percentage of their income online (AI-USA 2000) but the trends are promising. It seems inevitable that the web will play an increasingly central role in fundraising for Amnesty.

Additional Barriers to Online Activism: Issues of Representation and Access

ICTs contribute to the deterritorialization of activism by facilitating communication, the dissemination of information, co-ordination of action and mobilization of individuals across national boundaries. By the same token, however, ICTs have the potential to further exacerbate and entrench regional and socio-economic divides. Those who are engaged in online activism tend to represent the elite of the world, which begs the question: Just how grassroots or representative and accessible are these forms of activism?

ICTs do not operate independently of complex and interdependent sociopolitical, economic, or historical contexts nor does virtual space operate independently of relationships of power. Consequently, ICTs, which may be couched in terms of globalization and democratization or heralded as a panacea, tend to be accessible and beneficial to an elite minority while the majority has neither access nor voice. This so-called 'digital divide' is reflected at both national and international levels. The use and access to the internet is most widespread and inexpensive in industrialized countries, and within most countries the internet tends to benefit those who are already socially and economically privileged.

Industrialized nations account for 15 per cent of the world's six billion people, 88 per cent of whom are internet users, according to the United Nations (UN). (Bray 2001a, A25) 80 per cent of the world's population, on the other hand, has yet to place their first telephone call. (Bray 2001a, A25) Africa has less than two per cent of the globe's telephone lines, that is 2.5 lines for every 100 Africans, whereas there are 70 phone lines for every 100 Americans. More people use the internet in London than in all of Africa (Bray 2001a, A25) and, there are more users in South Africa than in the rest of the continent combined (Bray 2001b, A8).

Moreover, those who do have access to the internet may not have the same means or rights to publish their own views online, for example in countries where governments set up firewalls and monitor internet traffic. Internet users are also presented with volumes of contradictory bits of information, the reliability of which is often difficult to assess. Consequently, in spite of the vast quantity of information available on the internet, the quality of political discourse will not likely improve. Also, others will not necessarily welcome the values expressed on the web – a medium that remains profoundly Americanized. Many parts of the world view the web as representing consumerism, lax morality and the unrelenting drive of American culture. Ultimately, the assumption that the internet or ICTs are inherently inclusive and representative by virtue of their transnational nature continues to be one that is clearly unfounded.

As a means to begin to bridge the digital divide, Amnesty has committed itself to a multilingual approach to ICTs, as it has done with regard to the production of its hard copy reports and publications. Since one of the major hurdles to access is language, one of Amnesty's short-term internet strategies is to provide links to international AI sites in Arabic, French and Spanish as well as to national or section sites which operate in non-core languages. There is also a push toward establishing and maintaining regionally specific or thematic discussion groups in a number of languages. The more linguistically accessible AI is to the general public, the more inclusive it is likely to be as an international organization. The more diverse the contributions to the human rights discourse, the more likely the movement will break out of its Western mould.

Amnesty is also committed to aggressive improvement of its information technology support to sections. Most, if not all, of AI's poorest sections face exorbitant costs for hardware, internet access and telephone services. Combined with weak infrastructures and a need for skilled personnel, many sections are struggling to get online. Priority is now being given to ensuring reliable access to equipment and technical support. Resources garnered by the IS and wealthier sections are pooled and redistributed primarily according to identified needs, but also according to the strategic importance of a particular section. In other words, there may be heavier investments in sections that have the potential to wield a considerable amount of regional influence. In addition to this formal approach to resource redistribution, there is also some sharing of technological resources occurring informally, between AI sections. For example, a local Canadian Amnesty group donated a personal computer (PC) to AI's Jamaica section – its first and only PC to date.

However, the acquisition of equipment is no guarantee that a section will have the capacity to engage actively in transnational online activism as unreliable telecommunication infrastructures and the exorbitant cost of ISP services continue to limit access to the internet. Although AI is working to standardize technology across the movement so as to facilitate communication and increase speed of action, it recognizes that this may not be immediately feasible for a number of sections. Until, if ever, these limitations are addressed, AI will continue to use a variety of communication tools so as not to risk excluding a potential or existing section for, if ICTs inadvertently contribute to an over-representation of some countries over others, Amnesty may be (justly) discredited as a globally representative movement and its effectiveness may be compromised.

Organizational Challenges Raised by ICTs

AI has become increasingly reliant on information and communication technologies to carry out its activities internationally. As beneficial as some of these technologies have proven to be, others have been approached with trepidation and all have challenged the organization to rethink the shape and future of activism. However, the impact of ICTs has not been limited to strategy and action. Rather, these have had significant implications for AI's resources and for its managerial or organizational culture.

Wiring, upgrading and maintaining AI's technology is an expensive endeavour. The organization's commitment to standardizing technology across sections and supporting them requires a significant financial investment. There also needs to be an investment in training of existing staff and/or volunteers – time and effort that are often considered to be taxing on already burdensome workloads. On the other hand, the heavy investment in technology is also expected to 'pay off'. The cost of introducing new technologies is likely to be offset by the ability to recruit electronically and support more donors and members. Moreover, many programs, including the UAN, are beginning to see a decrease in discretionary costs of operation (such as postage, stationary, photocopying, or faxing).

The permeation of information and communication technologies at all levels of AI has also had a profound and lasting impact on Amnesty's managerial and organizational culture. Some age-old problems are exacerbated and new ones have emerged. No doubt, the means of communication have vastly improved, largely due to the widespread adoption of e-mail. However, actual communication and co-ordination between sections and structures, remains, as always, awkward or disjointed. This could be accounted for by AI's fragmented organizational nature. Structures have evolved to respond and reach out to particular constituencies – some localized, others transnational – but continue to have a poor record of communicating with each other. Consequently, the development of internationally representative or joint strategies also continues to be difficult. The web, in particular, is challenging AI to better integrate these relationships so that its public face will be one that is consistent and clearly defined.

This difficulty is compounded by the fact that Amnesty is gradually being drawn into becoming more reactive than it has been comfortable doing in the past. Historically, AI has established its positions and action agenda based on a lengthy research and approvals process. Now, the media and the public have come to expect that it will offer immediate commentary and opportunities for action on issues that, through the media, have captivated the public's imagination. In other words, a clear, common front must be agreed to quickly and made public with equal speed.

On the other hand, the membership is pulling Amnesty to respond to its evolving needs – needs that are also influenced by the opportunities new technologies afford it. For example, AI members who are electronically drawn together by a particular theme and/or language in a virtual, transnational and largely unregulated space, require some form of support, but it is not clear what kind of support or who, within the organization, is to provide it. Once again, Amnesty's loose organizational structure or 'organized anarchy' and the possibilities afforded to it by the internet, place competing demands on that very same structure. Consequently, the IS and AI sections are having to reinvent themselves. Managerial responsibilities, program areas including membership support and campaigning, and fundraising are all having to be redefined in direct response to changing members' needs. Again, this is no small feat for a large, unwieldy and disaggregated organization that, traditionally, has been resistant to profound change.

In addition to having to respond to a plethora of needs and competing priorities there are also important decision-making procedures that have yet to be established. Who makes decisions pertaining to the electronic medium? Is it the managers, who may not be familiar with the medium? Or is it the information technology staff, who may be more at ease with the mechanics of technology than with their potential strategic use? Then again, is it the campaigners or program staff, whose job it is to strategize and orchestrate action? Is AI to cultivate staff and volunteers with new sets of skills or has it come to expect that these individuals will have some basic experience using technology? Clearly, there are no straightforward answers to these questions as the experience and resources of each section varies so widely. However, as ICTs become increasingly integrated into Amnesty's broader mission, all levels of AI must, at some point or other, seriously engage in these debates.

Finally, the advent and widespread use of information and communication technologies is affecting Amnesty in yet another unexpected way. Some of those that AI purports to represent now have the means to speak for themselves. Human rights defenders, social justice advocates and local NGOs are actively using the internet, the web and e-mail, in particular, to access the general public directly and often do so more effectively than Amnesty. This development, whereby smaller human rights NGOs are appropriating a louder voice, is applauded by AI and is truly a coup for the human rights movement. Yet, the organization is led to ponder what this may mean for its role in the movement and for its relationship to victimized human rights defenders. Moreover, how will the public come to view and support AI's work in light of this development?

There is a negative aspect to this levelling effect of the internet, as well – one that is of great concern to Amnesty. All online activists, regardless of their cause, standards, legitimacy and systems of accountability, are vying for equal space on the web. Consequently, many tend to be viewed equally by the media and by the general public. Organizations like AI and Human Rights Watch, that have prided themselves on years of careful documentation and research, are now lumped together with that of groups whose mandates are entirely conflicting with AI's. In other words, civil society's heterogeneity may be levelled out by, and inaccurately represented in, cyberspace. Amnesty's challenge is to distinguish itself from groups that could potentially tarnish its commitment to human rights and, ideally, to reach out to those with whom it could collaborate as a means to further its cause in a meaningful and truly international or representational form.

Conclusion

Communication is absolutely fundamental to an organization, such as Amnesty, that is membership-based. The advent of information and communication technologies has vastly improved the speed with which data can be collected by AI and circulated internally and publicly. In turn, this has facilitated the co-ordination of action and the mobilization and delivery of organizational support to activists. However, ICTs also aggressively challenge AI to interact directly with the public in a still unfamiliar, unbounded, deterritorialized and transnational space. In response to the changing needs and expectations of its membership and the general public, Amnesty's online presence must extend beyond the comfort of a simple resource library or recruitment agent to become the leading online source for human rights. This is particularly important when one considers the levelling effect of the internet with various groups (or factions) within civil society, including opponents to the human rights movement, competing equally for virtual space. If AI is to adopt this new online persona successfully and if it is to be flexible and open to the changing nature of human rights discourse – nurturing a multi-vocal shaping of the international human rights agenda – it needs to make itself easily accessible and take concrete steps to bridge the digital divide. In so doing, however, Amnesty may be rendered more vulnerable to misinformation, misinterpretation and manipulation. Paradoxically, therefore, in order to open itself up to the public, Amnesty must be more protectionist – tightening its security controls and becoming ever more vigilant to occurrences of abuse.

Having experienced both the benefits and limitations of information and communication technologies, Amnesty has come to favour a utilitarian or pragmatic approach, rather than one that is particularly visionary. ICTs are a new communication medium and not a new world. They are most useful to AI when used in conjunction with other more traditional forms of communication, necessarily including face-to-face interaction.

Moreover, while the introduction of new technologies may have improved the medium they may also have posed unexpected organizational and financial challenges to and strains on AI. In particular, the existing structural gaps in Amnesty's fragmented organizational framework appear to be simultaneously bridged and widened by technology: ICTs facilitate communication between AI structures all the while nurturing expectations that Amnesty should offer both immediacy of action and even greater flexibility. In other words, online 'communities' or networks of members are demanding more flexible support. And, while AI's means of communication may have improved there is now a need to communicate even faster as it is expected to respond to crisis with even greater immediacy.

Ultimately, information and communication technologies have become an integral and valuable element of AI's strategy and commitment to the respect of international human rights. However, given the complexities embedded in the international human rights movement and the equally complex demands of those who contribute to it, technology cannot be accepted at face value but, rather, must be used strategically, as are all other campaign elements. Their limitations must be acknowledged and the challenges they pose to the organization must be identified if ICTs are to be effective, locally appropriate and inclusive across territorial and institutional boundaries. As long as these limitations and challenges are borne in mind, information and communication technologies are likely to continue to benefit Amnesty and its advocates.

Notes

Note on internet addresses (URLs): Websites tend to appear, change or disappear, often without warning. Addresses cited in this bibliography were accurate and active at the time of writing (January 2002) unless otherwise noted.

1. Amnesty's organizational structure is notoriously fragmented. Generally speaking, 'sections' refer to a national representative body of Amnesty. It may be managed by paid staff with the support of volunteers or, if resources are limited, it may be run exclusively by volunteers. Sections tend to act as intermediaries between the IS and local groups, networks and members.
2. In previous years, up to one-third of UA cases have had positive developments.
3. On average, four new UAs are issued daily. Updates on previously issued cases – updates calling for further action or, conversely, announcing an end to action – may also be issued. The latter may average two per day.
4. AI-USA and AI-Sweden are, to date, the only sections to openly post UAs online in their full text forms, including both recommended actions and authorities' addresses.

5   www.amnesty.org was expected to host over 8,400,000 visitor sessions in 2001 – a projection based on the first five months of 2001 – up from 1,400,000 in 1998. Although the numbers are truly impressive, the increase is entirely in line with the estimated general growth of internet use. In other words, Amnesty's popularity online has been maintained. It has neither increased or decreased in proportion to the web's overall traffic (AI 2001).
6   AI Canada's English-speaking section website, www.amnesty.ca, attests to the draw of Amnesty content for users. 2,800 and 2,437 pdf files were downloaded in May (out of 28,250 user sessions) and July 2001 respectively.

References

AI-USA (2000), Unpublished Internal Memorandum. 17 November.
Amnesty International. Computer Communications Working Group (2001), *Meeting Notes*, June.
Bray, Hiawatha (2001a), 'The Wiring of a Continent: Africa Goes Online', *The Boston Globe*, pp. A25, 22 July.
Bray, Hiawatha (2001b), 'The Wiring of a Continent: Entering the Queue', *The Boston Globe*, pp. A8, 23 July.
Johnson, Martin (1999), 'Non-Profit Organisations and the Internet', *First Monday: Peer-Reviewed Journal on the Internet*, Vol. 4(2), www.firstmonday.dk
United Nations. Department of Public Information (1948), *Universal Declaration of Human Rights*, DPI, New York, www.un.org/Overview/rights.html
Whaley, Patti (2000), 'Human Rights NGOs: Our Love-Hate Relationship with the Internet', in Steven Hick, Edward F. Halpin and Eric Hoskins (eds), *Human Rights and the Internet*, Macmillan Press, London, pp. 30-40.

Chapter 3

Scientists and Missile Defence: Organizing Against a Dangerous Plan

John Spykerman[*]

Introduction

After years of testing and months of heated debate, an American administration announces it will not deploy a controversial ballistic missile defence (BMD)[1] system designed to protect the country from an intercontinental ballistic missile (ICBM) attack. In defending his decision, the president cites arguments from the scientific community that the proposed system is beyond the reach of current technology and even if deployed, could not handle the decoys that an enemy warhead almost certainly would use. Moreover, deployment of such a controversial system that offers no true guarantee of protection would harm chances to achieve meaningful progress with Russia on nuclear weapons reductions and lasting stability. Even the most ardent BMD supporters find it difficult to endorse systems that simply do not work. For the time being, arms control supporters have won.

These events describe the public debate over President Bill Clinton's proposed national missile defence (NMD) system. On September 1, 2000, the President chose to defer an NMD deployment decision to the next administration despite immense pressure from the political right to begin construction immediately. But the above scenario is strikingly similar to other missile defence debates that preceded the Clinton administration. From the Sentinel and Safeguard systems of the 1960s and 1970s to President Ronald Reagan's Strategic Defense Initiative (SDI), the United States has repeatedly pursued BMD programs against the advice of the international community and several domestic actors. Time and time again, US leaders have pushed forward with ambitious new plans only to stop short of deployment, often citing problems with the technology. Several factors have changed, from the source of the threat to the technology under development, but the ideological arguments that drive BMD are a constant presence in US politics that makes missile defence deployment an issue for every administration.

Even the September 11, 2001 terrorist attacks against the United States had little effect on the ideological arguments driving the missile defence debate. Backers of a missile shield said the attacks proved the United States was vulnerable and needed to devote resources to protecting against the larger devastation that would result from a missile tipped with a nuclear warhead. Opponents, however,

---

[*] John Spykerman, who was formerly with the Global Security Program of the Union of Concerned Scientists, is writing in his own capacity.

pointed out that the attacks validated one of their chief criticisms of missile defence – that the threat of a missile attack is exaggerated. The September 11 hijackers showed that it is much easier to attack the United States from within, turning planes into suicidal weapons, rather than spending greater amounts of time and resources developing or acquiring nuclear and long-range missile capabilities. In the uncertainty of the aftermath from September 11, conservative backers of missile defence appeared to pull ahead, as the temporary bipartisan climate muted criticism from the left. Other concerns, however, such as the need to build international coalitions and the technological problems of rushing an unproven system toward deployment, have pulled the debate back toward the middle. While far-reaching in so many other ways, the terrorist attacks against the World Trade Center and Pentagon will in all likelihood result in no net gain or loss for either side of the missile shield battle.

Scientific arguments against BMD deployment made by nongovernmental organizations (NGOs) such as the Union of Concerned Scientists (UCS) have been an integral element in the effort to protect global stability against a move by the United States to deploy unworkable systems that threaten to ignite arms races. The successful campaign against the Clinton system contained many similarities to those that led to the 1972 Anti-Ballistic Missile (ABM) Treaty or opposed the SDI (better known as "Star Wars" by critics and supporters alike), but it also utilized many new aspects of information technology. For the first time, electronic organizing and use of the new internet-based media helped advance the scientists' argument that NMD was technologically flawed.

Information technology allowed UCS and other NGOs to create and develop their campaign on several levels, including:

- *Communication.* UCS, together with the Massachusetts Institute of Technology's (MIT's) Security Studies Program, produced the *Countermeasures* report, a technical assessment of the limited, ground-based BMD proposed by Clinton.[2] The report found several weaknesses in the system, especially in regard to its ability to overcome countermeasures from attacking missiles.[3] Released to the public and media in April 2000, it was the centerpiece of the NGO community's technological arguments and the work of 11 co-authors from a variety of fields in physics and engineering.
- *Research.* The website provided important access for research, as the 11 co-authors of the report relied on the Pentagon's unclassified open-source information on BMD programs to support their arguments.
- *Organizing.* As a participant in the Coalition to Reduce Nuclear Dangers, UCS and other NGOs utilized their web pages to distribute information relevant to a variety of anti-BMD arguments to each other, the public, and the media.
- *Activism.* At the grassroots level, UCS developed an e-mail network of scientists and engineers concerned with arms control and global security who could make effective arguments in their local media and to their representatives in Congress.

UCS and the arms control community won an important victory with Clinton's September 2000 decision. But with the election of President George W. Bush and a Republican Congress, the longevity of that victory is in doubt. Future campaigns against BMD may well be modeled on the high-tech use of information and organization employed against the Clinton system. However, their success will largely depend on the scientific and arms control communities' ability to maintain the political importance of technical arguments against BMD.

As the new US administration pushes ahead with plans for a global missile defence, it will not be the first time scientists must reorganize their efforts against BMD. On each occasion when the United States has been on the verge of BMD deployment, the arms control and global security communities have stepped forward to organize technology-based arguments against deployment. Other domestic NGOs (pacifists, religious and moral groups, and other dovish organizations) also have come forward equipped with their own arguments. Together, these civil society organizations produce an effective case against BMD. Many factors – chief among them domestic politics, international relations, and existing treaties – played a role in the official administration statement. But technological problems offer safe political cover – they allow for deferring deployment decisions in favour of continued research. In other words, deployment is put aside while more complicated political issues are dealt with.

Whether or not one agrees with the honesty of this logic, technological arguments against BMD help stop deployment and threats to arms control agreements that benefit US and global security. Because of this, it is important for scientists and NGOs such as UCS to advance their cause by combining high visibility and sound arguments. This chapter illustrates the importance of information technology and effective organizing in contemporary BMD debates. Beginning with an historical perspective on scientists and missile defences, the chapter moves on to the events leading up to Clinton's 2000 decision, the role played by scientists in the debate, and ends with lessons relevant for future BMD debates.

An Historical Perspective on Ballistic Missile Defence

Political Support for BMD

Few experts believe that President Clinton pursued his NMD plan by his own choice. His limited program, which even if functional would only have been capable of intercepting a few dozen warheads from an accidental launch or rogue state attack, was more the result of political pressure from the Republican Party. Republicans have been the chief supporters of BMD since the 1960s. While there have been no shortages of Democratic votes, the Democratic Party as a whole has been less receptive to deploying BMD systems in violation of the ABM Treaty. Talk of a BMD began as soon as German scientists launched rocket attacks against England. World War II ended before missile and nuclear weapon technologies could be used in tandem, but military strategists did not take long to realize the new threat the world faced. Nuclear weapons, combined with long-range missile technology, could threaten every nation from any place in the world. Six decades later, this strong psychological perception of vulnerability remains difficult for any movement to argue against.

A functional missile shield would give the US increased leverage to dictate foreign policy on its own terms. In the Cold War and thereafter, the US and other nations with nuclear weapons have relied on a policy of deterrence for protection from nuclear attacks. According to this concept, known as mutually assured destruction (MAD), one state is deterred from attacking another with nuclear weapons because it knows it would face an immediate and devastating counterattack. Faced with unacceptable damage from a retaliatory strike, states are deterred from launching an initial strike.

Effective arguments to political elites and the public rely on the ability to understand the motivation behind the pursuit of BMD. If the US were to deploy a functional BMD, it would no longer need to rely on MAD for protection against ICBM attacks from states with a low number of nuclear warheads. Isolationists argue that the US would be less vulnerable in an increasingly unstable global order. Unilateralists argue that with a missile shield the United States would not be deterred from asserting its leadership in regional conflicts where a rogue state might try to deter US involvement by threatening to launch one missile at a US city. For example, some question whether the US would have mounted such a relentless campaign against the Iraqi occupation of Kuwait if Saddam Hussein had possessed a long-range missile capable of reaching US territory during the Gulf War.

Thus, the dreams of a missile shield are very captivating and the supporting arguments difficult to overcome in the public arena for any group, but particularly for scientists, whose rational technical arguments often eschew the emotional and psychological factors that lead to BMD support. The fascination with BMD is not just held by political leaders. Asked simply whether they favor a missile defence, most Americans routinely support BMD (in fact, some polls show that a majority of Americans believe the US already has deployed a BMD).[4] The idea that the ruthless leader of an isolated state such as Iraq or North Korea could threaten American families in San Diego or Chicago does not sit well with the public.

These are difficult perceptions to counter in a public campaign against BMD deployment. To compensate for this, UCS and other groups must better understand the rationale supporters use for BMD deployment and continuously focus their criticism in ways that most effectively attack the credibility of these arguments in the eyes of elites and the public. As a participant in the research and development of defence programs, the scientific community has the access and expertise to shape policy debates among elites. But such arguments may not work among the public. Therefore, it is imperative for groups such as UCS to engage in public education and encourage media, especially local outlets, to further explore the many complicated issues associated with BMD. This can often mean two separate tracks of public activism, but the end result is always to reduce enthusiasm for deployment by examining the ability – or inability – of any BMD system to make the US more secure.

Missile defence proponents usually advocate the right of a state to define its security on its own terms. BMD supporters often reject the importance of multilateralism and the effectiveness of international institutions to solve crises and bolster the security of individual states. Their dream of an impenetrable missile shield is related to the belief in a "Fortress America" that can isolate itself from the chaotic fray on the global scene (Spencer & Scardaville 2000). Technologically speaking, proponents make an effective, although misleading, argument that the US, which landed humans on the moon, can eventually overcome any technological challenge and should not let such barriers stand in the way of research and deployment. They claim a shield that trumps so many threats to national security is well worth almost any cost.

While missile shields may seem initially promising to the public, opposition grows when more factors come into play. In the 1970s, when Cold War nuclear strategy meant that BMD launch sites would be among the first targets of a nuclear war, few citizens wanted these missiles anywhere near their home cities and towns. Gradually, public and elite support coalesced behind arms control initiatives. Scientists made consistent arguments against BMD on technological issues, while disarmament groups played a key role in drawing the attention of the national media to the nonproliferation regime. Technology-based counter-arguments against BMD can be difficult to make in the public arena, especially in electronic media. While BMD supporters can promote American ingenuity and cite past accomplishments, opponents must make the less romantic counter-arguments that, for example, the moon did not fight back against the Apollo program and that therefore, the analogy is irrelevant. Opponents of BMD have won many important victories, but a short history of the American flirtation with missile shields shows that they have yet to achieve a lasting victory.

A Brief History of BMD in the United States

From the 1950s to the 1970s, the Pentagon pursued several BMD intercept programs, spending more than $25 billion on systems mainly designed to rely on nuclear explosions to destroy an attacking missile or warhead (Schwartz 1998). The two global superpowers, the US and the Soviet Union, resorted to stockpiling and deploying many thousands of nuclear warheads in order to overcome any defence with sheer numbers. With advancements in multiple warhead technology, a defence system could never hope to field enough interceptors to counter each of the enemy's warheads. Before long, the Pentagon eventually began to lose hope in missile defence and grew to support the deterrence concept of MAD. Presidents Kennedy, Johnson, Nixon, and Ford all took steps, some more reluctantly than others, to reverse course from a BMD deployment. The highlight was the ratification of the Anti-Ballistic Missile (ABM) Treaty with the Soviet Union in 1972 under President Nixon.

ABM ratification was supported by many in the scientific community. Disillusionment with the Vietnam War fostered more political organization of scientists (UCS was founded in 1969) and many of the current arguments against BMD began to take their shape.[5] Arguments used then and now include: a missile defence will encourage rivals to build more warheads to overwhelm the system; the costs of developing and deploying such a system are vast; and a "perfectly" designed system cannot guarantee a perfect defence. Of course, the use of information technology has changed the manner in which scientists (and others in the arms control community) organize their issues and educate the public, media, and political leaders. Whereas scientists organized "teach-ins" at individual campuses during the Vietnam War, e-mail networks and websites are today used to organize members from a variety of locales.

Historically, the organization and visibility of BMD opponents have been proportionate to the nearness of a potential deployment. Domestic economic issues took hold in the US in the late 1970s and BMD fell off the political radar. However, the 1980 presidential election brought the conservative Ronald Reagan into office along with a Republican Senate. Reagan won over the public with his broad visions for renewed morality, economy and security, and in March 1983, his missile shield dream. As Frances FitzGerald writes in her history of Reagan and the Cold War, the President's career as an actor in 'simply told' movies and his fundamentalist religious beliefs contributed to broad notions of good versus evil and the role of the US as a saviour for humankind (FitzGerald 2000).

During his speech that introduced SDI, Reagan called on scientists, "those who gave us nuclear weapons", to now come together to build a multi-tiered defence against ballistic missiles. However, on the very same day he delivered this speech, Pentagon officials were testifying before a congressional committee that such technology was impossible, and that the military did not support further funding for such research. Reagan's plan called for an ambitious combination of space- and ground-based missile interceptors, laser technology and satellite systems. Many scientists were quick to oppose it, and arms control supporters accused Reagan of destabilizing reduction negotiations with the Soviet Union. While some objected in principle to the application of science to such a menacing cause, physicist Edward Teller, as he had done before for such causes, lent his support to Reagan and furthered a public perception of a divided scientific community.

Organizing against SDI was not always easy. Reagan had linked scientists with nuclear weapons and suggested there was a sense of obligation to Americans on the part of the scientific community to produce technologies for missile defences. While many scientists might have felt a sense of obligation to promote global security, many of them disagreed that that obligation involved missile defence deployment.

Participation and interest in Star Wars opposition was therefore heated. Several elder statesmen of the scientific community immediately moved to sever contact with the administration, and many young physicists pledged not to work on such programs that were capable of encouraging nuclear proliferation and destabilizing global security (Gottfried 1999, 46). But of course, there were plenty of scientists and engineers drawn to both Reagan's vision and lucrative government contracts, and the United States embarked on a six-year, $15 billion research phase that produced not one deployable lead on an effective technology for BMD (Schwartz 1998, 291).

By the beginning of the elder Bush administration, the dream of SDI had died. Instead, the focus moved to a more limited vision, theater missile defence (TMD). The Iraqi Scud attacks during the Gulf War showed that short-range missile technology had proliferated, and could pose a threat not affected by the US nuclear deterrent or relationship with the Soviet Union/Russia. With the threat of a destabilizing BMD deployment gone, it became less crucial for scientists to pursue a role in the public debate. The end of the Cold War, too, hastened BMD's exit from the public consciousness and very few paid attention to the progress of TMD development.

With their 1994 victories in Congress, Republicans tried to resurrect Reagan's enthusiasm for BMD. President Clinton had already reorganized the SDI program into the Ballistic Missile Defense Organization (BMDO) to deal with theater defence issues and to deflect the criticism "cold warriors" had thrown at an administration they saw as "weak on defense". The Republican Party's Contract With America[6] contained only one section relevant to defence or security, and that focused on deploying an NMD system. The push continued as Senate Majority Leader Bob Dole (Republican-Kansas) tried to win points in his 1996 presidential bid by making the Clinton administration's opposition to missile defence an issue. The public did not bite, but the president felt enough pressure to budget BMDO funds for NMD research (Cirincione 1997). Elections in 1996, 1998 and 2000 politicized the BMD issue further, but did little to spike public interest. While polls consistently show that technological arguments, cost, and the risk of breaking treaties all play important roles in turning the public against BMD, they also show the public gives a higher priority to domestic issues.[7] Still, Clinton's NMD plan responded to the wishes of many Republicans who saw a threat in so-called rogue states such as North Korea and Iran. But when Clinton made his September 2000 decision, public reaction was generally supportive, and the issue did not come up in any of the three presidential debates between then-Governor George W. Bush and Vice President Al Gore.

Civil Society and Scientists

The decades-old BMD debate in the US may seem repetitive. Indeed, the scenarios, issues, support, and criticism are often familiar to those who have watched this debate develop over the years. But the organizational tactics of civil society groups to oppose BMD have evolved into a very different game today than in earlier cycles, such as the one that led to the ABM Treaty of 1972. It is no coincidence that information technology plays a crucial role among scientists making technological arguments against BMD to the media, public, and political elites. Science and technology have always been linked, but the same cannot be said for science and politics.

Most scientists are reluctant to define their profession as a community with a stated, single view. Because of this, politically aware scientists oftentimes cannot compete in fervor and passion with other actors in BMD policy debates. The defence industry and neo-isolationist conservatives are capable of well-funded and organized campaigns to push their agendas and influence policy. Meanwhile, many scientists are unwilling to sacrifice their absolutism, idealism, or even the presumption of deeper understanding, for the compromises, half-steps, and spin control necessary in the shaping of public policy. As a result, it is quite difficult to organize a unanimous and well-funded campaign on behalf of the scientific community to compete with the defence industry and ideologues. One of the unique difficulties in fostering civil society activism among scientists is overcoming this reluctance to participate in highly political debates. For those who oppose BMD, the fact that the technology will not offer an effective defence should alone be enough to end the debate. But as 40 years of missile shield dreams prove, that is simply not enough.

Scientists have participated in global politics since the first years after the end of World War II.[8] Before World War II and the detonation of atomic bombs against Japan, scientists participated in US politics on a vastly different level. Initial organization of scientists developed mainly along two lines: quasi-governmental bodies such as the National Academy of Sciences, and specialized professional groups such as the American Physical Society. These organizations rarely took political positions, and concerned themselves more with the advancement of science itself. Interaction with the government and politics was often limited to advocating for more funding of research.

Scientists played a key role in the US war effort with the Manhattan Project and the development of nuclear weapons during World War II. But many members of the US nuclear effort and other scientists anticipated the ethical and moral problems of such weapons and re-examined their roles as society's technological experts. At first from insider positions as government advisers, and later as outside activists, scientists began to organize in support of peaceful and stable stewardship of the technology their knowledge produced.

Organizations such as the Federation of American Scientists (FAS) and UCS were formed between World War II and the end of the Vietnam War to enable scientists to play a greater role in politics outside of government service. Over the years, they have helped provide a unified platform for the portion of the scientific community that seeks to lend its voice and expertise to national debates over arms control and global security. The participation of scientists as political outsiders and grassroots activists has evolved in response to both NGO organizing and the advent of electronic media and information technology. Scientists played a key role in pushing for the ABM Treaty (making many of the same countermeasure arguments as today) and organized petitions against Star Wars-related work in the 1980s.

Interestingly, one of the greatest weaknesses of organizing scientists is also one of the greatest strengths in creating an effective message. Many scientists reject formalism, and the profession encourages the participation of individuals (Gilpin & Wright 1964). This strong individualism creates a difficult environment in which to forge the notion of a collective "scientific community", one whose members speak with one voice. The definition of a "scientist" itself is fuzzy – to suggest that certain political views are held by all, especially given such strong individualism, would be impossible.

Strong individualism can lead to power and influence. Accomplished scientists gain notoriety and the attention of important players in the national debate, such as political leaders and the media. Even for those without widely praised accomplishments or national fame, simply being a "scientist" is often enough to be respected locally as an expert whose wisdom is to be admired and heeded. Over the years, NGO organizers have learned the importance of encouraging scientists to approach their local media to give hometown angles to national stories. Also of note is the ability of respected scientists, such as Hans Bethe or Richard Garwin in recent years, to motivate mid-career and young scientists to lend their voices to political causes. A visible and respected scientist is important for campaigns to influence political leaders and national media, but local debates are won with numbers and strong grassroots activism.

Another obstacle to effective organizing is the difficulty of making of scientific arguments in the political arena. Scientists may be reluctant to "dumb down" their arguments for a lay audience, fearing a significant loss in the translation. Given the choice, many scientists would rather prove their point among colleagues who understand its technological aspects, rather than reducing their message to fit a more general audience. Arguing that BMD will not work because "the interceptor cannot see the warhead" may be good enough for some, but for many scientists it is much more rewarding and comfortable to discuss the intricate mathematical calculations and understanding of physics that lead to such conclusions. In fact, for many scientists, the discussion and understanding of such aspects are *vital* to making these arguments. Yet, for the majority of the public who lack the understanding of such physical and mathematical concepts, the arguments would fall on deaf ears.

In the larger national debate on BMD, scientists could never hope to take on BMD supporters with technological arguments alone. Political and science-based arguments are modeled on different worlds. As discussed above, politics can alienate and disturb members of the scientific community who are reluctant to involve themselves in politics.[9] To be more effective, science-based NGOs have learned to work in coalition with others. An umbrella group, the Coalition to Reduce Nuclear Dangers, utilizes the strengths of its member NGOs to create a multi-pronged attack on BMD.[10] Some, such as Peace Action and 20/20 Vision, bring grassroots expertise and a wide base of membership to the table. Others, such as the Council for a Livable World, share important political knowledge, research, and savvy. Finally, UCS and FAS provide the important technological expertise that commands the attention of political leaders and the national media.

Put together, this is civil society at its best: organizations and individuals working together to influence public policy and shape the national debate. In just 12 months, the conventional wisdom regarding Clinton's NMD deployment decision went from a sure thing to the shocking deferral to the next administration. Several factors other than civic activism led to Clinton's decision, namely the failure of two of the three NMD intercept tests conducted between 1999 and 2000. But the efforts of civil society, vastly aided by the use of information technology, played a vital role.

46 *Civil Society in the Information Age*

The Latest Campaign: Strategy and Resources

In 1999, morale in the NGO arms control community was low. Most experts believed Clinton would move ahead with deployment of his limited NMD before the 2000 elections in order to give political cover to the vice president from attacks on his defence policies. Even if technological criticisms were on target and the testing program produced few positive results (which turned out to be the case), many believed Clinton would still proceed with initial construction of the NMD system if only to "triangulate" congressional factions and pre-empt attacks on the Gore campaign. In October of that year, the US Senate rejected the Comprehensive Test Ban Treaty (CTBT) after just a few days of hearings and debate. The vote sent a strong signal that arms control opponents were asserting their muscle and that political arguments carried more weight than scientific support for treaties and verification measures.

Clinton's deployment decision was initially expected in June 2000. With less than a year remaining before his decision, arms control groups in the Coalition to Reduce Nuclear Dangers plotted a strategy to encourage postponement of the decision to the next administration.[11] Despite their belief that the technology for missile defence would not be able to offer a benefit to US security any time soon, the NGOs realized political factors would make termination of the program impossible. Postponement until a non-election year would put less pressure on an administration to deploy for political purposes and allow for more time to avoid actions that would destabilize relations with Russia and China. In the event that Vice President Gore succeeded Clinton, or that NMD opponents increased their numbers in Congress, there was also the chance that legislative pressure to deploy would subside.

Before the campaign began, the coalition plotted a strategy that showed it had learned its lessons from the failed CTBT effort, and identified factors to improve the NMD debate's chances for victory. NMD opponents would have to take several steps to make sure their message was organized, heard by the right people, and effective in the political arena. To organize, NGOs divided the work according to their respective strengths. UCS, with its technical expertise and credentials in the scientific community, took the lead in making the case against the feasibility of the proposed system. Other NGOs would focus on mobilizing grassroots activism and establishing contacts with key political leaders. Still others would seek to produce letters signed by well-known public figures and experts in national security. From an earlier statement by Clinton that deployment would be based on four criteria, the groups asserted that NMD failed on all counts: the status of the technology was not ready, it was too costly, the threat was exaggerated, and deployment threatened arms control agreements and international stability.

In retrospect, chances for victory were better for the arms control community with NMD than with the CTBT. However, the changing nature of the political debate over BMD during the last decade made this campaign more difficult than previous BMD debates. With the Cold War over and many in the public convinced BMD technology was within reach (and no threat to global security), technological criticisms would have a hard time gaining a sense of urgency. In 1998, North

Korea test-launched a medium-range missile over the territory of Japan, energizing BMD supporters with fresh evidence that long-range missile technology was proliferating and rogue states were an increasing risk to the US. Also, a healthy economy caused some to worry that the costs of BMD construction would not have the same impact as before. Even a system costing $60 billion over ten years would still amount to about just two per cent of annual US defence spending.

But in terms of crafting an effective campaign, there were more factors on the arms control community's side. During the CTBT ratification debate, treaty supporters were constitutionally required to get 67 votes in the US Senate. With Democrats in the minority and conservative Senator Jesse Helms (Republican-North Carolina) chairing the Foreign Relations Committee, it was too difficult to swing enough moderate Republican votes, and the treaty fell well short of ratification.[12] However, the target audience among political leaders for the NMD debate was much smaller, and victory did not require large support from both parties. Instead, the coalition knew the decision to deploy NMD rested solely with the President. If political cover for elections was a concern, the expanded target audience would then include those who could best influence the President's decision, namely key lawmakers from the Democratic Party, the national media, and important international allies. For the next several months, NGOs sought the best routes to gain access to these groups and pressure them to convince Clinton not to deploy.

Information technology played an important role in this campaign, helping NGOs craft their message and ensuring that it gained the necessary traction in the media and minds of elites and foreign allies. In preparing the campaign against Clinton's NMD, UCS and other organizations utilized information technology in a variety of ways that fall mainly into four categories: communication, research and collection of information, disseminating information, and organizing activism. The use of the internet helped connect physicists in Cambridge, Massachusetts with engineers in Stanford and allowed them to create, develop, and share the arguments that helped lead to Clinton's eventual decision not to deploy NMD during his term.

UCS's role in the campaign centred around two main initiatives. First, UCS produced the *Countermeasures* report (cited earlier), which analyzed the effectiveness of the planned system. Second, UCS developed the ArmsNet e-mail network, a network of scientists and engineers interested in arms control and global security who would be capable of providing scientific expertise to local and national media, and gaining access to their representatives in Congress. The *Countermeasures* report brought together 11 scientists and engineers with a variety of experiences related to BMD. The report would become the foundation of the arms control community's technological arguments and lead to a growing skepticism over NMD's ability to increase US security. ArmsNet, in turn, would help publicize the report's findings to a wider audience than would be possible from UCS's offices in Washington, DC, and Cambridge, MA. ArmsNet members, whose background in science prepared them to understand the complex arguments made in the report, could vouch for their accuracy and relevance to local reporters. As constituents of important lawmakers, they would have greater access to congressional offices where they could draw the attention of a senator and his or her aides to the report.

The Countermeasures Report

To those familiar with the highly technical methods of defeating missile defence systems, the UCS/MIT *Countermeasures* report may have been old news. But for most of the United States – politicians and media included – who had heard only from BMD experts at the Pentagon, the report was a strong rebuttal to the military's public confidence in the NMD system. The report found that the Clinton system, even in its most advanced stage of deployment, would be vulnerable to technically simple countermeasures. Moreover, the report found that such countermeasures would be readily available to enemy states and that the Pentagon's testing program was not challenging the system to function in realistic scenarios.

The report was the work of 11 scientists and engineers with a wide variety of expertise in physics, missile technology, arms control, and international security. Chaired by Andrew M. Sessler, a senior scientist at the Lawrence Berkeley National Laboratory and past president of the American Physical Society, the study group utilized public information and years of experience in BMD research and application to construct its criticism of the Clinton system. Spread out across the country and burdened with their own busy schedules and professional commitments, the co-authors often looked to e-mail and the web to quicken communications and coordination efforts.

Two UCS staff scientists, David Wright and Lisbeth Gronlund, first began the push for the report in the fall of 1998. After drawing up an outline and putting together the panel, the study group met for the first time in March 1999. Two months later, it would hold its only other meeting – leaving most of the communication between authors for e-mail. Gronlund and Wright, together with MIT's George Lewis, did much of the actual writing and conferred often in Cambridge. The web was also useful for research, as it contained information on BMD and other aspects of the debate on government and private-sector sites. While classification of sensitive material prevented the authors from delving deeply into many issues, declassified versions of many government reports, including the 1999 National Intelligence Estimate on the missile threat to the US, were readily available on the web.

After about one year of writing and exchanging drafts, the report was ready. On April 11, 2000, UCS and MIT published the report with funding from several foundations and sent copies to the media, political leaders, and other NGOs. The authors of the report and UCS staff met with several editorial boards at major newspapers, which initiated positive commentaries on the report's findings from *The New York Times, The Washington Post, The Boston Globe*, and others.

Initial reaction from the Pentagon rejected the *Countermeasures* report's findings. Citing their knowledge of "classified information", Pentagon officials claimed NMD would work regardless of the report's findings (Becker 2000, A12). However, without any concrete proof that NMD could overcome such countermeasures, the message that the Clinton NMD system would not offer a true defence began to gain a foothold in the national debate. Test failures, independent reviews, and production delays gave additional credibility to the report's conclusions.

The success of *Countermeasures* has created some concern, though, that effective use of declassified or potentially sensitive unclassified government reports will be less available to the public as the Pentagon attempts to cut off critics' access to information. Recently, the Defense Department has looked to classify more aspects of its testing process, fearing that independent scientific analysis will tip off hostile nations to the various weaknesses of BMD systems. One article reported that even the testing dates of future systems could be classified and withheld from the public.[13]

Shortly after the report's release, the American Physical Society (APS) took the unusual step for a professional association of issuing a statement on NMD testing. No deployment should be made, the APS agreed, until NMD is shown to be effective against countermeasures (APS 2000). The report also generated some support from within the Pentagon. Philip Coyle, then-director of operational testing and evaluation (DOT&E), scrutinized the testing schedule. None of the three intercept tests to be held before Clinton's expected decision, Coyle wrote, "were completely operationally realistic" (Coyle 2001). With a series of failed tests, mounting criticism from the media and the scientific community, and production delays in many of the system's components, the Pentagon has postponed future tests.

The report's analysis and findings were the result of a complex understanding of the physics of missile defence. Still, UCS took several steps to ensure that the report did not fly over the head of mainstream Americans. Scientists held press conferences and briefings with congressional offices to explain the intricate conclusions of the report, but in order to impact on the public debate, UCS knew that it would have to go deeper to drive home the message. UCS posted the entire 175-page report on its website, along with a four-minute animation detailing two of the potential countermeasures. The report and animation were also included on a CD-ROM, and a video of the animation was sent to several broadcast media outlets. The use of multimedia technologies broadened the reach of the report and played an important role in public education. The critical use of graphics simplified the making of a complex argument. Very few read the entire 175-page report, but very many saw the animation.

The ArmsNet E-mail Network

UCS created ArmsNet in March 2000 to foster communication and activism among scientists and engineers interested in arms control issues such as NMD. UCS knew that giving the report to validators – those who can vouch for a report's integrity via some degree of expertise in the field – would deepen the overall impact of the report in the national debate. Leaders in the scientific community and others with political experience in arms control would naturally be important validators for the national media. But in order to ensure that the *Countermeasures* findings reached the public consciousness (i.e., making sure the perception that NMD was unworkable became a household concept), it was important to make this same effort toward validation and publicity at the local level.

As an organization, UCS already knew the importance of organizing scientists to use local resources to affect a national campaign. In 1995, UCS founded the Sound Science Initiative (SSI) as a means for scientists to influence national policy on environmental issues through enhanced use of information technology. Recruiting from the UCS membership base and later branching out to professional organizations, universities, and elsewhere, SSI now consists of more than 2,000 scientists dedicated to promoting awareness and action on climate change and global environment issues. Scientists receive e-mail updates and directions to websites for materials useful for research and public education. Most of these scientists are from life science fields, have the important ability to understand the technical material and share their understanding with a wider base of the population who trust their expertise, including the media and their local members of Congress.

ArmsNet is the physical science sibling of SSI. It was created in a similar style, but aiming to foster participation of scientists in global security policy. During the Star Wars debate, there was a closer connection between academic physicists and Reagan's BMD program. SDI planned to rely on technologies not yet available – in fact, many of the technologies were so far off in the future that research was needed at the most basic and theoretical levels. This required the involvement of academics and other experts in theoretical and applied physics. But in the late 1990s, the Pentagon had already chosen the architecture of the NMD system and believed the operational effectiveness of its intercept technology was just around the corner. Research funding for the NMD system was contained within the Pentagon program and defence industry, and did not require outside academics to dream up new technologies. Therefore, most scientists did not face the same dilemma their counterparts did in the 1980s – whether or not to heed Reagan's call to defend the US from nuclear attack. Under President Clinton, there was no such catalyst for average scientists to join the public debate. ArmsNet, by design, seeks to organize scientists and give them the tools they need to make effective stands in favor of arms control and global security.

UCS initially sent an invitation e-mail from Kurt Gottfried and Richard Garwin, both well known activist-scientists, to several thousand scientists and engineers to join the e-mail network. Since then, membership has increased via word of mouth and appearances at American Physical Society events. ArmsNet members receive updates on BMD and nuclear weapons policy issues, as well as requests to take action to oppose deployment of the planned system. Activism has included writing Congress and the President to oppose NMD deployment based on the arguments of the *Countermeasures* report, authoring opinion columns and letters to the editor along similar lines, and participating in the educational efforts in Washington, DC.

UCS staff drew up a plan of action for ArmsNet in conjunction with the goals formulated earlier for the arms control community's campaign against NMD deployment. UCS would release its technical report and focus on ensuring that the report's message was an accepted and visible aspect of the media's NMD coverage. In addition, the report would be used to convince key congressional players that a deployment at that time would not offer an effective defence. In order to preempt a deployment decision that would give political cover to Democratic candidates, UCS sought to bolster the public's skepticism of NMD to soften charges of weakness on defence issues. After *Countermeasures* was released to the public, UCS would use its membership, particularly in ArmsNet, to bring the report's findings to their local media and representatives in Congress. Finally, UCS would mount a highly visible event in Washington, DC that combined local activism with a national stage.

The first ArmsNet project distributed and publicized the findings of the *Countermeasures* report to the media and Congress. ArmsNet members received via e-mail the key findings of the report and links to the UCS website for access to the entire report and other supporting information. Many members were not missile experts, but their understanding of technical concepts gave them an edge over the general public. Others had been involved in BMD programs or research, but had fallen out of the loop in recent years. For them, the UCS information and report were opportunities to brush up on the latest developments and familiarize themselves with the Clinton system. Still others were currently engaged in the NMD debate and used ArmsNet as a central focus for receiving and sharing information.

After members received the *Countermeasures* report, UCS asked that they bring this message into the national debate via the media and members of Congress. Members began publishing letters and opinion pieces in their local and national newspapers reinforcing the UCS message that NMD would not provide an adequate defence against likely attacks. Scientists with credentials in BMD research landed highly visible columns in major newspapers in Washington and San Francisco, while physics professors at universities played their role by providing hometown newspapers with 'local experts' for national stories.

Next, ArmsNet members traveled to Washington with UCS funding to make their case to Congress and the national media. In June 2000, the NMD Education Days brought 40 scientists and engineers from 16 states to Washington to oppose deployment of the planned NMD system. With one day scheduled for issues, media and lobbying workshops, and one day for meeting with members of Congress and the media, the scientists accomplished an impressive level of outreach to those in Congress and the media who might influence President Clinton's upcoming decision on NMD. The scientists met with lawmakers or aides from 63 offices, including both Senate offices from each of the 16 states. Aides and lawmakers responded with great interest to the meetings, and many took active roles in their discussions with the scientists, often asking for further information from a participant, or if the participant could serve as an advisor on technical issues in the future. It was an important achievement for the role of science in national politics, and a crucial engagement of scientists in the political process.

Throughout the summer of 2000, activism increased among the scientific and arms control communities by other means that utilized information technology. E-mail organizing led to the creation of several letters by experts opposed to NMD deployment. In July, 50 Nobel Laureates signed a letter organized by FAS to the President opposing NMD plans. Well-known experts on Russia, China, and US defence policy also signed similar letters to Clinton that summer. E-mail also played a large role in the arms control community, fostering an enhanced ability for rapid communication. With the click of a mouse, developing news reached the in boxes of everyone instantly. Because more people than ever had access to the latest news, the scope and nature of the debate created a larger forum for political involvement. In Congress, grassroots activism was beginning to show results as well. The arms control community knew they had achieved one of their goals when the Democrats demonstrated a clear cohesiveness by sticking together on votes for increased testing and signing letters to the president asking for a delay.[14]

Several specific events led to President Clinton's September 1 decision not to deploy NMD during his term. In his speech, he acknowledged the weaknesses of the testing program and the system's vulnerability to countermeasures, affirming the criticisms made by the UCS/MIT report and many other scientists and engineers.[15] But behind the scenes, other factors played a role, most prominently the overwhelmingly negative reception of US allies and others, especially Russia, to the NMD plan. Criticism of the NMD system weakened the confidence in the program among political elites and, with help from the media, the highly technical arguments of the *Countermeasures* report were validated and absorbed into the national consensus. The program's test failures, including the disastrous July 2000 test that barely made it off the ground, were highly publicized by television news programs and others in the media.

In 1999 and 2000, media coverage took a decidedly anti-NMD turn. *The Washington Post*, *The New York Times*, the *Los Angeles Times* and other influential newspapers editorialized against NMD. The media also gave an unprecedented high level of exposure to scientific reports and opinion pieces from scientists against the system, many of them the work of ArmsNet members. Seeing technical terms such as countermeasures printed in newspaper articles on international security and spoken by President Clinton in his speech restored many scientists' faith in the competence of the political process. For the time being, sound science and the integrity of global security prevailed. But with the historic November 2000 US elections, the battle would begin once more.

The New Debate and Lessons to Learn

President George W. Bush has declared his intention to deploy a robust and multi-layered BMD system to protect the US, US troops, and allies overseas.[16] Not for the first time, the arms control community finds itself confronted with an administration on the brink of deploying a missile shield. Arms control agreements and nuclear weapons reductions hang in the balance, and the international community remains skeptical of what it perceives as US unilateralism. Despite earlier victories, the scientific community has proven to be an inconsistent influence in the larger course of the BMD debate. The dreams of missile defences are quite durable, and politicians' and the public's faith in American ingenuity often surpasses the technical realities scientists have used to forge their arguments.

Working with the arms control community, scientists and engineers will once again step up efforts to convince President Bush that deploying technologically vulnerable defences will decrease overall US security and jeopardize the integrity of nuclear arms control agreements with Russia. Already, UCS has organized a second missile defence Education Days event, bringing ArmsNet members to Washington, DC, to hold press events and meet with members of Congress. But the campaign against Bush's BMD plans, which as of this writing (June 2001) had not yet been clearly defined, will be much more difficult.

The administration's national security team, including Vice President Dick Cheney and Secretary of Defense Donald Rumsfeld, is seriously committed to deployment, whereas President Clinton's motives were arguably more political. In addition, the new administration is less hospitable to the ABM Treaty, which restricts development and deployment of the various BMD systems being explored by the Pentagon. The push for deployment among members of the administration is so strong that some are advocating a "scarecrow" defence be deployed immediately and technological issues be addressed in later stages, improving on design flaws and adding more effective technologies when they become available.

Based upon initial reactions to the Bush BMD plan, the international community largely believes that this would be a negative development for global security. If the United States deploys a missile defence and abrogates the ABM Treaty, Russia will be less likely to dismantle its corroding nuclear weapons stockpile and take deployed missiles off high alert. Given that the cool international reception to the Clinton NMD plan played such a significant role in the 2000 decision, US arms control advocates would be wise to engage their foreign counterparts to pressure their governments to hold firm in their opposition to BMD. While Bush has declared that he will go ahead with a missile shield regardless of the reception it receives abroad, a strong rebuke from the international community could slow the deployment process and soften the damage it would do to arms control agreements.

Scientists who wish to prevent Bush's missile shield from destabilizing global security and igniting a new arms race must continue to involve themselves at all levels of the debate. The significance of a scientist as an expert in media coverage is greatly valued, but not only by BMD opponents. Supporters of BMD have already begun campaigns (funded in part by the defence industry) to recruit pro-BMD scientists and engineers to speak out in favor of deployment and vouch for the possibility that the systems could work and not endanger global security.[17]

To counter the Bush administration's deployment plans, then, it would be wise to work with technological experts in foreign countries. Scientists and engineers in other countries could begin their own campaigns to convince their political leaders and media that Bush's plans are a threat to security and (especially in the case of allies that may be included in a "global" BMD) will not function effectively enough to offer true protection. Currently, most national governments oppose the system out of concern for international agreements and security. If they are not educated on the technical vulnerabilities of such systems, they may lend their support if they eventually are swayed by political arguments from the Bush administration. Already, the new centre-right Italian government has endorsed Bush's plans, citing an increased threat to Europe from rogue state attacks.[18] If the new Bush BMD plan does not offer a true defence, it is imperative that scientists mount their campaign at home and abroad.

All actors who might oppose deployment must also commit to a stronger opposition in the early stages of the debate. Scientists have an important role to play, and must guard it well. Public and official confidence in technological arguments will only remain strong as long as the understanding of the long-term benefits and costs to US and global security are defined in rational, non-ideological terms – the methods that lead the public, media, and political elites to trust the scientific community.

Immediately following the September 11, 2001 terrorist attacks, it appeared that the increase in the President's popularity would result in muted criticism of missile defence from domestic actors. Moreover, international leaders appeared ready to make concessions and allow the United States to press ahead with further testing and deployment. However, as the nation calms in the months and years after the attacks, it will become apparent that a more rational debate on missile defence is preferred. With limited resources to spend, and the decisions of US defence planners now directly affecting the safety and security of the US population as never before, the public will demand an effective response to terrorism. In the past, scientists have waited until the final phases of BMD policy to make their voices heard. Efforts made by the arms control community, including the UCS ArmsNet e-mail network, show that highly organized activism and effective use of new information technologies can be the backbone of a potent political campaign. If President Bush does advocate a global missile shield, and sound scientific analysis shows that this will result in a decrease in overall security, US scientists will have to join with their counterparts in other countries to mount a campaign to prevent a dangerous deployment decision. The geographic and cultural challenges of such international activism and organizing on separate continents can only enhance the role information technology will play in this new debate.

Notes

Note on internet addresses (URLs): Websites tend to appear, change or disappear, often without warning. Addresses cited in this bibliography were accurate and active at the time of writing (January 2002) unless otherwise noted.

1. To clarify the use of acronyms in this chapter, I use BMD as a general term to describe any ballistic missile defence system. NMD, national missile defence, refers specifically to the system proposed under President Clinton that sought to provide a limited, ground-based defence for the territory of all 50 states. Theater missile defences (TMD) seek to protect smaller areas.
2. The full *Countermeasures* report, with an executive summary and demonstrative animation, is available at www.ucsusa.org/security/countermeasures.html

3   Countermeasures are steps attacking missiles used to foil a missile defence. In the case of the NMD system, which relies on so-called kill vehicles to smash into enemy warheads in the upper atmosphere, enemy countermeasures try to prevent the kill vehicle from finding the warhead in space or trick it into smashing into another object. The report analyzed several possible countermeasures, including the release of mylar balloons from the attacking missile, which stop the NMD system from distinguishing between a nuclear warhead and dozens of empty balloons; and submunitions, which are dozens of mini-warheads filled with chemical or biological agents mounted on one missile and capable of overwhelming any known defence.

4   Some 81 per cent of respondents polled by The New York Times and CBS News in March 2001 initially said it was important that the United States field a BMD system. When asked to consider that many scientists conclude the system will not work, support fell to 35 per cent. Also in a March 2001 New York Times/CBS poll, 64 per cent of respondents incorrectly believed the United States currently had a deployed NMD system.

5   Richard Garwin and Hans Bethe made one of the first key arguments using the countermeasures concept in 1968, writing in *Scientific American*. 218(3) pp. 21-31.

6   The *Contract With America* was the Republican Party's quasi-platform used in its successful 1994 congressional campaign. Most other elements of the contract dealt with social and economic issues.

7   A May 2000 poll by the Mellman Group found that just one per cent of the American public chose NMD deployment as a top priority, putting it behind education, tax cuts, and other domestic issues. More information on the polling can be found at www.clw.org/nmd/nmdpolldata.html. Poll data on the effectiveness of anti-BMD arguments is available at www.clw.org/nmd/bmdpoll0101.html

8   For an authoritative history of US scientists and public policy, see "Physicists in Politics", by Kurt Gottfried, *Physics Today*, March 1999, 52(3) pp. 42-48.

9   See *Citizen Scientist* by Frank von Hippel, especially p. 81, for more on the reluctance of scientists to participate in politics. American Institute of Physics, New York, 1991.

10 A complete listing of member NGOs in the Coalition to Reduce Nuclear Dangers can be found at www.crnd.org

11 For a summary of the CRND's year-long campaign against NMD deployment, see John Isaacs's "Anatomy of a Victory: Clinton Decides Against a Missile Defense" on the Council for a Livable World's website, www.clw.org/nmd/nmddelay.html, 5 September 2000.

12 On 13 October 1999, the Senate failed to give the required two-thirds majority support necessary for ratification. The final vote was 48-51.

13 See *Secrecy News*, "Increased Missile Defense Secrecy Proposed", 15 November 2000. *Secrecy News* is an e-mail publication of the Federation of American Scientists' Project on Government Secrecy. It provides informal coverage of new developments in secrecy, and security and intelligence policies. www.fas.org/sgp/news/secrecy/

14 On 13 July 2000, the US Senate voted 52-48 against an amendment offered by Senator Richard Durbin (Democrat-Illinois) and supported by UCS that would have required the NMD program to be tested against "realistic countermeasures". All 45 Democrats, plus three Republicans, supported the amendment. Later, key Democrats, including the Senate minority leader and ranking members of the armed services and foreign relations committees, held a press conference urging Clinton to reject a rapid deployment.

15 Clinton announced his decision to defer a deployment decision during a 1 September 2000 speech at Georgetown University.

16 President Bush declared his intention to deploy a system, abrogating the ABM Treaty if necessary, in a 1 May 2001 speech at the National Defense University.

17 The Safeguarding America for Everyone (SAFE) non-profit organization, which is partly funded by defence contractors, began a campaign in May 2001 to promote pro-BMD scientists in the media.
18 Silvio Berlusconi, the new Prime Minister of Italy, openly endorsed US NMD plans in May 2001, saying that President Bush "is right to take such precautions". See www.cdi.org/hotspots/issuebrief/ch8/index.html#update

References

American Physical Society (APS). National Policy Statement. (2000), 'National Missile Defense System Technical Feasibility and Deployment', 29 April, www.aps.org/statements/00.2.html

Becker, Elizabeth (2000), 'Citing Flaws in Concept, Experts Ask Delay in Missile Defense Plan', *The New York Times*, 12 April, p. A12.

Cirincione, Joseph (1997), 'Why the Right Lost the Missile Defense Debate', *Foreign Policy*, No. 106, Spring 1997, www.stimson.org/rd-table/fornpol.html

Coyle, Philip E. (2001), *FY2000 Annual Report of the Office of the Director, Operational Test & Evaluation*, www.dote.osd.mil/reports/FY00/index.html

Federation of American Scientists (2000), 'Increased Missile Defense Secrecy Proposed', *Secrecy News*, 15 November, www.fas.org/sgp/news/secrecy/

FitzGerald, Frances (2000), *Way Out There in the Blue: Reagan, Star Wars and the End of the Cold War*, Simon & Schuster, New York.

Garwin, Richard and Bethe, Hans (1968), 'Anti-Ballistic Missile Systems', *Scientific American*, Vol. 218(3), pp. 21-31.

Gilpin, Robert and Wright, Christopher (eds) (1964), *Scientists and National Policy-Making*, Columbia University Press, New York, pp. 281-282.

Gottfried, Kurt (1999), 'Physicists in Politics', *Physics Today*, Vol. 52(3), pp. 42-48.

Isaacs, John (2000), *Anatomy of a Victory: Clinton Decides Against a Missile Defense*, 5 September, Council for a Livable World, www.clw.org/nmd/nmddelay.html

Schwartz, Stephen I. (ed) (1998), *Atomic Audit: the Costs and Consequences of U.S. Nuclear Weapons since 1940*, Brookings Institution Press, Washington, DC.

Spencer, Jack and Scardaville, Michael (2000), *Missile Defense and the Arms Race*, 13 October, Heritage Foundation, http://heritage.org/views/2000/ed101300.html

Union of Concerned Scientists (2001), *Countermeasures: The Achilles Heel of Missile Defenses*, www.ucsusa.org/security/countermeasures.html

Von Hippel, Frank (1991), *Citizen Scientist*, American Institute of Physics, New York.

Chapter 4

Oxfam International

Peter I. Hajnal[*]

Introduction

Oxfam International (OI), established in 1995, was formally registered in 1996 as Stichting [not-for-profit foundation] Oxfam International, in the Netherlands. It groups together 12 autonomous affiliates in 11 countries. OI calls the group of Oxfams a confederation "working together to find lasting solutions to poverty, suffering and injustice".[1] Oxfam Great Britain (Oxfam GB) was the first of the 12 Oxfams. The latest, Oxfam Germany, was admitted to observer status in November 2000.

The recognition that globalization of trade, the economy, communications, conflicts, social trends and policies has had a major impact on the well-being of people was a contributing factor to Oxfam's decision to internationalize. OI came into being in order to strengthen co-operation and share resources among the independent Oxfams. An example of sharing is OI's proximity to Oxfam GB and its staff, resources and facilities, since both OI and Oxfam GB have their headquarters in Oxford. Similarly, OI's Washington Advocacy Office has benefited from the presence, in Washington, DC, of an Oxfam America office. A more recent example of sharing was the programme harmonization project which, in turn, led in 1999 to OI's strategic change objectives, providing for more integrated planning and programming by the Oxfams (OI 2001a, 3).

Oxfam GB was created in 1942 as the Oxford Committee for Famine Relief (hence the abbreviated name Oxfam) with the aim of helping to get food, clothing, medicine and other needed items to the people of war-torn Europe.[2] It has had gift shops and engaged in many fundraising and educational campaigns from its early years. Later, it gradually expanded its scope geographically (with projects in the Middle East, India, Korea, Hong Kong, Bangladesh, Africa and elsewhere), co-operatively (working with more and more international, national and local charitable and community organizations, governments and intergovernmental

---

[*] An earlier version of this chapter appeared in "International Nongovernmental Organizations And Civil Society", Peter I. Hajnal, *International Information: Documents, Publications and Electronic Information of International Organizations*, Vol. 2, 2nd ed., ed. by Peter I. Hajnal (Englewood, Co.: Libraries Unlimited, 2001). I acknowledge with thanks the information and insight kindly shared by Ernst Ligteringen, former Executive Director, Katy Fletcher, former Information Officer, and Julia Flynn, Head of Internet Development, Oxfam International; Sarah Totterdell, Publications Team Leader and Rosalind Buck, Librarian, Oxfam Great Britain; and Françoise Hébert, former Acting Executive Director of Oxfam Canada.

organizations), and in a range of activities (the most important change was a shift of emphasis to development issues, although disaster relief has remained an important concern). Oxfam GB still is the largest member of the Oxfam family, producing 37 per cent of the income of all Oxfams as of 1999 (Ligteringen 1999). The Oxfams are strategic funders of development projects; provide emergency relief in times of crisis; and campaign for social and economic justice.

The independent Oxfams are guided by a common philosophy and operate in largely similar ways but all participate in collective action, addressing inequality, injustice, hunger, poverty, armed conflict and natural disasters wherever these occur. All Oxfams subscribe to OI's strategic plan; the latest version of the plan is entitled *Towards Global Equity* and covers the period 2000-2004 (OI 2001d). The aim of this strategic plan is "to make a greater impact on the growing problem of the gap between rich and poor in our globalizing world". OI believes that closing that gap requires a fundamental shift in public opinion, and proposes to promote a broad global citizens' movement for social justice (OI 2001b). It makes the following three promises: "We will work to put economic and social justice at the top of the world's agenda ... We will co-operate in strengthening the emerging global citizens' movement for economic and social justice ... [and] We will significantly improve the quality, efficiency and coherence of our work" (OI 2001g).

The plan then sets out strategic change objectives for the following aims: the right to a sustainable livelihood; the right to basic social services; the right to life and security; the right to be heard; and the right to an identity.

The Oxfams, collectively, have projects in more than 80 countries, working mostly through local operational organizations. The relationship among the autonomous Oxfams is generally cordial but there have been strains; for example, in the 1960s and early 1970s Oxfam Canada not only showed its independence from Oxfam GB, but its radical activists were "influenced ... by ... their dislike of Oxford's paternalistic attitude towards its colonial offspring" and in their political stance "made a much stronger showing than their counterparts in Oxford" (Black 1992, 172).

OI considers that the total is greater than the sum of its parts; that is, it can have a larger impact in its work against poverty and injustice by working together with all member organizations. Citing the example of Oxfam's response to the November 1998 disaster in the wake of Hurricane Mitch in Central America, OI's 1998 *Annual Report* comments on the way "Oxfam affiliates and partners were able to join together–not only in delivering immediate assistance to those in most need but also to call for longer-term policy changes on the debt issue. ... Now we are all communicating about the same issues with the same message" (OI 1998, 3).

Mandate, Governance and Structure

OI's constitution is available on request from the OI Secretariat. Its mission statement is included in *Towards Global Equity* which states:

Poverty and powerlessness are avoidable and can be eliminated by human action and political will.
Basic human needs and rights can be met. These include the right to a sustainable livelihood, and the rights and capacities to participate in societies and to make positive changes to people's lives.
Inequalities can be significantly reduced both between rich and poor nations and within nations.
Peace and substantial arms reduction are essential conditions for development (OI 2001f).

Through its programmes, OI aims to:

address the structural causes of poverty and related injustice; ... work primarily through local accountable organizations, seeking to strengthen their empowerment; ... help people directly where local capacity is insufficient or inappropriate for Oxfam's purposes; [and] ... assist the development of structures which directly benefit people facing the realities of poverty and injustice and which are accountable to them (OI 2001f).

The main policymaking body of OI is the Oxfam International Board. It consists of the Chair and the Executive Director of each affiliated Oxfam, together with the Chair and Executive Director of OI. It meets annually to approve OI's plan and budget. The Committee of Executive Directors of each Oxfam plans and manages the implementation of Oxfam International Board decisions. It meets after the Board meeting and again in May, to prepare the OI plan and budget for the following year.

At the next level of OI governance are three committees: the Programme Directors' Committee, the Marketing Committee, and the Advocacy Committee. The OI Secretariat has a small staff of seven, plays a co-ordinating, facilitating and supporting role in the areas of co-operation and communication among the 12 member organizations; and promotes and monitors the implementation of OI's constitution and plans. The Secretariat is assisted from time to time by a number of working groups; for example, the [African] Great Lakes Working Group, the OI Campaign Consultative Group and the Middle East Harmonization Group. The Secretariat, headed by the Executive Director (executive directors are appointed by the Board), is located in Oxford. There is an Advocacy Office in Washington, DC – mentioned earlier – whose primary goal is lobbying the International Monetary Fund (IMF), the World Bank and the United Nations (UN),[3] as well as key advocacy staff in New York, Brussels and Geneva working on issues related to the UN, the European Union (EU) and the World Trade Organization (WTO), respectively.

Two of the national Oxfams, Oxfam America and Oxfam GB, have special consultative status with the Economic and Social Council of the UN. OI also has consultative status with the United Nations Conference on Trade and Development (UNCTAD), and OI and Oxfam America are associated with the UN Department of Public Information. Beyond the UN, OI has contacts with other international governmental organizations, for example the Organization of African Unity[4] (UN

ECOSOC 2001). Beyond that, and in order to fulfil its mission, OI needs a broad global alliance. In fact, the combined Oxfams were working with nearly 3,000 local partner organizations in some 80 countries in the year 2000.

Activities

OI is both an operational (service-delivery) and an advocacy organization. As mentioned earlier, it is involved in development, emergency response, and global advocacy. Its policy, based on its experience and its research, is to link these types of activities.

An example of emergency response at the end of 2001 is the humanitarian situation in Afghanistan following the September 11 terrorist attacks on the United States. Oxfam states that its "first concern is to minimize any further suffering or loss of life. We are gravely concerned by the vulnerability of Afghan civilians – men, women and children – who may be endangered by conflict in Afghanistan". The main goals in this emergency are to ensure adequate food distribution before the onset of winter; to minimize the impact on civilians of military action, population displacement and the disruption of aid; and to prepare for adequate support to all displaced people (OI 2001a). Earlier emergency projects included the Kosovo crisis of 1999, aid in Rwanda, help in Central America in the aftermath of Hurricane Mitch, among others. Such projects tend to involve Oxfam collaboration with other organizations active in the field.

One area of development work is Oxfam's fair trade initiative, pursued through several national Oxfams. As seen by the Oxfams, "[f]air trade is an alternative approach to conventional international trade. It is a trading partnership between producers, traders or buyers, and consumers which provides a more equitable and sustainable form of exchange. It does this by providing better trading conditions and by raising awareness of conditions endured by workers in many countries" (Oxfam Canada 2001). Looking beyond development itself, Oxfam GB characterizes fair trade as "both a development programme and a business which [h]elps people earn a living from their skills[, l]inks producers and consumers[; and h]elps people towards a better future through support and training" (Oxfam Great Britain).

An example of advocacy activity is "Education Now", the first global campaign of OI, launched in 1999 to promote universal primary education by the year 2015. The aim of the campaign is the realization of major policy changes to achieve education for all by removing the debt burden of developing countries; increasing aid for education, reforming IMF programmes of structural adjustment, and establishing a global action plan for basic education. The campaign targets policymakers, the media and the public. All Oxfams have collaborated in this campaign, with consensus-building an important part of the process (OI 1998, 6-7). The report of the campaign was issued as *Education Now: Break the Cycle of Poverty*.[5] Debt relief and poverty reduction – related to the education campaign – are an important part of OI advocacy work (OI 1999, 5).

A major concern for OI is how to optimize its collective effectiveness. The 1999 *Annual Report* refers to a project that sought to bring together programme staff of the Oxfams, notably in Southern Africa, around the themes of basic education, HIV/AIDS, armed conflict, resource extraction, gender and other inequalities, globalization, and disaster mitigation (OI 1999, 6). The project also covered information, communications and financial systems. Another example of how the Oxfams seek to co-ordinate their work to bring about increased impact can be seen in Oxfam's response to the East Timor emergency of late 1999.

> Under the umbrella of Oxfam International, ... Oxfam in Australia, CAA [Community Aid Abroad], is coordinating the Oxfams['] emergency response ... to provide protection and relief to the people of East and West Timor. With improved security, the Oxfam International response programme has now been implemented in East Timor, where ... [the] specialized team [is] working to provide water and sanitation, as well as shelter[6] (OId).

The Oxfams are committed to aligning their work and programme funding with the aims set out in the 2001-2004 Strategic Plan.

In 2001, OI's campaigns were:

> Cut the Cost... [h]elp the global drug industry focus on people, not profits, by making life saving medicines affordable for the poorest.
> Cut the Conflict ... the death toll for [sic] small arms 'in most recent years exceeds the toll of the atomic bomb that devastated Hiroshima and Nagasaki'.
> Drop the Debt Now – Rich countries have agreed to cancel 100% of debt owed by the poorest, but the IMF and World Bank have cancelled less than half ...
> Education Now ... 15 million children, the majority girls, are out of school [; and]
> Let Poor Countries Trade, Too – Many rich countries which demand 'free trade' mean they should be free to sell to the poor, but shouldn't have to buy from poor countries (OIa).

Financing

It is difficult to get a detailed picture of OI's finances. The 1999 *Annual Report* gives a statement of the financial activities of "Stichting Oxfam International", presenting the core budget only. This shows the total incoming resources for 1999 at US$1,224,088, made up of: contributions from affiliates (that is, the independent Oxfams), $851,000; campaign contributions, $100,000; donations received, $228,016; and other income, $45,072. Against this, resources expended during 1999 totalled $1,066,730, of which $228,447 was spent on Development Investment Fund projects; $101,499 on the Programme Support Operation; $404,604 on Secretariat costs; $282,207 on the Washington Advocacy Office; and $49,973 on campaigns. Funds on 31 December 1999 stood at $431,258. Another chart shows programme expenditures of a much higher amount – reflecting expenditures of all Oxfams for 1999 – US$297,094 million, of which $79,948 million was spent in Africa, $13,951 million in the Middle East, $60,516 million in

Eastern Europe, $51,805 million in Asia, $367 million in Oceania, $68,211 million in South America, and $22,296 million consisted of 'home country/international' expenditure (OI 1999, 11).

OI reports that full audited accounts of the core organizational budgets are available from the OI Secretariat. Inquirers are referred to individual Oxfams, each of which has its own financial basis "and is accountable for it's [sic] expenditure within an increasingly coordinated framework" and states that the "Oxfams themselves should be able to provide you with detailed information about their expenditure, either through their websites or if you contact them directly" (OI b).

Oxfam and Information Technology

The 2000-2004 strategic plan, discussed earlier, includes specific reference to its marketing and communications activities and the need to be consistent which extends to providing to managers and staff members of the Oxfams guidance for effective communication with the media and the public, and utilizing electronic media (OI 2001e). Work has begun on developing an internet strategy for OI which seeks to maximize the potential of the internet as a way of communicating with the public and using it as an effective tool for development. Implementation of the internet strategy will begin in 2002.

But in practice, OI has used the internet for several years. The website (www.oxfam.org; also www.oxfaminternational.org) went 'live' in September 1998 and was re-launched in March 1999 with OI's new logo. The site has good basic information about OI (though not enough for more detailed study), its mandate, structure and programmes.

The home page of the site is easy to navigate and its design is free of clutter. It has links to general information about OI ("About Oxfam International"), including the latest annual report. OI's first *Annual Report*, covering 1997, was on the website and was subsequently replaced each year by successive reports. At this writing (December 2001) the 2000 report is in preparation; it will, in turn, appear on the web. It is regrettable that older reports are not retained on the site, making it difficult to obtain multi-year information; due to the current level of resources available, the OI Secretariat does not find it possible to provide or retain data for research or to build a complete archive through its website.

In addition to giving an overview of what OI does and believes in, the website also serves as a gateway to the affiliated Oxfams and provides other useful links. It has, for example, a link to the latest strategic plan; here, too, retaining the earlier strategic plan (*Towards an Ever Closer Union: Strategic Plan, 1999-2000*) would have been useful for historical, comparative purposes. The page outlines OI's modus operandi: the rights-based approach; linking the global with the local; working with partners; and joining with other organizations.

The home page also leads the visitor to a brief description of OI's major types of activity. Campaigns, programmes and emergencies are described briefly on subsidiary pages. A particularly useful feature is the full-text version of OI policy papers. Many of these papers are published online through the Washington

Advocacy Office, but the underlying research is a collaborative effort. OI's website links to more than 20 papers spanning the years 1999-2001; commendably, policy papers – unlike annual reports – are retained on the website, and can be downloaded as Microsoft Word files. An even better resource is provided by Community Aid Abroad, the Australian Oxfam affiliate, which makes available 46 policy papers, produced from 1996 to 2001, in html format (OIc; Oxfam Community Aid Abroad). The papers are carefully researched and presented. They cover the following subject areas: debt, trade and investment; education; and conflict and emergencies.

As is usual on the web, the site has the latest news and other announcements. At this writing (December 2001), it has press releases, and news on campaigns and emergencies. The site does not yet have a search engine – a shortcoming that should be remedied as soon as possible. OI is in the process of examining this and other questions of web architecture.

To facilitate the goal of getting more people involved, the site provides information on volunteering, campaigning, making a donation to the Oxfams or to OI itself, and working for OI. It also allows the public to send e-mail messages to the Oxfams.

In addition to the public website, OI has created an intranet for internal communication within OI and among the Oxfams. Striving to ensure compatibility among the Oxfams, OI has set up a strong distribution system, with a contact person in each Oxfam office. Among the internal documents on the intranet are meeting documents and management information. (OI's public website also provides a link to a page concerned with the trade campaign in late 2001 and restricted to "allies and partners only"). As well, Oxfam working groups and the webmasters of the Oxfams use e-mail quite extensively; in fact, most internal communication among the Oxfams takes place electronically. OI also archives its electronic information for its internal use.

Thanks to the internet, OI can reach people everywhere, including countries where there is no resident/territorial Oxfam. Because the federation of Oxfam affiliates and their work extend to non-English speaking countries, there are practical problems involving language. As technology can be expensive, and it is costly to translate the contents of the website, the predominant language of the site remains English. It should be pointed out that the main working language of OI is English, but core documents of the organization are published in French, Spanish, Dutch and Chinese as appropriate. Affiliate websites reflect the language needs of the users of those sites. The internet strategy will develop thinking on how to address the language needs of audiences of OI.

Although OI's main information product is increasingly electronic, it issues a few publications in paper form; for example, the *Annual Report* and *Education Now: Break the Cycle of Poverty*. The latter, in document form, was published as a book by Oxfam GB in October 2000 with the title *The Oxfam Education Report*. This is not atypical; given OI's small staff and scarce resources, it is natural for it to use the facilities of Oxfam GB, located within a city block or so from OI's headquarters in Oxford. Oxfam GB is a major publisher, with a publications team of 13 members; it releases 15 to 20 books per year, plus two journals. The aims of the publishing programme are: to share learning and support good practice; to build capacity; to present evidence in support of Oxfam's advocacy and campaigning work; to increase public understanding of development and relief issues; and to contribute to changing ideas and beliefs about poverty. Since 1985, Oxfam GB's mandate has included a provision "to educate the public concerning the nature, causes, and effects of poverty, distress and suffering ..., to conduct and procure research concerning these and to publish or otherwise make the results thereof available to the public" (Black 1992, 256). Some publications are made available electronically, and the publishing team is currently exploring further electronic publishing initiatives. Through its publications, Oxfam communicates its accumulated experience, reflects its successes but also provides self-criticism.

Concluding Remarks

In the course of its long history (60 years in the case of Oxfam GB), the confederation of Oxfams has achieved an enviable reputation and some impressive results. With the internationalization of the movement, OI, during its briefer, six-year experience, has made considerable advances in co-ordinating the multifaceted work of the Oxfams in development, emergency response and advocacy. Oxfam, has chosen its targets and strategies thoughtfully and, in common with many civil-society organizations, has been able to respond to challenges in a speedy and flexible manner.

Information technology has been crucial for the entire existence of OI. It has played a major role in its internal work and public outreach. The organization's strategic plan for 2000-2004 recognizes the importance of technology, and provides for building on successes and addressing problems.

How well does OI's information output reflect the organization's mandate, programmes and aims? OI communicates to the public basic information about its programmes (both in the operational and advocacy areas), in order to arouse interest and help mobilize public support. Questions remain: How much concrete public support (financial support as well as getting involved as a volunteer) for OI is due to the information disseminated in print and via the internet? How has the information contributed to policy or programme changes by target governments and organizations?

How could OI improve its use of information technology? Useful and informative as OI's website is, its content should be enriched so that viewers could explore OI in more depth. Specifically, more information on the history, constitution and structure (to the level of working groups) would be helpful. More detail on OI's finances should be given, too; the organization is committed to transparency and is planning to have its annual reports reflect such details.

Technical improvements to the OI website should include installation of a search engine and provision (for faster access) of a non-graphic (text only) option. One should, of course, bear in mind that OI must weigh carefully how to balance its programmes and advocacy work and information activities, notwithstanding the role of information in both programmes and advocacy, given its limited resources.

Public information supporting OI's advocacy work is more comprehensive than information on programmes. This is illustrated by the full text of policy studies produced for the most part by the Advocacy Office in Washington and available on OI's website. These are thoroughly-researched, well-prepared and carefully-targeted papers. It is difficult to gauge the effect of these advocacy studies (or, indeed, of Oxfam's advocacy work itself) in changing the behaviour of policymakers in governments and international governmental organizations, especially the IMF and the World Bank. OI, itself, feels that it has had major successes through its advocacy work and that "[i]nternational institutions have come to accept [it] as a partner – a partner with a critical voice" (OI 1998, 3).

Notes

Note on internet addresses (URLs): Websites tend to appear, change or disappear, often without warning. Addresses cited in this bibliography were accurate and active at the time of writing (January 2002) unless otherwise noted.

1   The Oxfam member organizations are: Oxfam America, Oxfam-in-Belgium, Oxfam Canada, Oxfam Community Aid Abroad (Australia), Oxfam GB, Oxfam Hong Kong, Intermón Oxfam (Spain), Oxfam Ireland, Novib Oxfam Netherlands, Oxfam New Zealand and Oxfam Quebec. Oxfam Germany was recently admitted as observer. See Oxfam International's website at www.oxfam.org/what_is_OI/default.htm
2   For a useful and informative history of Oxfam GB, see Black 1992.
3   The address of Oxfam International's secretariat is Prama House, 2nd Floor, 267 Banbury Road, Oxford, OX2 7HT, United Kingdom (tel.: 44 1865 31 39 39; fax: 44 1865 31 39 35; OI has two identical websites: www.oxfam.org and www.oxfaminternational.org; e-mail: administration@oxfaminternational.org). The address of the Advocacy Office is 1112 16th Street, NW, Suite 600, Washington DC 20036, USA (tel.: 202 496-1170; fax: 202 496-0128; website: www.oxfaminternational.org; e-mail: advocacy@oxfaminternational.org).
4   See also United Nations, Department of Public Information, *Directory of NGOs Associated with DPI* www.un.org/MoreInfo/ngolink/ngodir.htm; Union of International Associations (1998/99), *Yearbook of International Organizations*, 35th ed., Brussels, Vol. 1, p. 1386; and Oxfam International.
5   Originally in document form entitled *Education Now: Break the Cycle of Poverty*; it was published as a book in October 2000: (Watkins 2000).
6   For more current information on East Timor, see Oxfam Community Aid Abroad (Oxfam Australia), *East Timor* www.caa.org.au/world/asia/east_timor/index.html

References

Black, Maggie (1992), *A Cause for Our Times: Oxfam, the First 50 Years*, Oxfam and Oxford University Press, Oxford.
Ligteringen, Ernst (1999), (former Executive Director of Oxfam International), interview with author, 29 July.
Oxfam Canada (2001), *Fair Trade in Coffee*, www.oxfam.ca/campaigns/fairTrade.htm
Oxfam Community Aid Abroad, *Oxfam International Policy Papers*, OCAA, www.caa.org.au/oxfam/advocacy/index.html

66 *Civil Society in the Information Age*

Oxfam Great Britain, *About Oxfam Fair Trade*, www.oxfam.org.uk/fairtrad/aboutft1.htm
Oxfam International (a), *Campaigns: Change the World*, OI, Oxford www.oxfam.org/what_does/advocacy/default.htm
Oxfam International (b), *How Are Oxfam's Funds Used?*, OI, Oxford, www.oxfam.org/involve/donations.htm
Oxfam International (c), *Policy Papers*, OI, Oxford, www.oxfam.org/what_does/advocacy/papers.htm
Oxfam International (d), *The Timor Crisis and the OI Response*, OI, Oxford.
Oxfam International (1998), *Annual Report, 1998*, OI, Oxford.
Oxfam International (1999), *Annual Report, 1999*, OI, Oxford, www.oxfam.org/what_is_OI/a_report/default.htm
Oxfam International (2001a), *Afghanistan*, OI, Oxford, www.oxfam.org/news/afghan.htm
Oxfam International (2001b), 'Foreward', *Towards Global Equity: Strategic Plan, 2001-2004*, OI, Oxford, www.oxfam.org/strategic_plan/intro3.htm
Oxfam International (2001d), 'Introduction', *Towards Global Equity: Strategic Plan, 2001-2004*, OI, Oxford, www.oxfam.org/strategic_plan/index.htm
Oxfam International (2001e), 'Marketing and Communications', *Towards Global Equity: Strategic Plan, 2001-2004*, OI, Oxford, www.oxfam.org/strategic_plan/business3.htm
Oxfam International (2001f), 'Mission Statement', *Towards Global Equity: Strategic Plan, 2001-2004*, OI, Oxford, www.oxfam.org/strategic_plan/intro2.htm
Oxfam International (2001g), 'Our Three Promises', *Towards Global Equity: Strategic Plan, 2001-2004*, OI, Oxford, www.oxfam.org/strategic_plan/humane6.htm
Union of International Associations (1998/99), *Yearbook of International Organizations*, 35th ed., Brussels
United Nations, Department of Public Information, *Directory of NGOs Associated with DPI*, UN, www.un.org/MoreInfo/ngolink/ngodir.htm
United Nations, Economic and Social Council (2001), *NGOs in Consultative Status with ECOSOC*, UN, 29 November, www.un.org/esa/coordination/ngo/pdf/INF_List.pdf
Watkins, Kevin (2000), *The Oxfam Education Report*, Oxfam GB, Oxford.

Chapter 5

The Working Life of Southern NGOs: Juggling the Promise of Information and Communications Technologies and the Perils of Relationships with International NGOs

Juris Dilevko[*]
Copyright © Juris Dilevko

Introduction

The astronomical increase in the number of citizen groups, civil society movements, and nongovernmental organizations (NGOs) in the period 1980-2000 represents a fundamental transformation in the relationship of ordinary citizens to governing authority. Roberts (2000) reports that, at the end of the twentieth century, over 30,000 international NGOs existed, while "domestic ones are counted in the millions". As one instance of this phenomenal growth, Bornstein (1999) notes that registered nonprofit organizations grew from 18,000 to 58,000 between 1989 and 1996 in the Philippines. Examples of this kind could be adduced for every country in the world. What explains this explosive growth? One common explanation is long-standing citizen frustration with existing government structures. Governmental bodies are either too corrupt, too weak, too unresponsive, too bureaucratic, or too inward-looking to understand the aspirations of their citizens and to help in providing effective solutions to a myriad of social, cultural, and political problems (Lindenberg & Dobel 1999). Whatever the reason, governments — whether national or local — no longer have a monopoly on social action. To be sure, there have always been innovative and far-reaching nongovernmental social movements that have been initiated by dynamic individuals. These movements were all the more noteworthy and memorable for being isolated occurrences. What is different at the beginning of the 21st century, however, is the vast number of such movements and the fact that they have become key structural players in solving a host of local and national problems that governments no longer have the capacity or the will to address. Indeed, their unavoidable presence on the world stage may

---

[*] I would like to thank Ms Moya Mason for her invaluable help as a Research Assistant for this project.

be seen as evidence of a widespread feeling that fundamental social change will only come about through the auspices of nongovernmental actors.

William Drayton, the founder of Ashoka, an organization named for an altruistic emperor of India that provides support to nongovernmental citizen movements in many countries in Africa, Asia, and South America, views this trend in terms of "social entrepreneurship" (Bornstein 1999, A17). In the business world, when individuals or small groups see an opportunity to provide a product or service that a larger corporation or entity is not capable of providing, they seize their opportunity and step in to fill the vacuum. They become small business entrepreneurs, competing to win financing in order to bring their product or service to market and to attract others to their vision and product so that, eventually, they can expand their offering of wares. In much the same way, NGOs may be seen as "social entrepreneurs", filling the vacuum created by retreating or unwieldy governmental bodies that are too slow in providing necessary services. And just as small businesses must be fleet of foot to outdistance their rivals, the substantial increase in the number of the NGOs means that they too must compete for funding, staff members, and local support to stay alive and remain relevant. As Drayton has recognized with his venture-capital approach to funding worthy small local NGOs, there is a move away from a charity-based approach to problem-solving to an approach that is more market-oriented.

Seeing the rise and proliferation of NGOs through the prism of small business growth also means recognizing that many small businesses struggle and, ultimately, fail. While there is no dearth of people with innovative and useful ideas, it is an unfortunate fact of life that the number of innovative and useful ideas that can plausibly be executed and sustained in any one given location is limited. There is no room for a dozen hot-dog vendors on a busy street corner. At best, two or three of them will survive financially. Exponential growth does not necessarily lead to long-term productivity gains. The same holds true for NGOs. It does not necessarily follow that fast-paced growth in the number of NGOs leads to long-term sustainable productivity gains, as measured by social progress. Indeed, a number of scholars have bluntly stated that there are too many NGOs and that, to be truly effective, they must merge in order to avoid duplication and waste. The goods – in this case, social change – must be delivered "at a cost that is appropriate for its performance" (Bornstein 1999, A17).

Against this backdrop of skyrocketing growth and competition among NGOs of all types, an important cog is the southern NGO, that is, an NGO which is based in and operates in developing countries. Just as large international NGOs compete for funds from donors, foundations, and governmental agencies at all levels, southern NGOs invariably compete for the attention, expertise, technical resources, infrastructure, and money that international NGOs can provide. How are they faring in this environment? Do they think that information and communications technologies (ICTs) help them carry out, and succeed in, their work? How can their relationship with international NGOs be characterized? In other words, what was it like to be a southern NGO in 2001?

Increased access to and use of ICTs by southern NGOs has often been identified as an important step toward effective action in their relevant fields. For instance, Lal (1999, para 1), writing about the African situation, suggests that ICTs can help to "support tasks that involve complex decision making, communication and decision implementation..., automate tedious tasks done by humans, and ... support new tasks and processes that did not exist before". Castells (1998, para 2), citing econometric studies showing a close statistical relationship between diffusion of information technology, productivity and competitiveness for countries, regions, industries and firms, notes that "the availability and use of information and communication technologies are a pre-requisite for economic and social development in our world". On the other hand, Hamelink (1997, para 29) worries that the spread of ICTs contributes to "cultural globalization" and reinforces "current patterns of cultural colonialism". Summarizing much of his previous work, Heeks (1999, para 15, 17-18) marshals a large body of evidence showing that "the majority of ICT-based initiatives end in total failure of a system that never works; partial failure in which major goals are unattained or in which there are significant undesirable outcomes; sustainability failure that succeeds initially but then fails after a year or so; or replication failure of a pilot scheme that cannot be reproduced". He reminds us that investment in ICTs must be seen as an opportunity cost. Because investing in ICT means "explicitly not investing in other development areas", advocates of ICTs often neglect "to demonstrate how ICT-based information represents a more important resource than water, food, land, shelter, production technology, money, skills or power in the development process". In addition, focusing on ICT also means that "organic information systems and indigenous knowledge – the systems and knowledge which arise from within poor communities – are being systematically ignored and overriden". Smillie (1999, para 13) declares that "one of the greatest dangers in the promotion of ICT is that Southern organizations will be drawn too quickly into the purchase of expensive and sophisticated technology that they can neither afford nor sustain, beguiled by the hope that it will solve problems that it cannot". Taking a middle position, Ballantyne, Labelle, and Rudgard (2000, para 3, 9) argue that ICTs contribute to development goals if and only if they are used properly, that is to say, if they are "based on local needs" in such a way as to create local content using "local networks of expertise, traditional knowledge resources and local information, often in local languages" to serve local partners so as to "build up an experienced cadre of local experts who themselves can address local capacity building challenges".

Just as there is an ongoing debate about the value of ICTs for developing countries, there are also questions about the efficacy of the relationship between southern NGOs and international NGOs. Although most international NGOs profess that they have real partnerships with southern NGOs, a report by the International Forum on Capacity Building (1998) observes that most Southern NGOs believe they have little influence with their international NGO partners and that local NGOs in Africa are particularly concerned that co-operating with international NGOs has a detrimental effect on their missions and managerial autonomy. In a study of four African NGOs that had partnerships of between two and ten years with northern NGOs, Ashman (2001) found that, while the northern NGOs described the relationships in terms of such metaphors as a "crew team rowing together" and "two wheels of a bicycle", the southern NGOs described those same relationships in images that "included an element of power difference" such as husband-wife or parent-child. More specifically, southern NGOs complained that the funding contracts linking them to northern NGOs were too short to have long-term developmental impacts and emphasized "upward accountability" to the northern NGOs rather than "mutual accountability" to affected communities (Ashman 2001, 79-80). In addition, southern NGOs complained that their northern NGO partners rigidly adhered to signed partnerships agreements, that staff turnover at northern NGOs was too high to ensure productive continuity, and that northern NGOs were simply too large and bureaucratic. Edwards (1999) discusses eight studies showing that minimal levels of flexibility and innovation characterize the work of some international NGOs, that international NGO accountability procedures are distorted towards the needs of donors rather than beneficiaries, that capacity-building efforts of international NGOs have been weak, and that partnerships between international NGOs and southern NGOs are highly unequal (Edwards 1999, 27). Dichter (1999) explains the underlying philosophical conflict between southern and northern NGOs as emanating from the desire of southern NGOs "to want credit for their own work; they do not want to carry the water for international NGOs, for whom they have often been subcontractors or grantees, but want to run development projects on their own" (Dichter 1999, 47).

To say the least, the relationship between southern NGOs and their northern international counterparts is fraught with tension and pitfalls. So, too, is the relationship with ICTs. As Ballantyne, Labelle, and Rudgard (2000) maintain, ICTs must be imbued with as much local-ness as possible in order to produce sustained change. Accordingly, the way in which southern NGOs define and manage their relationship with international NGOs and ICTs will, for all intents and purposes, define their level of success in achieving their development goals.

Methodology

To answer some of the questions about the way in which southern NGOs are dealing with ICTs and international NGOs based in northern "developmentally-advanced" countries, a small-scale exploratory survey research project was undertaken. An initial list of 500 NGOs working on sustainable human development, poverty, or environmental issues in countries having membership in the Group of 77 or having been part of the former Soviet Union was established using the *Yearbook of International Organizations* (36th edition), and a search of the web was performed using the search string "Country XYZ and NGO". According to its website (www.g77.org), the Group of 77 is a third-world coalition within the United Nations that "provides the means for the developing world to articulate and promote its collective interests and enhance its negotiating capacity on all major economic issues ... and promote economic and technical co-operation among developing countries". NGOs working in these countries are typically referred to as southern NGOs. E-mail messages were sent to a random selection of

150 southern NGOs in March-April 2001 inviting them to go to a website that housed an English-language survey and to complete a series of questions. In addition to three preliminary questions that elicited basic demographic data, the survey consisted of 16 questions on two topics: (i) the way in which southern NGOs perceived and used information and communication technologies and (ii) the relationship of southern NGOs with international NGOs. Southern NGOs were told that, if they chose to participate in the survey, they would be eligible for a draw for one of three prizes of $100 USD each. Nine messages bounced back immediately, a sign that the address was no longer operational. A total of 141 southern NGOs thus received the initial survey solicitation. Survey responses were received from 37 southern NGOs – a response rate of 26.2 per cent. Because this survey was sent to a limited number of southern NGOs and because the response rate was relatively low, conclusions drawn from this survey should be used carefully. Survey responses were received from the following geographical areas: Africa (10); South America and the Caribbean (4); South-Eastern and Far Eastern Asia (13); and the Trans-Caucasian area (10). As one indicator of their size and operating capacity, southern NGOs were asked how many "paid workers" they employed. Seven southern NGOs employed 1-5 paid workers (18.9 per cent), five NGOs employed 6-10 paid workers (13.5 per cent), nine NGOs employed 11-20 paid workers (24.3 per cent), 11 NGOs employed 21 or more paid workers (29.7 per cent), and five southern NGOs were entirely volunteer (13.5 per cent). All contacted and responding southern NGOs had an e-mail address and a website. All questions were asked in an open-ended format to allow survey respondents as much latitude as possible in their answers. Data were compiled and results categorized based on the answers received to the open-ended questions. To preserve the confidentiality inherent in the survey, NGOs are referred to by number, not by name.

Use of and Opinions About ICTs by Southern NGOs

Basic Data

Although all 37 survey respondents possessed and used some form of ICT infrastructure, defined as "equipment that allows you to connect and make use of the internet, World Wide Web, and e-mail", they had a fairly wide range of available equipment. As displayed in Table 5.1, 18 southern NGOs (48.6 per cent) had either one or two computers, complemented by one or two peripherals such as a printer, scanner, or fax machine. Another eight southern NGOs had three computers, while seven southern NGOs had anywhere from four to ten computers. Four southern NGOs had a server, with at least three networked computers. There was relative homogeneity in spending on ICT equipment in the previous 12 months as 28 respondents (75.6 per cent) stated that they spent less than $2,500 USD, and only two southern NGOs spent more than $10,000 USD on ICTs (Table 5.1). Accordingly, most southern NGOs are making do with what many observers in western countries would term minimal resources, but which, in the context of "developing" countries, may be adequate. For instance, NGO 1 has "two computers with modems, two colour printers, one scanner, two unlimited internet accounts", while NGO 4 has three Pentium computers, three 486 DX computers, two scanners, one photocopier, one fax machine, and two printers.

When asked how their NGO "benefits from using ICTs", the responding NGOs, taken as a whole, indicated that they literally could not function without them. The speed and low cost of e-mail was mentioned repeatedly, as in the following extract from a response from NGO 1: "all our communication internally and externally is done through e-mail. It is cost efficient, secure, and quick, everything our national postal service isn't". E-mail is also used for dealing with volunteers, sending reports to benefactors and partners, tracking queries, sharing ideas, and networking with other development organizations. The web and their own websites also play an essential role in the life of southern NGOs. They are used to share project experiences, to electronically sell "third-world" craft products, to find out general information about other organizations, to search for donors and apply for funding, and to publish information about local activities. In more general terms, websites have allowed NGO 19 to gain "credibility" because of the "quality of information provided and the high quality of the site". It has also led to a significant increase in membership because "travelers coming to visit [this country] want to become members [and] one of our major funders found us through this site". Finally, websites and e-mail have helped NGOs 32, 34, and 37 to "create awareness of [their] plight", contribute to higher literacy levels, and help to ensure that "education is now possible for our children".

Table 5.1 ICT Infrastructure and Annual Spending on ICT in 2000-2001 by Southern NGOs

ICT equipment used by Southern NGOs		Spending on ICT equipment in previous 12 months (USD)	
1 computer with 1 or 2 peripherals (e.g., printer, scanner, fax machine)	10 (27%)	Less than $1,000	16 (43.2%)
2 computers and at least 2 peripherals	8 (21.6%)	$1,000 - $2,499	12 (32.4%)
3 computers and at least 2 peripherals	8 (21.6%)	$2,500 - $4,999	3 (8.1%)
4-5 computers and at least 2 peripherals	3 (8.1%)	$5,000 - $9,999	4 (10.8%)
6-10 computers and at least 2 peripherals	4 (10.8%)	$10,000 - $19,999	2 (5.4%)
Server, at least 3 networked computers, and at least 2 peripherals	4 (10.8%)	$20,000 or more	0
Total	37 (100%)	Total	37 (100%)

Social and Cultural Consequences of ICT Use

When asked if ICTs had caused positive or negative changes in the decision-making processes of their organizations, a large majority of respondents stated that the change had been positive or that there had been no noticeable change. As shown in Question 1 of Table 5.2, 24 southern NGOs (64.9 per cent) felt that changes in the decision-making processes occasioned by ICTs were positive, 24.3 per cent felt that such changes were neutral, and only 5.4 per cent of responding NGOs thought that such changes were negative. According to NGO 4, e-mail facilitates the act of gathering the opinions and ideas of other members of the organization before any decision is taken. In addition, it allows for a "documented record of conversations" and ensures that contradictory interpretations of a particular decision or a meeting do not occur so that when, for example, "the executive director consults the steering committee through e-mail ... everyone gets the same message". NGO 18 believed that "using technology has helped us become more organized and focused", while NGO 28 was of the opinion that, because of ICTs, "we have less time for gossip, which is good". NGO 30 suggested that decision making is not only more streamlined and prompt because of ICTs, but also more inclusive: "at the beginning, we were handling e-mails by two persons. But gradually [we] came to the conclusion that a team should [do so] and that at least two colleagues from the leadership must [be] included in the team so that urgent decisions could be made". Moreover, NGO 30 continued, "it has created new jobs to be considered" – a possible reference to how ICTs may help broaden the range and scope of an organization's activity simply by making it aware of new information and issues. NGO 20 simply concludes that ICTs "give us more options" before a decision is taken. NGO 14 concurred, writing that "we can help each other more quickly and respond to crises. We can fix things that we might have let go, for better or worse. We can take advantage of more opportunities. We can pool expertise and apply synergistic energy to improve projects and offer psychological support to each other". A discordant note among the overwhelmingly positive responses to this question came from NGO 15, which recognized that, while "international relationships and networking is developing rapidly", the frequency and quality of "internal relationships within the organization are decreasing" – a circumstance which has led to a "dictatorship attitude in the organization ... where the organization's decisions are undertaken by one head and not participatory".

Respondents were nearly unanimous in answering the questions contained in Questions 2-6 of Table 5.2. For example, they did not feel (94.6 per cent) that the use of ICTs lowered staff morale (Question 2). Indeed, many southern NGOs were adamant that it had heightened the morale of staff members because they have become computer-literate and thus more connected to world issues. In short, ICTs have "created more enthusiasm", "made our morale rise and made us feel more powerful", and made us "feel less alone".

Table 5.2 Views on the Social and Cultural Consequences of ICT Use
(n=37)

Question	Positive change	Negative change	Both positive and negative	No change
1. Has the use of ICTs led to any changes in the decision-making processes of your NGO?	24 (64.9%)	2 (5.4%)	2 (5.4%)	9 (24.3%)

	Yes	No	Yes and No	Not applicable
2. Has the use of ICTs led to a lowering of staff morale at your NGO?	1 (2.7%)	35 (94.6%)	-	1 (2.7%)
3. Has the use of ICTs eroded your use of indigenous and informal communication channels?	4 (10.8%)	28 (75.7%)	-	5 (13.5%)
4. Has the use of ICTs led to a decrease in local initiatives for the design of developmental efforts?		35 (94.6%)	2 (5.4%)	
5. Has your use of ICTs caused you to give too much priority to "first-world" solutions to "third-world" problems?	2 (5.4%)	35 (94.6%)	-	
6. Has spending on ICTs by local and international NGOs consumed funds that could be more usefully spent in other areas?	4 (10.8%)	29 (78.4%)	4 (10.8%)	-

	Yes	No	Yes and No	Phenomenon already present
7. Has the use of ICTs raised class barriers between those who know how to use ICTs and those who do not?*	12 (32.4%)	14 (37.8%)	4 (10.8%)	5 (13.5%)
8. Has the use of ICTs contributed to the propagation of the English language and western culture?	7 (18.9%)	17 (46%)	4 (10.8%)	9 (24.3%)

* There was one reply (2.7%) of "not applicable" and one reply (2.7%) of "don't know" to this question.

There was slightly less unanimity about whether the use of ICTs had eroded the use of indigenous and informal communication channels: 28 southern NGOs (75.7 per cent) felt that it had not done so (Question 3 of Table 5.2). Most of the NGOs stated that they were able to distinguish between indigenous communication channels and ICT-based channels, using the former for one purpose and the latter for a different purpose. For example, NGO 19 stated that "when we need to consult with villagers about their concerns, we meet with them", NGO 36 declared that "we keep those separate", and NGO 13 observed that most of the beneficiaries of its help are illiterate and so the NGO must be careful to preserve traditional communication channels. In fact, NGO 14 remarked that "we are working very hard to accomplish just the opposite – enhance [indigenous] channels and preserve the entire basis of [our organization], which is interpersonal relationships rooted in communities. As we introduce telecentres to villages we are trying to establish a graduated, step-by-step way to avoid depersonalizing such relationships and leapfrogging from village level communication in the flesh to worldwide communication via electrons ... We are [thus] working on a project to strengthen indigenous communication via the web by having local community websites and self-reflecting (individual, groups, schools, villages) presentation of village life on the web – in the service of the community rather in an effort to escape community". Southern NGOs who believed that ICTs have eroded traditional communication channels were, unfortunately, not very forthcoming with details. For instance, NGO 31 noted that "sometimes there are better answers out there", but provided no further observations.

In their replies to Questions 4 and 5 of Table 5.2, Southern NGOs were very clear that, despite the wealth of information available through the web and other ICT sources, they had neither neglected local initiative in the design of development efforts (94.6 per cent) nor had they given too much priority to "first-world" solutions for "third-world" problems (94.6 per cent). While most answered with a simple "no" to both questions, some NGOs were more expansive with their comments. Admitting that "many of the initiatives come from outside the local area", NGO 1 nevertheless felt that ICTs had actually contributed to local initiative because "there weren't many initiatives coming locally before ICT was available and now I see that local people are doing things on their own initiative, something unlikely to have happened had the outside initiatives not [first] taken place". NGO 5 and NGO 19 related similar experiences, noting that ICTs have had a small, though no less real, impact on opening up political processes in countries with no tradition of public consultation, especially with respect to "fledging attempts to organize communities to fight unwanted development projects". With regard to the imposition of "first-world" solutions for local problems, many southern NGOs declared that they were sufficiently wise to tailor "ready-made" solutions to local exigencies: "first-world solutions can be adapted to our needs". NGO 7, for example, stated that "we believe that there is no first-world solution [that can be] prepared for us". NGO 12 was even more adamant, remarking that "if the first-world thinks that they can provide all the solutions through the Net, let them have the satisfaction of believing it [but] the ground reality is different. All societies ... have always had a local solution to their problems". NGO 32 observed that the very multiplicity of proposed solutions available through ICTs was a clear benefit: "all and every solution is good to hear before you choose one that is best".

Expenditures on ICTs by both local and international NGOs was not considered wasteful by 78.4 per cent of the responding southern NGOs (Question 6 of Table 5.2). NGO 23 declared that "ICT spending is a small fraction of our organizational budget". In fact, both NGO 5 and NGO 29 felt that such spending, no matter how small, had many "indirect benefits for the poor [because] it helps in raising funds", "helps us make more money by networking", and increases efficiency in "managing organizational affairs including accounts and research data". NGO 27 too felt that ICT expenditures were well worthwhile insofar as they serve as a "media for advocating and building a campaign strategy and influencing public opinion". Perhaps NGO 33 summarized best the prevailing opinion on this question: "To be in the running, we need to have the right tools. It is money well spent". Nevertheless, there was some criticism of excessive ICT spending. Consider the views of NGO 4: "there are some NGOs [in our country] that use funds to purchase computer equipment and internet access but do not use the equipment to its full potential. For example purchasing a new top of the line computer ... to check the e-mail every few days". Three separate NGOs noted that education, food and irrigation systems, and health care were more immediate concerns than ICT equipment. Of the respondents who replied "yes and no" to this question, NGO 18 simply stated that "we need so much that it is hard to answer", NGO 22 noted that "there are better and worse ways to spend the money, but we feel we need it". In general, given the relatively small percentage of funds devoted to it in the budgets of southern NGOs, ICT spending is a sound investment that has the potential to pay for itself through increased donations and funding opportunities.

In response to Question 7 about whether the introduction and use of ICTs is in danger of raising class barriers between those who know how to use ICTs and those who do not, opinion was almost evenly divided: 14 southern NGOs disagreed with this assertion (37.8 per cent), while 12 agreed (32.4 per cent). Four southern NGOs (10.8 per cent) replied both affirmatively and negatively, while five southern NGOs (13.5 per cent) stated that such barriers already existed. Within the group of NGOs who thought that class barriers would not result because of ICTs, a common theme was that, given adequate training, ICTs would alleviate class divides. NGO 5, for example, felt that "ICT is actually contributing to increasing productivity [and] it is actually bridging the gaps between poor and the rich as most poor/middle class people are now moving toward ICT education". NGO 13 believed that, because "ICT is just too simple to use", the creation of class barriers is impossible because "with basic education anyone absolutely can know how to send e-mails or surf the web". NGO 7 also discounted the creation of class barriers, especially "if [our] government sets up a network of public access Internet cafes". Of the four southern NGOs that answered both yes and no to this question, education was again the predominant theme. That is to say, if there is little commitment to ICT education, class barriers will be a problem; on the other hand, greater efforts at ICT education will forestall the erection of such barriers.

The primary concerns of those who felt that the formation of new ICT-related class barriers was a real possibility (12 NGOs representing 32.4 per cent of the sample) were very similar to the concerns expressed by those who thought that class barriers were already present in their country and that the introduction of ICTs would not alter a pre-existing situation (5 NGOs representing 13.5 per cent of the sample). NGO 15 insisted that "technology in general creates gaps between haves and have-nots. Roads, farming systems knowledge, financial planning, telecommunications, basic services etc. are all unequally provided". NGO 19 concurred, observing that "ICTs, like all new technologies, come first to those with the money to buy them or invent them in the first place. All third-world countries have rich people, just as all developed countries have poor people. So the rich/poor split is both international and within each country, and it is widening". NGO 11, while agreeing that ICTs have a tendency to create socio-economic barriers, noted that "these are more or less the same barriers as you have between those who have had an education and those who have not". NGO 29 concluded that "barriers will always be a given".

There were two specific social cleavages that, in the opinion of three southern NGOs, are exacerbated by the introduction of ICTs. NGO 4 worried about the increasing divide between young and old people as a result of ICTs. Whereas young people are very much at home in the world of ICTs, older people often have great difficulty orienting themselves in a technology-filled universe. Formerly respected for their accumulation of wisdom and traditional cultural knowledge, older people are now in danger of becoming shunted aside and marginalized. NGO 1 commented upon the increasing divide between rural and urban centres. Rural schools are already poorly equipped from the standpoint of books and supplies in comparison with urban schools; the introduction of ICTs in urban schools will only put rural children at a greater disadvantage. Adopting a more nuanced position, NGO 14 felt that, while urban youth are currently far ahead of rural youth in their understanding of ICTs, the gradual penetration of ICTs into the village level has caused "some awakening among rural teenagers about biodiversity and environmental concerns that is very exciting ... and totally boring to well-to-do urban youth. What's helping with this, not incidentally, is our use of the web, e-mail and digital cameras to encourage and support rural youth in their efforts". In other words, while social divides and class barriers may indeed exist on the surface – urban populations in contrast with villages – knowledgeable and wise use of ICTs may aid in creating sophisticated village-level solutions that could have a significant positive effect on cities.

Southern NGOs were also not very worried that ICTs contribute to the propagation of the English language and western culture at the expense of other languages and indigenous cultures (Question 8). Seventeen NGOs (46 per cent) said that they were not at all concerned, four NGOs (10.8 per cent) were both concerned and not concerned, seven NGOs (18.9 per cent) were seriously concerned about this issue, and nine southern NGOs (24.3 per cent) declared that the influence of the English-language and western cultural systems was already well-entrenched and inescapable through the spread of such media as television and films. Of the 26 NGOs who did not feel threatened by the English language and its attendant values or who declared that such influence was already pervasive, many indicated that they were quite pleased to be able to learn English, which they thought opened a whole new world to them and gave them an educational advantage. For example, NGO 4 wrote that "we are eager to expand our English capabilities, but still respect and maintain our ... culture and heritage". NGO 3 noted that "even if we didn't have computers we would still have to communicate in English [but] this does not mean adopting Western values. We very much stick to the use of [our] customs and values". NGO 6 also agreed, stating that "it is good to use other languages [and] people can benefit from other cultures and languages and yet not be colonized". NGO 8 was even more enthusiastic, suggesting that the internet is "unfolding the unknown [because] it's a source of learning, expanding knowledge and a matter of inspiring experiences". Admitting that English is a powerful tool that "can contribute to adopting new values", NGO 9 stressed that "we work very hard to conserve and rescue the traditional activities". Accordingly, NGO 9 made a subtle distinction between using English as a means towards increased knowledge and socio-economic betterment but not as a means for fundamental transformation of indigenous culture and traditional values. Taking English-language use for granted, NGO 23 remarked that the real "challenge is to develop multiple language capacities which actually enhances ones participation in and contribution to global culture. We do not feel colonized by the English language and we are actively engaged in the process of reflexivity with respect to values – especially the values embedded in specific paradigms and world views. In this mode of cognition, we can never be colonized".

On the other hand, a handful of southern NGOs thought that they were already "colonized", but insisted that it did not much matter. NGO 12 declared that the "English language has always opened more doors and opportunities for the people than any ... vernacular language". NGO 33 insisted that, even though English-language use has become so assimilated into the practices and mores of its home country that it has become second-nature, "our culture and ethnic languages remain intact". NGO 33 added that, because "there are thousands of sites in Chinese, French, or German", there is much room for the cultural expression of other groups even with the predominance of English. In sum, being open to and using English does not mean that local languages and cultures are in danger of being forsaken. To judge by the testimony of these southern NGOs, quite the opposite seems to be occurring. Universal use of English is so much a given that it is no longer a contentious philosophical issue. These southern NGOs have learned how to balance use of English as a working language with the equally important goal of strengthening their community, defined as a nexus of local language, tradition, and culture.

Still, a fairly large minority of southern NGOs (29.7 per cent) was, to varying degrees, disturbed by the implications of the proliferation of the English-language and western cultural systems. Admitting that English was probably the best language "for international exchange", NGO 34 was troubled by the fact that "if you can't speak English, you can't write a proposal or a report that looks like you're competent [and] you don't look like you 'deserve' funding and support". In other words, facility in English is becoming the chief criterion by which to measure worthiness, regardless of true merit. Is there a solution to this problem? The only recourse for "third-world" countries is to "promote English using computer-assisted, self-paced technology", but this takes "assets" that are currently not available on a widespread basis and is, for all intents and purposes, a "post-colonial" solution that has been dictated by "necessity [and] imperative". NGO 25 seems to have adopted the same resigned outlook: "but what can we do. We are powerless to change the tides". NGO 15 lamented the fact that, due to the constant promotion of and emphasis on ICTs, the popularity of English-language schooling is becoming greater and greater, with the result that local-language instruction suffers: "People are much more interested to learn English and parents are more interested to send their girls and boys to English schools though it is not possible for them due to financial problems. After [only] some days parents are unable to bear the high cost of education so that they do not know either English nor [our native language]". NGO 29 worried that "ICTs will further spread the blind lusting of third worlders for western affluence and fashions and following these, values. (Picture a broken-down village, clay oven in the back, *The Young and the Restless* on the TV inside.) On the other hand, perhaps once as yet unknown critical mass is reached in terms of third-world access to ICTs, we may see a sudden geometric increase in effectiveness of those of us around the world working for the good of all".

A final question asked whether there were any negative aspects of ICTs that had not been discussed in previous sections of the survey and 19 NGOs (51.4 per cent) replied that they could not think of any additional drawbacks to ICT. The issues raised by the remaining 18 southern NGOs echo, in many ways, the range of concerns raised by western users of ICTs. Five NGOs mentioned the detrimental influence of easy access to pornography through the web; two NGOs rued the fact that employees used the web for personal business and were caught up in its many distractions; and another two NGOs complained about viruses and false e-mails. NGO 3 worried about the eyesight and posture of staff members sitting in front of computers all day. NGO 18 reflected that, after "we get used to ICTs", they invariably "breakdown". NGO 23 noted that "the main negative aspect is information overload and difficulty in managing and utilizing (rather than collecting) the information". NGO 26 lamented that ICTs "show people everything that is available in the world, most of which they will never have for themselves". NGO 2 concurred, declaring sadly that its members were "frustrated" because "we cannot keep up with the development" of western countries. NGO 6, noting that "ICTs are a tool for literate people whereas in our Sub-Saharan region, more than 50 per cent of the population are still more illiterate and living under the poverty line. We are [therefore] not sure that the ICTs are contributing positively to the alleviation of poverty". NGO 27 felt discomfort with "the lack of human touch and sense" of ICTs. Finally, NGO 36 expressed doubts about systemic structural issues connected with ICTs: "The huge investment that it takes to jump forward to each new technological level means that we are beholden to such forces rather than to the touchable, breathing people that we know and see each day. That's very sad".

Still, despite this myriad of troubling issues, ICTs remain a lifeline for southern NGOs. Simply put, they have learned to cope, and have made strenuous

80 *Civil Society in the Information Age*

efforts to focus on the positive aspects of ICT use. Accordingly, southern NGOs prefer to see ICTs as a new "work tool" (NGO 1) in their arsenal rather than an ideological Trojan horse for western culture and values. Results from this survey suggest that they are not overwhelmingly concerned about tangential philosophical questions connected with ICT use. The general sense of the responses could be summarized as follows. It does not matter much who invented the shovel, or for what purposes, or if the inventor is becoming rich because of his or her invention. The shovel has been invented, it exists, and the shovel is useful to me even though it has some faults of which I am very well aware but which I have learned to compensate for and work around. Therefore I use the shovel quite often because I need to build something to improve life in my country. To be sure, this is a simplification of the complex views expressed in survey responses. Yet, to a very great extent, it captures the essence of the results. In other words, southern NGOs are very pragmatic and realistic in their understanding and use of ICTs.

Relationship of Southern NGOs with International NGOs

Frequency of Contact

Of the 37 survey respondents, eight southern NGOs (21.6 per cent) had "very frequent" contact (at least once a day) with large international NGOs in the previous 12 months, 12 southern NGOs (32.4 per cent) had "frequent" contact (10-20 times per month), six southern NGOs (16.2 per cent) had "moderate" contact (4-7 times per month), and nine southern NGOs (24.3 per cent) had "infrequent" contact (1-2 times per month). A majority of the respondents (20 out of 37) therefore had 10 or more contacts per month with international NGOs (Column 2 of Table 5.3). For the purposes of this survey, contact was defined as in-person, telephone, fax, or e-mail contact between any member of the responding organization and a large international NGO. By far the most common type of contact was e-mail, which was mentioned by 17 southern NGOs. Fax contact was mentioned by nine southern NGOs, and in-person contact was mentioned by seven southern NGOs. The following response from NGO 8 is representative of many of the answers given by those southern NGOs with "very frequent" and "frequent" contacts: "Most contacts are made through e-mails; very few by fax and telephone. Postal mails mainly cover big reports and other printed materials ... Subjects usually include – mutual agreement for various development issues, share reports, studies and evaluations, field visits ... During December 2000, a consultant from [international NGO X] visited our working area to assess the necessity to further extend support for our eye care project".

Many of the southern NGOs with "very frequent" or "frequent" contacts were working on numerous concurrent projects, and were therefore in touch with more than one international NGO at the same time. In fact, 13 southern NGOs (35.1 per cent) mentioned that they had contacts with two or more international NGOs. NGO 8 listed the names of ten international NGOs whom it considers to be "partners". NGO 2 stated that it had "intensive" or "very intensive" contact with five international NGOs; sometimes such contact lasted as little as four weeks, but often such contact stretched to eight or even 12 months. NGO 10 wrote that it had over "2400 contacts per year through e-mail, telephone, fax, and postal service" with five international NGOs. Three southern NGOs stated that they made grant applications to large international NGOs in the past year, and that the intensity of e-mail and postal contact increased sharply during the grant-writing phase. Two southern NGOs noted that they had been invited to attend the headquarters of international NGOs for seminars or to give a series of speeches about a particular local issue to a "developed-world" audience.

In-person visits by representatives of international NGOs were especially valued. NGO 4 stressed that two of the international NGOs with which it is in contact had sent volunteers to establish and deepen an "ongoing relationship". NGO 19 has been fortunate enough to have three in-person contacts with three separate large international NGOs. Two of these contacts have been visiting experts who gave presentations about environmental issues; the third in-person contact happened when a representative of an international NGO "was vacationing in our country, heard about us, and offered to set up a partnership involving their members volunteering to work with us on a project to be funded by a government agency".

In overall terms, there is a considerable amount of contact between southern NGOs in "developing" countries and international NGOs. As mentioned above, e-mail contact is the most common type of contact, followed by fax, phone, postal mail, and in-person contacts. No matter the type of contact, the overarching concern was money, as in the following comment from NGO 19: "Through the internet I came across Rainforest Action Network (RAN) several years ago, who were offering assistance through their Rainforest Action Group programme. We joined and received a few newsletters. This programme seemed to offer help to small groups who wanted to work with/for RAN, using RAN materials to work locally to preserve rainforests, but we never got too far with this. We are constantly struggling with finding resources (money) to deal with local environmental crises". In other words, there may be all sorts of contact, but if money is lacking to follow up such contact, the contact, even if very frequent, is not of much use. Indeed, the experiences of NGO 13 are an eloquent testimony on this point. Although it had contacted over 150 international NGOs via fax and e-mail, "nothing worth referring to came out of these contacts. We had contacted these NGOs to work with us on specific development projects relevant to the national developmental objectives of [our African country]. The response from [them] is always 'We regret we cannot be of help or we are dealing directly with governments!'". The only financial support received by this NGO is participation in one seminar in Europe and a grant from an international foundation "with strings attached". Speculating as to the reasons behind its failure to secure more funding, NGO 13 was convinced that "NGOs in the developed world now seem to have little or no faith in NGOs in third world countries. Generally, there is donor fatigue from the developed world not so much because NGOs in the third world are not efficient in performing their responsibilities, but because NGOs in the developed world are more engaged in addressing most of their very luxurious administrative needs rather than effectively co-operating with local NGOs in the third world in addressing the needs of the disadvantaged...". Of course, most of the responding NGOs were not as scathing in their assessment of their contacts with large international NGOs; most had complimentary or neutral things to say about their experiences with large international NGOs. Nevertheless, the concerns raised by NGO 13 – and to a lesser extent by NGO 19 – are forceful reminders that, while frequency of contact between southern NGOs and large international NGOs is a positive sign, it must be matched by an ongoing commitment to provide adequate resources and monetary support if the contact is to prove fruitful and beneficial in the long term.

Negative or Frustrating Experiences

When asked whether they had had "any negative or frustrating experiences with large international NGOs", 17 of the southern NGOs replied in the affirmative. As a percentage of the total sample of the 37 responding NGOs, this is a rate of 45.9 per cent; as a percentage of the 35 southern NGOs that have had at least one contact per month with international NGOs, this is a rate of 48.6 per cent. As shown in Column 3 of Table 5.3 below, southern NGOs that had "very frequent" contact (25 per cent) or "frequent" contact (41.7 per cent) with international NGOs were less prone to report "negative or frustrating experiences" than were southern NGOs that had "moderate" (66.7 per cent) or "infrequent" contact (66.7 per cent). It is noteworthy, however, that no matter the level of contact, a significant number of southern NGOs in each "frequency of contact" subdivision described "negative or frustrating experiences" with international NGOs. On the other hand, these figures suggest that, as southern NGOs enter into more and more frequent contact with international NGOs, the rate of "negative or frustrating experiences" tends to decrease, either because there is a greater mutual understanding or because there is a greater awareness, on the part of the southern NGO, of the realities and limitations involved in a relationship with an international NGO. The size of the southern NGO, as measured in paid employees, also influenced the way that they perceived international NGOs. As summarized in Table 5.4, of the 17 NGOs that have ten or fewer paid workers, ten (58.9 per cent) have had negative or frustrating experiences with international NGOs. Conversely, of the 20 NGOs that have 11 or more paid workers, only seven (35 per cent) claimed to have had such experiences. As the number of employees in a southern NGO increases, there may be a concomitant formalization and systematization of working relationships, leading to greater inter-organization understanding and professionalization.

The two most common complaints revolved around a lack of financial support – mentioned by six southern NGOs – and various administrative impediments and headaches, which were mentioned by five southern NGOs. NGO 2, an organization with "very frequent" contacts with international NGOs, had the following typical interconnected litany of complaints: "Conflict of interests (differences in points of view concerning advocacy issues); spending too much time in preparing and writing the proposals [because] the target is not sure to get it; decline in executing the previous commitments; refusing to fund essential jobs, such as management, marketing, financial and administrative jobs". NGO 1 (frequent contact) wrote that it was frustrated because one international NGO is "very slow in processing its administrative work [because] between project approval and receival [sic] of money nearly a year passed". It also complained that another international NGO with which it worked "has had a high turnover in its administrative staff [and] consequently there are interruptions in the communication". NGO 9 (frequent contact) complained that "most of the time we made programs with a specific budget, however this support is arrive [sic] late or they decide to suspend the payments and it limited that activities". NGO 13 (very frequent contact) described its innovative "Communal Farming System approach" in agricultural sector development, and then lamented that international NGOs have not been "helpful and would scarcely collaborate" even though they "have the money". NGO 6 (moderate contact) had a very similar set of frustrations: "Yes, when our request of funding is rejected because they say it does not fulfil the criteria of selection and when the communication is one way direction [and when] there is no feed back reports after a field visit".

Table 5.3 Effect of Frequency of Contact Between Southern NGOs and International NGOs on the Type of Relationship Between Southern NGOs and International NGOs

Frequency of contact by Southern NGOs with international NGOs	Number of Southern NGOs having such contact	Southern NGOs having negative or frustrating experiences with international NGOs	Southern NGOs not sufficiently consulted by international NGOs on matters of local concern	Southern NGOs that feel international NGOs are more interested in disaster relief than capacity building
Very frequent contact (at least once a day)	8 (21.6%)	2 (25%)	2 (25%)	4 (50%)
Frequent contact (10-20 times per month)	12 (32.4%)	5 (41.7%)	5 (41.7%)	4 (33.3%)
Moderate contact (4-7 times per month)	6 (16.2%)	4 (66.7%)	3 (50%)	5 (83.3%)
Infrequent contact (1-2 times per month)	9 (24.3%)	6 (66.7%)	5 (55.6%)	7 (77.8%)
No contact	2 (5.4%)	-	1 (50%)	-
Total	37 (100%)	17 (45.9%)	16 (43.2%)	20 (54.1%)

84 *Civil Society in the Information Age*

Five southern NGOs complained about what could be termed philosophical and ethical lapses in the international NGO community. NGO 22 (moderate contact) stated that "the frustrating part is the way they try to make you feel lower than they. That they are the experts and we know nothing about our country and its problems. It is really infuriating". NGO 21 (moderate contact) wrote that "Yes, sometimes these people can be very negative". NGO 25 (infrequent contact) maintained that negative experiences with international NGOs depended on "what they want from us and how much". NGO 16 (infrequent contact) addressed the structural problem of networking, noting that "[i]t is hard to work with them unless you know the members well". NGO 15 (infrequent contact) was highly critical of an international NGO whose representative expressed "his hidden desire that there be a sexual relationship with some of our female staff" even though "the open sexual relationship in our country is not of our culture". When the sexual advance was rejected, this southern NGO found that "our project proposal was rejected [even though] it had documentary evidence". Equally troubling were the following cryptic comments received from four southern NGOs with "infrequent" contacts and one southern NGO with "frequent" contacts when asked whether they had "negative or frustrating experiences with international NGOs": "Yes, but we would rather not be specific"; "We have had our problems and would rather not say them more than that in this open forum"; "We hope for better days and pray"; "More often than not"; and "Yes, we have but we figure, as women, we must expect adverse conditions and will endeavor to keep guard against it".

Table 5.4 Effect of Southern NGO Size As Measured by "Paid Workers" on the Type of Relationship Between Southern NGOs and International NGOs

Size of Southern NGO as measured by paid workers	Number of Southern NGOs of this size	Southern NGOs having negative or frustrating experiences with international NGOs	Southern NGOs not sufficiently consulted by international NGOs on matters of local concern	Southern NGOs that feel international NGOs are more interested in disaster relief than capacity building
All volunteer	5 (13.5%)	3 (60%)	4 (80%)	4 (80%)
1-5 paid workers	7 (18.9%)	3 (42.9%)	3 (42.7%)	2 (28.6%)
6-10 paid workers	5 (13.5%)	4 (80%)	2 (40%)	5 (100%)
11-20 paid workers	9 (24.3%)	3 (33.3%)	2 (22.2%)	5 (55.6%)
21 plus paid workers	11 (29.7%)	4 (36.4%)	5 (45.5%)	4 (36.4%)
Total	37 (100%)	17 (45.9%)	16 (43.2%)	20 (54.1%)

To be sure, 18 southern NGOs (48.6 per cent if all 37 responding NGOs are included in this calculation; 51.4 per cent if the 35 NGOs that have had at least some contact with international NGOs are included in this calculation) specifically stated that they had not had "negative or frustrating experiences". Typical comments were as follows: "We have always received all possible co-operation"; "Never"; "We have received nothing but help and information"; and "We have not had any bad experiences. At times, due to misunderstandings we have had minor disputes (deadlines on reports) but nothing worth talking about. We work very well with [them] and are thankful for their support". Despite this group of satisfied southern NGOs, it is nevertheless clear that a significant array of problems – some stated, some unstated – remains to be solved. While problems with financial matters are front and centre in the relationship between southern NGOs and international NGOs, the results of this survey suggest that there are other disturbing issues that are contributing to a residual, often festering, tension. As southern NGOs and international NGOs come to know each other better, these tensions may be become less acute, although it is clear from Table 5.3 that they will likely never disappear.

Consultation on Matters of Local Concern

When southern NGOs were asked whether "you feel that your NGO is sufficiently consulted by large international NGOs on matters of local concern about which your local NGO has special expertise", 16 survey respondents (43.2 per cent) replied in the negative, which included one southern NGO that wrote "sometimes". The same sort of pattern noted with regard to the previous question also pertains to this question. That is to say, the more frequent the contact between a southern NGO and an international NGO, the less chance there is that the southern NGO will claim that it has not been sufficiently consulted on matters of local concern. Conversely, the less frequent the contact, the more chance there will be that southern NGOs will feel that they have not been sufficiently consulted. As shown in Column 4 of Table 5.3 above, while 35 per cent of southern NGOs with "very frequent" or "frequent" contacts (7 out of 20 NGOs) state that they have not been sufficiently consulted, this figure rises to 53.3 per cent in the case of southern NGOs with "moderate" or "infrequent" contacts (eight out of 15 NGOs). Again, one explanation may be that, as working relationships between southern NGOs and larger international NGOs intensify, both sides develop confidence in each other – a circumstance which lends itself to increased co-operation and teamwork. And while 52.9 per cent of the southern NGOs having ten or fewer paid employees (nine out of 17) did not feel sufficiently consulted (Column 4 of Table 5.4), only 35 per cent of the NGOs having 11 or more paid employees held this view (seven out of 20). The larger the organization in terms of paid employees, the more chance there may be for fruitful avenues of consultation and collaboration.

NGO 14 (frequent contact) was perhaps the most eloquent respondent to this question, including themes and concerns in its answer that would be alluded to more briefly by other survey respondents. NGO 14 declared that, instead of bringing an attitude that could be characterized as "we come to learn from you, share with you", donors often "emphasize strategies and projects of their own choosing" because they "have the money and expertise". On a more concrete level, NGO 14 asserted that "evaluation and monitoring" are a big problem because "a lot of [international] NGOs are very good at looking good but not necessarily having the kind of programs and services that make a big difference. The groups that look good get the money; other groups tend to have extensive services that have an impact on many people but they are not so good at reporting or putting on the dog and pony show that impresses donors". Recognizing that some kind of balance must be achieved, NGO 14 nevertheless rued the fact that, for many donors, "a key issue is competency in English and editorial/PR skills". Finally, NGO 14 is quite caustic about the propensity of international NGOs to hire outside consultants to evaluate projects that they have supported. Admitting that "donors rightfully want accountability from the recipients of their largess[e]", NGO 14 nonetheless observed that "outside consultants and firms" hired as project evaluators "often cost much more or as much as the projects they support". More specifically, "we have seen evaluation consultants who know very little about the culture and context of the programs they are evaluating come for a quick one-or-two-week whirlwind site visit, return home, write a report which is only marginally understanding of the realities of the field, and charge anywhere between ten and 200 times as much as the people they evaluate are paid". Such soaring consultancy costs, NGO 14 concluded, make it a "challenge to write grants that pay decent salaries to local staff and also have enough in the budget for professional evaluators who have both skill and credibility".

Although more laconic in their assessment of the situation, many other surveyed NGOs essentially agreed with the remarks of NGO 14. For example, NGO 34 (frequent contact) wryly noted that "we feel bad for the international NGOs sometimes. The people who work in them often live in big cities halfway around the planet from here, but seem to know what life is like for us". NGO 6 (moderate contact) remarked that "they can get information from different sources and they [therefore] take their own decision and judgement without consulting the local partners". NGO 12 (moderate contact) was critical of international NGOs for relying "on big NGOs in the countries where they fund" either because of "convenience or lack of personnel". Noting disparagingly that "the favourite term that is bandied [about] for such an arrangement [is] outsourcing of expertise", NGO 12 remarked that an unintended consequence of such practices is that "so-called small NGOs find it very difficult to develop their own human resources". NGO 35 (infrequent contact) was exasperated that "they try to tell us what we need to know about our environment!". NGO 37 (infrequent contact) asks "Consult us? Now that is amusing!". NGO 19 (frequent contact) declared that "we have never been directly consulted by [an international NGO] regarding anything". Speculating as to why international NGOs may not consult as much as they might, NGO 16 (no contact) noted that "there is a lot of politics in the international NGO environment ... and they will not contact local NGOs where they feel that the local NGO may be able to outcompete them for funds". NGO 36 (infrequent contact) in effect summarized these negative views by observing that international NGOs "just try to give us orders".

This list of negative experiences, however, should be not be viewed as representative of the situation of all southern NGOs. After all, 22 southern NGOs (59.5 per cent) stated that international NGOs did consult with them. Taking stock of its relationships with international NGOs, NGO 8 (very frequent contact) concluded that "everything is decided by mutual consultation". NGO 8 was particularly laudatory about the "fresh graduates" that international NGOs have sent for internships: "they try to have acquaintance with local people, learn the local culture; they study, collect information and gather practical experiences of local expertise. Internees have always expressed that their stay ... was interesting, uplifting and inspiring experience which would be an asset for their future career". NGO 3 (frequent contact) too felt "very comfortable with amount of consultation we are given. The large NGOs with which we deal trust us in the expertise we have and let us do our work without too much interference". NGO 17 (frequent contact) was very enthusiastic about the regional and sectoral meetings sponsored by international NGOs that brought together many southern NGOs from various countries in an effort to share knowledge and find common solutions, often through cross-border projects. In sum, while some international NGOs are making a concerted effort to be sensitive and to establish respectful links with southern NGOs, other international NGOs remain ensconced in a paternalistic and hierarchical relationship model. Judging from the answers provided for this survey, the longer that a southern NGO has worked with an international NGO, the greater the chances for mutually satisfactory consultation. Similarly, the more intense the contact between southern NGOs and their international counterparts – through intern programs or regional meetings, for example – the more opportunity there is to develop an atmosphere of meaningful two-way communication.

Disaster Relief at the Expense of Capacity Building

Asked whether they thought that "international NGOs are more interested in disaster-relief or service provision than in capacity building", 20 of the 37 responding NGOs (54.1 per cent) felt that this was indeed the case (Column 5 of Table 5.2). In a now familiar pattern, southern NGOs with "very frequent" or "frequent" contacts with international NGOs (eight out of 20 NGOs) were less likely to take this view (40 per cent) than were southern NGOs with "moderate" contacts or "infrequent" contacts (80 per cent) (12 out of 15 NGOs). In addition, southern NGOs with 11 or more paid employees (nine out of 20 NGOs) were less likely to take this view (45 per cent) than were southern NGOs with ten or fewer paid employees (64.7 per cent) (11 out of 17 NGOs). A central theme that appeared repeatedly in the replies of these 20 southern NGOs was that disaster relief was much more glamorous than the thankless hard work necessary to achieve capacity building. NGO 12 (moderate contact) felt that international NGOs gravitate to issues that are "mainstream and that give ample photo opportunities". NGO 24 (frequent contact) agreed, noting that "disaster relief is more tangible, more organizable, offers more opportunities for categorical funding with physical (e.g., can be collected, bought, donated, shipped, even photographed) consumed (items). Disasters come and go, and are more marketable in terms of 'get in/get out' compassion. They are attractive to Americans and others who like to 'fix' things". Capacity building, on the other hand, is "less measurable, less easy to get closure on, harder to get the sense that you're having an impact, harder to prove you are really accomplishing something". In summary, NGO 24 remarked that "the mere fact that most funders don't want to pay for operational expenses is the indication that disasters and crises are more marketable. Not to be cynical, but a lot of the support game is about framing ongoing needs in marketable terms". NGO 26 (moderate contact) complained that "we can't even get small grants for really good causes, no recognition, until a news-catching incident happens in the area". NGO 25 (infrequent contact) attributed the focus on disaster relief to the "edutainment mentality that is so pervasive in today's culture". NGO 33 (infrequent contact) wondered "where is the spotlight for capacity building? It is only the disasters that are illuminated". NGO 31 (moderate contact) concurred: "Most international NGOs don't know one thing about building capacity, and don't want to learn. Why? No way to generate the big bucks or get the cameras rolling". NGO 34 (frequent contact) declared that "it is terrible to want a disaster to happen so help and money will be forthcoming, but that is the case for many of us". NGO 35 (infrequent contact) was just as blunt, noting that "large major disasters make money for international NGOs". Finally, as NGO 6 (moderate contact) recalled, the presence of international NGOs after a disaster, while welcome, is a decidedly short-term affair that does not solve structural problems: "Take the example of Rwanda in 1994, after the genocide, more than 200 international NGOs entered the country, but six years later we remain with only about 50 NGOs and few of them deal with development work".

Overall Assessment of the Role of International NGOs

Southern NGOs were also asked how they would "in general characterize the work done by international NGOs". As shown in the first two columns of Table 5.5, "helpful" and "indispensable" were the two adjectives used most frequently to describe international NGOs and their work. 22 of the 37 survey respondents (59.5 per cent) used these adjectives either separately or together. Only seven survey respondents (18.9 per cent) chose to use the word "patronizing" to describe their relationship, and five of these conceded that international NGOs had nevertheless been "helpful" despite their patronizing attitude. And, as shown in Columns 3 and 4 of Table 5.5, the range of help provided by international NGOs to southern NGOs is impressively wide. When asked whether they had had "any positive experiences" or had been "helped" in some way by international NGOs, 29 (78.4 per cent) cited at least one such occurrence, and many southern NGOs cited two or more. Financial help, either alone or together with some other kind of help, dominated the list, with 20 southern NGOs (54.1 per cent) stating that they had been helped financially by international NGOs. Seven southern NGOs (18.9 per cent) mentioned that they were grateful to international NGOs for free satellite web access, web hosting, and computer equipment. Volunteer help was also much appreciated, as was the ability to participate in international seminars and conferences. In addition, several southern NGOs were grateful that they were receiving newsletters and reports from international NGOs, and one southern NGO praised an international NGO for "publishing a book of ours for farmers on the topic of pesticide-free, biodynamic agriculture".

Table 5.5 Overall Characterization of International NGOs by Southern NGOs and the Types of Help They Received from International NGOs

Adjectives used to describe work of international NGOs		Types of help received from international NGOs	
Helpful	13 (35.2%)	Financial help	9 (24.3%)
Indispensable	4 (10.8%)	Free equipment, including computers, and other technical help	3 (8.1%)
Helpful and indispensable	5 (13.5%)	Skill training and education through seminars/ conferences/workshops	4 (10.8%)
Patronizing	2 (5.4%)	Financial help and contact-building	3 (8.1%)
Helpful and patronizing	5 (13.5%)	Financial help and donations of equipment, including computers	4 (10.8%)
Overrated	3 (8.1%)	Financial help and skill training	1 (2.7%)
Helpful and inauthentic	1 (2.7%)	Financial help and sending volunteers or experts on site visits	3 (8.1%)
Indispensable, but needs to be guided	1 (2.7%)	General advocacy	2 (5.4%)
No answer	3 (8.1%)	No help/no positive experiences	8 (21.6%)
Total	37 (100%)	Total	37 (100%)

Despite the general high esteem with which international NGOs are held by southern NGOs, there were heartfelt words of advice. NGO 5 (frequent contact) complained that international NGOs are "sometimes ... too much biased toward their established client NGOs and less attention [is given] to new NGOs. Often they have biased country advisors who give them wrong advices [sic]. These advisors recommend financial support to NGOs run by their relatives or friends and not on the basis of merit of work. These advisors are exactly like government employees (white elephants) in the developing countries". NGO 9 (frequent contact) wanted international NGOs to be more sensitive to the cultural and social context of the countries in which they operate. In the opinion of NGO 9, it was too often the case that "the projects have to go by the politics and laws that they establish, but sometimes this politics does not apply for different reasons, depending of [sic] the people, the climate, the geographic position, etc". NGO 30 (frequent contact) was also concerned about the over-politicization of international NGOs, almost all of which have "their own political agenda and contrary to their tall claims of being "non-political", they are very much biased [in that] they are helpful, but they are "more helpful" to certain parties". NGO 14 (frequent contact) perhaps best summed up the prevailing situation by contrasting the "palatability" of international NGOs with government organizations and corporations, both of which have political and economic objectives. Nevertheless, NGO 14 warned that "to the extent that they are havens for ex-pats who can't make it in their home countries and live separate from the cultures they profess to serve, [international NGOs] are dispensable. The organizations that deserve our admiration are those that strike a balance between true service, reasonable public relations, little chest-beating, a feeling of partnership and trust, respect for local culture, marginal imposition of foreign values on local situations".

Discussion and Conclusion

The portrait that emerges of southern NGOs from even this small survey is of a constant competition to attract the intellectual and financial attention of international NGOs. In this competition, ICTs are the tools of choice. More than half (19 out of 37) of the surveyed organizations had three or more computers, but only 56.8 per cent of them (21 out of 37) spent more than US$1,000 on ICT equipment in the previous 12 months. E-mail was by far the most common application of ICTs; it is indispensable for networking, fundraising, and general advocacy. Websites aided in establishing the credibility of southern NGOs. To a large extent, ICTs have brought about positive change in the decision-making processes of southern NGOs, making them more focused and informed. Staff morale has not been lowered because of the introduction of ICTs; in fact, it has often soared as individuals successfully grapple with new concepts. Belying the concerns of Heeks (1999), there was near unanimous agreement that ICTs had not eroded the use of indigenous and informal communication channels, had not led to a decrease in local initiatives for the design of developmental efforts, and had not caused southern NGOs to give too much priority to "first-world" solutions to "third-world" problems. Not afraid to learn about all possible perspectives and solutions to specific problems or challenges, southern NGOs nevertheless remained grounded in the reality of their local situations and worked hard not to lose sight of the particular circumstances of their socio-economic environments. In addition, southern NGOs felt that ICTs had not consumed funds that could have been spent more usefully in other more pressing areas, mainly because the percentage of their total operating budget devoted to ICTs is relatively small. Opinion was about equally divided on the question of whether ICTs create or exacerbate a class divide, with many southern NGOs believing that such social divides were already in existence due to many other factors. In partial substantiation of Hamelink (1997), there was some worry that ICTs contributed to the propagation of the English language and western culture, but, for the most part, southern NGOs were resigned to the fact that, for better or worse, the cultural influence of English had to be accepted, given its unassailable position as the world's working language. The almost complete and wholehearted acceptance of the value of ICTs as a "work tool" by southern NGOs is one indication that ICTs have reached critical mass on a worldwide scale. Indeed, there were many indications that ICTs were facilitating the creation of what Ballantyne, Labelle, and Rudgard (2000) referred to as "local networks of expertise".

While embracing ICTs, southern NGOs are more leery of their contacts with international NGOs. More than 40 per cent of southern NGOs recounted negative or frustrating experiences with international NGOs and said that they had not been sufficiently consulted on matters of local interest. More than 50 per cent of them said that international NGOs were still more interested in disaster relief than capacity building. And although they pragmatically recognized that the work of international NGOs was, on the whole, helpful, and at times indispensable, there was a gnawing sense that many aspects of the relationship left much to be desired. But, as indicated in Tables 5.3 and 5.4, the southern NGOs that had the fewest misgivings about international NGOs were those that had the most frequent contacts with them and that had the largest complement of paid staff members. Organizational size and intensity of contacts do seem to matter. And, given the fact that, for many southern NGOs, international NGOs are an important, if not vital, source of financial and technical support, it might be useful for smaller, free-standing southern NGOs to consider organizational and structural changes that would allow them to put in place the preconditions necessary to a more positive working relationship with international NGOs. To be sure, it is also incumbent upon northern international NGOs to work towards making their partnerships with southern NGOs more effective by adopting policies and procedures that result in open, trusting and flexible partnerships, and an in-depth comprehension of local needs and local situations. As described by Offenheiser, Holcombe, and Hopkins (1999), the most forward-looking international NGOs are embarking upon efforts to "build partnership arrangements that capitalize on trust to optimize partners' capacity to achieve real impact on their own terms" and "to operationalize the linkages between local realities and global policy formulation in ways that optimize the voices of southern partner organizations in and through ... advocacy work" (Offenheiser et al. 1999, 127-128). Lindenberg and Dobel (1999) identify five main organizational types – separate independent organizations, independent organizations with weak umbrella co-ordination, confederations, federations, and unitary corporate organizations – and discuss how these structures will respond to the challenges of globalization, noting that they have great potential for the long term "only if they can maintain community-based flexibility, adaptiveness, and diversity while maintaining more general universal standards" (Lindenberg & Dobel 1999, 13). Foreman (1999) examines the relatively new governance structure of the global bumblebee federation,[1] observing that, despite its advantages, it carries with it the risk of the "franchising" of NGOs in developing countries (Foreman 1999, 193).

Yet, the very fact that there are literally hundreds of thousands of NGOs in developing countries competing for attention and resources suggests that many of them – most likely the smallest ones with the fewest staff members who may not necessarily have the time nor the accumulated body of knowledge needed to deal fruitfully with international NGOs – will find it difficult to have their voices heard, thus depriving diverse communities and constituencies with pressing developmental problems of spokespersons and willing intermediaries. Given the wide attention paid to reforming the governance structures of international NGOs, it is odd that comparatively little has been said about the need to organize southern NGOs into alliances and collaborative networks of their own where they are not mere adjuncts of northern international NGOs. The range of development issues tackled by southern NGOs on a daily basis is vast. They speak with many and varied voices, and while they make good use of ICTs in an effort to advance their respective programs, they are often not heard. And if they are heard, it may be the case that they are not heard in the right places by the right people or it may be the case that their relationship with an international NGO is marred by unequal power relations. It stands to reason, then, that southern-initiated, southern-based, and southern-controlled cross-border networks that allow for multi-purpose development issues to be highlighted and addressed would not only increase the organizational strength, efficacy, and visibility of individual member NGOs, but also allow them as a group to compete, on a more equal basis, for funds from the same donor communities as northern international NGOs. It would also allow them to deal with northern-based NGOs from a position of new-found strength and it would help in creating an atmosphere where projects could become self-sustaining and where capacity building would not be an empty slogan. The Grameen Bank and the Bangladesh Rural Advancement Committee are among the few examples of such southern-based organizational networks and alliances. Why not more? Without such southern-based cross-border and cross-theme organizing efforts, many southern NGOs may fall by the wayside, unable to surmount the barriers strewn before them. If the principle of "collaborative accountability" outlined by Ashman (2001) is to become widely used, replacing the principal-agent concept whereby the giver of resources has substantially more say in defining accountability procedures, it would be advantageous for southern NGOs if they were operating from a position of strength. After all, successful and sustainable development projects depend as much on external financial resources as local indigenous knowledge. An accumulation of such local indigenous knowledge – an accumulation resulting from the formation of southern-based NGO alliances and networks – would go a long way towards ensuring collaborative accountability. And while it is true that a single individual southern NGO may enter into a collaborative accountability agreement with its northern international NGO partner, it is not outlandish to suggest that a broadly-based alliance or network of southern NGOs has more of a chance in bringing about true collaboration and ensuring real collaborative accountability.

Note

Note on internet addresses (URLs): Websites tend to appear, change or disappear, often without warning. Addresses cited in this bibliography were accurate and active at the time of writing (January 2002) unless otherwise noted.

1   The term "global bumblebee federation" refers to the intricate network of influence and interaction between member organizations and a central or international organization head office (such as World Vision) whereby the central authority devolves to the affiliates over time (Foreman 1999, 181). This type of federation is characterized by the members' strong belief in the mutual benefit of ceding power to a strong central organization where the Board membership is not based on a member's capacity to raise resources but, rather, on the geographic region or other non-resource criteria. In turn, the various national offices are encouraged to fulfil all aspects of the NGO's mission including fund-raising and delivery of services (Lindenberg & Dobel 1999, 17).

References

Ashman, Darcy (2001), 'Strengthening North-south Partnerships for Sustainable Development', *Nonprofit and Voluntary Sector Quarterly*, Vol. 30(1), pp. 74-98.

Ballantyne, Peter, Labelle, Richard and Rudgard, Stephen (2000), *Information and Knowledge Management: Challenges for Capacity Builders*, www.oneworld.org/ecdpm/pmb/b11_gb.htm

Bornstein, David (1999), 'A Force Now in the World, Citizens Flex Social Muscle', *The New York Times*, July 10, pp. A15, A17.

Castells, Manuel (1998), *Information Technology, Globalization and Social Development*, Paper presented at the UNRISD Conference on Information Technologies and Social Development, Palais des Nations, Geneva, June 22-24, 1998 www.unrisd.org/infotech/conferen/castelp1.htm

Dichter, Thomas W. (1999), 'Globalization and its Effects on NGOs: Efflorescence or a Blurring of Roles and Relevance?', *Nonprofit and Voluntary Sector Quarterly*, Vol. 28(4), pp. 38-58.

Edwards, Michael (1999), 'International Development NGOs: Agents of Foreign Aid or Vehicles for International Cooperation?', *Nonprofit and Voluntary Sector Quarterly*, Vol. 28(4), pp. 25-37.

Foreman, Karen (1999), 'Evolving Global Structures and the Challenges Facing International Relief and Development Organizations', *Nonprofit and Voluntary Sector Quarterly*, Vol. 28(4), pp. 178-197.

Hamelink, Cees J. (1997), *New Information and Communication Technologies, Social Development and Cultural Change*, www.unrisd.org/engindex/publ/list/dp/dp86/dp86.htm

Heeks, Richard (1999), *Information and Communication Technologies, Poverty and Development*, Working Paper 5 of the Development Informatics Working Paper Series. Manchester, England: University of Manchester.

International Forum on Capacity Building. (1998), *Southern NGO Capacity-building: Issues and Priorities*, New Delhi, India: International Working Group on Capacity-Building of Southern NGOs.

Lal, Bhavya (1999), *Information and Communication Technologies for Improved Governance*, www.abtassociates.com/reports/governance/ict.pdf

Lindenberg, Marc and Dobel, J. Patrick (1999), 'The Challenges of Globalization for Northern International Relief and Development NGOs', *Nonprofit and Voluntary Sector Quarterly*, Vol. 28(4), pp. 4-28.

Offenheiser, Raymond, Holcombe, Susan and Hopkins, Nancy (1999), 'Grappling with Globalization, Partnership, and Learning: a Look Inside Oxfam America', *Nonprofit and Voluntary Sector Quarterly*, Vol. 28(4), pp. 121-140.

Roberts, Adam (2000), 'International NGOs: New Gods Overseas', *The Economist*, Vol. 49, pp. 79-81.

Smillie, Ian (1999), *Narrowing the Digital Divide: Notes on a Global Netcorps*, www.unites.org/reference/smillie0.html

Chapter 6

Essential Partners: Landmines-Related NGOs and Information Technologies

Kenneth R. Rutherford

[T] *he involvement of civil society and the information technology revolution are the foundations on which a profound democratization of international politics is being built.* Lloyd Axworthy (1997), Statement by the Canadian Foreign Minister to the NGO Forum on Banning Anti-Personnel Landmines, Oslo, 7 November.

Introduction

On 16 December 1993, information technology helped save my life, when I was injured by a landmine and was able to use a hand-held radio to call for help. I said "Kilo Romeo (my radio call sign). I've been injured by a land mine. I'm bleeding. I'm 'O' positive. Send for an airplane". The local UN radio operators then co-ordinated with a Kenyan-based plane, which was in transit to Somalia on a medical aid drop off, to divert to pick me up and then evacuate me to a hospital in Nairobi.

The main point of this story is that information technologies in the form of a hand-held radio made the difference between life and death for me. Most other landmine victims, of whom more than 50 per cent die before reaching medical help, never have access to hand-held radios. Little did I realize that information technologies based primarily on the internet would soon help ban the weapon that almost killed me, and maims and kills more than 20,000 people each year. This NGO-led prohibition took the form of the Mine Ban Treaty (MBT), which was signed in 1997 by more than 130 states.[1]

This chapter examines how nongovernmental organizations (NGOs), specifically the International Campaign to Ban Landmines (ICBL) and the Landmine Survivors Network (LSN) utilized information technologies to help achieve the treaty.[2] The study of how they used these tools is important to international relations because it highlights how a coalition of NGOs in the form of the ICBL helped for the first time to achieve a ban on a weapon in widespread use and in the face of opposition by the major world powers. Moreover, it also shows how LSN used information technologies to successfully prod the international community to address landmine victim assistance issues.

The first section provides a background to the landmine issue and recounts a brief history of NGOs' role in promoting the issue and the various attempts to get the international community to address problems caused by landmines. The second section addresses the ICBL and the role of information technologies in banning landmines. The third section examines how the LSN made use of information technologies to achieve their goals of increasing resources for victim assistance. It concludes that the ICBL and LSN use of informational technologies opens up new avenues by which these technologies can be used to influence the making of foreign policy.

Background

The achievement of the MBT marks an incredible accomplishment: It is the "first time, the majority of the nations of the world will agree to ban a weapon which has been in military use by almost every country in the world" (Chrétien 1997). It also did not have the support of many major powers, which is contrary to the way most multilateral disarmament agreements are achieved.[3] At this writing (December 2001), more than 140 states have signed and more than 120 have ratified the convention (International Campaign to Ban Landmines). When it entered into force 1 March 1999, it became the fastest that a major international agreement ever came into force in history (International Campaign to Ban Landmines). Academics, (Price 1998) diplomats (Cameron 1998) and NGO representatives (Williams 1998) call the MBT's genesis and negotiations an innovative model for the future development of international law. Even the Nobel Committee recognized this unique coalition by awarding the ICBL and its co-ordinator Jody Williams the 1997 Nobel Peace Prize, in part for helping to create a fresh form of diplomacy.

State military forces traditionally used landmines for defensive purposes, primarily to protect strategic locations or channel enemy forces into specific fire zone areas. Restricted to these particular military uses, landmine casualties were primarily confined to military personnel during combat engagement or related operations. Beginning with the Vietnam War, however, landmines have become more widely used by poorly trained military forces and more offensive in military practice. Since many wars are now "long-running, internal, and low intensity, [they] often involv[e] cash-starved militaries for whom low-technology, low-cost landmines are a weapon of choice ... [c]onsequently, in wars today, mines are frequently placed in areas of high civilian concentration rather than being confined to discrete battlefields of limited size" (Human Rights Watch 1993, 9). The result has been an increasing level of destructiveness to civilian communities. For example, the top three states hosting landmine-disabled populations are recently emerging from decades of internal conflict that entailed the use of mines by all parties.[4] According to the US State Department, there are between 59-69 million landmines currently deployed[5] (United States 1998, 9), thereby making them "one of the most toxic and widespread pollution[s] facing mankind" (United States 1993, 2). Moreover, the State Department finds that landmines exacerbate regional conflicts, hinder post-conflict reconstruction, seriously undermine infrastructure, and deny land to civilian use thereby leading to overuse of existing land (United States 1998, 8-9, 11). Furthermore, each year landmines kill more than 24,000 people (International Committee of the Red Cross 1999, 16), most of whom are civilian (United States 1998, 1).

While landmine use among most state professional forces has declined recently (International Campaign to Ban Landmines 1999b, 3), there are notable exceptions. The most noticeable exceptions are Russian landmine use in Chechnya, (Ward 1997) Dagestan, (International Campaign to Ban Landmines 1999a) and Georgia,[6] and landmine use by Eritrea in its conflict with Ethiopia[7] (International Campaign to Ban Landmines 1999b, 196-97). During the 1990s, there were also a few cases of landmines deployed by professional troops in which civilians were purposely targeted. In Bosnia during the period 1993-94, Bosnian Croat and Serb forces used mines to discourage the return of refugees of other ethnic groups, and so did Serbian forces in Kosovo in 1999 to harm returning Kosovar refugees. Nevertheless, many non-state military forces still rely upon them to achieve their objectives. Recent and current internal wars, such as those in Afghanistan, Bosnia, Cambodia, Rwanda, Somalia and Uganda are further examples that landmines are not being used to conquer the opposing force, but rather the goal is economic and social destabilization or prevention of the return of refugees. In Afghanistan, for example, "[g]uerrilla forces used mines to force populations off the land and reduce potential support for their opponents" (United Nations 1999, 10), while in Cambodia the Khmer Rouge used landmines "to destabilize contested areas" (United Nations 1997, 6). Such strategies have resulted in these countries hosting some of the highest concentrations of landmines in the world. It is estimated that Afghanistan currently hosts between five to seven million landmines (United States 1998, 58) while Cambodia hosts between four to six million landmines (United Nations 1997, 38).

Initial NGO interest in the landmine issue began in the 1970s when the International Committee of the Red Cross (ICRC) determined that some weapons should be prohibited both "by customary and treaty-based international humanitarian law because landmines cause superfluous injury and unnecessary suffering (damaging effects disproportionate to the military purpose) and that they are of an indiscriminate nature (no distinction between civilians and combatants)" (Sand-Trigo 1997). These legal discussions will be reviewed at greater length in the next section, but for our current purposes, it suffices to say that the ICRC discussions in the 1970s eventually resulted in minimal international legal restrictions being placed on landmine use through the Landmines Protocol of the 1980 Convention on Conventional Weapons (CCW). This particular protocol was strengthened, as the Amended Protocol II adopted at the final CCW Review Conference in Geneva on 6 May 1996, when it became apparent that NGOs had the public support to push through a ban.[8] Prior to the CCW, landmine use was not a topic of concern for the media, NGOs or policymakers.

Even though the landmines protocol of the CCW was signed in 1980, it remains relatively unnoticed by the international community as reflected by the fact that after 15 years only 52 states had ratified it (Wren 1995, A6). Upset at the lack of universal support for the CCW and the effects of landmines, the ICBL started in 1991 when the Washington, DC-based Vietnam Veterans of America Foundation (VVAF) and the German medical NGO MEDICO decided to form a broad-based international campaign to speak with one voice supporting the ban. It was officially launched in October 1992, by "six NGOs, which had taken a number of individual and joint steps in the direction of the ban campaign by issuing a 'Joint Call to Ban Antipersonnel' landmines and hosting the first NGO-sponsored international landmine conference in May of 1993".[9]

International Campaign to Ban Landmines

Investigating the process through which the ICBL utilized information technologies as a tool to achieve its goals has important substantive implications. This section shows some of the ways that the ICBL accomplished this. The broader implications are how NGOs can play important roles in getting other issues, such as the environment and human rights, addressed by the international community.[10] Furthermore, landmines are a key policy problem, as they cause many injuries and deaths in regional conflicts, hinder post-conflict reconstruction, seriously undermine infrastructure, and deny land to civilian use thereby leading to overuse of existing land (United States 1998, 8-9, 11).

While international NGO policymaking entrepreneurial skills and lobbying strategies – promoting their messages through the media, taking public protesting actions, and mass letter writing campaigns – are well-known in other international issue areas such as the environment and human rights, the ICBL case yields relatively new information-technology strategies that are briefly described below.

Media Technologies

The ICBL's use of media technologies greatly contributed to moving states toward the landmine ban position. The campaign had the technical ability to research and publicize information quickly and early enough in the agenda setting process of international conferences to affect state landmine policy development. By controlling the agenda – what was to be discussed and how – the ICBL established the context of the landmine debate as humanitarian rather than military. The ICBL used communications technologies to disseminate information about the effects of landmine use to the international community, other ICBL members, their respective governments, the media, and the public. This effort greatly influenced the landmine positions of many states, especially Canada. Canadian Foreign Minister Axworthy commented that states can no longer "ignore the power and reach of new information technologies that allow the experience of Angola and Cambodia to be brought into people's living rooms" (Axworthy 1997). Axworthy's implication is that these technologies allow for information collection and dissemination in an issue area once monopolized by states, namely security, and in faraway places to be brought to the public and their governments.

E-mail Communications

The ICBL was able to utilize a few communications technologies across a range of dissemination and communications strategies, especially in the latter years of the campaign. Initially, the ICBL internal communications framework used telephones and fax machines. It was more than five years into the campaign (in 1996) that e-mail became a more widespread communications tool as the primary method for ICBL leaders to co-ordinate strategies among the members of the campaign. These leaders emphasize that e-mail is primarily used for internal ICBL communications rather than "for communications outside of the campaign" (Williams 1998, 24-25).

Web Pages

Another form of communications technology that the ICBL employs in its campaign is the World Wide Web. Web pages help provide the media and interested public and policymakers with easy access and information on a 24-hour basis. It also helps to generate governmental respect for the ICBL (International Campaign to Ban Landmines 1997). Moreover, websites greatly enhance the ability of NGOs to compile central information and make it available rapidly to activists. Specifically, it allows individuals working from their homes and/or private locations to pressure governments (Engardio 1999). Beyond being an information source for governments, members and the media, the sites also provide the public with a source for updated landmine information. Most of these sites are hyper-linked to each other thereby increasing total 'hits' or 'visits'. Similar to the results from external e-mail communications, the benefits of using the web were at first minimal. The ICBL did not have a website until March 1996, (Vitagliano 1999) when VVAF donated some of its organizational web pages to the ICBL in the capacity of housing the United States Campaign to Ban Landmines (USCBL) campaign co-ordinator (Wareham 1999). This initiative came in part from Mary Wareham, the USCBL Co-ordinator from 1995 to 1998, who wanted a few pages to store the USCBL and ICBL website. Only afterwards did the major organizations in the ICBL start acquiring websites (Wareham 1999). It was not before early 1998 that the ICBL created its own website, which is maintained in Oslo, Norway by a young Norwegian webmaster, Kjell Knudsen, hired by the ICBL (Wareham 1999).

Reducing Coalition-building Costs

Communications technologies also helped NGOs reach out to each other across geographical space (Engardio 1999). Broadening the membership base was deemed by ICBL leadership as an essential priority in order to achieve a nearly universal ban. One of its strategies was to generate more public pressure on states through continual membership expansion by either supporting the creation of new country landmine ban campaigns or attracting existing NGOs to join. The ICBL's creation of a wide-ranging coalition of broad ethnic, geographical, organizational and religious diversity was one of the campaign's major accomplishments. Most of this credit should go to the ICBL leaders who "did a fantastic job of identifying opportunities to advance the campaigns goals and alerting to its global network of supporters through newsletters, e-mail, [and] the web" (Lumpe 1998, 86).

Reducing Communication Costs

In addition to helping the ICBL reduce coalition-building costs, these technologies also helped reduce the costs associated with communications. Communication technologies helped ICBL members to overcome geographical separation among the ICBL members who come from more than 70 different states, and to counteract government control of information at a lower cost than would be the case with traditional forms of communications. These technologies were especially important to the ICBL in 1997 as more southern NGOs joined the campaign and as the early December treaty signing date neared. While traditional forms for communication, such as telephone, fax and postal mail, were instrumental in ICBL's formative years, they required a tremendous amount of time and money. Once established on the internet, ICBL leaders were able to send more information in shorter time at a lower cost through e-mail. During the initial phase of the campaign, for example in 1992 and 1993, Jody Williams, the ICBL Co-ordinator, would take meeting minutes and talking points by her laptop computer, then disseminate them by fax and then later by e-mail (Murphy 1998, F4). Geographical distance no longer matters as much as it did when information technologies were logistically challenging and financially burdensome to allow individuals and NGOs to communicate on a regular basis across borders and regions.

This section's broader significance for the study of international relations is that it may help predict the success or failure of current NGO efforts to address other security issues, such as banning child soldiers, ratifying the treaty establishing the International Criminal Court and restricting the use of small arms and light weapons. If NGOs indeed play a significant role in getting the international community to address the landmine issue, it becomes more relevant to examine the conditions under which the ICBL was able to effectively use information technologies as a tool to get the landmine issue addressed.

Landmine Survivors Network

Subsequent to my landmine accident, another landmine survivor, Jerry White, and I founded the LSN in order to promote landmine victim assistance and rights within the mine ban movement. LSN's mission is to help landmine survivors help themselves. It is the first international organization created by landmine survivors for landmine survivors. We also both realized how our own personal situations (having access to good medical and other resources) were unlike those of hundreds of thousands of landmine victims around the world. In many mine-infested countries, people make less than US$5,000 per year.

Besides amplifying the voice of survivors, we wanted to assist mine victims and their families worldwide to recover, heal and resume their roles as participating and contributing members of society. With few rehabilitation resources and many survivors many, we saw tremendous power in helping survivors help survivors. However, we were faced with many dilemmas, including lack of financial resources and means to disseminate our survivor message worldwide.

An example of how the internet was used by NGOs to speak with a collective voice was LSN's 1 March 2000 appeal to President Bill Clinton urging him to ban landmines. We used the internet to invite landmine survivors to sign-on to the appeal by sending e-mails directly to survivors and/or NGOs working with them, and through the ICBL e-mail network. In turn, survivors e-mailed their approval to be included as signatories to the LSN Washington, DC home office. By using the internet, we were able to write the appeal to President Clinton and then forward it to survivors and their caregivers around the world for their review and support. The result was that within several weeks, we had collected more than 1,300 landmine survivor signatures from 15 countries, including those heavily mined such as Afghanistan, Angola, Bosnia, Cambodia, Ethiopia, Eritrea, Jordan, Mozambique, Russia and Vietnam.

Joined by two US World War II landmine survivors, John Wack, a deminer who lost his leg in Italy in 1943, and Duane Robey, who lost his foot in Germany in 1944, Jerry and I released the appeal at a United Nations press conference on 1 March 2000, the one-year anniversary of the entry into force of the Mine Ban Treaty. The survivor action appeal was also disseminated through the LSN website and e-mailed by the ICBL co-ordinator, Liz Bernstein, to more than 1,300 ICBL members, allowing them to follow up quickly with thank-you notes to survivors and those who assisted LSN on the appeal. Regular fax, telephone and mail correspondence would not have been as effective in responding quickly to the various survivor appeal supporters or disseminating the release worldwide. For example, the telephone and mail system structures of many of these countries, such as Angola, Afghanistan and Vietnam are very fragile or non-existent.

The internet also helped keep landmine survivors active at ICBL conferences. LSN organized landmine survivor press conferences at international landmine gatherings, such as those held in Geneva, Brussels, and Johannesburg. We created press releases that highlighted problems confronting landmine survivors and those populations living in landmine-infested countries. We would then use the internet to e-mail the releases to ICBL members, governments and the media.

The use of e-mail was also crucial in planning large international landmine conferences, especially those in southern countries, such as Cambodia, Mozambique and Jordan. These conferences were very important to LSN's and ICBL's desire to broaden the campaign from primarily Northern NGOs to Southern NGOs. In July 1998, LSN hosted the Middle East Conference on Landmine Injury and Rehabilitation, which was primarily planned through e-mail. To organize the Jordan conference, LSN staff used the internet to extend invitations and to arrange visa and travel logistics for nearly 40 landmine survivors and more than 30 international public health experts from nearly every Middle Eastern country. Besides the information and professional exchanges among a host of rehabilitation specialists, landmine survivors and governing authorities, including representatives from the Taliban in Afghanistan, the conference provided a platform from which Her Majesty Queen Noor announced that Jordan would sign the treaty, thereby becoming one of the first Arab countries to do so.

After the 1997 treaty-signing, LSN created landmine survivor networks. This was greatly assisted by using information technologies. Funding for some of these technologies came from the Landmines Project at the Open Society Institute (OSI), which supported some communications costs for NGOs. Individual NGOs, such as the Mines Advisory Group (MAG), supported procurement of communication technologies by forming a small grants project funded by Comic Relief, which raises money every other year for African development projects. MAG gave some of these funds to ban landmine activists requesting "grants for the purpose of equipment purchase or e-mail/modems or fax machines ... or towards communications costs" (Carstairs 2000).

At LSN, we used the internet to help co-ordinate and collect landmine survivor and assistance information from five LSN peer support networks in landmine-infested countries: Bosnia, Ethiopia, Eritrea, Jordan and Mozambique. Before establishing the networks, we had found that in heavily mined countries there was little continuity as to who is doing what, with whom, where and with what result. While it was often noted that there needs to be greater collaboration and communication among international organizations, local groups and government ministries to avoid service duplication or competition, and to promote co-ordinated action to address urgent need, information technologies were not integrated into the process of trying to solve these challenges. To address this problem, we began collecting documented information regarding the roles of locations of organizations, groups and ministries involved in support for victims of landmines. Governments and NGOs could then apply the information directly in facilitating referrals to existing services for those in need. This information could also be used as a reference tool for those interested in services directly applicable to victim assistance actions. The information was then entered into an easy-to-use database published over the internet. The information on the needs of survivors and the organizations that help them was then readily available to those working in the field and to everyone with access to the internet.

E-mail also facilitated our efforts to increase attention to the plight of landmine victims and assistance on both the ICBL and international agendas. For example, in late 1995, very few people in the ICBL were pushing for victim assistance. Several NGOs, such as VVAF, Handicap International and the International Committee of the Red Cross were, of course, providing prosthetics and other assistance in the field, but NGOs were not lobbying for such assistance to be part of the talking points for solving the landmine problem. In October 1996, we demonstrated a prototype of the first database to track the needs of mine victims worldwide and the limited resources to help them. The LSN database slowly started to serve as a small clearinghouse of information and resources. In 1997, we proposed to create a landmine survivor register and caregiver database on the internet, to be used by the media, policymakers, international organizations, deminers, the military, landmine survivors and individuals who wished to become more involved in the campaign to ban landmines, or simply rehabilitate mine victims. By 1998, the database contained profiles of scores of landmine survivors and their families in Mozambique, Angola, Bosnia, Cambodia, Jordan, Lebanon, and Afghanistan. It also contained detailed information on over 1,000 organizations and was used by media and NGOs alike as a source of information about the world's mine-affected people and communities. One of the tangible results of our landmine victim and assistance strategies was the inclusion of landmine victims and victim assistance in the Mine Ban Treaty, which makes it the first time in the world's history that a disarmament treaty incorporated victim assistance language for victims of the weapon being banned.

Seeing the necessity also to focus efforts on tracking existing resources and programmes worldwide in order to ensure that the MBT's victim assistance obligations are monitored, in March 2000 we launched an online database (www.landminesurvivors.org) profiling four mine-affected countries – Bosnia and Herzegovina, Eritrea, Jordan and Mozambique. The database includes: a *Service Directory*, providing contact information for caregivers and support programmes available for all persons with disabilities; background information on *Landmine Affected Countries*, including landmine statistics, victim assistance and rehabilitation profiles; and a list of landmine related *References*, including bibliographic sources and website links.

While LSN's internet-based activities, including its database, are useful to keep track of and promote landmine survivor needs, they cannot meet those needs nor ban landmines. Only by engaging governments would our efforts to ban landmines and help survivors be successful. At LSN we found that by incorporating information technology into our organization, we were better able to communicate messages and strategy among landmine survivors and their care providers. The internet also allowed us to communicate directly with many landmine survivors, who live mostly in the South. As discussed earlier, we used e-mail to send invitations to and arrange logistics for more than 40 landmine survivors to come to Amman, Jordan in 1998 for the First Middle East Conference on Landmine Injury and Rehabilitation. And recently we used e-mail to collect more than 1,300 signatures of landmine survivors to appeal in March 2000 to President Clinton to ban landmines. Both of these actions would have been extremely difficult and expensive without e-mail.

While I believe from my landmine experience that the internet cannot substitute for people-to-people interaction, it remains important in getting issues addressed. The internet does provide an information technology that has enhanced LSN's advocacy practices and overseas management of its field offices. Most important, it has helped us hold, or at least more readily counter, vague commitments and double-speak by governments, especially on victim assistance. We are continuing to use the internet to help monitor government behaviour, as evinced by LSN's online database, which tracks international actions for survivors in a range of selected mine-infested countries. Our use of internet-based information technologies, such as the online database, e-mail appeals to international leaders, and conference planning, shows how "virtual activism" helps ensure that the weapon that disfigured our bodies and took away the innocence of daily life is banned and proper rehabilitation services become available worldwide. Unlike most NGOs, we do not want to see LSN's constituency grow. Instead, we are using the internet to help disseminate landmine victim and assistance information worldwide, and to help rehabilitate the thousands of innocent and often impoverished mine victims around the world.

Conclusion

Since the end of the Cold War, state sovereignty has continually been challenged by NGOs concerned with transnational problems that states have been unable or unwilling to manage. Because of the need for co-ordinated international action on these problems, the increasing ease of instant communication has helped increase inter-state communications and "expand the number of NGOs at the global level as well as their role in multilateral diplomacy" (Aviel 1999). In other words, the rapid development of communication technologies has helped transform NGOs into important international actors that have the ability to influence international politics. As Jessica Mathews, President of the Carnegie Endowment for Peace, recently stated: "[t]hese technologies have broken governments' monopoly on the collection and management of large amounts of information and have taken away from governments the deference that they enjoyed because of that monopoly" (Mathews 1999). Corroborating this observation are a "growing number of other scholars and analysts who also point out that breakthroughs in telecommunications and transportation have undermined state authority by ending the state's monopoly on information; that there is an increasing reliance on nonstate entities such as NGOs for focus and direction, drafting, and implementation of declarations, platforms, and treaties on crucial international issues, including human rights, the environment, and the proliferation of land mines" (Reitano 1999). The potential implications are that these technologies are allowing NGOs greater power in issues traditionally monopolized by states.[11]

As information technologies continue to develop, come online, and increasingly become available to the public, the result for international policymaking will be profound. This chapter shows how information technologies facilitated ICBL and LSN communications and reduced networking costs. Moreover, these technologies helped the ICBL maintain a unified and co-ordinated campaign and broadened it to more than 70 states, while also helping LSN create networks of survivors in mine-infested countries. Understanding the ICBL and LSN's use of information technologies is important because it highlights implications for international relations and future NGO coalitional efforts to address transnational issues.

Notes

Note on internet addresses (URLs): Websites tend to appear, change or disappear, often without warning. Addresses cited in this bibliography were accurate and active at the time of writing (January 2002) unless otherwise noted.

1. Officially known as The Ottawa Convention on the Prohibition of the Use, Stockpiling, Production and Transfer of Anti-Personnel Mines and on their Destruction.
2. The Campaign consists of over 1,000 arms control, development, environmental, humanitarian, human rights, medical and religious NGOs representing some 60 countries.

3   For further information on these and other unique features of the Ottawa Convention see Ken Rutherford, (1999), 'The Hague and Ottawa Conventions: A Model for Future Weapon Ban Regimes?', *Nonproliferation Review*, Spring-Summer 1999, Vol. 6(3), pp. 36-50.
4   The ICRC estimates that Afghanistan, Angola and Cambodia host the largest numbers of those disabled by landmines.
5   In their *Hidden Killers 1994* report, the US Department of State estimated that there were 80-110 million landmines in at least 64 countries (United States 1994, v).
6   In November 1999, Russian military forces dropped mines in northern Georgia hoping to block Chechen militants' potential escape routes (Russians 1999, A36).
7   It should be noted that the Ethiopian defense forces claim not to have used anti-personnel landmines in the conflict. According to the ICBL, "[t]here is no evidence to the contrary" (International Campaign to Ban Landmines 1999b, 147).
8   The Landmines Protocol was attached to the CCW as Protocol II and is officially known as the Protocol on Prohibitions or Restrictions on the Use of Mines, Booby Traps and Other Devices. The two other Protocols were Non-detectable Fragments (Protocol I) and Prohibitions or Restrictions on the Use of Incendiary Weapons (Protocol III). The CCW Review held in Vienna in September 1996 adopted Protocol IV that called for restrictions on the use of laser weapons, while the landmines protocol was amended at the third and final CCW review held in Geneva. The four protocols are regulated by the provisions of the Weapons Convention.
9   The six NGOs were Handicap International (France), Human Rights Watch (United States), Medico International (Germany), Mines Advisory Group (United Kingdom), Physicians for Human Rights (United States), and the Vietnam Veterans of America Foundation (United States) (Williams 1998, 22).
10 See Paul J. Nelson (1997), 'Deliberation, Leverage or Coercion? The World Bank, NGOs, and Global Environmental Politics', *Journal of Peace Research*, Vol. 34(4), pp. 467-472; William Korey (1998), *NGOs and the Universal Declaration of Human Rights: A Curious Grapevine*, St. Martin's Press, New York; Paul Wapner (1995), 'Politics Beyond the State: Environmental Activism and World Civic Politics', *World Politics*, Vol. 47(3), pp. 391-425.
11 For a practical example how a variation of the ICBL model is being applied to other transnational issue areas, see Stefan Brem and Ken Rutherford (2001), 'Walking Together or Divided Agenda? Comparing Landmines and Small-Arms Campaigns', *Security Dialogue*, Vol. 32(2), June, pp. 169-186.

References

Aviel, JoAnn Fagot (1999), 'NGOs and International Affairs: A New Dimension of Diplomacy', in James P. Muldoon, Jr., JoAnn Fagot Aviel, Richard Retiano, and Earl Sullivan (eds), *Multilateral Diplomacy and the United Nations Today*, Westview Press, Boulder, pp. 156-166.

Axworthy, Lloyd (1997), Statement by the Canadian Foreign Minister to the NGO Forum on Banning Anti-Personnel Landmines, Oslo, 7 November.

Brem, Stefan and Rutherford, Ken (2001), 'Walking Together or Divided Agenda? Comparing Landmines and Small-Arms Campaigns', *Security Dialogue*, Vol. 32(2), June, pp. 169-186.

Cameron, Maxwell A., Lawson, Robert J. and Tomlin, Brian W. (1998), 'To Walk Without Fear', in Maxwell A. Cameron, Robert J. Lawson, and Brian W. Tomlin (eds), *To Walk Without Fear: The Global Movement to Ban Landmines*, Oxford University Press, Toronto, pp. 1-17.

106 Civil Society in the Information Age

Carstairs, Tim (2000), Mines Advisory Group, e-mail interview with author, 31 January.
Chrétien, Jean (1997), Statement by the Canadian Prime Minister at the Signing Conference for the Ottawa Convention, Ottawa, 3 December.
Engardio, Pete (1999), 'Activists Without Borders', *Business Week*, 4 October, no. 3649, pp. 144-150.
Human Rights Watch and Physicians for Human Rights (1993), *Landmines: A Deadly Legacy*, The Arms Project of Human Rights Watch and Physicians for Human Rights, New York.
International Campaign to Ban Landmines, www.icbl.org
International Campaign to Ban Landmines (1997), Recorded notes from workshop discussion on "Using the Campaign as a Model for Other Issues", in *ICBL Report: NGO Forum on Landmines*, Oslo, 7-10 September.
International Campaign to Ban Landmines (1999a), 'Islamic Extremists in Dagestan are Also Using Landmines' Press Release, Geneva, 13 September (from 'Russian Troops Clearing Dagestan Rebel-Planted Mines', Foreign Broadcast Information Service, Transcribed Text, Moscow *Interfax*, Report #LD2508105399, 25 August 1999).
International Campaign to Ban Landmines (1999b), *Landmine Monitor Report 1999: Toward a Mine-Free World*, Human Rights Watch, New York www.icbl.org/lm/1999/
International Committee of the Red Cross (1999), *Overview 1999: Landmines Must Be Stopped*, ICRC 1 March.
Korey, William (1998), *NGOs and the Universal Declaration of Human Rights: A Curious Grapevine*, St. Martin's Press, New York.
Lumpe, Lora and Donarski, Jeff (1998), *The Arms Trade Revealed: A Guide for Investigators and Activists*, Federation of American Scientists, Washington, DC.
Mathews, Jessica Tuchman (1999), Statement to the 75th Anniversary Symposium, Harvard School of Public Health, Boston, 25 September,
www.hsph.harvard.edu/digest/mathews.html
Murphy, Caryle (1998), 'The Nobel Prize Fight', *Washington Post*, 22 March, p. F4.
Nelson, Paul J. (1997), 'Deliberation, Leverage or Coercion? The World Bank, NGOs, and Global Environmental Politics', *Journal of Peace Research*, Vol. 34(4), pp. 467-472.
Price, Richard (1998), 'Reversing the Gun Sights: Transnational Civil Society Targets Land Mines', *International Organization*, Vol. 52 (Summer), pp. 613-644.
Reitano, Richard and Elfenbein, Caleb (1999), 'Diplomacy in the Twenty-First Century: Civil Society Versus the State', in James P. Muldoon, Jr., JoAnn Fagot Aviel, Richard Retiano, and Earl Sullivan (eds), *Multilateral Diplomacy and the United Nations Today*, Westview Press, Boulder, pp. 234-244.
'Russians Drop Mines in Georgia' (1999), *Washington Post*, 18 November, p. A36.
Rutherford, Ken (1999), 'The Hague and Ottawa Conventions: A Model for Future Weapon Ban Regimes?', *Nonproliferation Review*, Spring-Summer 1999, Vol. 6(3), pp. 36-50.
Sand-Trigo, Ariane (1997), International Committee of the Red Cross Delegation to the United Nations, letter to the author, 3 March
United Nations. Department of Humanitarian Affairs (1997), Robert Eaton, Chris Horwood, and Norah Niland (eds), *Cambodia: The Development of Indigenous Mine Action Capabilities*, UN DHA.
United Nations. Office for the Coordination of Humanitarian Assistance (1999), *Mine Action Programme: Afghanistan*, UNOCHA.
United States. Department of State. Political-Military Affairs Bureau. Office of International Security Operations (1993), *Hidden Killers: The Global Problem with Uncleared Landmines*, Washington, DC.
United States. Department of State. Office of International Security and Peacekeeping Operations (1994), *Hidden Killers: The Global Landmine Crisis*, 1994 Report to the U.S. Congress on the Problem with Uncleared Landmines and the United States Strategy for

Demining and Landmine Control, Washington, DC, Department of State Publication 10225, January, www.state.gov/www/global/arms/rpt_9401_demine_toc.html
United States. Department of State. Bureau of Political-Military Affairs. Office of Humanitarian Demining Programs (1998), *Hidden Killers: The Global Landmine Crisis*, Washington, DC, Department of State Publication 10575, September, www.state.gov/www/global/arms/rpt_9809_demine_toc.html
Vitagliano, Marissa (1999), US Campaign to Ban Landmines, telephone conversation with author, 19 October.
Wapner, Paul (1995), 'Politics Beyond the State: Environmental Activism and World Civic Politics', *World Politics*, Vol. 47(3), pp. 391-425.
Wareham, Mary (1999), Senior Researcher, Human Rights Watch and former Coordinator, US Campaign to Ban Landmines, telephone conversation with author, 19 October.
Williams, Jody and Goose, Steve (1998), 'The International Campaign to Ban Landmines', in Maxwell A. Cameron, Robert J. Lawson, and Brian W. Tomlin (eds), *To Walk Without Fear: The Global Movement to Ban Landmines*, Oxford University Press, Toronto, pp. 20-47.
Wren, Christopher S. (1995), 'U.N.-Backed Drive to Restrict Land Mines Fails at Talks', *New York Times*, 13 October, p. A6.

Chapter 7

The Power of Global Activist Networks: The Campaign for an International Criminal Court

William R. Pace and Rik Panganiban[*]

> *The NGO Coalition for an International Criminal Court brought together a network of hundreds of NGOs and international law experts to develop strategies and foster awareness. Their efforts paid off when we witnessed the signature of the ICC statute in Rome three weeks ago. Again, a key to their network was e-mail and the World Wide Web.* Statement by Kofi Annan, Secretary-General, United Nations, to the World Youth Forum, Braga, Portugal, 7 August 1998.

If the claim is true that nongovernmental organizations allied with 'middle power' countries are the new 'superpower', (Williams 1997) then it is the internet that is their arsenal. On their own, civil society organizations[1] usually have scant monetary and physical resources, are often under-staffed and over-mandated, have no special access to information, and have no particular political authority beyond moral suasion. Nevertheless, acting together, civil society groups have shown again and again that they have the ability to affect the outcomes of the most high-level and far-reaching intergovernmental negotiations.

The central aim of this chapter is to show how information technology enables networks of nongovernmental organizations to operate less hierarchically and more federatively – in short, as a multi-polar network. We will use the NGO Coalition for an International Criminal Court as a case study in how these networks can function. We argue that information technology in conjunction with a more federative and broad-based organization greatly increases the political influence that civil society can have over intergovernmental policy-making.

The Coalition for an International Criminal Court is a broad-based network of more than 1,000 nongovernmental organizations supporting the creation of a just, effective and independent International Criminal Court. The Coalition co-ordinates its work through a small secretariat office based in New York and two recently-added affiliate offices in Brussels, Belgium and Lima, Peru.

Information technology has been used by the Coalition for many of its activities, including: outreach to the public and media, communication with its members and other NGOs, information-gathering about the official ICC

---

[*] William R. Pace and Rik Panganiban are both currently with the World Federalist Movement but are writing in their own individual capacities.

110 *Civil Society in the Information Age*

negotiations and disseminating that information, and collaboration among its leadership and members. By looking at the history of the Coalition, a number of key aspects of the role of information technology can be shown:

1. to facilitate collaborative decision-making among diverse partners;
2. to reach a broad public;
3. to create an informed and co-ordinated activist network;
4. to facilitate the development of active regional and national networks.

This chapter is divided into three sections that follow the development of the Coalition and serve to elucidate these aspects of the role of information technology. We start by discussing the creation of the Coalition and the beginnings of an international network of groups and individuals supporting the International Criminal Court. Then we discuss the role of information technology during the official treaty conference on the ICC in Rome in 1998. Beyond the Rome Conference, we discuss the 'devolution' of the Coalition into more developed and active regional and national networks. We close with some comments on possible lessons to be learned from the experience of the Coalition.

Creating the Campaign

Like many initiatives, the Coalition had humble beginnings.

In the Fall of 1994, recently appointed executive director of the World Federalist Movement (WFM), William Pace, had been monitoring closely the Sixth Committee (Legal) of the UN General Assembly. For many years the World Federalist Movement had been following the International Criminal Court issue, holding meetings and conferences on this proposal. Pace sensed that there was the potential for the Sixth Committee to act on a resolution calling for a Preparatory Committee to study the possibility of the creation of an International Criminal Court. However he felt pressure needed to be exerted upon Sixth Committee government delegates to support this resolution or it risked being buried for another year, as it had been for decades.

Pace drew up a list of NGOs that he felt might act quickly on this issue. He drafted a memorandum and sent it out via fax broadcast and e-mail to some 30 groups, mostly in the New York area. On February 25, 1995, a small group of nongovernmental organizations met in New York to discuss the status of the International Criminal Court proposal. Pace was asked to chair the meeting. Among those in attendance were representatives of Amnesty International, Parliamentarians for Global Action, the Quaker UN office, No Peace Without Justice International, and Human Rights Watch.

Pace updated the participants on recent discussions within the UN Sixth Committee on the International Criminal Court. He suggested that there was the possibility of the issue gaining a higher profile than it had received in the several decades it had been discussed within the legal committee. He outlined the possible steps that could be taken by the Sixth Committee to make the International Criminal Court a reality, if enough pressure could be put upon them to act.

No one was particularly confident at that meeting that the discussions would move beyond the theoretical level, but nonetheless, the issue was important enough that it deserved to be closely monitored by groups that supported the idea of a permanent International Criminal Court.

It was decided to create an informal coalition of supportive nongovernmental organizations, for the purpose of strategizing, sharing information, and working together to support the creation of this idealistic new institution. It was agreed that the Coalition for an International Criminal Court (as it was later called) would take no positions on behalf of its member organizations, but that it would serve to help its members to disseminate their own positions and papers. The WFM was requested to act as the secretariat for the Coalition, and William Pace was asked to serve as the 'convenor' of the Coalition.

At the time, the view of most UN experts was that the International Criminal Court would not be created anytime soon. More optimistic estimates were that if the Court were created as a 'permanent ad-hoc tribunal' subordinate to the UN Security Council, it could begin operations in five to ten years. More conservative estimates from many international affairs experts imagined a Law of the Sea-type process that could take from 25 to 50 years to complete!

The Beginnings of a Global Information Network

Prior to the meeting, most of the correspondence between groups was conducted via fax and postal mail. E-mail was still a relatively new technology for many nongovernmental organizations. The web was still in its infancy, but newsgroups, computer conferences, and gopher document servers were becoming quite popular with many NGOs.

At that first meeting, Rik Panganiban of WFM was asked to develop a database of groups and individuals who were interested in being kept informed about the International Criminal Court issue. Many participants at that initial meeting felt that there were many NGOs not present who would support the issue if they knew about it.

Panganiban suggested that a fax broadcast list and an e-mail list be set up quickly, since many of the developments on the ICC were often quite sudden and unexpected. He volunteered to look into setting up a gopher server and a website for groups that could access information that way. The participants agreed that this seemed to be a good course of action.

Around the same time, the World Federalist Movement was working with a Washington-DC based group called the Coalition for International Justice (CIJ) to support the work of the newly-created International Criminal Tribunal for the Former Yugoslavia. This international court was created by the Security Council to "prosecute persons responsible for serious violations of international humanitarian law committed in the territory of the former Yugoslavia since 1991". One of WFM and CIJ's first actions was to create a website and gopher server to provide information on the Yugoslav tribunal to anyone on the internet. So WFM was already experienced with the technical and political aspects of setting up an NGO website.

Soon after the February 1995 meeting, Panganiban contacted the Institute for Global Communications (IGC), an internet service provider based in San Francisco that specializes in assisting not-for-profit organizations. IGC at the time had several hundred computer conferences on their own network that enabled members to post information and discuss issues relevant to the topic. Many groups active at the United Nations had accounts with IGC, so they could access the computer conferences there. So it seemed logical to create a computer conference called 'UN.ICC'.

In addition, WFM created an e-mail list called 'icc-info' to e-mail out information on the ICC. This e-mail list quickly became the primary means of getting out timely information on the issue. An important initial decision of the Coalition was to keep the icc-info list and the un.icc computer conference open and unmoderated, meaning that any group or individual with an e-mail address could subscribe themselves to the list and any subscriber could freely send out an e-mail to the list that was immediately distributed to all the subscribers. This initial openness and inclusiveness was to characterize all of the Coalition's use of information technology.

From 1995 to 1997 the e-mail list steadily grew in subscribers, including civil society organizations from around the world, professors of international law, students of law and political science, foundations, and individual activists. Traffic on the e-mail list also steadily increased from short occasional updates from the Coalition secretariat to event notices from other NGOs to lively debates on the various legal issues surrounding the proposed Court. From an initial subscriber base of about 50 addresses, it had grown by 1997 to several hundred e-mail accounts.

WFM also created a fax broadcast to send out fax information to the Coalition's network. This was an important tool since not every member of the Coalition had e-mail. And prior to the prevalence of scanners and Adobe Acrobat PDF files, most documents were not available in digital form.

The Early Days of the Web

From the beginning, one major consideration of the Coalition in its information dissemination strategy was accommodating the various levels of technical expertise of its audience. Although geared toward a nongovernmental organization membership, we were aware that legal experts, students, activists, governmental and United Nations officials would be using our information.

The main challenge that we have faced and continue to face is the often great disparities in access to information technology among the different constituencies we serve. The levels of access ranged from activists in the developing world who mostly correspond by post to well-financed government ministries who used the World Wide Web on a daily basis. This meant that a great deal of information was duplicated over print, fax, e-mail and website.

For our website, this also meant that we always had an eye toward the user who was using a text-only interface, or who only had a relatively slow bandwidth connection to the internet. 'Text-only' was our priority, only in special circumstances putting out documents in HTML, Word, spreadsheet, or later PDF formats. This became an incredible challenge when dealing with gigantic documents with hundreds of footnotes. Many organizations at the time were familiar with gopher, so we used a gopher server to deliver many of the documents we gained access to.

Our free print publication *The ICC Monitor* was becoming a major news source for many people who were interested in the negotiations. We began publishing online version of the *Monitor*, initially as text-only and later HTML with photos and images. Although our print version was quite popular, the web version was also downloaded with increasing frequency.

Access to UN and Government Documents

Getting United Nations and government documents in a digital format was a challenge in the early days of the Coalition. Often they were unwilling to give out diskettes containing their documents even though the text was available in print form. One UN legal official claimed this was because there were concerns that groups might try and falsify documents if they obtained the original digital versions.

But slowly the Coalition secretariat staff gained a rapport with the UN secretariat services who often gave us documents on diskette the same day they were released in print. We immediately placed these documents online, where they could be downloaded and read by hundreds of our colleagues who otherwise would have to wait for the United Nations to mail the documents to them. In this way, the Coalition made it possible for many groups to stay informed up-to-the-minute of ICC developments.

In early 1997, the Coalition was informed that it could download many of the United Nations documents through the UN's 'Optical Disk System', a comprehensive database of UN official documents updated daily and accessible at the UN's law library and many other locations. Using the Optical Disk System, the Coalition greatly increased its output of documents available on its website.

Government documents still had to be obtained by 'sneaker net', i.e. walking over to government delegates and asking them for the documents on diskette. More often, the documents had to be re-typed or scanned, a labourious but necessary process that was very much appreciated by NGOs in the field.

The importance of NGOs in the Coalition being able to obtain these documents online cannot be over-emphasized. As national NGOs were beginning to be seized of the ICC issue, they had the capability to have in front of them the actual text being debated by governments, plus informal drafts and proposals being discussed. By studying the real texts and coming up with their own positions, national NGOs could speak with authority and expertise to government foreign ministries and diplomats.

In other UN negotiations, it has been the practice of some larger organizations with offices in New York or Geneva to not share documents with other NGOs. Sometimes this was because organizations were given confidential documents by sources within government delegations and told not to reveal that they had them. Also it was simply not a part of the culture and operating procedures of some NGOs to even think of sharing the document with other groups. And prior to the internet, it was costly to disseminate documents to groups that were not based where your office was.

Regardless of the reasons, the result was that prior to the 1990s it was common for smaller groups based outside of New York and Geneva to come to General Assembly meetings, special sessions, and preparatory committee meetings totally unprepared for what was being discussed. Meanwhile, larger groups that had been following the negotiations closely had no real interest in sharing the documents with smaller groups.

But growing questions of inequity among NGOs and a growing North-South divide among civil society forced many networks and coalitions to deal with these problems.

The positive attitudes of both large and small NGOs to the Coalition for an ICC was due in large part to our willingness to share all documents with every single member of the Coalition. Slowly, NGOs began to realize that the Coalition had no interest in hoarding documents. So when they began receiving drafts and working papers being written by governments from their own sources, they began sharing those documents with the Coalition. Soon, NGOs understood that the Coalition was valuable because we were the first to receive most documents, and we were the quickest at getting those documents out to the population of groups monitoring the International Criminal Court negotiations, including government delegates.

The great irony was that because the Coalition had members from around the world sharing documents with us the Coalition often had key information before several government delegations did.

Bringing Like-Minded Groups[2] Together

Beyond simple information dissemination, information technology facilitated collaboration and co-ordination among a disparate and diverse body of NGO activists. The website, e-mail list and computer conference increased the exposure of the Coalition and its message to a broad population of civil society organizations. Slowly, civil society organizations concerned with a wide variety of issues were joining the Coalition, including religious groups such as the World Council of Churches, the Women's Environment and Development Organization and other women's organizations, peace groups such as the Lawyers Committee on Nuclear Policy, victim's rights groups – for example, Redress – and groups concerned with the persecution of ethnic and other minority groups such as the East Timor Action Network.

As more of these groups joined, their level of activity increased. Many subscribed to the e-mail listserv. Some groups sent representatives to Preparatory

Commission (PrepCom) meetings. Papers and position statements were sent to the Coalition to be uploaded to the website and distributed at PrepComs. Discussions on relevant issues increased in the listserv and groups found each other agreeing on common strategies.

Eventually, caucuses and networks began forming around common themes, such as the Women's Caucus for Gender Justice, bringing together women's organizations concerned with violations of human rights specifically affecting women and the incorporation of gender concerns into the structure of the proposed Court. A Victim's Rights Working Group was formed to bring together groups that worked with victims of human rights violations such as torture and rape. Peace groups began meeting together and engaging in e-mail discussions. Common positions were being worked out and proposals were being generated, often over e-mail, to then be used in lobbying governments participating in the PrepComs.

Also, regional networks began forming among groups interested in the International Criminal Court. As early as 1997, African, Latin American and European NGOs began meeting together and sharing information. The Coalition European Co-ordinator Pascale Norris in 1997 went on a whirlwind tour of Europe, leading to the creation of ten national networks on the ICC. Similar efforts in Africa and Latin America resulted in dozens of national networks sprouting up in those regions. Asia was more complicated, given the less active civil society movements in many of the countries in the region, but networks were begun in India, the Philippines, Australia, New Zealand and Japan.

The importance of these regional and sectoral caucuses should not be minimized. The ability of different groups of varying capability and expertise to work together was critical to the effectiveness of the Coalition. In particular, the New York and Geneva-based organizations with more expertise on the complex politics and language used in United Nations negotiations were able to combine their voices with groups in the 'grassroots' who had more connection to real victims of human rights abuses and actual court cases that were setting precedents for how the International Criminal Court might operate.

The internet facilitates sign-on processes and collaborative position drafting by NGOs, where groups that generally share similar viewpoints can easily exchange positions and come to common agreements on language to push for. Then as these common positions get distributed via e-mail and the web to other groups, more sign-ons are gained. When the resulting common statement is given to government delegations, it carries the weight of a broad consultative process involving many groups from around the world.

Getting out the Information on the Rome Conference

Against expectations, and due in some part to pressure from civil society, government delegates decided at the third PrepCom in February 1997 to convene a "UN Conference of Plenipotentiaries on the Establishment of an International Criminal Court" from June 15 to July 17, 1998. This was great news for the Coalition, but it gave the organizers very little time to plan a major world conference.

Because the PrepCom secretariat was already overburdened with making arrangements for government participation, much of the logistics of nongovernmental organization participation at the conference was handled by the Coalition. The principal challenge was getting the news out to as many NGOs around the world as possible to ensure maximum public pressure upon government delegations to negotiate a strong treaty. It was felt that without a substantial presence by a body of NGOs from all regions of the world and all sectors of civil society, it was unlikely that the voice of NGOs would garner much attention or credibility by government negotiators.

The Coalition secretariat mobilized an intensive information dissemination campaign, using every medium of communication, from word-of-mouth, postal mail, and telephone, to fax broadcasts, e-mail broadcasts, and web alerts. The goal was to bring NGOs from as many states participating in the negotiations to Rome as possible, particularly from the developing world. The result was that 235 NGOs were accredited to attend the Rome Conference. And many more groups were able to participate as part of other umbrella groups, such as the Fédération Internationale des Ligues de Droits de l'Homme and WFM, bringing the total up to about 500 civil society organizations.

And more importantly, there was a growing global awareness, at least among civil society, of the significance of the conference.

The Rome ICC Conference – Multi-polar Advocacy

In terms of information technology, the Coalition had three main goals at the Rome Treaty Conference. The primary goal was to act as an information network within the conference to enable government representatives, NGO participants, and UN staff to exchange information effectively with one another. The second, though no less important, goal was to act as an alternative information source for national media and our networks of activists and NGOs who were interested in monitoring the treaty conference. The third objective was to provide access to communications technology to all the NGO participants so they could report to their own home offices and receive instructions. These were daunting tasks for our small Coalition secretariat, so we needed to enlist some partners to work with us in Rome.

Connecting the Conference to the World

We knew that unless there was world attention upon the conference, there would be little pressure upon delegates to the conference to come out with a strong treaty. A small number of international press sent reporters to the conference, but there would be no sustained public eye upon the proceedings unless civil society acted.

First, the Coalition organized dedicated teams of NGO monitors who followed certain specific issues and parts of the draft text and issued detailed reports on the progress (or lack of progress) in those areas. On each of the teams were legal experts who had followed these issues from their beginnings in the Sixth Committee, through the Preparatory Committee, up to the conference, bringing not only a strong legal background but also an understanding of the debates to date. These exhaustive 'Team Reports' were published on the web as soon as they became available, for consumption by activists and legal experts around the world (the same version was used for both audiences).

Because of this team structure, the Coalition quickly became one of the few 'delegations' that were able to monitor the entire conference. During certain hectic periods, there were ten to twelve simultaneous meetings going on, which even the largest government delegations were sometimes not able to cover. So our Team Reports became really the only mechanism for both NGOs and governments to get up-to-date information on the status of all the issues being discussed.

In addition, a group of activists and journalists calling themselves "The Advocacy Project" approached the Coalition and offered their services as reporters at the conference, broadcasting their articles on the internet. We agreed to work with them and charged them with the difficult task of highlighting from the negotiations the key political issues and areas of controversy and serving as an alternative news outlet from the conference.

The Advocacy Project created an e-mail bulletin, called *On the Record*, that amassed several hundred subscribers from around the world. The Advocacy Project reporters prepared daily reports and interviews on the critical subjects being debated at the Treaty Conference in a more user-friendly format than the 'legalese' used in the Team Reports.

The Coalition also approached the *Inter-Press Service (IPS)* to assist with reporting at the conference because of their long record of reporting at various UN summits and conferences. IPS agreed to send a team of journalists to Rome to publish a daily print newspaper at the conference which would also be published on the web. They supplemented this reporting with news from their reporters on various human rights situations around the world.

In addition, the Coalition brought to Rome its own print and web publication, *The ICC Monitor*, to continue reporting from a strictly NGO perspective. The *Monitor* served as a space for NGOs to publish their own position statements and announce meetings with government delegations and with each other.

And of course, individual NGOs were communicating with their home offices via e-mail and fax and receiving further instructions, position statements, and background documents, which they then shared with government delegates in Rome.

The World Responds

From the hundreds of individuals who were receiving the e-mail broadcasts from the Coalition and the Advocacy Project and the articles appearing in the press around the world, it was clear that news from the conference was getting out to thousands and thousands of people around the globe. NGOs were getting much of the press coverage because they were not as shy as government delegates about 'naming names' and pointing fingers at specific delegations they felt were being obstructionist or held positions they opposed.

The Coalition decided to publish some of the e-mails it had been receiving from individuals expressing their concern about the status of the negotiations. As one individual wrote from Saint-Sixt, France:

> Je tiens à dire de manière solennelle que j'espère la création d'une Cour Internationale aux pouvoirs réels. De nombreuse personnes de mon entourage familial et professionel ont le même espoir. Je comprends mal la position de mon pays qui, après avoir initié cette démarche, s'est montrée ensuite trés négative et a tout tenté pour que cette création n'ait pas lieu ou pour que la Cour n'ait pas de pouvoir. [I must state solemnly that I hope that an International Court with real power will be created. A number of people of my family and professional circles have the same hope. I fail to understand the position of my country which, having initiated this advance, subsequently showed itself to be very negative and tried to see that the Court is not established or, if established, will not have power.]

Or as one South Korean woman wrote:

> I sincerely urge in the strongest of terms for the governments of both sides of Korea – and all governments likewise – to support a strong International Criminal Court, independent, autonomous, effective, with access to resources, protecting the rights of both the accused and victims of crimes. Governments must not forget the victims of crimes both of the past and those that could come in the future if we fail.

It is difficult to measure what effect all this reporting and information dissemination had on the official proceedings. It is clear that government delegates knew that their decisions and actions were being widely reported by NGOs, often NGOs who were from their own home countries and who were reporting directly to their counterparts in their capital.

In more than one instance, a government appears to have changed its position after NGOs at the conference co-ordinated actions with NGOs in that government's capital. The Latin American Caucus of NGOs was a very active presence at the conference, working directly with several Latin American government delegations that were more progressive on many issues, and dialoguing frequently with those Latin American delegations who were not as ready to move forward. The government of Mexico posed some problems for NGOs because of its opposition to the inclusion of crimes committed during internal armed conflicts.

The Latin American Caucus alerted Mexican NGOs in Mexico City to the position the Mexican government was taking. Many e-mails were sent back and forth between Rome and Mexico City, reporting on developments and suggesting strategies. The Mexican NGOs were successful in getting several news reports into several major newspapers in Mexico that criticized the government's position. Within days the Mexican delegation had shifted its position to not oppose the inclusion of crimes committed during intra-state conflicts.

Similarly, the delegation from the United Kingdom was influenced by the co-ordinated lobbying activities of the NGO network in the UK and the NGOs at the Rome Conference. The United Kingdom had come into the Rome Conference as a new member of the more progressive 'Like-Minded' group of countries. The UK

Foreign Minister Robin Cook had recently come out with his "Foreign Policy with a Human Face" policy statement, including among other things greater support for human rights and in particular the International Criminal Court.

However, early information suggested that the UK delegation in Rome was divided in its support for a strong and independent Court. Some within the delegation appeared to be attempting to re-establish closer ties with the more conservative positions of France and the United States. In particular, the United Kingdom delegation in negotiations on what constituted a war crime signaled its opposition to the inclusion of the use of landmines as a war crime under the ICC statute.

The Coalition in Rome informed the UK NGO network of these developments. The UK network in turn leaked this information to several newspapers in London, which published stories on how the UK delegation in Rome was going back on commitments that the UK foreign minister had just recently stated.[3] This was particularly embarrassing for the UK foreign minister, since he had been praising Britain's role in pushing for a global ban on the use of landmines. The following day, Robin Cook reportedly called the UK delegation, re-iterated his position, and sent over two of his staff from London to ensure that his instructions were implemented.

Less dramatic shifts in the positions of other government delegations were reported by other national and regional caucuses. One might never know exactly why certain governments changed their positions, but several progressive governments noted at the end of the conference that the pressure from civil society groups, both within the conference and back in their capitals, was essential to the success of the negotiations. As Sylvia Fernandez of the Argentinean delegation noted:

> I am convinced that the successful adoption of the Rome statute is largely due to the work of the Coalition and the partnership that you managed to develop between NGO's and governments during the four years of your work. The fluid dialogue between delegations and representatives of civil society was indeed essential to identify goals and preoccupations and to design the best strategies to achieve them (Fernandez 1998).

The Numbers and The Virtual Vote

In the final days of the Rome conference, there were indications that a small number of powerful governments, in particular China and the United States, would be able to face down the rest of the conference and water down the treaty. The Coalition decided to report on the large disparity between the positions of the most conservative minority and the large majority of countries that were ready to move forward with a strong treaty. William Pace suggested that the Coalition publish the actual positions of all the countries, showing the percentage of support for key issues, based on statements they had made in the Committee of the Whole. The result was two reports called *The Numbers* (NGO Coalition 1998a) and *The Virtual Vote* (NGO Coalition 1998b).

The Numbers and *The Virtual Vote* showed for example that 75 per cent of states supported the inclusion of internal armed conflicts within the definition of war crimes, 83 per cent supported a *propio motu* more independent prosecutor for the court, and 75 per cent supported automatic jurisdiction for all three core crimes of genocide, war crimes and crimes against humanity. This was accompanied by detailed breakdowns of each country's positions on several key issues in a large table. This data showed in stark detail that there was very little support for the United States positions calling for the exclusion of internal armed conflicts from war crimes, a less powerful prosecutor, and 'opt-in' clauses for war crimes and crimes against humanity.

Diplomats had remarked to Coalition members that *The Numbers* and *The Virtual Vote* were faxed back to national capitals by several government delegations to show where the key issues stood. It was also made clear to delegations that this data was being shared with NGO networks and media sources from around the world. From this perspective, it became clear to many delegations that the majority position was the most progressive one.

Then, on July 17, 1998, the last day of the conference, at about 10 p.m., Chairman Philippe Kirsch lowered the gavel, indicating that the Rome Statute on the International Criminal Court was adopted in a recorded vote of 120 in favour, seven opposed and 21 abstentions.[4]

Post-Rome: The Coalition Goes Global and Local

The Coalition had achieved a major success at the Rome Treaty Conference, concentrating and co-ordinating the massive force of hundreds of civil society organizations supporting the ICC. After the Conference, the challenges had not diminished but multiplied. Now the task had become garnering the necessary 60 ratifications of the ICC Treaty for it to enter into force and for the Court to come into being. In addition, the Coalition sought to ensure that the strongest possible domestic implementing legislation was developed after ratification to allow for full compliance with the Court. To accomplish these goals would require the expansion and deepening of the Coalition's activity at the regional and national levels on all five continents. Again, information technology was essential to the achievement of these objectives.

Prior to the Rome Conference, the general strategy of the Coalition was to maintain a fairly low profile. There was fear that if the ICC gained too much media attention too early, reactionary, nationalistic, and pro-military factions would arise to try and undermine the process. Information technology enabled the Coalition to get out its information strategically to those groups who were likely to support the Court, without broadcasting the news to groups who were likely to try and destroy it.

In this post-treaty phase, the strategy had changed. Now broadened constituencies among several sectors of civil society, parliamentarians, and the media were needed. Education and awareness became the primary goal of the Coalition.

Again, this feat would have been astoundingly difficult without the access to information technology. Even with information technology, supporting national ratification campaigns in 60 to 80 countries around the world would be an awesome task.

To facilitate a global ratification campaign, the CICC website was greatly enhanced. The expansions to the website in 1999-2000 included:

- making the site more interactive, with enhanced searching capabilities;
- expanding the country-by-country information and updating it on a weekly basis;
- adding a new section on the process and status of implementation in each country;
- adding a calendar of ICC-related events around the world;
- and making available the contact information for the Coalition's national and regional networks.

New information and documents are being added to the site weekly, including UN Preparatory Commission and other UN documents in the six official languages of the UN; ratification bills; documents on implementation of the Statute; government and NGO papers on substantive issues; and government and NGO press releases. Original photographs of key events including signatures and ratifications are also uploaded to the site.

New links have been established to sites with ICC-related information in Portuguese, German, Russian, Arabic, Polish, Spanish and French. This was in addition to the links to the sites of other NGOs working on the ICC and to a University of Chicago site with an extensive bibliography of online and off-line resources and publications on the ICC.

Meanwhile, the Coalition e-mail listserv expanded greatly after the high-profile Rome Conference. The list grew from approximately 800 subscribers in 1998 to 1250 in 2000. As a result, the list is now moderated by the Coalition to ensure the relevance of postings and the maximum interest of the list for its readers. Daily postings to the English listserv include summaries of all relevant media coverage, updates on progress towards ratification and implementation, and announcements of key events.

The Coalition also added separate listservs for various regions, caucuses and languages. A listserv in Spanish was developed in 1999 and a French listserv was created in 2000. Postings are made on a daily basis to the Spanish and French lists; some are translations of the key documents posted to the English list, while others are news articles and other information originally in Spanish and French. Members of the Coalition were assisted in developing specific e-mail listservs for issues of relevance in Europe, Poland, South Africa and Asia. Separate listservs are maintained for the Victims' Rights Working Group, the Steering Committee on Children and Justice, and the Faith-Based Caucus. The existence of these specialized lists allows the Coalition Secretariat and individual subscribers to send more detailed information of particular interest to a region or caucus, without overloading other members of the list with e-mails outside of their areas of interest.

An important service was also added at the request of members of the Coalition: a relational country information database system that is password-protected. This allows Coalition members to share sensitive country-specific information on the progress of ratification and implementation of the Statute. In this way, NGOs seeking to work with existing national networks can obtain online current information on the status of the ratification campaign and who the relevant contacts are, both within the government and among NGOs.

The Coalition also began producing a bulletin, *The ICC Update*, to provide up-to-date information between issues of the *ICC Monitor*. Each issue was mailed, faxed, and e-mailed to government delegates, UN officials, NGOs, media representatives and the more than one thousand subscribers to the ICC information listserv. These were also distributed at intergovernmental and civil society meetings and events worldwide. A separate update newsletter was produced monthly by the European office, with additional events and information specific to Europe. These were distributed to hundreds of subscribers by e-mail, fax and mail, including government representatives, international organizations and NGOs based in Europe, as well as at European events and meetings.

Finally, the Coalition began conducting daily searches of Lexis-Nexis in English, French and Spanish and posting summaries of news coverage to the ICC listservs in the three languages. A bi-weekly summary of the key media coverage was then provided in *The ICC Update*.

At this writing (January 2002) there are 48 ratifications to the ICC Treaty, with 12 more necessary for the treaty to enter into force. The Coalition has set a target date of July 2002 for the completion of the ratification process.

Conclusion

As this brief recounting of the development of the NGO Coalition has shown, information technology is becoming increasingly integral to the functioning and effectiveness of civil society as a voice in international decision-making. For a small network of NGOs with a small secretariat in New York to grow into an international global campaign with more than 1,000 members and 25 active national campaigns in every region, fast and reliable communications technology was essential.

The International Criminal Court, once it is in operation, will be a test case for the limits of global transparency. The Coalition plans to continue to be involved in the initial process of setting up the Court in The Hague, Netherlands. And once it is in operation, the Coalition will be expected to follow the cases the way it has followed the UN negotiations. Human rights groups involved in cases that the ICC is trying will want to know in real-time how the investigations and court proceedings are going. The internet makes this possible, but the bureaucracy needs to make it available.

We should not overstate the case of the importance of information technology. Effective global civil society campaigns have been organized prior to the existence and availability of much of the information technology that global networks like the Coalition for an International Criminal Court utilize. Examples include the global anti-apartheid movement, the anti-slavery movement, and international campaigns against nuclear weapons.

However the availability of information technologies has made the speed and scope of civil society activity so much greater. It simply was not possible a decade ago for far-flung activists to receive up-to-the-second reports on the status of international negotiations and then communicate instantly with local media and government officials their responses. Now this is a common occurrence.

In addition, traditional means of communication will still be a necessary component of global civil society campaigning. In the sometimes competitive and demanding world of civil society organizations, trust and common understanding have often only been built through face-to-face meetings among members of the Coalition. The Coalition was begun largely through goodwill among a small set of NGO actors within the UN system. It continues largely because of continued goodwill among the larger set of NGO actors who come to New York periodically for the ICC Preparatory Commission meetings.

Also, paper continues to be a useful medium. The *ICC Monitor* as a print publication continues to be much in demand, at conferences, universities, libraries, and government missions. A newsprint newsletter is still much more accessible to interested individuals than a web page. The actual paper versions of UN documents are still requested by NGOs, often even if the digital equivalent is available. This is particularly important for a truly global movement, since access to information technology is still limited in some countries and regions.

The Coalition is a case study of what we view as a larger socio-political trend toward multi-polar, less-hierarchical networks of civil society groups facilitated by information technology. Whether these federative local-global networks succeed or fail will have to be observed and measured over a long period of time. The experience of global nongovernmental networks concerned with, for example, sustainable development, racism, and child soldiers should be studied and compared to see what lessons can be learned for future campaigns and networks. The organizational structures are driven often more by necessity than design, as larger numbers of civil society organizations seek to work together in larger and larger groupings.

In addition, as the technology improves, becomes less expensive, and becomes more available to civil society, the nature of these international networks will change. Teleconferencing will be replaced by live video over the internet. There will be more pressure on the United Nations and other intergovernmental bodies to broadcast public meetings on the web or make transcripts available online. Activists will be able to receive instant messages on their personal data assistants and mobile phones and instantaneously send e-mails and place phone calls directly to the decision-makers at UN conferences.

Postscript

Many commentators have noted that were the International Criminal Court in place, it could have had jurisdiction over the crimes against humanity committed by the perpetrators of the September 11, 2001 attacks. As human rights activists, the pressure on us to complete the work of establishing the Court has intensified and our commitment to our goals has deepened. Support for the ICC from governments has never been higher, with several states pointing out the urgent need for such a tribunal in their interventions to the UN General Assembly in the year 2001.

Recent events have also shown that one person's tool is another's weapon. We have witnessed how such apparently benign technologies as commercial airplanes, cellular phones, e-mail, video broadcasting, and digital encryption can be used by criminal and terrorist organizations for their own malevolent ends. Technology alone cannot save us. Our hope is that the international community can unite to create sensible and effective global instruments to safeguard future generations from these kinds of horrific assaults.

Editor's Note

The Rome Treaty establishing the International Criminal Court achieved the required number of ratifications on 11 April 2002 when 10 countries submitted their instruments of ratification to the UN simultaneously. Now that this milestone has been reached, the Treaty will officially enter into force on 1 July 2002, 60 days after the receipt of the 60th ratification. The Court will be located at The Hague, Netherlands. (United Nations 2002, www.un.org/News/facts/iccfact.htm and www.un.org/law/icc/index.html.)

Notes

Note on internet addresses (URLs): Websites tend to appear, change or disappear, often without warning. Addresses cited in this bibliography were accurate and active at the time of writing (February 2002) unless otherwise noted.

1   For the purposes of this paper, the terms 'nongovernmental organizations' and 'civil society organizations' are used interchangeably.
2   Not to be confused with the 'Like-Minded Group' of country delegations to the ICC negotiations. The Like-Minded Group of countries was a loose group of government delegations that generally supported more progressive views toward the International Criminal Court.
3   See Binyon, Michael (1998), 'Britain Opposes War Crime Status for Landmines', *The Times* (London), 6 July, p. 11; and Hooper, John and Black, Ian (1998), 'Self-interest Brings Court into Contempt', *The Guardian* (London), 15 July, p. 17.

4   For a good description of the last hours of the conference, see Roy Lee's account in (1999), 'The Rome Conference and its Contribution to International Law', in Roy S. Lee (ed), *The International Criminal Court: The Making of the Rome Statute*, Kluwer Law International, Boston, pp. 23-26; and Lawrence Weschler's account in (2000), 'Exceptional Cases in Rome: The United States and the Struggle for an ICC', in Sarah B. Sewall and Carl Kaysen (eds), *The United States and the International Criminal Court: National Security and International Law*, Rowman & Littlefield, Lanham, MD, pp. 85-111.

References

Annan, Kofi (1998), *'Act on Your Ideals'*, *Secretary-General Urges Young People at World Youth Forum*, UN Press Release, SG/Youth/1, 7 August, World Youth Forum, Braga, Portugal, www.un.org/events/Youth98/pressrel/sgyouth.htm

Binyon, Michael (1998), 'Britain Opposes War Crime Status for Landmines', *The Times* (London), 6 July, p. 11.

Fernandez, Sylvia (1998), Argentinian delegation to the Rome Conference, correspondence with the authors.

Hooper, John and Black, Ian (1998), 'Self-interest Brings Court into Contempt', *The Guardian* (London), 15 July, p. 17.

Lee, Roy S. (1999), 'The Rome Conference and its Contribution to International Law', in Roy S. Lee, (ed), *The International Criminal Court: The Making of the Rome Statute*, Kluwer Law International, Boston, pp. 1-39.

NGO Coalition for an International Criminal Court. (1998a), *The Numbers: NGO Coalition Special Report on Country Positions*, 10 July, www.igc.apc.org/icc/rome/html/rome_other.html

NGO Coalition for an International Criminal Court. (1998b), *The Virtual Vote: NGO Coalition Special Report on Country Positions on L.59*, 15 July, www.igc.apc.org/icc/rome/html/rome_other.html

Weschler, Lawrence (2000), 'Exceptional Cases in Rome: The United States and the Struggle for an ICC', in Sarah B. Sewall and Carl Kaysen, (eds), *The United States and the International Criminal Court: National Security and International Law*, Rowman & Littlefield, Lanham, MD, pp. 85-111.

Williams, Jody (1997), *The International Campaign to Ban Landmines: A Model for Disarmament Initiatives?* Oslo, Speech by Jody Williams, International Campaign to Ban Landmines, accepting the Nobel Peace Prize. www.nobel.se/peace/articles/williams/index.html

Chapter 8

AIDS, Médecins Sans Frontières, and Access to Essential Medicines

James Orbinski
Copyright © James Orbinski

In early 2001 I was in South Africa visiting a Médecins Sans Frontières (MSF) clinic. MSF had been trying – but up to that time without success – to start antiretroviral (ARV) treatment for people living with HIV/AIDS.[1] I was examining a 20-year-old man. If he were virtually anywhere in the Western world, he would be just starting his life. But his life is nearly over. He was so weak that two friends had to help him onto the examining table. The foul odor of his breath was so severe – his lungs were filled with infection that was not responding to antibiotics – that one nurse was forced to leave the room. As he sat on the examining table gasping for air, he asked me: "Why do you come here with only kindness when what I need is medicine to stop this AIDS? Your kindness is good but it will not help this AIDS. They have such medicine in your countries – why not here in South Africa?".

People ask similar questions all over the developing world, the vast majority of whom have no access to ARV therapy, a proven and effective treatment for HIV/AIDS. Since the beginning of the HIV/AIDS epidemic, 20 million people have died. Worldwide, 40 million people now live with HIV, and 95 per cent of these are in the South (UNAIDS 2001). With HIV/AIDS, as with so many other illnesses, what happens to adults impacts on children. Today, in Africa alone, there are 13 million children orphaned because of a parent who has died of AIDS. In many countries 1 in 4 women have HIV infection, and most will pass this on to their newborn children. Globally, five million people were newly infected in 2001, and at least five million will be newly infected in 2002. India, Russia and the other former Soviet republics, and Asia stand on the brink of a potential HIV explosion. AIDS is not just an epidemic. It is a global catastrophe that is already a rival to the Black Plague of the Middle Ages. And yet unlike the Black Plague, it is a treatable infectious disease. But who has access to that treatment? At least 38 of the 40 million people with HIV/AIDS do not. Until last year, nor did they have any hope of gaining access to essential life-saving ARVs in their HIV-limited lifetimes.

Among health-oriented nongovernmental organizations (NGOs), there have been few recent issues more galvanizing than that of access to ARVs for the treatment of HIV/AIDS. MSF and a coalition of other NGOs – including Consumer Project on Technology (CPT), Health Action International (HAI), ACT UP, ACCESS in Thailand, Treatment Access Campaign (TAC) and OXFAM – have taken on this issue with a clarity of vision and an immediate fast-track impact previously unknown in international issues. This has both taken advantage of and reconfigured new post-Cold War relations between states, civil society organizations and other non-state actors such as multinational pharmaceutical corporations. All of this has taken place in the 'theatre' of globalization – with characters and themes that represent both the realities and discontents of so-called globalization. For MSF this meant taking on this issue under the rubric of our Access to Essential Medicines Campaign. The 'how' of this action cannot be understood without first understanding the 'why'. Undoubtedly, the 'why' will differ slightly in its articulation for each NGO. NGOs are not homogeneous in their raison d'être, nor in their organization or methods. I describe here only my view of MSF's experience with this issue, and make no attempt to speak for others.

In 1999 the Norwegian Nobel Committee awarded the Nobel Peace Prize to MSF "in recognition of [its] pioneering humanitarian work on several continents". More particularly, it recognized the special characteristics of MSF that differentiate its work from other humanitarian organizations. There are two main aspects to this that combine to define humanitarian action for MSF. The first aspect is that MSF brings direct medical action to bear to people in need, in situations of egregious suffering, in war or in situations of political neglect. This is direct medical action that seeks to relieve suffering in the first instance. This medical relief is offered with the intention of seeking to restore the autonomy of people who suffer, so they can then make their own decisions about their own destiny. The act of providing humanitarian assistance is not divorced from this intention with which it is offered. MSF believes that humanitarian action is not simply a technical act, not simply a matter of providing relief or providing a material service for an identified need.

The second aspect touches on MSF's commitment to witnessing and to describing publicly its direct knowledge and experience of the human reality of suffering in war or in situations of political neglect or failure. For MSF, the humanitarian act responds to human needs, and as such, it is the most apolitical of acts; but if its actions and morality are taken seriously, it has the most profound of political implications. This is a kind of paradox that describes the place or space where MSF finds and continues to reinvent its identity. I think that it is a fair and accurate description. It is, in my mind, the essence of what MSF represents and the essence of what the Nobel Committee recognized in MSF. Adhering to that vision has had dramatic implications for the practice of humanitarianism since MSF began in 1971. MSF started and continues to exist in an ethic of refusal – a refusal to accept fatalistically the reality of human suffering, as well as a refusal to accept that such suffering should go without at least an equally human response. It is our duty as human beings to respond to that suffering and to ensure that people's dignity is recognized and honoured, and that it is at the centre of the political project.

In the last thirty years, MSF has taken on various issues – various 'themes' – but in our own minds we had never constructed these as campaigns *per se*. An example of a continuing MSF concern is the rights of refugees and the responsibilities of states and others to respect, promote and protect those rights. We have also assumed a direct role in identifying populations in danger, trying to ensure that the reality of their lives is a part of the public political debate on the responsibilities of government, and the role of states. One could also look at particular countries and particular wars. For example, in the Sudan the effort of MSF centres on direct provision of humanitarian assistance and an advocacy effort that tries to keep the human reality of civil war in that country in the public political domain.

Another MSF 'theme' is street children. The problems they live with and the reality of their existence have been a focus for MSF in various ways. There have been many such themes. Only recently, in 1999, did we, for the first time, launch a formal campaign, focusing on increasing people's access to essential medicines.

Until roughly 1996 to 1998, in our work with AIDS patients around the world, we had to face the fact that there was no proven effective treatment. We largely provided treatment for opportunistic infections, and did all that we could to help people with HIV/AIDS live and die in dignity, and to bring their plight to public knowledge. But in 1997, when it became obvious that ARV therapy could prolong life, we took on a new battle. As doctors we cannot remain silent while a viable treatment exists, but the people we are working with do not have access to it. Until early 2001, the cost of patented drug therapy for HIV was US$15,000 per year for a single person. At that price you can be sure that only a handful of people are treated, and you can be sure that entire nations outside of the wealthy West will go untreated. In the last three years, MSF and a plethora of other NGOs have been successful in generating generic competition and therefore in bringing the market price of generic ARV for HIV down to a cost of less than US$300 per year. We did this through national and international public political pressure on governments, international government organizations (IGOs), and on the pharmaceutical industry. We have worked with coalitions of patient groups around the world, with NGOs, with certain governments and with certain members of the pharmaceutical industry to force this change.

A continuous challenge for MSF and other NGOs is to define our role, our capabilities, our responsibilities, and our limits. In this one example of access to ARVs (and there are many other such examples), even with all the volunteers in the world and a manifold increase in our budget of US$300 million, 82 per cent of which comes from private citizen donations, MSF could not have faced the challenge of paying for and providing access to patented treatment for HIV/AIDS. And as a humanitarian organization, this is neither our role nor our responsibility. This is fundamentally a political issue, and we first had to identify it as such, then provoke it, and be careful not to engage in premature partnerships with industry and governments before our goal is reached. NGOs and social movements can respond to and can shape their social and political environments in many ways. They must be clear about their own roles, responsibilities, capabilities and limits as well as about the roles, responsibilities, capabilities and limits of both the private sector and government. This is particularly challenging today in a global neoliberal political climate where the very nature of relationship between civil society, government and the private sector is changing, and what were once public services, are either downloaded to the voluntary sector or privatized. Here, for MSF, the humanitarian act is very clear. It seeks to relieve suffering, to restore autonomy, to witness to the truth of injustice, and to insist on political responsibility (Orbinski

1999). It is this understanding that led MSF to take on the issue of access to ARVs for all people living with HIV/AIDS in the way that we are doing, and to join with others in this struggle.

The Access to Essential Medicines Campaign

Over the years, MSF has seen that our patients in the South have less and less access to essential medicines. We witness this reality and see our patients dying needlessly every day. The medicines that are available for certain diseases are increasingly archaic, increasingly ineffective because of drug resistance, and increasingly lacking in genuine innovation, so that no new treatment becomes available, for example for Leishmaniasis and other diseases. As well, medicines that exist are often no longer produced because of the virtually non-existent purchasing power of the people who suffer from tropical diseases like African Sleeping Sickness. Finally, medications are often priced out of the reach of the majority of people who need them. Here, the best example is the majority of patients – 38 million of 40 million – with HIV who do not have access to ARV drugs. We recognized that these broad categories of issues were related, and created the Access to Essential Medicines Campaign to attempt to address them in very specific ways.

Based on our analysis of HIV/AIDS and access to ARVs, we recognized that the most significant issue was not the commonly argued lack of infrastructure for the delivery of health care, but the excessive price of ARVs that puts the question of infrastructure beyond consideration. If you cannot even afford to buy the medicine, why would you build an infrastructure that could never deliver it? The question of access to ARVs, which are largely patented medications, also reveals, in a very real and human way, the impact of patents on people's access to the fruits of medical research and medical knowledge.

When one looks at the lack of research and development (R&D) for neglected diseases in the South, the excessive pricing of patented medication that is a barrier to people's access to medicine, and the lack of production of listed medicines that are no longer commercially viable, one can see that the issue of patents is an excellent entry into larger questions about the role, interests and responsibilities of the private sector, of other non-state actors such as NGOs, and of government. Considered this way, the issue of patents raises some very specific questions. Is a patent simply a mechanism to reward innovation, or is it also more than this? What is the purpose of the apparent social contract that is embodied in the patent system? Is it not also intended as a mechanism to stimulate innovative research and development of new drugs for priority diseases, and not simply diseases or lifestyle conditions (like hair loss and obesity) that have a lucrative market? Are not patents also a mechanism to ensure a balance between private interests and public goods – the public goods being the fruits of medical research and medical knowledge itself – and access to these? When viewed in this way, the broader question becomes 'Patents to what end?'. States have a duty to promote, protect and enhance people's access to health care. They also have a duty to find the right relationship between public and private interests. I use the word 'relationship' rather than 'balance' because putting this in terms of balance does not address the question of ends. The end should be to ensure that people have access to health care. At the same time, there has to be a viable mechanism to both reward and stimulate priority innovation to serve the end of ensuring people's access to improving health care.

When we started the Access to Essential Medicines Campaign, we had a clear intention of bringing the issue to the pinnacle of debate at the World Trade Organization (WTO). Why? Because the WTO is the most significant IGO since the end of World War II. It is the only IGO that has enforcement power. It therefore has the ability to alter the very economic and political fabric of a given society or a regional collection of nations. The power that is invested in the WTO, until the resolution on public health protection passed at the Doha ministerial meeting in late 2001 [see Appendix for the full text of the Doha Declaration on the TRIPS Agreement and Public Health], was rooted exclusively in self-referential trade rules that excluded the possibility of other considerations – social policy, health, environment, labour standards – that must be part of any meaningful and just vision. Therefore, we set out to challenge the singular focus on trade and the singular focus on patent protection as a means of rewarding innovation. We also set out to ensure that the question of access to health care, access to the fruits of medical knowledge, and, first and foremost, the question of people's right to exist, become part of the equation. We wanted to insist that public health considerations, as decided upon by a legitimate political entity (a nation state), will trump trade interests or the self-interests of non-state actors (for example, corporations).

An NGO Coalition

Much of what has been achieved in the area of public health, and on the right relationship between public health considerations and trade considerations, has been dependent on a process whereby civil society groups have organized themselves systematically around a set of principled ideas: the right of people to exist, the right of access to health care including the fruits of medical knowledge, and the necessity of ensuring the priority of public health interests over trade interests. NGOs have engaged in a global process of activism that has had several dimensions: raising public awareness; the mobilization and catalyzing of government responsibility at regional, national and international levels; confronting the simplistic and rapaciously self-interested arguments of many private-sector companies, and confronting the intransigence of largely Western governments to represent the interests of society as a whole as opposed to those of simply self-interested actors.

MSF has been one of many players in a coalition that was not as formally constructed as some international relations scholars would like to believe. Rather, it was a global issue-specific coalition of localized actors who were linked through modern technology (largely the internet and mobile telephones) as well as through regular meetings devoted to specific questions. A vital aspect of the coalition was that it was able to bridge the North-South divide through such linkages around shared, principled ideas.

In conducting the Access to Essential Medicines Campaign, MSF sponsored a series of meetings on very particular questions, spread over time so that people could come together to share ideas. For example, we held a meeting in Geneva in March 1999 on compulsory licensing where we brought together experts as well as NGOs from all over the world. It was a relatively small meeting of about sixty people who discussed the nature, state-of-the-art and implications of compulsory licensing and its implications for WTO's Trade-related Aspects of Intellectual Property Rights (TRIPS) agreement and its adjudication processes. We discussed what compulsory licensing under TRIPS could mean for people in the South in terms of access to essential medicines. In other words, people came together on an issue they were concerned about, and they shared, acquired and created knowledge – all of which strengthened a fluid NGO coalition.

The Geneva meeting was followed by another, larger and very important meeting in Paris in October 1999, about the crisis in access to essential medicines. The next meeting in November 1999, in Amsterdam, had some 350 representatives mostly of NGOs but also representatives of industry, of government and of IGOs (for example the World Health Organization, WHO; and United Nations Development Programme, UNDP). That meeting reviewed and accepted an action plan that focused on the TRIPS agreement and on the specific changes required for the developing world. Then there was the Seattle ministerial meeting of the WTO in late 1999. MSF was present at the meeting, participating informally in the discussions, and supporting developing world delegates with information. There were subsequent meetings in Europe, in Africa, South America, and Asia on various subjects – for example, the Bangui agreement for West Africa, which is essentially a 'TRIPS plus' agreement that the EU was pushing and MSF was opposing. MSF lobbied governments not to sign it. The outcome of this is still uncertain; some signed, some did not. Other elements of the MSF campaign continue to include a focus on stimulating research and development for neglected diseases, addressing the lack of commercial viability of medicines that exist but are no longer being produced, and other issues.

Other crucial actions include ongoing participation and advocacy at specialized conferences, professional workshops and public events that deal with relevant access issues. Equally important, and vital to the success at Doha, was both lobbying and supporting developing-world governments with technical expertise and the latest information on rapidly evolving positions and perspectives of relevant state and non-state actors locally and internationally. This began in the weeks following the 1999 Amsterdam conference. It meant many private and public meetings and informal contacts with ministers and government officials all over the world, and peaked in Doha in the final minutes leading up to the actual ministerial declaration.

The tactics that MSF uses to address issues seek to create common vision where it is possible, and to galvanize public support for those issues. They also seek to create and galvanize government responsibility. Again, we push governments to assume their political responsibility. At the same time, we work to bring these issues into the public domain. MSF insists on the right to speak and the right to be heard. If that takes the form of a peaceful demonstration, so be it. MSF does not use violence as a means of achieving a political end. This is why, for example, in Genoa, during the G8 Summit in July 2001, MSF denounced violence by some elements of the demonstrators – while at the same time also denouncing provocative violence used by police and security forces.

The series of meetings I have described, as well as many others hosted by other NGOs, created a space for people to come together, share ideas, and to build and strengthen clarity of vision. At the same time, MSF, Health Action International and Consumer Project on Technology engaged public advocacy and targeted lobbying of governments, IGOs, and members of the pharmaceutical industry. OXFAM joined the coalition, and this clearly increased the coalition's strengths and viability. Treatment Access Campaign, a grassroots activist organization from South Africa, ACT UP, ACCESS in Thailand, similar grassroots NGO coalitions in South America, India, and elsewhere all engaged local actions that provoked local and international political responses. The coalition is not formally governed, but is issue- and opportunity-specific, held together by clearly articulated principled ideas and a clear vision of what we seek to achieve. Each actor works according to its own methods and its own understanding of what is required in its particular circumstance.

These issues all coalesced to create an environment where public awareness grew around the actual consequences of the TRIPS agreement as it was being implemented according to Washington- and Brussels-based political goals. These questions became public questions, and part of the political debate. This appealed to people the same way as the Landmines Convention campaign had. Here, there is something distinctively unjust about the long-term presence of landmines after a particular conflict is over – and a civilian who then loses her legs. There is something inherently obvious about the moral incongruity or moral unacceptability of that outcome. People understand that and react to it, because as human beings, it requires a response. The same holds true for access to essential medicines. People understand the incongruity between the existence of a medicine and the lack of access to that medicine, particularly in the case of those who suffer and die from HIV/AIDS in such huge numbers. People can empathize with that; they can see themselves in that situation. And this is why MSF's commitment to witnessing is so important. You can touch people with your own experience; you can relate people's suffering to your reality. This is a key element of the campaign that we try to keep in focus: the human reality of the lack of access to essential medicines.

When you think about war, for example, about the Geneva Conventions, international law, the questions of sovereignty versus individual autonomy, the questions of charity versus duty, these are complicated, abstract concepts. Academics and philosophers can and do work during their whole life analyzing such questions. But if you speak to the human reality of war and the consequences of not adhering to the principles and rules of war, then people understand. They also understand that therefore the rules of war must be followed – something that often is not happening. Similarly, one can talk about the role of the pharmaceutical industry, about TRIPS, about compulsory licensing, about quality assurance, the

R&D pipeline, genomics, proteomics, and so forth. These are all very complicated concepts that on the surface are unappealing. But ultimately, if you can keep the focus on the human reality of injustice, then people will understand the problem and will bring themselves to inquire about these more complicated issues. So, that has been the major focus of the campaign: to keep it rooted in the human reality. This is one of MSF's key contributions to the question of access to essential medicines. Many organizations have been working on this for many years. They have done highly significant work on the technical issues, on the legal issues, on industrial development analysis, and so on. What MSF has brought to the campaign is the human reality, as well as a significant investment in developing and disseminating some of the more technical issues and aspects that are part of the proposed solution to these human realities.

The Role of Information and Communication Technology in the Campaign

The internet and web-based electronic mail have had a huge impact on the speed and scope of the campaign. The ability to share the latest information virtually instantaneously – in an open and transparent manner – changes the political equation locally and globally. Also important is the ability to have private, or at any rate less public, exchanges and to share information – for example, via listservs such as the one administered by CPT. The fact that the internet allows individuals to engage in worldwide communication in very short time frames has been enormously significant. Finally, mobile phones have been critical; one can talk virtually to anyone, at any time in order to clarify a point, receive immediate information, or clear up contentious issues even faster than via the internet.

It is important to recognize that technology is not an end in itself, but a means that must facilitate something. The ends are the principled ideas around which people gather. People come together around ideas that they believe in. And they stay together when there is a discernible, visible and viable political goal. Coalitions generally fall apart unless there is intentionality with reasonable potential to become reality. Lacking that intentionality, people's commitment will vary and will not necessarily achieve the kind of result that, for example, has been achieved at Doha. So, the set of principled ideas and the viability of a politically desirable outcome are key to the integrity and vitality of such coalitions. Another consideration is that once people have come together, they share ideas and come to trust one another–and that cannot really be achieved via the internet, over the telephone, with a fax machine, or through television. People have to meet face to face, and have to have an opportunity to define and articulate a shared vision of what they want to achieve.

Information and communication technology (ICT) has enhanced the legitimacy of civil society in a variety of ways. ICT has allowed posting on the web one's position on issue X, as well as the rationale and evidence for that position. Posted references can be followed up so that web-users can decide for themselves if the information makes sense. For example, when visitors to MSF's website can read the latest document on compulsory licensing, or an analysis of the AIDS epidemic, or of access to treatment for African Sleeping Sickness, they can determine to their own satisfaction whether the organization's position is accurate and credible. This kind of exchange should not be for a closed circle of experts, and should not exclusively use the language of specialists. Most of MSF's position papers are written for the general public. Members of that broad audience can contact MSF if they wish, they can comment, they can join or contribute. MSF as a whole has no formal process for a web-based dialogue, but some MSF sections do, and people can send questions. MSF does its best to respond. This transparency and the consequent credibility enhances legitimacy because the position is not only morally compelling, but defensible using credible argument and evidence. By posting information, by describing your rationale and your evidentiary framework, you are doing something very powerful. People expect a certain level of analysis and integrity, and, if those expectations are met, they see your work as legitimate. The inevitable consequence is that people are able and want to engage an informed debate that clearly has political implications. Of course, the subsequent debate is a political process, so some people will agree and others, disagree.

By Way of Conclusion: The Aftermath of September 11

What has changed after September 11? Fundamentally, September 11 has not changed the underlying issues that call into question people's access to essential medicines. What it has changed is the context in which those issues are addressed or fail to be addressed. The issue of access to essential medicines is a question of basic justice, of the recognition of people's basic rights as human beings, and of recognition of their dignity – which stands even before rights. These are the most basic of humanitarian issues. But if their meaning is taken seriously, then this has profound political implications. That has not changed after September 11. MSF is not ready to accept trade without careful consideration of health interests as part of the political equation. After a long process, this was recognized, at least in principle, at Doha. It is a beginning that addresses the injustice inherent in the question "they have such medicine in your countries – why not here in South Africa?". This is a very significant achievement for the NGO coalition – a coalition that will continue to struggle until people with HIV/AIDS actually have access to ARVs, and until all people have viable access to essential life-saving medicines.

Appendix

WORLD TRADE ORGANIZATION
MINISTERIAL CONFERENCE, FOURTH SESSION
DOHA, 9-14 NOVEMBER 2001
DECLARATION ON THE TRIPS AGREEMENT AND PUBLIC HEALTH

Adopted on 14 November 2001

1. We recognize the gravity of the public health problems afflicting many developing and least-developed countries, especially those resulting from HIV/AIDS, tuberculosis, malaria and other epidemics.
2. We stress the need for the WTO Agreement on Trade-Related Aspects of Intellectual Property Rights (TRIPS Agreement) to be part of the wider national and international action to address these problems.
3. We recognize that intellectual property protection is important for the development of new medicines. We also recognize the concerns about its effects on prices.
4. We agree that the TRIPS Agreement does not and should not prevent members from taking measures to protect public health. Accordingly, while reiterating our commitment to the TRIPS Agreement, we affirm that the Agreement can and should be interpreted and implemented in a manner supportive of WTO members' right to protect public health and, in particular, to promote access to medicines for all.
In this connection, we reaffirm the right of WTO members to use, to the full, the provisions in the TRIPS Agreement, which provide flexibility for this purpose.
5. Accordingly and in the light of paragraph 4 above, while maintaining our commitments in the TRIPS Agreement, we recognize that these flexibilities include:
   a. In applying the customary rules of interpretation of public international law, each provision of the TRIPS Agreement shall be read in the light of the object and purpose of the Agreement as expressed, in particular, in its objectives and principles.
   b. Each member has the right to grant compulsory licences and the freedom to determine the grounds upon which such licences are granted.
   c. Each member has the right to determine what constitutes a national emergency or other circumstances of extreme urgency, it being understood that public health crises, including those relating to HIV/AIDS, tuberculosis, malaria and other epidemics, can represent a national emergency or other circumstances of extreme urgency.
   d. The effect of the provisions in the TRIPS Agreement that are relevant to the exhaustion of intellectual property rights is to leave each member free to establish its own regime for such exhaustion without challenge, subject to the MFN and national treatment provisions of Articles 3 and 4.

6. We recognize that WTO members with insufficient or no manufacturing capacities in the pharmaceutical sector could face difficulties in making effective use of compulsory licensing under the TRIPS Agreement. We instruct the Council for TRIPS to find an expeditious solution to this problem and to report to the General Council before the end of 2002.
7. We reaffirm the commitment of developed-country members to provide incentives to their enterprises and institutions to promote and encourage technology transfer to least-developed country members pursuant to Article 66.2. We also agree that the least-developed country members will not be obliged, with respect to pharmaceutical products, to implement or apply Sections 5 and 7 of Part II of the TRIPS Agreement or to enforce rights provided for under these Sections until 1 January 2016, without prejudice to the right of least-developed country members to seek other extensions of the transition periods as provided for in Article 66.1 of the TRIPS Agreement. We instruct the Council for TRIPS to take the necessary action to give effect to this pursuant to Article 66.1 of the TRIPS Agreement.

Source: World Trade Organization (2001), *Declaration on the Trips Agreement and Public Health*, 14 November, WTO, Doha, Qatar, WT/MIN(01)/DEC/2, www.wto.org/english/thewto_e/minist_e/min01_e/mindecl_trips_e.htm

Note

1 ARV treatment has since started in the project.

References

Joint United Nations Programme on HIV/AIDS (UNAIDS) (2001), *AIDS Epidemic Update*, December, www.unaids.org/epidemic_update/report_dec01/index.html#full

Orbinski, James (1999), *The Nobel Lecture*, Oslo, 10 December. Speech by James Orbinski, Médecins Sans Frontières, accepting the Nobel Peace Prize. www.nobel.no/eng_lect_99m.html

World Trade Organization. Ministerial (2001), *Declaration on the Trips Agreement and Public Health*, 14 November, WTO, Doha, Qatar, WT/MIN(01)/DEC/2, www.wto.org/english/thewto_e/minist_e/min01_e/mindecl_trips_e.htm

PART II

CIVIL SOCIETY IN RELATIONSHIP WITH INTERGOVERNMENTAL INSTITUTIONS

Chapter 9

The United Nations and Civil Society

Barbara Adams

Introduction

During the 1990s the United Nations (UN) system witnessed a dramatic upsurge in the involvement of a diverse range of nongovernmental organizations (NGOs) in its work. While this was most visible in the cycle of UN world conferences, there are many areas of UN endeavour, such as international development co-operation, human rights, women's equality, disarmament, peace-keeping, emergencies and refugees, and many UN activities, including policy-setting, standards and normative work, operational activities, advocacy and information work, in which NGOs now participate to an unprecedented degree.

NGO contributions to the UN are multifaceted and often impossible to trace. In addition to being valuable partners in, for example, operational development and emergency activities, or human rights and election monitoring, NGOs are the source of vital experience, expertise and information. They provide new insights and approaches in most areas on the UN agenda. It is increasingly acknowledged that governments and intergovernmental organizations cannot, acting alone, successfully deal with the enormous challenges posed by poverty eradication, sustainable development and other global issues.

Historically NGOs were viewed by the UN primarily as providing public support for the UN system and participating in the implementation of some of its programmes. Over the last ten years, however, a new element has been added to the work done by NGOs: their substantive contributions and their contributions to the policy-setting processes and fora of the UN. The monitoring activities of NGOs contribute significantly to the democratization of international relations and international co-operation, making the work of the UN more transparent and accountable to a wider public than has been the case in the past.

Formal mechanisms for NGO presence and participation (and assessment of performance) at the UN are very limited compared with the breadth and depth of NGO involvement in world affairs. Formal procedures have changed little since the founding of the UN and do not readily facilitate the insights, experience and expertise of NGOs as a contribution to decision-making and policy-setting other than as communicated through governments.

Formal NGO Relations

NGOs have been active in the UN since its founding. They interact with the UN Secretariat, programmes, funds and agencies, and they consult with the member states. NGO work related to the UN comprises a number of activities including information dissemination, awareness raising, development education, policy advocacy, joint operational projects, and providing technical expertise and collaborating with UN agencies, programmes and funds. This work is undertaken in formal and informal ways at the national level and at the UN. Official UN Secretariat relations with NGOs fall into two main categories: consultations with governments, and information servicing by the Secretariat. These functions are the responsibility of two main offices of the UN Secretariat dealing with NGOs: the NGO Unit of the Department of Economic and Social Affairs (DESA), and the NGO Section of the Department of Public Information (DPI). Formal interaction and consultation between NGOs and the UN are governed by the UN Charter and related resolutions of the Economic and Social Council (ECOSOC).

The Preamble of the UN Charter affirms the aims and purposes that "We, the peoples of the United Nations" are committed to realize through the organization. Article 71 says: "The Economic and Social Council may make suitable arrangements for the consultation with non-governmental organizations which are concerned with matters within its competence. Such arrangements may be made with international organizations and, where appropriate, with national organizations after consultation with the Member of the United Nations concerned" (United Nations 1989).

This article and the arrangements established by ECOSOC form the basis for NGO consultation with governments at the UN and establish guidelines for the UN Secretariat when dealing with NGOs. These procedures and arrangements also govern or guide other UN agencies and programmes in their relations with NGOs. An annex to this chapter gives specific details of the rights and responsibilities of NGOs in relationship with ECOSOC and DPI.

Consultative Status with ECOSOC

Arrangements for consultation with NGOs are governed by ECOSOC resolution 1996/31 adopted on 25 July 1996. This resolution defines NGOs as "any international organization which is not established by a governmental entity or intergovernmental agreement" (United Nations 1996a). 'Organization' refers to NGOs at the national, subregional, regional and international levels, except where expressly stated otherwise. Resolution 1996/31 also specifies certain principles for NGOs concerning their consultative status with ECOSOC, as well as NGO consultations with the Secretariat. The resolution establishes three categories of consultative status for NGOs. General consultative status is for large, international NGOs whose area of work covers most of the issues on ECOSOC's agenda. Special consultative status is for NGOs that have special competence in a few fields of ECOSOC's activity. The third category, which is inclusion on the roster, is for NGOs whose competence enables them to make occasional and useful contributions to the work of the UN and that are available for consultation upon request. NGOs on the roster may also include organizations in consultative status with a specialized agency or other UN body.

The ECOSOC Committee on Non-Governmental Organizations is the only intergovernmental committee in the UN system that focuses exclusively on relations with NGOs. The committee is composed of 19 member states and meets every year. Its main function is to review NGO applications for consultative or roster status, request changes in status, and submit its recommendations on applications to ECOSOC.

The committee may consult with organizations in consultative status on specific items on the ECOSOC agenda or other matters and reports to ECOSOC on these consultations. It is also responsible for "regular monitoring of the evolving relationship between non-governmental organizations and the United Nations", and holds annual consultations with NGOs about that relationship. Reports on such consultations are to be transmitted to ECOSOC for appropriate action.

Association with DPI

In addition to consultative status with ECOSOC, appropriate NGOs may seek associative status with the UN Department of Public Information. The importance of working with NGOs as an integral part of UN information activities was recognized when DPI was established in 1946. The General Assembly (GA), in resolution 13 (I) of 1946, instructed the department and its branch offices to "actively assist and encourage national information services, educational institutions and other governmental and non-governmental organizations of all kinds interested in spreading information about the United Nations. For this and other purposes, it should operate a fully equipped reference service, brief or supply lecturers, and make available its publications, documentary films, filmstrips, posters and other exhibits for use by these agencies and organizations" (United Nations 1946).

Organizations eligible for association with DPI are those that share the ideals of the UN Charter; operate solely on a non-profit basis; have a demonstrated interest in UN issues and a proven ability to reach large or specialized audiences, such as educators, media representatives, policymakers and the business community; and have the commitment and means to conduct effective information programmes about UN activities through publication of newsletters, bulletins, backgrounders and pamphlets or through the organization of conferences, seminars and roundtables and by enlisting the co-operation of print and broadcast media. Close to 1,600 NGOs with effective information programmes on issues of concern to the UN are associated with the department, which gives the UN valuable links to civil society worldwide.

Changing Patterns of NGO-UN Relations in the 1990s

The UN/NGO relationship exploded in the early 1990s primarily through a series of UN global conferences. NGOs had long been recognised for their work in development projects at the field level and for their role in education and information dissemination. Human rights groups have been active since the founding of the UN in promoting its standard-setting work. Women's organizations have been focusing on the UN as a global forum to advance women's rights since the International Women's Year in 1975. They had mobilized national and grass-roots constituencies for the International Women's Decade (1976-1985), and for the mid-term conference in 1980 in Copenhagen and the End-Decade Conference in Nairobi in 1985. However, their mobilizations did not focus on the official UN deliberations. In 1985 over 15,000 women and men went to Nairobi for the parallel NGO Forum, but fewer than 400 NGOs were accredited to the official conference. One decade later for the Fourth World Conference on Women in Beijing, China, the number of accredited NGOs had ballooned to over 2,600.

The turning point for NGOs in developing new ways of working and focusing on the intergovernmental negotiations was the UN Conference on Environment and Development (UNCED) that took place in Rio de Janeiro in 1992, and its preparatory process. NGOs, primarily from the environment movement, were determined to influence UN policy and hence the outcome of the governments' negotiations. They realized that this required their participation, monitoring and lobbying before the conference itself – during its two-year preparatory process – and set about learning how international policy-making took place.

The UNCED Secretariat actively encouraged the participation of NGOs in the UNCED process, and together the UN and NGOs achieved an unprecedented degree of international mobilization around the conference agenda. In bringing together large numbers of environment and development NGOs from around the world, UNCED revealed that there was a global constituency for the issues on the UN agenda and highlighted the powerful mobilizing force of the NGOs. The successful efforts of the UNCED Secretariat ensured funding for a large number of Southern NGOs, and the UNCED Preparatory Committees provided a series of meetings for NGOs to exchange information, build trust and develop their common agenda.

Member states also showed unprecedented recognition of the vital contribution of NGOs in Agenda 21, the major outcome document adopted at UNCED. This comprehensive blueprint devoted ten of its 40 chapters to elaborating ways to involve various "major groups" in the follow-up, further development and implementation of sustainable development (United Nations 1992).

The focus of NGOs on official UN deliberations and the international policy agenda continued and was evident at a number of major UN conferences and their preparatory meetings that took place in the first half of the 1990s. These conferences attracted an unprecedented number of NGOs and this was reflected in the official accreditation to those official conferences: approximately 2,600 to the Fourth World Conference on Women (Beijing, 1995), 1,300 to the World Summit for Social Development (Copenhagen, 1995), over 1,000 to the International Conference on Population and Development (Cairo, 1994), 1,400 to the UN Conference on Environment and Development (Rio de Janeiro, 1992).

Alongside traditional activities such as circulating documents, formally addressing plenary sessions, organizing briefings and publishing daily bulletins and newspapers, NGOs put more effort into working with and lobbying government delegations, both during intergovernmental meetings and at the national level. An increasing number of government delegations to world conferences included representatives of national NGOs.

The preparatory process for the UN Conference on Human Settlements (Habitat II) that took place in Istanbul in 1996 broke new ground by officially inviting representatives of NGOs and local authorities to participate in the informal drafting groups which drew up the Declaration and Programme of Action, and by proposing that local authorities and their international representative bodies be accorded a special, semi-official status at the conference.

The evolution of the NGO-government relationship in the global conferences was accompanied by developments in inter-NGO and North-South NGO relationships and in their self-organizing. NGOs organized themselves into working groups or caucuses by region, constituency, and issue. These caucuses, in particular the women's caucus, divided up the work of monitoring the negotiations, drafting alternative language, and engaging relevant delegates. They enabled NGOs to better manage their participation in the international policy dialogue and have been adapted to other international venues to facilitate NGO co-operation.

In some cases NGO involvement was a significant factor in the ability of major UN conferences to achieve an international consensus reflecting current thinking and commitments of governments on difficult policy challenges. This was particularly true with the issues related to women's rights and reproductive health. Women's organizations campaigned successfully to ensure that the World Conference on Human Rights (Vienna, 1993) included women's rights. During the preparatory process for the International Conference on Population and Development, they succeeded in changing the framework for population policies from a focus on demographics and the promotion of birth control to a focus on the primacy of the role of women and their needs, and their reproductive health and rights.

As the decade of the 1990s progressed NGOs continued their policy focus in a number of areas. They formed coalitions and played a significant role in the accords to ban anti-personnel landmines and to establish the International Criminal Court. As the decade ended, the Jubilee campaign for debt relief also began to explore possibilities at the UN to advance its concerns.

Impact on UN Arrangements for NGOs

The impact of the large presence and contributions of NGOs to the UNCED process and the participation of a constituency new to the UN resulted in an agreement among member states to review the UN arrangements for NGOs.

The ECOSOC Review

In February 1993 the ECOSOC decided to establish the parameters and mandate for "a general review of current arrangements for consultation with NGOs, with a view to updating them" (United Nations 1993). The focus of the review was twofold: to examine and update the provisions of ECOSOC Resolution 1296 (XLIV) that had governed the rules and procedures concerning NGO consultative status with ECOSOC and its subsidiary bodies since 23 May 1968; and to examine the question of the participation of NGOs in "all areas of work of the UN" (United Nations 1968).

The review took place from February 1993 to July 1996, and concluded when ECOSOC adopted, by consensus, resolution 1996/31 and decision 1996/297. ECOSOC resolution 1996/31 included: eligibility of national, regional and sub-regional NGOs for consultative status; including national affiliates of international NGOs; change in the nomenclature concerning categories of consultative status from Category I and II to General and Special consultative status; agreement of a standard procedure for NGO accreditation to and participation in international conferences convened by the UN; and expansion of the role of the ECOSOC Committee on NGOs while streamlining its procedures (United Nations 1996a;b).

Addressing the second aspect of the review, the ECOSOC decision 1996/297 requested the GA to examine at its next session "the question of the participation of NGOs in all areas of work of the UN" (United Nations 1996b), with the caveat that 'all areas' would not be understood to extend beyond what the GA itself was empowered to consider under Articles 10 and 12 of the UN Charter. These articles addressed matters that were dealt with in the Security Council, and the USA, in particular, had been very concerned throughout the review process that any changes in NGO access should not be extended to the Security Council.

One of the most significant outcomes of the ECOSOC review was that it firmly established the eligibility of national, subregional and regional NGOs, including the national affiliates of international NGOs, to accede to consultative status. This development stemmed in part from the experience of the UN conferences, where many national and regional NGOs demonstrated an international perspective and programme of work. Their direct experience of conditions within their country or region gave depth and reality to discussions on global issues.

The other significant outcome of the ECOSOC review was its emphasis on the need for increased participation from NGOs from developing countries and to achieve a better North/South balance in NGO participation. The review recommended the establishment of a Trust Fund to support Southern NGO participation in UN processes.

New Rules and All Areas

The ECOSOC decision 1996/297 was adopted at a time when the GA was examining many aspects related to UN reform. The GA had set up a number of working groups including the Working Group on the Strengthening of the United Nations System and on the UN's financial situation. To take up the ECOSOC recommendation and consider how to expand NGO participation in all areas of the UN's work outside of the ECOSOC, the President of the GA, Ambassador Razali Ismail of Malaysia, established a sub-group of the Working Group on the Strengthening of the United Nations System.

The sub-group began its first round of negotiations on 29 January 1997. Unlike the proceedings during the ECOSOC review of NGO arrangements, NGOs were not permitted to monitor the sub-group's deliberations on the scope of its work. They presented a common statement expressing their view that ECOSOC resolution 1996/31 could form the basis for arrangements in the GA and its main committees, and that arrangements for UN conferences as contained in part VII of the resolution should provide the basis for arrangements in GA special sessions. The Chair of the sub-group, Ambassador Kamal of Pakistan, organized sessions especially to hear their inputs.

As the deliberations started, governments were unable to define the scope of the exercise. The United States and the European Union sought to limit the mandate solely to NGO participation in the GA, its main committees and, as a concession, special sessions of the GA. The Group of 77 developing countries and the Non-Aligned Movement (NAM), working together, insisted that 'all areas of the work of the UN' meant examining all bodies of the UN system, including the Bretton Woods institutions and the Security Council.

After months of negotiation, the sub-group failed to reach agreement on a mandate and was disbanded. Expressing frustration with the impasse, GA President Razali Ismail noted that the question of NGO participation has become a political football in this group, and that plays into the hands of governments who do not want anything to happen with NGOs.

As it became clear that consensus could not be reached on extending NGO status, the GA, under Canada's guidance, adopted a decision that called for a report from the Secretary-General on current arrangements and practices with NGOs throughout the system, as well as legal and financial implications of any change in arrangements. Ross Hynes of Canada, who chaired the GA negotiations on the participation of NGOs, said that he hoped the Secretary-General's report would generate momentum and show that many parts of the UN system were already 'way ahead of the GA' in their collaborative work with NGOs.

The Secretary-General's report, *Arrangements and Practices for the Interaction of Non-governmental Organizations in All Activities of the United Nations System* (A/53/170), was issued on 10 July 1998 for consideration at the 53rd session of the GA. The report also contained proposals toward enhancing participation of NGOs in all areas of the UN system, including: harmonizing existing UN databases on NGOs to facilitate exchange and compilation of information on NGOs across the system; ensuring that NGO sections and liaison offices are appropriately staffed and allocated the necessary logistical and financial resources; and sharing best practices and experiences to promote coherence and efficiency in dealings with civil society. The report cited UN efforts to expand information dissemination through the internet, and requested member states to review funding for the UN's optical disk system (ODS) to allow for wider access by NGOs. It also requested member states to establish a trust fund to facilitate participation of NGOs from developing countries in UN activities. While informative on the work of the UN system with NGOs, particularly at the operational level, many NGOs felt that the report was cautious on the matter of NGO status with the GA, requesting simply that member states consider additional measures such as allowing NGOs with consultative status to occupy seats in the GA during public debates on items in social or economic fields (United Nations 1998).

The same political impasse that had stalemated agreement on the mandate of the working group continued during deliberations of the GA. Consensus could only be found on a decision to request another report from the UN Secretariat, asking member states and others, including NGOs, for their views on the Secretary-General's report.

In preparing the new report, the UN Secretariat circulated a questionnaire to all NGOs in consultative status with ECOSOC and to some networks of NGOs, and it made the questionnaire available electronically. The new report, issued in September 1999, was entitled *Views of Member States, Members of the Specialized Agencies, Observers, Intergovernmental and Non-governmental Organizations From All Regions on the Report of the Secretary-general on Arrangements and Practices for the Interaction of Non-governmental Organizations in All Activities of the United Nations System* (A/54/329) (United Nations 1999).

In their responses many NGOs expressed their support for extending NGO status to the GA. However, a few member states expressed opposition to such a development, emphasizing the intergovernmental nature of the UN. NGOs continue to advocate for official status with the GA. To date the GA has not taken any further action on 'regularizing' NGO status, and any arrangements, regarding for example NGO participation at special sessions of the GA, continue to be on an *ad hoc* basis.

New Practices and Experiments for NGO Participation

As attempts to establish new rules and new areas of access for NGOs were foundering, there has been a proliferation of ad hoc measures and new practices to enable NGOs to participate more fully in the work of the UN. These practices have included the participation of NGO representatives in hearings, panels, regular briefings and dialogues with governments. The GA in its consideration of economic and finance matters in 1996, for example, organized panel presentations with representatives from NGOs, academics and business representatives. The Commission on Social Development has introduced dialogue segments with NGOs. The Commission on the Status of Women, the ECOSOC and other bodies have included NGO representatives on panels.

The Commission on Sustainable Development (CSD) has instituted multi-sector dialogues in its current five-year work programme. In 1998 CSD set up a multi-stakeholder committee to prepare a review of the voluntary initiatives and agreements. In 1999, the dialogue focused on tourism and the agreed conclusions from the dialogue sessions were incorporated in the initial text prepared by the CSD Chair for negotiation by governments. In 2000, the subject of the dialogue was sustainable agriculture and in 2001 the subjects were energy and sustainable development.

In addition to pioneering the concept of multi-sector dialogues, the 19th UN GA Special Session to review and appraise the implementation of Agenda 21 (Rio+5) in June 1997 agreed for the first time in UN history to invite 10 representatives of major groups to address its plenary session. This matter of NGOs addressing the plenary of a GA session became a lightning rod in the debate concerning NGO participation in the GA and was seen by some governments as symbolic of increasing NGO power.

As there are no regular rules governing the participation of NGOs in the GA and its special sessions, sometimes lengthy negotiations have had to take place to address the participation of NGO representatives at a special session undertaking a five-year review of a major conference. Resolutions have been adopted inviting NGOs to address the plenary for the following special sessions held to review the implementation of the Programmes of Action of: the International Conference on Population and Development (ICPD+5) in 1999; the Global Conference on Small Island Developing States (SIDS+5) in 1999; the Fourth World Conference on Women (Beijing+5) in 2000; the World Summit for Social Development (WSSD+5) in 2000; and the 2nd UN Conference on Human Settlements (Habitat II+5) in 2001.

Intergovernmental deliberations have been less contentious regarding NGO participation in major UN conferences as these are not bodies of the GA and do not seem to be challenging its authority. It is accepted that NGOs will be accredited to and can address UN conferences; their access to informal meetings has varied enormously. On a few occasions NGOs have had access to informal negotiating sessions, and rarely during informal meetings; and always at the discretion of the chair, NGOs were permitted to comment upon the proceedings.

Recent UN conferences have added to negotiating meetings sessions addressing the themes of the conference and have experimented with hearings and roundtables. In November 2000, the UN held two days of civil society hearings as a contribution to preparations for the Financing for Development Conference, scheduled for March 2002 in Monterrey, Mexico.

The UN GA Special Session on HIV/AIDS, in June 2001, held four roundtables presided over by government ministers. These roundtables included NGO representatives among a limited number of high-level participants.

In addition to the development of new practices for NGO interaction with member states, most agencies and bodies of the UN system have reviewed their relations with civil society organizations in recent years. The establishment of a focal point for NGOs and civil society matters in the Office of the Secretary-General has given added authority and priority to the question of the UN's relations with NGOs.

New forms of governance have been established that involve the participation of NGOs. The governing body of the Joint UN Programme on HIV/AIDS (UNAIDS) has five seats for NGOs and the Inter-Agency Standing Committee on Humanitarian Affairs has three places for NGOs.

In 2000, ECOSOC established, as a subsidiary body, a Permanent Forum for Indigenous Issues that will consist of 16 representatives, of whom eight will be from indigenous groups and organizations.

Civil Society and Global Governance

Developments concerning UN-NGO relations during the 1990s have not taken place in a vacuum, but in the broader context of shifting international political scenery at the end of the Cold War. The climate became more favourable for issues of people-centred development. The priorities of the international community included new definitions of security that included achieving sustainable development and focusing on non-military approaches to problem-solving and decision-making.

The presence and participation of NGOs not only provided technical input and expertise on the issues under consideration; it increased public awareness and linked the national deliberations to the positions taken by governments at the international level. NGO advocacy brought transparency and accountability to the positions of governments.

This contribution to democracy at the international level was recognized and praised by Secretary-General Boutros Boutros-Ghali. He recognized the political changes that their participation signified. Addressing NGOs at a UN conference on 19 September 1994, he said: "Non-governmental organizations are a basic form of popular participation in the present-day world. Their participation in international organizations is, in a way, a guarantee of the political legitimacy of those international organizations" (Boutros-Ghali 1994).

He went on to comment on the impact this has had on UN diplomacy: "The United Nations was considered to be a forum for sovereign States alone. Within the space of a few short years, this attitude has changed. NGOs are now considered full participants in international life" (Boutros-Ghali 1994).

In 1995, the year of the fiftieth anniversary of the UN, the Commission on Global Governance contributed a report to its discussion on global reform. The report, *Our Global Neighbourhood*, addressed ways of improving the world's governance and advocating giving civil society a greater voice in governance. It recommended the establishment of an annual civil society forum to contribute to the deliberations of the UN GA (Commission on Global Governance 1995).

In July 1997, Secretary-General Kofi Annan presented his report on *Renewing the United Nations: A Programme for Reform*, in which he acknowledged the emergence of a global civil society and its essential role: "a vibrant civil society is critical to processes of democratisation and empowerment" (United Nations 1997).

Kofi Annan has frequently addressed the valuable role of NGOs and their significance in the changing political dynamic. At a press conference on 27 June 2001 during the UN GA Special Session on HIV/AIDS, he praised the commitment of HIV/AIDS activists:

> I am ... even more impressed by the strong participation of non-governmental activists – within national delegations, at a wide range of parallel events, in the Round Tables, and as observers in the plenary sessions. You can feel their presence and you feel the presence of these activists everywhere, and they really have transformed the atmosphere of the building – as they do at all the best United Nations events. I am more than ever convinced that such partnerships are essential to our success in the new century. Of course they bring problems and controversy with them, but so does every new idea (Annan 2001).

As an active civil society is seen as an essential component to tackle the democratic deficit in international decision-making, NGOs have historically believed that a strengthened UN will also contribute to international democracy. Some NGOs have seen the UN as vital in the strengthening of international law and respect for human rights. For other NGOs critical of the governance and policies of the Bretton Woods institutions, the UN was seen as a positive alternative.

In the era of globalization, however, some NGOs now believe that there is a shift in the role that the UN is playing in economic matters – a shift from challenger to convenor. Compared with the UN's previous work, for example on structural adjustment (*Adjustment with a Human Face*, the Economic Commission for Africa's (ECA) alternative approach to structural adjustment), some NGOs and social movements see the UN as pursuing a more pragmatic approach. This has included energetic attempts to co-ordinate programmes with the Bretton Woods institutions and the donor governments of the OECD, and to establish partnerships with the private sector, including the Secretary-General's initiative on the Global Compact.

The Millennium Summit, which took place at UN headquarters in September 2000, was heralded as a milestone by member states and UN agencies; it is the basis for their follow-up and implementation. However, it had very little NGO input. The Millennium NGO Forum organized by NGOs a few months before the Summit attracted little attention from the NGO policy activists from the UN conferences of the 1990s or from the member states at the Summit.

In September 2002, the UN will convene the World Summit for Sustainable Development in Johannesburg, South Africa. In setting up the high-level meeting 10 years after UNCED, the UN Secretariat recommended the inclusion of a number of stakeholder dialogues during the preparatory committees and at the Summit itself. This recommendation came before member states for decision in a climate of detailed examination of arrangements for NGOs and protracted and sometimes hostile positions from some large states. These arrangements were adopted surprisingly quickly by all member states.

The UN Conference on Environment and Development in Rio de Janeiro in 1992 ushered in a decade of new and innovative relations between the UN and NGOs that have transformed the international policy-setting arena. These developments have not been translated into new rules for NGO participation and, at the beginning of the new century, there is some back-tracking on behalf of some member states and some hesitation on the part of social movements about the role of the UN in the era of globalization. The World Summit for Sustainable Development will be the occasion to move to the next stage of relations between the UN and civil society.

Annex: Rights and Responsibilities of NGOs' Relationships with ECOSOC and DPI

Economic and Social Council

The following are the formal rights and arrangements for the participation of NGOs in consultative and roster status with ECOSOC and its subsidiary bodies.

- The provisional agenda of the Economic and Social Council shall be communicated to organizations in general, special and roster status.

- NGOs with general status have the right to place items on the agenda of ECOSOC and its subsidiary bodies.
- Organizations with general and special status may designate authorized representatives to sit as observers at public meetings of ECOSOC and its subsidiary bodies. Those on the roster may have representatives present at such meetings concerned with matters within their field of competence.
- Brief written statements can be submitted by organizations in general and special status and can be published as UN documents and circulated to members of the council or subsidiary body. These statements will be circulated by the Secretary-General in the relevant UN working languages and also maybe translated into any of the official languages of the UN upon request by a member government. NGOs on the roster may be invited to submit written statements.
- The ECOSOC Committee on NGOs shall make recommendations to ECOSOC concerning which NGOs in general status make an oral presentation during the session; NGOs in special status may also address ECOSOC, provided there is no ECOSOC subsidiary body with jurisdiction in a major field of interest to the council and to an organization in special status. No provision is made for NGOs on the roster to address ECOSOC.
- Commissions and other subsidiary organs of ECOSOC may consult with NGOs in general and special status; such consultations may be arranged on the request of the NGO. Organizations on the roster may also be heard by the commissions or subsidiary organs on the recommendation of the UN Secretary-General and at the request of the commission or other subsidiary organ.
- A commission of ECOSOC may recommend that an NGO with special competence in a particular field undertake studies or investigations or prepare papers for the commission.
- NGOs shall be able to consult with officers of the appropriate sections of the Secretariat on matters of mutual interest or concern. Such consultations shall be upon request of the NGO or the Secretary-General.
- The Secretary-General may request organizations in general, special and roster status to carry out studies or prepare papers.
- The Secretary-General is authorized to offer facilities to NGOs in consultative relationship, including:
    - prompt and efficient distribution of documents of ECOSOC and its subsidiary bodies as the Secretary-General considers appropriate;
    - access to UN press documentation services;
    - arrangement of informal discussions on matters of special interest to groups or organizations;
    - use of UN libraries;
    - provision of accommodation for conferences or smaller meetings of consultative organizations on the work of ECOSOC; and
    - appropriate seating arrangements and facilities for obtaining documents during public meetings of the General Assembly that deal with matters in the economic, social and related fields.

NGOs in consultative status with ECOSOC must report every four years on their activities. The reports are submitted to the committee on NGOs, which can revoke an organization's consultative status if:

- it fails to submit reports;
- it "abuses its status by engaging in a pattern of acts contrary to the principles of the Charter of the United Nations including unsubstantiated or politically motivated acts against Member States";
- "there exists substantiated evidence of influence from proceeds resulting from international recognized criminal activities such as the illicit drugs trade, money laundering or the illegal arms trade"; and
- within the preceding three years, an organization has not made a positive or effective contribution to the work of the UN, in particular ECOSOC and its subsidiary bodies.

Department of Public Information

Association with the department can be initiated with a written request to the NGO Section of DPI. The request should be accompanied by documentary evidence attesting that the applying organization meets the criteria indicated above. A profile of the organization, based on the information received, is submitted to the senior Departmental Committee on Non-Governmental Organizations for review at its annual session.

The DPI/NGO Section provides associated NGOs with a number of services. For example the section organizes, in collaboration with the NGO/DPI Executive Committee (an 18-member executive committee of associated NGOs that maintains liaison for the NGOs with DPI), the Annual DPI/NGO Conference, the premiere NGO-related event at headquarters each September; organizes weekly briefings on UN-related issues; conducts an annual orientation programme for newly accredited NGO representatives; organizes quarterly communications workshops for NGOs; processes NGO applications for associative status with DPI; and publishes the *Directory of NGOs Associated with DPI*. The section maintains a website hosted on the UN homepage (www.un.org/MoreInfo/ngolink/dpingo.htm), and the NGO Resource Centre offers access to current UN documents, press releases as well as DPI and UN system publications; a video lending library with a collection of UN system videos; monthly mailings of UN information materials to associated NGOs, and it processes UN passes for NGO representatives.

NGOs that enjoy consultative status with the Economic and Social Council are granted association with the department, upon written request and demonstration of an active information programme, without going through the review process mentioned above.

References

Note on internet addresses (URLs): Websites tend to appear, change or disappear, often without warning. Addresses cited in this bibliography were accurate and active at the time of writing (January 2002) unless otherwise noted.

Annan, Kofi (2001), *Opening Remarks at Press Conference*, (UN General Assembly Special Session on HIV/AIDS) UN, New York, 27 June.
Boutros-Ghali, Boutros (1994), *Speech to the DPI Annual Conference*, UN, New York, 19 September.
Commission on Global Governance (1995), *Our Global Neighbourhood: The Report of the Commission on Global Governance*, Oxford University Press, Oxford.
United Nations. Department of Public Information (1989), *Charter of the United Nations and Statute of the International Court of Justice*, UN, New York, DPI/511 www.un.org/Overview/Charter/chapte10.html
United Nations. Economic and Social Council (1968), *Arrangements for Consultations with Non-governmental Organizations*, UN, New York, 27 May, E/RES/1296 (XLIV).
United Nations. Economic and Social Council (1993), *Review of the Arrangements for Consultation with Non-governmental Organizations*, UN, New York, 12 February E/1993/214.
United Nations. Economic and Social Council (1996a), *Consultative Relations between the United Nations and Non-governmental Organizations*, UN, New York, 25 July, E/RES/1996/31 www.hri.ca/uninfo/resolutn/res31.shtml
United Nations. Economic and Social Council (1996b), *Non-governmental Organizations*, UN, New York, 25 July, E/DEC/1996/297.
United Nations. General Assembly (1946), *Establishment of the Department of Public Information of the Secretariat*, UN, New York, 13 February, A/RES/13 (I).
United Nations. Secretary-General (1997), *Renewing the United Nations: A Programme for Reform*, UN, New York, 14 July, A/51/950.
United Nations. Secretary-General (1998), *Arrangements and Practices for the Interaction of Non-governmental Organizations in All Activities of the United Nations System*, UN, New York, 10 July, A/53/170.
United Nations. Secretary-General (1999), *Views of Member States, Members of the Specialized Agencies, Observers, Intergovernmental and Non-governmental Organizations from All Regions on the Report of the Secretary-General on Arrangements and Practices for the Interaction of Non-governmental Organizations in All Activities of the United Nations System*, UN, New York, 8 September, A/54/329.
United Nations. Sustainable Development (1992), 'Agenda 21: Programme of Action for Sustainable Development, Rio Declaration on Environment and Development, Statement of Forest Principles : the Final Text of Agreements Negotiated by Governments at the United Nations Conference on Environment and Development (UNCED)', Rio de Janeiro, 3-14 June, ST/DPI/1344,
www.un.org/esa/sustdev/agenda21text.htm

Chapter 10

Thoughts on Religious NGOs at the UN: A Component of Global Civil Society

Benjamin Rivlin[*]

The general focus of this volume is "Civil Society in the Information Age". Religious Nongovernmental Organizations (NGOs) are an important part of civil society. This essay concerns itself with dual questions of the role of religious NGOs in global civil society and how the "information age" has impacted on religion.

The Context: Global Civil Society

During its more than half-century of existence, the United Nations (UN) has gone through various phases: the first, focused on peace, peacekeeping and disarmament issues, within the context of the Cold War; the second, still within the Cold War context, marked by the expansion of the UN membership as a result of decolonization, changing its nature from a North-dominated organization to one with a strong role for the peoples of the South; the third, the ascendance of social and economic issues, such as economic and human development manifested in placing 'human security' on a par with 'the maintenance of international peace' as the *raison d'être* of the UN system and holding a series of multilateral global conferences on specific social issues, for example population, the environment, the status of women, social development and human rights. This last phase of quasi-parliamentary diplomatic gatherings emerged simultaneously with the electronic age revolution that is marked by ease of physical communications and computer networking. The presence of large numbers of knowledgeable NGOs, including religious groupings, at the world conferences arose not only from cheap and rapid air travel but also from the extensive use of e-mail and the World Wide Web.

NGOs can be said to have become more visible and active participants in UN affairs during this phase when, in the words of the Security Council Summit of January 1992, "non-military sources of instability in the economic, social,

---

[*] Author's note: I am grateful to the many religious NGO representatives and UN Secretariat members who took the time to talk with me about the subject of this essay. I also owe thanks to Stephanie Sapiie for her research assistance and to Paul D. Numrich, Abraham Bargman, Leon Gordenker, Bernard E. Brown, Nancy Okada and this volume's editor, Peter I. Hajnal, for their comments and suggestions on earlier versions of this essay. Any errors in fact or interpretation are purely my own.

156 *Civil Society in the Information Age*

humanitarian and ecological fields" were declared as "threats to peace and security" (UN Security Council 1992). A shift in the UN agenda was evident. Social and economic issues gained in prominence. The Rio Conference on Environment and Development (1992) set the stage for NGOs to assume an unprecedented public role in shaping the outcome of the meetings. This was followed by the conferences on Human Rights (Vienna, 1993), Population (Cairo, 1994), Social Development (Copenhagen, 1995), Status of Women (Beijing, 1995), and Human Settlements/Habitat II (Istanbul, 1996). All of these were attended by thousands of accredited NGO representatives who influenced the outcome of these conferences. In addition, NGOs were instrumental in the adoption of the Mine Ban Treaty (Ottawa, 1997), the Protocol to the UN Framework on Climate Change (Kyoto, 1997) and the Statute of the International Criminal Court (Rome, 1998).

Gradually emerging from these meetings was an innovation in international life – a 'global civil society', alternatively called 'transnational civil society' and commonly referred to as 'international civil society'. The latter term, international civil society, is a misnomer because it implies interactions among states whereas the innovative activities undertaken in civil society are by non-state actors.[1] This new phenomenon is part of the universe of civil society made up of thousands upon thousands of non-governmental actors, mostly NGO advocacy groups, operating within countries throughout the world and focusing essentially on domestic public policy issues. Drawing a line between domestic civil society and international, global or transnational civil society is very tricky. Such issues as human rights, development, population, and global warming are both domestic and global political issues. Depending on the issue and the occasion, local NGOs work with international NGOS to form a coalition of forces seeking to influence both national and international public policy. Thus, an international civil society network specific to the subject at hand arises, e.g. on landmines. The UN and particularly the world conferences it has organized provide the venues in which representatives of civil society are active, helping to set agendas and framing the debate. An empirical analysis of the participation and effectiveness of NGOs in three world conferences notes "it is as yet unclear whether the increase in the number of NGOs with shared transnational goals can be equated with an emerging global civil society" and concludes that "[t]here is no denying that NGOs are on the world stage to stay. It is too soon, however, to declare that a global civil society has definitively emerged" (Clark 1998).

Ad-hoc coalitions of domestic NGOs and international NGOs, often involving church-based organizations, form the global, transnational or international civil society. The major concerns of international civil society are the impact of globalization, the implementation of the international human rights covenants, the establishment of an International Criminal Court, control of armaments including the ban of landmines, the environment, the shift from inter-state to intra-state conflicts, poverty and human development. The prominence and success of 'global civil society' in shaping the international agenda has led to talk of a 'new diplomacy' that fills the gaps left by the weakening of sovereignty under the pressures coming from the consequences of globalization and interdependence[2] (Brown 2001). The rising voices and increasingly effective performance of NGOs were challenging the monopoly of governments and IGOs in determining international public policy. Former Secretary-General Boutros Boutros-Ghali recognized this propensity when he wrote in *An Agenda for Peace*, "peace in the largest sense cannot be accomplished by the UN system or by Governments alone. Non-governmental organizations, academic institutions, parliamentarians, business and professional communities, the media and the public at large must be involved" (UN Secretariat 1992, para 84). Less than a decade later, the new Secretary-General Kofi Annan declared in his *Report to the Millennium Summit*, "global affairs are no longer the exclusive province of foreign ministries, nor are states the sole source of solutions for our small planet's many problems ... The more complex the problem at hand – whether negotiating on landmines, setting limits to emissions that contribute to global warming, or creating an International Criminal Court – the more likely we are to find non-governmental organizations, private sector institutions and multilateral agencies working with sovereign states to find consensus solutions" (UN General Assembly 2000b, para 315). Religious organizations, led by those active at the UN, are part of the amalgam that constitutes global civil society often joining with their secular counterparts in intense lobbying, presenting their particular view on issues of interest to them.[3]

Related to the 'new diplomacy' is the emergence of the concept of 'multi-track diplomacy' or 'second-track diplomacy' as a response to the rise of various forms of intra-state violence which challenge the conventional means of conflict resolution by states and IGOs which "seem outdated and powerless" (Van Tongeren 1998). Multi-track diplomacy involves, besides governments and IGOs, professional organizations, business groups, churches, the media, private citizens, including eminent persons, training and educational institutes, activists and private funding agencies. These non-official actors, particularly NGOs and religious organizations, often stand a better chance of breaking logjams on the local level than do official agencies because of their familiarity with the local situation and grassroots movements. Notable examples include the successful efforts of the Italian-based Catholic lay Community of Sant'Egidio in bringing Mozambique's warring parties together and the Moravian church and Protestant leaders facilitating negotiations in Nicaragua in 1988 (Van Tongeren 1998).

Religion and the UN Agenda

Religion is one of the major social forces in the world. While by no means monolithic or uniform, it is ubiquitous. A common theme, running through a recent exploration of religion in international relations in the new millennium by more than a dozen scholars, is that we are witnessing a resurgence and an increasing visibility of religion on all levels of social activity, including world affairs.[3] The global revival of religion is attributable to a disillusionment with modernity – the shortcomings of science and rationalism to live up to the promises of a good life – among millions who find in religion and spirituality answers to their quest for meaningful identity and a sense of empowerment that is denied to them by their marginalized existence. This is no less true in the most advanced industrialized societies than in the poorest parts of the world. Clearly, religion is one of the major components of all societies, often an essential unifying force but, at times, also divisive. The global resurgence of religion is manifested by "the growing saliency of religion in the politics of countries throughout the world".[4]

Religious adherents and their traditions make a valuable contribution to social order, and at times disorder and tension, which they do in their singular way through distinctive rites, symbols, myths and beliefs. This has led one student of religion to observe that a characteristic of religion in our contemporary world is "The Persistence of Religious Plurality" (Brasher 2001, 11) or as another scholar pointed out the "twentieth century, or perhaps its last half, and the first half of the twenty-first, might possibly be named the Multi-religious Century or Era" (Jack 1993, 369). Most religions aim at promoting eternal truths to provide answers to humanity's longing to understand the universe and the individual's place in it. Since this is achieved through the agency of mere mortals, religious diversity ensues, and since some religions claim to have a monopoly on truth, the stage is set for perpetual theological competition among some religions, particularly those with strong proselytizing inclinations. Theological and sectarian differences have led throughout history to an array of ethnic identity contestations and turf wars.

Our contemporary world is blessed, or perhaps cursed, with a plethora of ethno-religious conflicts and tensions. A partial listing includes: the Arab-Israeli struggle over Palestine, the Kashmir dispute between India and Pakistan, the Catholic-Protestant discord in Northern Ireland, the clash within a number of Islamic states over fundamentalism, the Hindu-Muslim tension within India, the ill-will between Roman Catholics and Russian Orthodox churches, civil war in the Sudan between the Muslim north and the mainly Christian/animist south, the Muslim-Christian conflict in the Philippines, the mutual slaughter of Muslims and Christians in Indonesia, the confessional political struggle within Lebanon, the escalating violence in Nigeria between Muslims and Christians, the rift within Israel between secular and ultra-orthodox Jews, Buddhist and Muslim dissidence in China, religious tensions in parts of the former Soviet Union, i.e. Armenia-Azerbaijan over Nagorno-Karabach and Muslim rebellion in Chechnya and most recently the *jihad* of Osama bin Laden.

Despite the prevalence of religious pluralism and interreligious tensions, a common ethical core exists in all or nearly all religions, i.e. the pursuit of human compassion, peace, justice and social harmony. Together they constitute a universal set of standards for moral conduct. On the surface, there is a categorical affinity between these universal principles and the ideals of the UN as enunciated in the UN Charter, most notably in its Preamble, "We the Peoples". Practically all substantive issues on the agenda of the UN – the maintenance of peace, conflict resolution, disarmament, development, human rights and other social issues – fall within the purview of one or another of the universal religious tenets. Below the surface, however, there are basic disagreements among most religions, even within particular religions, over the meaning and applicability of some or all of the basic tenets of the UN ideals: human rights, democracy, pluralism, religious and ethnic tolerance, peacekeeping, and free speech. The differences, which are basically ideological, are reflected in the positions taken by states and religious NGOs on particular issues, such as women's rights.

Given the affinity between UN ideals and some universal religious ethics, it is not surprising that even before the creation of the UN, religious groups provided part of the input into the drive to establish a peaceful and just post-World War II order. Constituent churches of the World Council of Churches (WCC), which was in the process of formation towards the end of World War II, played an active role in this effort, pressing for the inclusion of the "We the peoples of the UN" preamble to the Charter as well as provisions on human rights and consultation with nongovernmental organizations (World Council of Churches 1999, 31). Parallel to the very active lay Commission to Study the Organization of Peace was the Commission on a Just and Durable Peace sponsored by the equally active Federal (National) Council of Churches. It was headed by John Foster Dulles, then an elder of the Presbyterian Church who was to become an adviser to the US delegation at the 1945 UN founding San Francisco Conference. Voices from several religious organizations were among the 42 American consultative citizens' organizations who attended this conference at the invitation of the US delegation. Foremost among the religious consultants, championing the need to include social and human rights values in the Charter as it was being drafted, were Dr. O. Frederick Nolde, representing the Federal Council of Churches and Judge Joseph Proskauer and Jacob Blaustein of the American Jewish Committee (Korey 1998, 32-34).

The UN Charter that was drafted in San Francisco in 1945 was clearly in the tradition of liberal-progressive thinking that harkened back to the nineteenth-century claim of the primacy of science over religion, to Woodrow Wilson's dream of an organized democratic world, Franklin D. Roosevelt's "Four Freedoms", the Atlantic Charter and Wendel Willkie's *One World*. The UN Charter's inclusion of major organs devoted to social and economic progress and the welfare of colonial peoples was in direct line with the thinking of Roosevelt's New Deal. However, Winston Churchill's metaphor for the UN as "a true temple of peace in which the shields of many nations can be hung, not merely a cockpit in a Tower of Babel" (Churchill 1946) could be taken as a hint of a symbiosis between religion and the world organization. While the UN is clearly in the secular tradition of the separation of church and state, the high ideals proclaimed in it are traceable to religious as well as to secular moral principles.

Within the UN Charter, religion is included in Articles 1 and 55 as one of the "human rights and fundamental freedoms". That the UN headquarters does not have a chapel but rather a "meditation room" bespeaks the UN's religious neutrality and the recognition of the difference between "faith" and "church". Given the fact that the organization is made up of member-states with differing and hostile religious orientations ranging from those with official state religions to those espousing atheism, this is not surprising. In the words of Dag Hammarskjöld, "The UN stands outside – necessarily outside – all confessions. But it is nevertheless an instrument of faith. As such, it is inspired by what unites not by what divides the great religions of the world".[5] However, a visible presence of religion was established across the street from the UN headquarters on First

Avenue when, in 1963, the United Methodist Church opened the Church Center for the United Nations at 777 United Nations Plaza. The 11-storey building, popularly referred to as "777", houses, in addition to a chapel, offices of numerous religious NGOs.

The Universal Declaration of Human Rights and the ensuing International Covenants reiterate the Charter provisions on freedom of thought, conscience and religion. Religious NGOs pressed for a more specific affirmation of religious freedom. In 1981, after nearly 20 years of study and debate in the Commission on Human Rights, the General Assembly adopted a *Declaration on the Elimination of all Forms of Intolerance and of Discrimination Based on Religion or Belief*[6] (UN) General Assembly 1981). The Declaration proclaims that everyone shall have the right to freedom of thought, conscience and religion, that no one shall be subject to coercion that would impair that freedom, or to any discrimination on the grounds of religious or other beliefs. It also specifies the right of parents to organize family life in accordance with their religion, and the right of children to have access to religious education in accordance with their parents' wishes. Freedom of religion encompasses the freedom to worship or assemble, to establish charitable institutions, to make, acquire and use ritual articles, to write, publish and disseminate religious publications, to teach a religion or belief, to solicit financial contributions, to designate religious leaders, to observe holidays and ceremonies and to communicate with others on religious matters at the national and international levels. The story of the adoption of this declaration provides insight into understanding the difficulties inherent in forging a common approach to religious freedom at the UN. Before this declaration could be adopted, there were substantive objections coming from religious Islamic states on the right to change one's religion, opposition from some Soviet Bloc states, and the failure of "most states from Africa, Asia and Latin America to show interest in the issue" since "they had different priorities, from the eradication of apartheid to economic and social development" (Jack 1993, 269).

Twenty years after the adoption of this declaration, the UN General Assembly adopted a second major pronouncement on religion, a resolution entitled *Protection of Religious Sites* (UN General Assembly 2001b). The origins of this resolution were a decade-long effort to promote peace and religious conciliation in the Balkans by the Appeal of Conscience Foundation, a New York-based ecumenical coalition working on behalf of religious freedom and human rights throughout the world.[7] In December 2000, it issued "A Call to Stop Desecration of Holy Sites" which reiterated its earlier declarations calling "for an end to the confiscation, desecration and destruction of houses of worship and of holy and sacred places of whatever religion". The call was signed by participating Catholic, Greek Orthodox, Serbian Orthodox, Armenian, Anglican/Episcopalian, Muslim and Jewish religious leaders. The General Assembly resolution was adopted unanimously in the wake of ransacked mosques and churches in the Balkans and the destruction of giant Buddhas in Afghanistan by the Taliban government. It also came within the context of the "UN Year [2001] of Dialogue Among Civilizations" which is concerned with the "collective heritage of mankind" that provides "a source of inspiration and progress for humanity at large", of which religious values are a significant component. But religion *per se* is not mentioned in the resolutions regarding this dialogue; only the preamble to one resolution makes reference to "diversity of belief"[8] (UN General Assembly 2001c).

The UN Design for International NGOs and the Role of Religious NGOs Within It

The UN Organization established by the Charter is an intergovernmental organization (IGO) of member states that operates within the framework of long-established diplomatic modalities. Politics in the UN, as practised at its inception and in its early years, was essentially manoeuvring among its member states, particularly among its most powerful – the five permanent members of the Security Council. Although, "the Charter avoided granting non-governmental organizations [NGOs] formal status ... Article 71, applied amidst initial controversy ... offered a narrow formal opening in the wall of governmental representation" in enabling the Economic and Social Council (ECOSOC) to "make suitable arrangements for consultation with non-governmental organizations which are concerned with matters within its competence"[9] (Gordenker 1995; 127). A political space was thus provided for NGOs at the UN which was slowly entered. The world of international NGOs that emerged was tremendously complex, lacking a hierarchical structure, made up of a disparate group of essentially voluntary social associations, often grassroots and reflecting a diversity of interests and foci.[10] In the case of religious NGOs, they represent some traditional religions with a long history of concern for social justice and peace as well as newer creeds, generally offshoots of the older established religions.

It is interesting to note that despite the fact that religion plays such a significant role in society, a search of the literature on international NGOs fails to reveal many references to religious entities. Religion and the UN is a vast and complicated subject which can receive only a rudimentary analysis within the constraints of this chapter. A comprehensive treatment of the subject is in the process of being prepared at the Park Ridge Center for the Study of Health, Faith, and Ethics as part of the Religion Counts initiative (Park Ridge Center 2002).

Consultative status with ECOSOC was "generally accorded to those non-governmental organizations which are not in principle opposed to the objectives of the United Nations" (Commission to Study the Organization of Peace 1957, 97). At the outset in 1947, ECOSOC admitted seven organizations to Category I, 33 to Category II and 3 to Category III.[11] By 1985, 852 organizations had been granted consultative status by ECOSOC, 34 in Category I, 268 in Category II and 450 in Category III and by 1999 there were 111 organizations in General Consultative Status (formerly called Category I), 918 in Special Consultative Status (formerly Category II) and 672 on the Roster (formerly Category III). Still another category of NGOs is that of observer status with the UN Department of Public Information (DPI). In 2001, the number of NGOs accredited to the UN numbered in the thousands. Of these, under 10 per cent, some 150, are religious NGOs that have formal affiliation with the UN. Not all religious nongovernmental bodies concerned with UN affairs have sought formal consultative status. A number of purposeful generic nongovernmental organizations exist, actively engaged with UN issues but outside the framework of ECOSOC or DPI. The aforementioned Appeal of Conscience Foundation is an example of a generic NGO.

Activities of Religious NGOs

Broadly speaking, religious or church-based NGOs (formal or generic), engage in three types of activities: 1) interfaith coalition building with an ecumenical commitment which seeks to further mutual understanding among religions and to foster common positions in support of the UN, particularly in the promotion of peace and the betterment of the human condition; 2) denominational particularistic concerns focused on serving their institutional needs and that of their congregants by exploring the relationship (good or bad) between the UN and their world view as it affects their congregants; 3) humanitarian relief service in many distressed regions of the world. The agendas and activities of religious NGOs vary. It is far beyond the scope of this essay to delve into the nuanced differences found among religious NGOs or to examine their individual activities in detail.

During the UN's first 40 years, religious NGOs played a limited role in setting policies or in their execution. This was also true of their more numerous secular counterparts in the NGO community except for relief and development organizations which have intimate connections with the United Nations High Commissioner for Refugees (UNHCR), the World Food Programme (WFP) and the United Nations Development Programme (UNDP). At the outset, after the mechanism of NGOs was established by ECOSOC, the early religious NGOs that appeared on the scene were largely those that shared the liberal-progressive orientation of the UN Charter. This was true of the interfaith coalitions, such as the World Conference on Religion and Peace as well as the early denominational NGOs who saw in the UN an organization committed to their own values of peaceful reconciliation among nations, a just world order, and the promotion of human welfare. They identified with the UN and sought accreditation as NGOs with consultative status. It should be stressed that a theological rationale draws religions to the UN since peace is a core belief of most religions.

At the outset, primarily American religious bodies, with international ties and experience, became active supporters and promoters of the world organization. Strongest interest in the UN came from the non-evangelical Protestants, some Catholic groups, and by most Jewish bodies, until the adoption in the General Assembly of the "Zionism as Racism" resolution. From less than a dozen at the outset, the number of religious NGOs having consultative status with ECOSOC and DPI grew to approximately 150 by 2001. In addition to so-called "peace churches", e.g. the Mennonites and Quakers, who have pacifism as part of their creed, nearly every Christian denomination and other world religions, as well as numerous interfaith groups comprise the community of religious NGOs. As do their secular counterparts, the religious NGOs, in acceding to consultative status, "undertake to support the work of the UN and to promote knowledge of its principles and activities, in accordance with its own aims and purposes and the nature and scope of its competence and activities" (UN Economic and Social Council 1996). Over the years, most religious NGOs have fulfilled this commitment by broadly supporting UN peace operations and its social and economic development initiatives.

The broadest agenda is perhaps that of the World Conference on Religion and Peace (WCRP) whose prime mission "based on the principle of profound respect for religious differences ... is solely dedicated to *multireligious* cooperation for peace" and whose approach to the UN is total or holisitic. Preliminary discussions in the 1960s among a broad spectrum of religious leaders in the United States led to establishing an inter-religious organization and taking it to other parts of the world. Meetings were held in Geneva, Rome, Tokyo, Istanbul, New Delhi, Dedham and Kyoto between 1967 and 1970. At the Kyoto Assembly, the WCRP was formed on a truly inter-religious basis. Participating were Christian, Buddhist, Hindu, Shintoist, Muslim, Jewish, Bahá'í, Zoroastrian, Sikh, Jainist, and Confucian delegates. From its outset, the WCRP operated on the principle of the holistic approach to the promotion of peace plus three cautions: no theology, no proselytizing and no syncretism.[12]

Religious NGOs, supportive of the idealistic goals of the UN, cannot concern themselves with all UN activities. The range of UN activities is so vast that it is beyond the resources of any one religious NGO to cover all of them. Rather, each tries to give priority to those issues in which it has a special interest and expertise and where it feels it can make a contribution to the UN and strengthen its own programme.[13] An examination of mission statements issued by several religious NGOs reveals a common set of objectives for the activities of a church-related office in the UN setting: 1) to bear witness – share concern and accountability for world peace and justice; 2) to advocate the positions of the church on issues of international significance on the UN agenda; 3) to educate church members about the UN and global issues through seminars, publications, speaking engagements, etc. and to assist them in linking with UN agencies; 4) to monitor and study issues of concern to the church, such as the eradication of poverty, human rights, conflict and war; 5) to network and co-operate with UN agencies, other NGOs, and interfaith groups on areas of common concern.[14] In addition, many religious NGOs are active in providing important humanitarian assistance and relief in various troubled areas of the world in keeping with their theological calling to provide succor to the poor and disadvantaged.

The activities of religious NGOs in the field, such as local training, conflict prevention, promoting non-violence, mediation and peace-building through development, are beyond the scope of this chapter. A broad overview of these activities was the subject of a day-long workshop on 20 June 2001 held at the United States Institute of Peace in Washington, DC (Smock 2001).

A significant number of religious NGOs have felt a need to reach out to fellow religious NGO's by establishing in 1972 the Committee of Religious NGOs at the United Nations (CRNGO) "to serve as a forum to inform and educate our constituencies about the global challenges of our time, and the constructive role the UN can play in addressing those issues [and] as a forum for exchanging and promoting shared religious and ethical values in the deliberations of the world organization" (Committee of Religious NGOs 2000). CRNGO holds monthly meetings at the Church Center for the UN at which it promotes networking for religious NGOs and sponsors speakers and panel discussions on such topics as "Are Human Rights Really Universal?", "Women's Rights are Human Rights", "The Situation in Sierra Leone" and "Challenges and Hopes for Freedom and Religion and Belief in the New Millennium", "Human Rights From a Religious Perspective" and "The Internet's Impact on Globalization and Values". Interestingly, these meetings of religious NGOs open, not with a prayer, but a "meditation gong". Some 60 religious NGOs from various branches of Christianity, Judaism, and Asian religions are members of the committee. Membership in this committee is voluntary and its membership list does not include a number of prominent Christian groups nor any Muslim NGO.

Since its inception CRNGO has had thirteen presidents coming from diverse groups such as the World Conference on Religion and Peace, Unitarian Universalist Association, Pax Christi International, World Union for Progressive Judaism, Evangelical Covenant Church, Baptist World Alliance, and Won Buddhism International. The current president comes from the Bahá'í International Community. The Committee publishes a *Survey of Activities of Religious NGOs at the United Nations* which is based on mission statements supplied voluntarily by the member organizations. An examination of the mission statements of the CRNGOs as reported in the latest survey reveals a strong tendency towards interfaith dialogue, plus, in order of frequency, the following sets of purposes: 1) social, educational, agricultural and humanitarian assistance; 2) peace and justice; 3) furthering the goals of the UN; and 4) information and support services.[15] While this survey does not constitute a full account of the activities of NGOs, since it reports on less than one third of the NGOs with consultative status, it is indicative of the perspectives of most religious NGOs that do not restrict themselves to a single issue. A stark exception is presented by the Catholic Family and Human Rights Institute (CFHRI), an NGO with an office on UN Plaza but without consultative status which primarily focuses its activities on a single issue – abortion.

The past decade, with the convening of the series of UN-sponsored conferences on social issues and the growing trend towards globalization, saw a shift in the UN agenda that brought to the fore basic social issues such as human rights, population control, and the status of women, that emanated from the Cairo Conference on Population, the Copenhagen Conference on Social Development and the Beijing Conference on Women. Noticeably, these programmes have pitted right-wing conservatives against the more liberal among both Protestant and Catholic NGOs. They have also roused a growing hostility to the UN social and economic development initiatives, as witnessed by a newspaper headline, "The UN Quietly Wages War on Religion: Does This Respected Body Suppress Monotheism in Order to Regulate Global Values?". This article condemns the UN Secretariat as composed of "secular humanists" who "aspire to world government" (Woodard 2001, OSO8) and reflects the rise of increasing right-wing collaboration and the formation of a pro-life coalition among conservative evangelicals, conservative

Catholics, Mormons, Muslims and conservative Orthodox Jews (Editorial Preface 2000, 1). The most contentious issue arousing the strongest passion has been not only over women's reproductive rights, but over the unorthodox, intimidating tactics, for the UN arena, used by the pro-family and anti-abortion proponents which one observer noted turned "UN conferences into something of a religious battleground" (Engh 2000). Leading the fray is the Catholic Family and Human Rights Institute, whose president, Austin Ruse, boasted that "we broke every rule of UN lobbying ... attended all the women's meetings and essentially took them over"[16] (Ruse 2000). Ruse was referring to Cairo+5 and Beijing+5, the five-year reviews of the Cairo Program for Action adopted at the 1994 Population and Development Conference and the Platform for Action adopted at the 1995 Status of Women Conference, held at UN headquarters. Ruse, who networks with many Muslim delegations at the UN, contends that he is acting in compliance with the calling of the Holy See, whose observer status at the UN grants him access to UN grounds (Ruse 2001). The credibility of the Catholic Family and Human Rights Institute has been challenged by other Catholic groups, notably Catholics for a Free Choice which accuses it of engaging in disinformation, disrespecting the UN rules of procedure and of having "consistently shown itself to care little about the issue of human rights, but to be involved in single-issue opposition to safe and legal abortion and family planning"[17] (Catholics for a Free Choice 2001, 32).

The controversy stirred up on women's rights and related issues, while arousing strong emotions, did not succeed in eclipsing the main thrust of religious NGOs. A much heralded manifestation of religious presence at the UN came with the convening of the Millennium World Peace Summit of Religious and Spiritual Leaders on 28 August 2000. Although meeting in the UN General Assembly hall for two days and addressed by Secretary-General Kofi Annan, this religious summit was not an official UN-sponsored event. It was organized by members active within what may be called "an interfaith group of non-governmental organizations" and which was largely underwritten by the media millionaire Ted Turner, the conclave's honorary chair, with additional support from a number of foundations. Bawa Jain of the International Mahavir Jain Mission and the Interfaith Center of New York was its energetic and sometimes controversial secretary-general. Following two days of speeches in the General Assembly, two more days of roundtable meetings were held at the Waldorf Astoria Hotel. These sessions were characterized by an absence of structure and strict rules of procedure leading to such primitive tactics as the jockeying for the podium by unscheduled speakers. Some roundtables were carried out in an orderly fashion; others were marked by near bedlam.

This assemblage represented an effort on the part of religious leaders to bring to bear their influence on the conduct of world affairs. This represented the latest such effort, going back to perhaps the earliest universal interfaith dialogue, the World's Parliament of Religions held in Chicago in 1893 in connection with the Columbian Exposition.[18] More than a quarter-century before the establishment of the League of Nations and a half-century before the UN, this gathering had among its purposes "to promote and deepen the spirit of human brotherhood among religious men of diverse faiths, to discover ... what light religion has to throw on the great problems of the present age especially the important questions connected with temperance, labor, education, wealth and poverty, and to bring the nations of the earth into a more friendly fellowship in the hope of securing permanent international peace".[19]

Although the organizers of the 1893 meeting "could not overcome their Christo-centrism", the Parliament had a thin semblance of universality, for, in addition to religions of the Judeo-Christian tradition, Buddhism, Hinduism, Islam, and Shintoism were also represented, even though sparsely (Jack 1993, 423). In contrast, the Millenium assemblage of 2000 boasted participation by a wide array of religious dignitaries from some 50 religions that stretched far beyond the Judeo-Christian-Muslim tradition. In addition to Francis Cardinal Arinze (President of the Pontifical Council for Inter-Religious Dialogue at the Vatican), Rev. Konrad Raiser (Secretary-General of the World Council of Churches), Patriarch Karekin II (Armenian Orthodox Church), Njongonkulu Ndungane (Archbishop of Cape Town), Abdullah Salaih Al-Obaid (Secretary-General of the World Muslim League), Sheikh Ahmad Kuftato (Grand Mufti of Syria), Rabbi Isaac Meir Lau (Ashkenazic Chief Rabbi of Israel), the list included Buddhists, Confucians, Hindus, Shintoists, Zoroastians, Mormons, Sikhs, Taoists, Jains, traditional African and Native American religions, and worshippers of nature. Notably missing was the Dalai Lama, the spiritual leader of the Tibetan people, whose presence was blocked by China. The Dalai Lama's "exclusion undermined the summit's strong articulation of support for religious freedom" (Love 2001, inside back cover). Evangelical Protestants, who were all but absent, complained that Eastern religions were over-represented at the summit. The failure by the organizers to invite a number of Christian groups, such as the world-wide Seventh-day Adventists, was questioned.[20]

Kofi Annan called "this summit of religious and spiritual leaders ... without doubt one of the most inspiring gatherings ever held here" (UN Secretary-General 2000). The colourful array in the General Assembly hall of so many religious leaders of divergent faiths – priests, ministers, patriarchs, metropolitans, muftis, sheikhs, swamis, monks, rabbis and chieftains – sitting side-by-side and mingling in the corridors, each dressed in his or her distinctive vestments and regalia, was a most impressive sight and a symbol of what might be. But this was essentially a surface visage of harmony under which lay resentment and friction. Particularly irritating to representatives of indigenous peoples and delegates from eastern religions, notably Hindus, were the proselytizing practices of Christianity and Islam (Numrich 2000). The lone evangelical to be invited to speak was the Rev. Anne Graham Lotz, daughter of Billy Graham, who provided a jarring note when she told the gathering that "the way to world peace was through acceptance of Jesus as 'the prince of peace'".

The formal outcome of the summit was the "Commitment to Global Peace", a comprehensive statement of lofty principles bordering on platitudes and touching on every tribulation confronting humanity, that concludes:

We, as religious and spiritual leaders, pledge our commitment to work together to promote the inner and outer conditions that foster peace and the non-violent management and resolution of conflict. We appeal to the followers of all religious traditions and to the human community as a whole to cooperate in building peaceful societies, to seek mutual understanding through dialogue where there are differences, to refrain from violence, to practice compassion, and to uphold the dignity of all life.[21]

The organizers of the summit had planned to establish an International Council of Religious and Spiritual Leaders as an advisory panel to the UN. The idea was stillborn, as was the notion that a department of religious affairs be established in the office of the UN Secretary-General.

Judging by the unwieldiness and the outcome of the religious summit, a role for religious interfaith activity in the pursuit of the goals for world peace and social justice, enunciated as far back as the 1893 World Parliament of Religions, remains a persistent and elusive challenge in the 21st century. Yet, in a world where conflicts with religious undertones persist, attendees of the religious summit contend that the promotion of reconciliation and harmony among peoples of different faiths is intrinsically a step in the right direction. Moreover, "the fact that the meeting took place without any extreme conflict was an achievement in itself" (Cole 2000, 14).

Religious Groups and Information Technology

With the plethora of new and easily accessible means of communication, the information age can be liberating by opening new opportunities for religious institutions to promote their messages through cassettes, CDs, internet chat rooms and websites. These techniques have been used very effectively by various religious groups. However, once connected to the internet, access is gained to an almost indescribable wealth of information. As networking has "come of age" with the internet, the undermining of religious parochialism and insularity may set in. Because of the religious freedom climate it nurtures, the door is opened to the dissemination of derogatory challenging perspectives, so much so that there is a great deal of trepidation within religious circles over the potential effect of the burgeoning information revolution. Throughout the centuries, beginning with the invention of the printing press, advances in technology have had great significance for religions in delivering their messages and in mobilizing their adherents.

> When a new technology unleashes massive cultural change, the challenge to traditional religion is immense. In the West, established and new religions alike have vied to fulfill their conserving and articulating functions by exploiting innovation in communication technology that accompanied cultural change. The printing press, radio, film and television each attracted religious virtuosos who drew on the innovation in communication to conserve past values or express new ones amid the landscape

wrought by cultural change. ... [O]nline religions (traditional and new) represent ... the latest site of cultural challenge and change ... (Brasher 2001, 12-13).

Most religions and their affiliated NGOs are involved in cyberspace, having websites and making extensive use of e-mail. Has this contributed to "greater solidarity" among religious NGOs? The new means of rapid communications and transportation, hallmarks of the information age, have certainly facilitated religious interaction and dialogue. Familiarity contributes to mutual understanding but it also breeds contempt. The existence of divergent creeds establishes conditions for inducing conflicts. It is still too early to understand fully the impact of the information age in reinforcing, what Hans Küng called, "the ongoing dialogues among the world religions in order to achieve and strengthen an interreligious world ethic" (Hasenclever 2000, 642). Certainly, information technology – extensive use of e-mail, faxing and the internet – is bringing about changes in the *modus operandi* of religious NGOs. However, as evidenced by the Millennium World Peace Summit of Religious and Spiritual Leaders and the controversy over women's rights, it has not brought about the goal articulated by Rev. Konrad Raiser of the World Council of Churches for the millennium meeting to "deny the sanction of religion to those who seek to make it a tool of violence" (World Council of Churches 2000).

By Way of Conclusion

Given the broad spectrum of religious NGOs, it is not surprising, that they pursue differing strategic goals. Some are outwardly directed, strongly committed to the "UN idea"; others are more inwardly directed, focused on their parochial concerns; and still others are more dedicated to service and humanitarian relief. The dividing lines among these activities are not rigid. Religious NGOs may pursue one or all of these goals, depending on the issue at hand. The question at the end of this exercise is whether the activities of religious NGOs make a substantial mark in contemporary global civil society. Are they effective players within the 'New Diplomacy'?

As noted above in the discussion of 'multi-track diplomacy', churches, i.e. religious institutions, comprise one of numerous categories of nongovernmental actors involved. Religious NGOs constitute less than ten per cent of the approximately 2000 NGOs with consultative status with ECOSOC and DPI. Often some religious NGOs constitute part of a coalition on a particular issue. In these instances, they are rarely on the forefront of the undertaking, such as the drafting of the International Criminal Court Statute, the Kyoto Protocol on Global Warming or the landmines ban. The lead in these efforts was usually taken by advocacy NGOs with specific expertise. Those religious NGOs which participate in the coalition play a supporting role, not necessarily a negligible one. Religious NGOs make their presence felt by inspiring people to act and at times taking action themselves, such as lobbying. On certain volatile social issues, regarding women's rights and abortion, there is rabid contentiousness marked by disunity and incivility among religious NGOs.

A study concerned with the influence of NGOs in the UN system is entitled *The Conscience of the World* (Willets 1996). Surely, this aptly describes religion's claim to its preeminence as the source of universal ethics and morals. Ironically, the book, which contains chapters on a wide range of NGOs, states that it is difficult "to understand more fully the role that religion plays in the international public policy arena and identify what works and what doesn't in the interactions of religious NGOs and the UN" (Numrich 2001, 54). To try to understand the interrelationship between religion and the UN, a project, *Religion Counts*, has been undertaken by the Park Ridge Center, supported by a grant from A Better World (Numrich 2001, 54). One of the initiators of this project, Martin Marty, has noted that "For all the problems that have appeared when public discourse includes religious themes, it is also clear that the texts and traditions of faith communities have much to offer by way of including calls for effecting social justice, working toward healing, and provoking profound thought" (Numrich 2001, 67). Changing and influencing the agenda to be debated in the world arena is a prime function of global civil society. A central question on the world's agenda concerns the devastating aspects of globalization, adversely affecting large numbers of people who "see their position systematically eroded by economic and political forces which work to the benefit of a small proportion of the world's population" (Edwards 2000, 605). Meeting this challenge is the obligation of all value-based NGOs, religious and secular. The extent to which religious NGOs will play a meaningful role in international society's dealing with this crucial issue of the twenty-first century is very much dependent on how religions live up to their theology and overcome their complicity in conflicts around the world.

Notes

Note on internet addresses (URLs): Websites tend to appear, change or disappear, often without warning. Addresses cited in this bibliography were accurate and active at the time of writing (January 2002) unless otherwise noted.

1. See Thomas Risse-Kappen (1995), *Bringing Transnational Relations Back In: Non-State Actors, Domestic Structures and International Institutions*, Cambridge University Press, Cambridge.
2. See also Kofi Annan (2000), 'Partnership With Civil Society Necessity in Addressing Global Agenda', UN Press Release, SG/SM/7318, 29 February.
3. See *Millennium: Journal of International Studies* (2000), Vol. 29(3). Special Issue, 'Religions and International Relations'; see also Jonathan Fox (2001), 'Religion as an Overlooked Element of International Relations', *International Studies Review*, Vol. 3(3), pp. 52-73.
4. See Scott M. Thomas (2000), 'Taking Religious and Cultural Pluralism Seriously: The Global Resurgence of Religion and the Transformation of International Society', *Millennium: Journal of International Studies*, Vol. 29(3). Special Issue, 'Religions and International Relations' pp. 815-841.

170 *Civil Society in the Information Age*

5   Quoted by Secretary-General Kofi Annan in his address to the Millennium Summit of Religious and Spiritual Leaders (UN Secretary-General 2000).
6   The long tortuous path leading to the adoption of this declaration is described by Jack 1993, Chapter 12.
7   The Appeal of Conscience Foundation was founded by Rabbi Arthur Schneier in 1965. It has held numerous interfaith conferences on peace, tolerance and conflict resolution and has sent missions to various countries, including interfaith initiatives in Russia and China. Information about the foundation and its activities can be found on the internet, www.appealofconscience.org
8   The other resolutions dealing with dialogue are UN General Assembly 1998 and UN General Assembly 2000a.
9   See also Thomas G. Weiss and Leon Gordenker (eds) (1996), *NGOs, the UN and Global Governance*, Lynne Rienner Publishers, Boulder; and Peter Willetts (ed) (1996), *The Conscience of the World: The Influence of Non-Governmental Organizations in the UN System*, Hurst, London.
10 For a discussion of the relationship between national and international NGOs see Willets 1996, pp. 2-3.
11 Initially the three status categories were designated as "a", "b", and "c". Later the designations were changed to "I", "II" and "III". More recently they became "G" (General), "S" (Specialized), and "R" (Roster). The distinctions among the three remained the same: category "a", "I" or "G" indicate organizations that are concerned with most activities of ECOSOC and its subsidiary bodies; category "b", "II", or "S" connote organizations that have a special competence in, and are concerned specifically with only a few fields of activity; and category "c", "III" or "R" refers to other organizations that can make occasional and useful contributions to the work of ECOSOC and its subsidiary bodies. To all intents and purposes, the distinction among all categories of NGOs has all but disappeared.
12 See (Jack 1993) for a detailed history of the evolution and activities of the WCRP.
13 This is a paraphrase of the statement by the Lutheran Office for World Community (1990), *Lutheran Work With the United Nations*, New York.
14 This is based on publications of the Presbyterian United Nations Office and the Lutheran Office for World Community, both located in the Church Center for the United Nations, 777 United Nations Plaza.
15 The first edition of the survey covered 1995-1996; the second 1998-1999 and the latest is for 2000-2001.
16 For a description of the pro-life lobbying at the UN see Jennifer Butler (2000b), 'For Faith and Family: Christian Right Advocacy at the UN', *The Public Eye*, Vol. 9(2/3), pp. 1,3-17; and Jennifer Butler (2000a), 'The Christian Right Coalition and the UN Special Session on Children: Prospects and Strategies, *The International Journal of Children's Rights*, Vol. 8(4), pp. 351-371.
17 For a critical analysis of the pro-life coalition see Institute for Democracy Studies (2000), *The Global Assault on Reproductive Rights: A Crucial Turning Point*, IDS, New York, May.
18 The Columbian Exposition or the Chicago World's Fair of 1893 was held to commemorate the 400th anniversary of the landing of Christopher Columbus in the Western Hemisphere.
19 The full text may be found in Jack 1993, pp. 431-432.
20 See Adventist Press Service (2000), 'World Religious Summit Brings Mixed Responses', Adventist Press Service, 2 September, Basel, www.stanet.ch/APD.

21 The full text may be found on the internet at:
www.millenniumpeacesummit.org/declaration.html Secretariat of the Millennium World Peace Summit of Religious and Spiritual Leaders

References

Adventist Press Service (2000), 'World Religious Summit Brings Mixed Responses', Adventist Press Service, 2 September, Basel, www.stanet.ch/APD
Annan, Kofi (2000), *Partnership With Civil Society Necessity in Addressing Global Agenda*, UN Press Release, SG/SM/7318, 29 February, Wellington, New Zealand.
Brasher, Brenda E. (2001), *Give Me That Online Religion*, Jossey-Bass, San Francisco.
Brown, Bernard E. (2001), 'What is the New Diplomacy?', *American Foreign Policy Interests*, Vol. 23, pp. 3-21.
Butler, Jennifer (2000a), 'The Christian Right Coalition and the UN Special Session on Children: Prospects and Strategies, *The International Journal of Children's Rights*, Vol. 8(4), pp. 351-371.
Butler, Jennifer (2000b), 'For Faith and Family: Christian Right Advocacy at the UN', *The Public Eye*, Vol. 9(2/3), pp. 1,3-17.
Catholics for a Free Choice (2001), 'Bad Faith at the UN: Drawing Back the Curtain on the Catholic Family and Human Rights Institute', CFFC, Washington DC.
Churchill, Winston (1946), *Sinews of Peace*, speech delivered at Westminster College, Fulton, Missouri, March 5. www.winstonchurchill.org/sinews.htm
Clark, Ann Marie, Friedman, Elisabeth J. and Hochstettler, Karen (1998), 'The Sovereign Limits of Global Society: A Comparison of NGO Participation in UN World Conferences on the Environment, Human Rights, and Women', *World Politics*, Vol. 51(1), pp. 1-35.
Cole, Patrick (2000), 'UN World Peace Summit Draws Colorful Array of Religious Leaders', *Chicago Tribune*, 30 August, p. 14.
Commission to Study the Organization of Peace (1957), *Strengthening the United Nations*, Harper & Brothers Publishers, New York.
The Committee of Religious NGOs at the United Nations (2000), *Survey of Activities of Religious NGOs at the UN, 1989-1999*, New York www.rngo.org
'Editorial Preface' (2000), *The Public Eye*, Vol. 9(2/3), p.1.
Edwards, Michael and Sen, Gita (2000), NGOs, Social Change and the Transformation of Human Relationships: A 21st-century Civic Agenda', *Third World Quarterly*, Vol. 21(4), pp. 605-616.
Engh, Gabrielle (2000), *Conservative Religious Groups Complain of Prejudice by UN, NGOs*, Ecumenical Women 2000+, www.ew2000plus.org/OTRPanelArticlePrint.htm
Fox, Jonathan (2001), 'Religion as an Overlooked Element of International Relations', *International Studies Review*, vol 3(3), pp. 52-73.
Gordenker, Leon (1995), 'NGOs and the United Nations in the Twenty-First Century', in *Envisioning the United Nations in the Twenty-First Century*, The United Nations University, Tokyo pp. 124-134. Proceedings of the Inaugural Symposium on the United Nations System in the Twenty-first Century 21-22 November.
Hasenclever, Andreas and Rittberger, Volker (2000), 'Does Religion Make a Difference? Theoretical Approaches to the Impact of Faith on Political Conflict', *Millennium: Journal of International Studies*, Vol. 29(3), pp. 641-674.
Institute for Democracy Studies (2000), *The Global Assault on Reproductive Rights: A Crucial Turning Point*, IDS, New York, May.

Jack, Homer A. (1993), *WCRP: A History of the World Conference on Religion and Peace*, World Conference on Religion and Peace, New York.
Korey, William (1998), *NGOs and the Universal Declaration of Human Rights*, St. Martin's Press, New York.
Love, Janice (2001), 'Religion in Politics: Reflections on the UN's Millennium World Peace Summit of Religious and Spiritual Leaders', *International Studies Perspectives*, Vol. 2(1), inside back cover.
Lutheran Office for World Community *(1990), Lutheran Work With the United Nations*, New York.
Numrich, Paul D. (2000), *Religion Counts Looks at the Summit: One Observer's View of the Millennium World Peace Summit of Religious and Spiritual Leaders*, The Park Ridge Center for the Study of Health, Faith and Ethics, Chicago.
Numrich, Paul D. (2001), 'United Religions at the United Nations', *Second Opinion*, Vol. 8, pp. 53-68.
Park Ridge Center for the Study of Health, Faith and Ethics (2002), *We the Religions: The Role of Religion in the United Nations System*, Park Ridge Center, Chicago.
Risse-Kappen, Thomas (1995), *Bringing Transnational Relations Back In: Non-State Actors, Domestic Structures and International Institutions*, Cambridge University Press, Cambridge.
Ruse, Austin (2000), President, Catholic Family and Human Rights Institute, Speech to the Cardinal Mindszenty Foundation, St. Louis, March.
Ruse, Austin (2001), Personal interview with author, 29 May; and memorandum, 'The Ways of UN Pro-Life Lobbying'.
Smock, David (2001), *Faith-Based NGOs and International Peacebuilding*, United States Institute of Peace, Washington DC, 22 October.
Thomas, Scott M. (2000), 'Taking Religious and Cultural Pluralism Seriously: The Global Resurgence of Religion and the Transformation of International Society', *Millennium: Journal of International Studies*, Vol. 29(3). Special Issue, 'Religions and International Relations' pp. 815-841.
United Nations. Economic and Social Council (1996), *Consultative Relationship Between the United Nations and Non-governmental Organizations*, E/RES/1996/31, 25 July, part I(3).
United Nations. General Assembly (1981), *Declaration on the Elimination of All Forms of Intolerance and of Discrimination Based on Religion or Belief*, UN, New York, A/RES/36/55, 25 November.
United Nations. General Assembly (1998), *United Nations Year of Dialogue Among Civilizations*, UN, New York, A/RES/53/22, 16 November.
United Nations. General Assembly (2000a), *United Nations Year of Dialogue Among Civilizations*, UN, New York, A/RES/54/113, 7 February.
United Nations. General Assembly (2000b), *We the Peoples: The Role of the United Nations in the 21st Century*, Secretary-General's Report to the Millennium Summit, Press Release GA/9704, 3 April.
United Nations. General Assembly (2001b), *Protection of Religious Sites*, UN, New York, A/RES/55/254, 11 June.
United Nations. General Assembly (2001c), *United Nations Year of Dialogue Among Civilizations*, UN, New York, A/RES/55/23, 11 January.
United Nations. Secretariat (1992), *An Agenda for Peace : Preventive Diplomacy, Peacemaking and Peace-keeping*, Secretary-General's Report Pursuant to the Statement Adopted by the Summit Meeting of the Security Council, UN, New York, ST/DPI/1247, 31 January.

United Nations. Secretary-General (2000), *Secretary-General Addresses Millennium Summit of Religious, Spiritual Leaders, Urges Participants to Set Example of Interfaith Cooperation*, UN, New York, UN Press Release SG/SM/7520, 29 August.

United Nations. Security Council (1992), *Provisional Verbatim Record of the 3046th Meeting: Security Council Summit*, UN, New York, S/PV.3046, 31 January.

Van Tongeren, Paul (1998), 'Exploring the Local Capacity for Peace: The Role of NGOs', *The Courier ACP-EU*, 168(March-April), 70-72.

Weiss, Thomas G. and Gordenker, Leon (eds) (1996), *NGOs, The UN and Global Governance*, Lynne Rienner Publishers, Boulder.

Willetts, Peter (ed) (1996), *The Conscience of the World: The Influence of Non-Governmental Organizations in the UN System*, Hurst, London.

Woodard, Joe (2001), 'The UN Quietly Wages War on Religion: Does This Respected Body Suppress Monothesism in Order to Regulate Global Values?', *Calgary Herald*, 11 August, p. OSO8.

World Council of Churches (1999), *The Role of the World Council of Churches in International Affairs*, WCC, Geneva.

World Council of Churches, Office of Communication (2000), *Press Update*, Geneva, 30 August, PR-00-27, www.wcc-coe.org/wcc/news/press/00/27pu.html

Chapter 11

Expanding the Trade Debate: The Role of Information in WTO and Civil Society Interaction

Heidi K. Ullrich[*]

In 1999, up to 50,000 members of civil society demonstrated in Seattle at the Third Ministerial Meeting of the World Trade Organization (WTO). The following year this number doubled to 100,000 in Prague during the annual meeting of the World Bank and International Monetary Fund. In 2001, this number again doubled to approximately 200,000 people at the Group of Eight (G8) Summit in Genoa. While diverse in many respects, the demonstrators shared three factors. Firstly, they were members of a growing number of civil society organizations (CSOs), and more specifically, representatives of nongovernmental organizations (NGOs). Secondly, they were critical of the current system of economic global governance symbolized by these international institutions. Thirdly, their prime means of communicating with each other, organizing the demonstrations, and spreading their message was through the use of information/communication technology (ICT).

Given the great diversity among various CSOs, an all-encompassing definition is problematic[1]. However, CSOs may generally be seen to consist of groups of individuals, within one or more countries who voluntarily organize themselves with the purpose of pursuing selected politico-economic or social objectives. NGOs are part of civil society. The term NGO incorporates a large number of groups and institutions that vary considerably in their objectives, activities, effectiveness and even ethics. This study identifies as trade-related NGOs such diverse groups as pro-business associations, labor unions, environmental groups, agricultural and consumer organizations and anti-capitalists. Some argue that rather than defining NGOs, it is better to distinguish them by identifying key elements including their goals, membership and staff, sources of funding, and their activities (Simmons 1998, 85). While NGOs are not normally associated with governments, some of these organizations, particularly those involved in operational activities rather than advocacy,[2] at times have connections with governments. Broad-based NGOs have been active for decades. More recently, the fears associated with globalization, including concern over the relationship of trade and sustainable development, labor, human rights and consumer rights have led to the creation of issue-specific civil society actors forming NGOs and other coalitions to express their concerns.

---

[*] The author would like to thank Peter I. Hajnal and Sylvia Ostry for their invaluable comments on earlier drafts of this paper.

Through facilitating communication and the exchange of information between members, the rapid advances in ICT have given NGOs a new platform on which to express their demands concerning among other issues, the multilateral trading system.

For nearly 50 years, the multilateral trading system within the framework of the General Agreement on Tariffs and Trade (GATT) operated in relative obscurity. Trade negotiations over the reduction of tariffs on manufactured goods were considered the realm of government and industry representatives. Neither the GATT nor NGOs made any significant attempts to interact. However, the multilateral trading system and the manner in which trade policy was developed changed dramatically with the establishment of the WTO on 1 January 1995. Incorporating the elements of the 1947 GATT, the WTO also covers several new issue areas including trade in services, intellectual property rights and trade-related investment measures as well as an enforceable Dispute Settlement Procedure (DSP). Furthermore, the agenda of the Third WTO Ministerial in Seattle included the contentious issues of trade-related environmental and social issues such as labor rights. These powers, present and potential, as well as accusations of lack of transparency, have been the cause of the increased NGO attention to the WTO. The sophisticated use of ICT by these groups has provided the means to enable this attention to be widespread.

While traditional media such as television, radio and newspapers remain important for the spreading of information, the phenomenon of large numbers of newly active members of global civil society demanding a voice in multilateral trade policy coincides with the emergence of the internet and other forms of ICT in the public realm. In fact, Ostry suggests that a 'protest business', which she terms 'dissent.com', "could be a new market created by the internet" (2000, 14). The first target of an 'NGO swarm'[3] was the Multilateral Agreement on Investment (MAI) negotiated by the Organisation for Economic Co-operation and Development (OECD) in the mid-1990s. The placing of a leaked copy of the draft agreement on the website of Public Citizen's Global Trade Watch (GTW) in 1997 led to a large number of NGOs publicly criticizing the MAI. Following the collapse of negotiations in October 1998, these NGOs claimed their first ICT-inspired victory. In 1999, they turned their attention to the WTO.

This chapter investigates the role of information, specifically ICT, in the interaction between the WTO and civil society. The first section places trade-related NGOs within a typology enabling a basis for their analysis. Section two provides an overview of recent WTO reforms intended to increase the dialogue with civil society and trade-related NGO representatives. Section three describes the use of ICT by both the WTO and trade-related NGOs and its impact. Several case studies reflect the diversity in outlook and approach to the use of ICT of selected trade-related NGOs. Section four discusses the means of facilitating communication between the WTO and trade-related NGOs. Included in this discussion are the inherent limitations and challenges of this interaction. The investigation concludes by offering the WTO and trade-related NGOs a series of recommendations for how their interaction and use of information could be more effective thus resulting in the type of knowledgeable and two-way dialogue that is necessary for the expansion of the trade debate.

Classifying NGOs: Toward a Typology of Trade-Related NGOs

Given the considerable increase in the numbers of trade-related NGOs in recent years often with varying beliefs, objectives and manners of operation, it is useful to offer a typology. Such a distinction allows officials of member governments and the WTO Secretariat, trade negotiators and other members of civil society to better understand the objectives, actions and approaches of these groups. Due to its broad applicability, this study utilizes the categorization of trade-related NGOs as developed by Scholte, O'Brien and Williams. (1999) This typology consists of:

- Conformists. These groups generally support the objectives of trade liberalization and the basis behind the activities of the WTO. According to Scholte, O'Brien and Williams: "Conformers only interrogate the outputs of the existing global trade regime, not its foundations" (1999, 113). Conformist NGOs regularly interacting with the WTO include corporate business associations such as the International Chamber of Commerce (ICC) and the European Union (EU) Committee of the American Chamber of Commerce; commercial farmers' associations such as the American Farm Bureau and the International Policy Council on Agriculture, Food and Trade, and economic research institutes such as the World Economic Forum.
- Reformists. While generally agreeing with conformists on the need for a multilateral trade regime, reformists wish to alter the current neo-liberal approach to trade. Reformist groups seek to transform trade policies to take into account such issues as sustainable development and labor rights as well as to modify WTO operating procedures in order to make the organization more accessible to civil society (Scholte et al. 1999, 112). Reformist groups include trade unions and human rights advocates such as the International Confederation of Free Trade Unions, the World Confederation of Labour, International Labor Rights Fund, and the International Centre for Human Rights. Campaigning for increased consideration of development issues are Greenpeace, Oxfam, World Wide Fund for Nature, Third World Network and International South Group Network.
- Radicals. Members of radical groups aim to limit the rule-making powers of the WTO with some fringe groups demanding that the WTO be eliminated. This category also includes the 'uncivil society' groups Hajnal describes as "a relatively small group of thugs and extreme anarchists" (2001, 1). Radical groups do not normally approach WTO Secretariat officials or member government representatives. In turn, WTO officials are at times unable to communicate with these NGOs through means of ICT due to being blocked from entering their chat rooms. Radical coalitions of civil society include Peoples' Global Action (PGA), the Ruckus Society and the Black Bloc.

Using this typology, the majority of trade-related NGOs are conformists and reformists. However, as seen in the various mass demonstrations during meetings of international institutions involved in managing the global economy, the destructive actions of a relatively small group of radical members of civil society often make the headlines rather than the carefully planned information campaigns of more moderate NGOs.

In a similar classification focusing on the demonstrators present in the streets of Seattle during the 1999 WTO Ministerial, Bayne divides them into three groups: 1) Orderly – calculated to have the largest groups of between 20,000 and 25,000; 2) Obstructive – roughly 10,000; and 3) Destructive – between 200 and 300 people. (2000b, 136)

Although the Scholte, O'Brien and Williams typology offers a general distinction among trade-related NGOs, it is somewhat limited due to various reasons. First is the lack of emphasis on the differences within the various categories. For example, among reformist groups, particularly Northern and Southern NGOs, differences exist in the type and degree of reform sought as well as in the use of ICT. Among Southern NGOs there is a growing belief that calls by Northern NGOs for greater environmental standards and labor rights to be incorporated within multilateral trade rules are merely a form of protectionism. Additionally, given the greater numbers and much higher operating budgets of Northern NGOs, fears abound concerning their dominance over Southern NGOs.[4] Regarding interaction with the WTO, although most reformist groups are willing to interact with the WTO, there are some who consider such action as a form of co-optation. Among radical groups, there is a growing divide between Left and extreme-Right groups.

A second point of weakness of the Scholte, O'Brien and Williams typology is its lack of distinction between their functional activities. In analyzing pre- and post-Seattle NGO websites Ostry (2000) identifies three functional types of networks:

- Mobilization networks. These networks are loose coalitions of NGOs frequently with interests at odds with one another. However, they share a dedication to operating in an unstructured organizational environment based on participatory democracy (Ostry 2000, 13). Examples of mobilization networks include the People's Global Action (PGA), discussed in a case study later in this chapter, and the International Civil Society Opposing a Millennium Round (ICS).
- Technical networks. The objective of these organizations is to have some degree of impact on policy. Thus, technical networks tend to work within both governmental and intergovernmental channels (Ostry 2000, 16). Such groups include the Institute for Agriculture and Trade Policy, the International Centre for Trade and Sustainable Development and the International Institute for Sustainable Development that are briefly discussed within this study.
- Networks forming a 'virtual secretariat' to developing countries. These networks, based both in the South and North, work together to exchange information, offer assistance, create cohesion and strengthen the bargaining

position of Southern NGOs. The diverse groups forming this 'virtual secretariat' include the Southern-based Third World Network, highlighted in a case study, and Focus on the Global South, as well as various Northern development organizations such as Oxfam (Ostry 2000, 17).

Typologies serve as useful explanatory tools. However, as these varying typologies illustrate, such categorizations tend to focus on only a few defining factors while leaving others out. In the multi-dimensional environment of NGOs, while the application of only one typology may reduce complexity, there is also the danger of ignoring critical elements. Thus, rather than the strict use of a specific typology, an approach incorporating the general understanding of various means for distinguishing the diverse types of NGOs may be more appropriate. Such an approach is attempted in the case studies presented later in this chapter.

From Monologue to Dialogue: Institutional Aspects of the WTO's Interaction with NGOs

Before discussing the institutional aspects of the WTO's interaction with NGOs and other members of civil society, it is useful to clarify the organization's institutional structure and decision-making procedures. The WTO is an intergovernmental institution in which the member governments, (144 as of January 2002) rather than WTO Secretariat officials, agree on the policies to be implemented.[5] Member governments are guided by the rules set out in the Agreement establishing the WTO signed in Marrakesh in 1994. Agreement is generally taken by consensus within the General Council, consisting of the members' trade ambassadors or by trade ministers at the ministerial meetings held at least every two years. According to a WTO External Relations official, the division that has primary responsibility for relations with civil society, the WTO Secretariat is limited to the role of "a facilitator – but a proactive one. It operates with a modest mandate, trying to draw the attention of the members' delegates" (Kuiten 2001).

Unlike the GATT, the 1994 Agreement establishing the WTO addresses the issue of interaction with other international organizations as well as NGOs. Article V states in part:

1. The General Council shall make appropriate arrangements for effective cooperation with other intergovernmental organizations that have responsibilities related to those of the WTO.
2. The General Council may make appropriate arrangements for consultation and cooperation with non-governmental organizations concerned with matters related to those of the WTO (GATT 1994, 9).

Between 1995 and mid-1996, WTO interaction with trade-related NGOs was limited. On the initiative of some WTO members and the staff of the External Relations Division, further progress in WTO relations with NGOs was approved after almost a year of deliberation with other WTO members on 18 July 1996 with the General Council adopting the document entitled *Guidelines for Arrangements on Relations with Non-Governmental Organizations* (WTO 1996a). Members acknowledged the "role NGOs can play to increase the awareness of the public in respect of WTO activities" (WTO 1996a). According to these guidelines, members of the WTO pledged to increase transparency and improve communication with NGOs by faster de-restriction of official documents[6] and the use of ICT to encourage WTO interaction with NGOs. The WTO Secretariat received a mandate to "play a more active role in its direct contacts with NGOs". Accordingly, trade-related NGOs would henceforth be able to attend Secretariat-organized symposia, interact with WTO staff, and attend WTO ministerial meetings (WTO 1996a, Pt. IV).

NGO Participation at WTO Ministerial Conferences

WTO Ministerial Conferences, held at least every two years, bring together trade representatives, including the trade ministers, from all WTO members to discuss and take decisions on critical issues surrounding the activities of the WTO. Due to the high-level of discussion that takes place during these meetings as well as the surrounding publicity, Ministerial Conferences potentially serve as prime forums to NGO representatives for influencing government officials as well as increasing public awareness on the activities of the WTO.

However, participation at the first two WTO ministerial conference was both minimal and unbalanced. Only 235 individuals representing 108 NGOs attended the 1996 Singapore Ministerial while the 1998 Geneva Ministerial managed to draw 362 individuals from 128 NGOs. Additionally, at both of these meetings, business groups outnumbered environment, development, trade unions and consumer groups by a large margin.[7] That the WTO's efforts seemed to be resulting in limited interaction with NGOs was apparent. At the June 1998 Geneva WTO Ministerial, United States President Bill Clinton proposed that the WTO should "provide a forum where business, labor, environmental and consumer groups can speak out and help guide the further evolution of the WTO. When this body convenes again, I believe that the world's trade ministers should sit down with representatives of the broad public to begin this discussion" (WTO 1998a, 9-10). One month later WTO Director-General Renato Ruggiero announced further actions intended to represent the WTO's "on-going collaboration with partner NGOs" (WTO 1998b). Although these plans included the establishment of NGO briefings by WTO staff, there was also a deliberate focus on using ICT-based tools. This included enhancing the WTO website as a means of interaction, creating an NGO section, and making official NGO submissions available for downloading by interested parties.

Despite the efforts of the WTO to accommodate NGOs in the negotiations at the 1999 Seattle Ministerial, including organizing a symposium for 1,500 accredited NGO representatives, it was nevertheless overwhelmed by the 50,000 members of civil society that descended upon the streets of Seattle. Immediately following the ministerial, the Chairman of the General Council, Tanzanian

Ambassador Ali Mchumo, reflected on the lessons of Seattle: "Seattle has provided a wake-up call for all of us to reflect and re-examine how we need to evolve a more inclusive and participatory system of decision making even when consensus remains the basic principle of decision making" (WTO 2000a, 5).

Despite the stated need for increased participation, the WTO announced that the Fourth Ministerial Conference would be held in Doha, Qatar in November 2001. NGOs were highly critical of the decision given the restricted number of NGO representatives that would be allowed to officially attend as well as the inability of NGOs to hold demonstrations in Qatar. Space limitations forced the WTO to restrict the number of delegates of eligible NGOs to one per accredited organization. Due perhaps to the heightened security in the wake of the September 11 terrorist attacks on the US, only approximately 360 from the 647 accredited NGOs attended the 9-14 November Doha Conference. Rather than indicating a decrease in NGO activity related to WTO issues, the Doha Conference perhaps signaled a shift in the manner in which civil society approaches its large-scale interaction with the WTO. Instead of converging on the conference site, hundreds of events took place in WTO member countries throughout the ministerial to highlight the opinions of various NGOs. However, notably as in the run-up to the Seattle Ministerial, almost all were organized using some form of ICT.

Post-Seattle reforms The WTO's post-Seattle reforms resulted in significant changes in the daily interaction between NGOs, the WTO, and member governments. According to an NGO representative, "The change is apparent. Firstly, in the relation with the Secretariat and NGOs and secondly, in the attitude of the member governments".[8]

The changes in the Secretariat are largely due to the realization that WTO interaction with civil society must be transparent, consistent and take the form of a two-way dialogue. The efforts of the WTO's External Relations Division have also been noteworthy. In September 1999, Bernard Kuiten became the WTO's first full-time civil society liaison official. As part of their efforts to increase WTO/NGO interaction, in April 2001 the WTO Secretariat initiated a series of regularly scheduled NGO briefings given by WTO staff.[9] These informal briefings, scheduled immediately following important meetings of WTO members, allow for a candid exchange of information. The External Relations division also regularly organizes NGO presentations and symposia covering topics of interest to NGOs.

The change in member governments' attitudes toward interaction with civil society has been less visible due to differences in approach among various members. However, members have supported greater WTO outreach to both civil society and government officials, particularly in developing countries.

Increased pressure to bring about institutional reform to encourage greater interaction between the WTO, its member governments, and civil society has primarily come from outside the organization – from civil society itself. Member governments, encouraged by WTO staff, have responded by adopting a series of measures intended to increase interaction. While the impact of these reforms remains to be determined, the substantial impact that ICT has had on the shape of WTO/NGO interaction is evident.

The Impact of ICT on the WTO and Trade-Related NGOs

In the closing years of the 20th century, Keohane and Nye predicted: "In the next century, information technology, broadly defined, is likely to be the most important power resource" (1998, 87). As the case studies in this section demonstrate, information itself cannot generate power. If it is to be an effective source of power, information must be transformed into knowledge and shared with others. Thus, ICT has the potential to be a resource for empowerment.

Over the last decade, there have been numerous developments in ICT. Perhaps the most significant in terms of increasing the ease, volume and speed of information exchange has been the internet that allows communication via e-mail and on-line forums, as well as the World Wide Web that facilitates document exchange and the transfer of images. ICT also includes mobile telephones, successive generation of mainframes and ever smaller and more powerful personal computers. Recognizing neither the boundaries of sovereign states, nor space and time, ICT has brought about a borderless, even virtual, world.

This section describes the various ICT tools employed by the WTO and trade-related NGOs. An initial attempt at assessing the impact of these tools on the overall interaction between the WTO and NGOs is also included. Case studies evaluating the various manners in which NGOs use ICT tools in their interaction with the WTO are incorporated to demonstrate the degree of diversity that currently exists.

WTO

Only in recent years has the WTO implemented a series of initiatives that offer interested parties a full-range of ICT options for increasing their interaction with the WTO. These include a re-designed, interactive website; on-line trade forums; the holding of virtual meetings; use of electronic mail; and the establishment of reference centers. Reasons for the relatively slow development of a comprehensive approach to ICT include a lack of resources, political will and vision on the part of some members. However, the post-Seattle WTO has recognized the advantages ICT can offer its member governments and all members of civil society in terms of expanding the trade debate. A WTO spokesman notes: "Information communication technology has allowed us to have a broader audience ... and do a better job" (Rockwell 2001).

Website The WTO's substantially redesigned website (www.wto.org) has evolved into an extraordinarily rich source of readily-available information on the background, structure and activities of the institution. While first launched in 1996, the revamped website offers member governments and civil society a comprehensive selection of information on the WTO. As of August 2001, the site included guides to the organization and operation of the WTO, over 100,000 official derestricted documents in the three official languages of the WTO (English, French and Spanish), an interactive Community Forum, press releases, the 'Focus' newsletter, member governments' proposals, committee, council and panel reports, and the results of Trade Policy Reviews.

The WTO website includes an 'NGO room' (www.wto.org/english/forums_e/ngo_e/ngo_e.htm) that provides NGOs with specific information of interest to them relating to the activities of the WTO as well as posting NGO position papers for downloading. Additionally, in order to stimulate discussion between civil society and the WTO, the WTO website has a chatroom (www.wto.org/english/forums_e/chat_e/chat_e.htm). As of late November 2001, the chats initiated by users (971) far outnumbered those initiated by the WTO (11). Topics ranged from "Should the WTO have so much power?" to "Third World Views on the WTO". As part of the WTO's efforts to expand the trade debate, the WTO recently added a 'Trade Resources" page offering general information on the main issues of the multilateral trading system and trade statistics of WTO members. However, still in an early stage of development, the page remains limited in its usefulness.

The prime motives for the redesigned website were to make it more current and user-friendly. These objectives have been accomplished through the continuous updating of the site, a more logical layout and the inclusion of a useful search engine. Whether due to the growing interest in the WTO by civil society or to the new features of its website, the WTO's site has registered a phenomenal rise in visitors. As of June 2001, the WTO homepage was getting over 400,000 total users a month compared to approximately 100,000 per month in 1999 (Carrier 2001).

On-line forums In October 2000, the WTO and World Bank, through the jointly operated Trade and Development Centre, hosted a month-long on-line forum on the topic of "Trade and Sustainable Development". This forum was the first event of the WTO Network that brings together trade officials, academics and members of civil society to discuss current trade issues. More than 1,300 individuals, from students to government officials, participated in the forum. According to Jean-Guy Carrier, manager of WTO Internet Resources, the forums are "an on-going process to enable NGOs to have input. Discussion, any discussion, is good on these forums ... These forums have been a test for us on how to improve on-line communication" (Carrier 2001). Due to budget and time restrictions surrounding the November 2001 Doha Ministerial, additional forums have not been scheduled in the near-term.

Virtual conferences/webcasts In order to facilitate communication with members of civil society that are unable to attend personally WTO-sponsored events in Geneva, two virtual conferences have been held to date. These virtual conferences, broadcast via the internet, have had several hundred people logging on each time. Webcasts allow WTO experts to provide up-to-date information on specific trade issues and respond to questions from civil society. However, these virtual conferences have several drawbacks including high cost and being susceptible to deliberate interference from some more aggressive NGOs who aim to cut all lines of communication with the WTO.

Electronic mail/mailing lists Two of the most effective means of interaction between the WTO and civil society are the use of electronic mail (e-mail) and electronic mailing lists. E-mail allows anyone with access to a telephone and a modem to contact the WTO directly at low cost. While no directory currently exists on the WTO website, adding division and staff e-mail directories would likely serve to increase personal interaction. An additional advantage of sending messages via e-mail is that the recipient is able to forward the message on to other interested members of civil society thus allowing messages to rapidly reach broader audiences. The WTO relies on vast NGO networks to spread news and information.

Electronic mailing lists are much faster and cost-effective than conventional mail – and even the sending of facsimiles (faxes) for organizing events – due to their capacity to send a message to large numbers of e-mail addresses at the touch of a button. Several WTO officials cited the WTO Symposium on Issues Confronting the World Trading System held 6-7 July 2001 as a successful example of the advantages of electronic communication. Through using electronic mailing lists, the WTO Secretariat was able to arrange the participation of approximately 450 members of civil society including many NGOs.[10] Electronic mailing lists may also be used to keep trade-related NGOs informed of WTO activities. The External Relations Division sends monthly bulletins to the approximately 1,400 trade-related NGOs on its mailing list. Due to the limited resources of the WTO Secretariat, it is necessary for NGOs to contact the WTO (ngobulletin@wto.org) in order to be placed on the NGO mailing list and receive the bulletin. However, according to Carrier, there is an automated registration system that allows users of the WTO website to select the specific type of information they would like to receive from the WTO. Users have the freedom to change their preferences on-line (Carrier 2001).

Despite the ease of communicating electronically, the WTO continues to communicate with some NGOs via traditional postal services, especially those located in developing member states due to still limited internet access in these countries. However, as access to the internet becomes ever more widely available throughout the world, the WTO reports that communication with civil society is increasingly through various ICT tools.

Reference centres In 1997, the WTO initiated a programme of establishing reference centers in some of the less economically developed member countries as part of an on-going effort of capacity-building. These centers involve the installation of computers and training in the use of the internet and the operation of other sources of trade policy information such as CD-Roms. While such centers are generally located in the ministries of trade or industry, they are available to all citizens. The WTO encourages trade officials in these member countries to share the resources of the reference centers with other government ministries, businesses, unions and NGOs. As of Autumn 2001, there were 104 reference centers supported by special trust funds provided by several Western member governments.

Impact and limitations of information/communication technology for the WTO The WTO's use of ICT in its interaction with NGOs has evolved according to the changing demands of civil society as a whole. Prior to 1999, the percentage of NGO representatives contacting the WTO was relatively small compared to the number of government officials, academics, and business group representatives. However, according to Carrier, over the last several years there has been a dramatic increase in the number of NGOs seeking information on WTO activities. He acknowledges that even though Secretariat staff members are constantly working to increase their on-going exchange with the public, and especially NGOs, they still are "not accomplishing miracles" (Carrier 2001).

Some more radical members of civil society who are opposed to globalization and the activities of the WTO continue to hinder the impact of IT-based information exchange between the WTO and other members of the public. Highly adept at using the very ICT tools that enable globalization, hackers have on several occasions attempted to interfere with the operation of the WTO's website, webcasting sessions, and e-mail system. For example, in the run-up to the 1999 Seattle WTO Ministerial, a very convincing copycat website[11] was launched by an NGO opposed to the WTO immediately prior to the 1999 WTO Ministerial. In order to prevent such activities, the WTO has been forced to use a large portion of its technology budget to increase IT security rather than expanding its ICT-based services. Despite the large amounts of information that ICT can store and transmit, individuals are still ultimately responsible for determining the degree of its impact. Carrier concludes: "We are dealing with humans – and human nature" (2001).

NGOs

Information/communication technology has had a tremendous impact on NGOs, particularly trade-related NGOs that tend to focus on advocacy rather than operational activities. The degree of this impact varies greatly due in part to the often substantial differences in approach, technical capacity, and objectives of trade-related NGOs. Another determinant is an NGO's financial capacity. Some of the larger NGOs such as Greenpeace and the World Wide Fund for Nature (WWF) have annual budgets that are substantially larger than the WTO's budget (Robertson 2000, 1123). These relatively well-resourced NGOs have been able to develop extensive ICT-based information and communication systems. Despite the differences in resources and objectives, most trade-related NGOs have experienced similar ICT-related changes in three activities: modes of operation; campaigning; and information exchange and education. However, while the advances in information technology have produced a qualitative shift in the operation and effectiveness of trade-related NGOs, traditional communication, including personal discussion, remains the core means of interaction.

Modes of operation As the case studies below suggest, trade-related NGOs, regardless of approach, rely heavily on ICT-based tools, such as the internet, World Wide Web, mobile telephones and personal computers in their daily operation. Even some of the more extreme anti-trade NGOs have developed sophisticated websites that serve as both a source of information for members as well as to increase public awareness of their particular operational objectives.

Whether trade-related NGOs are involved in analysis and research, lobbying, or public awareness, ICT enables these groups to carry out their operations more efficiently regardless of geographical location. As a long-time WTO observer notes: "the advantage of a physical presence in Geneva is diminishing as modern information technologies allow groups throughout the world to monitor and contribute to WTO debate" (Esty 1998a, 725-726). This is particularly important to Southern NGOs.

Advances in ICT have also encouraged the linking of NGOs with similar or complementary objectives. In the same way that e-mail facilitates communication between the WTO and NGOs, it also allows NGOs operating throughout the world to form coalitions with each other. ICT is particularly effective in linking NGOs from developed and developing countries. Such partnerships greatly effect campaigning and the spread of information.

Campaigning As the recent large-scale protests against the global economic system demonstrate, there has been a fundamental change in the way NGOs campaign due to the development of ICT-based tools. The large turnouts of anti-globalization and anti-trade demonstrations were largely organized by the use of e-mail, websites and mobile telephones. Many NGO members have become experts in the use of both traditional and ICT-based media to advance their views, at times surpassing the ICT capabilities of officials within international organizations. The need for ICT skills has led to a handful of civil society groups specializing in assisting activists to stage effective, technology-based demonstrations. For example, the Ruckus Society hosted the first annual Tech Toolbox Action Camp in June 2001 to offer instruction in the use of the internet and other forms of ICT for use in campaigning.

However, according to research on the impact of ICT on NGO campaigning, "while activists recognize the impetus the internet provides their lobbying efforts, they do not suggest that electronic networking should, or even can, supplant the street-level education and organization characteristic of this century's most effective citizen movements" (O'Neill 2000, 198). These results are supported by Lori Wallach, Director of Public Citizen's GTW, who, although a self-confessed ICT convert, explains "Even though the internet is used to share information, the real deep planning and organizing is still done person to person".[12]

In addition to the periodic headline-grabbing demonstrations, many trade-related NGOs campaign year-round at both the domestic and international levels. Some trade-related NGOs, such as GTW, offer ready-made talking points and pre-written letters to be sent to policy-makers or funding agencies on their websites to encourage more effective, albeit pre-packaged, campaigns year-round.

Information exchange and education Information/communication technology provides almost limitless potential for expansion in the activities of information exchange and education. The benefits of ICT over conventional forms of communication technology include cost-effectiveness, interactivity and the ability to rapidly exchange large amounts of information (O'Neill 2000, 194). Although a small number of NGOs have the luxury of substantial budgets, many trade-related

NGOs operate with limited resources. However, ICT, when used in conjunction with a well-planned and targeted information campaign, offers all NGOs the ability to have their voices heard regardless of the size of their budget or number of staff. Thus, in the competitive world of trade-related NGOs, ICT allows NGOs to operate on a level playing field.

With vast amounts of storage available on websites, NGOs are able to provide visitors with continuously growing archives of their press releases and other trade-related information. For example, the ICC has archives dating back to 1997 while GTW's archives begin in 1999. NGOs often give visitors the opportunity to extend their information sources by offering links to related sites. Many NGOs limit the available links to sites displaying similar views, but some offer a broad selection including the WTO and domestic trade policy sites.

To spread their information as far as possible, trade-related NGOs increasingly are providing multilingual websites. English, French and Spanish, the official languages of the WTO, are the most common, with English taking the lead. However, some are true polyglots such as Peoples' Global Action (PGA) that offers documents in 7 different languages.

In addition to the importance of exchanging information, many trade-related NGOs also aim to serve an educative function by offering policy analysis to other members of civil society and at times to trade policy-makers. As is to be expected, the analysis tends to reflect their particular approach to the trade debate rather than offering a wide range of views. However, there are exceptions. The coverage of the recent WTO Symposium on Issues Confronting the World Trading System by the International Institute of Sustainable Development (IISD) is a fair and objective summary despite the IISS report being funded by the WTO. Several trade-related NGOs including GTW, the ICC and Third World Network (TWN) produce reports and books supporting their specific standpoint on trade that are prominently advertised on their websites.

Impact and limitations of information/communication technology for NGOs As shown, ICT has had a significant impact on the modes of operation, campaigning and information exchange and education activities of NGOs. The equalizing effect that ICT provides to the full spectrum of trade-related NGOs have profoundly influenced their growth, membership and activities. However, although ICT offers NGOs many benefits, there are also drawbacks.

Three-quarters of the world's population do not own a telephone – let alone a modem with which to connect to the internet. This digital divide exists between developed and developing countries as well as within developed countries. Although efforts are being made to reduce this gap, as long as significant numbers of NGOs and civil society do not have access to ICT, conventional forms of communication will remain crucially important to NGOs.

The ability to send or store large amounts of information using ICT is generally considered a fundamental breakthrough in the operation of NGOs. However, the resulting massive increase in the volume of available information can serve to strain the resources of an NGO due to the time needed to gather, sort and analyze the material. Additionally, the lack of regulation covering internet postings by either governments or members of civil society can lead to questions over the reliability of information (O'Neill 2000, 198).

Case Studies of Selected Trade-Related NGOs: Use of ICT in Interaction with the WTO and Civil Society

Trade-related NGOs, whether single-issue or broad-based, generally are involved in one or more of the following three activities: 1) analysis of trade policy; 2) lobbying in favor of or against one or more trade issues; 3) public awareness. Although trade-related NGOs share many similarities, differences in approach and means can be vast. As noted by Robertson, during the 1999 demonstrations against the WTO in Seattle the "unity against a single target suggested a strength of purpose, but differences among the protesting groups probably were greater than their differences with the WTO ... To present 'civil society' as a united force is quite inaccurate" (2000, 1119-1120).

However, there have been attempts at forming loose networks among NGOs. The demonstrations in Seattle witnessed initial efforts at diverse groups of civil society forming loose coalitions (Ostry 2000). Networks involving agricultural organizations, environmental NGOs, labor unions and human rights activists evolved both on the ground and through cyberspace. In the run-up to the Fourth WTO Ministerial held in Doha, Qatar, coalitions again formed. In response to the WTO-imposed restrictions allowing only one delegate from each of the NGOs eligible for accreditation, the US-based Institute for Agriculture and Trade Policy proposed a pooling of slots that would allow an elected and unified NGO delegation to attend. However, due to reasons such as the differences in views as well as the competitive nature of many trade-related NGOs, significant support for the plan did not emerge. In the opinion of WTO NGO Liaison official Kuiten, in order for the large numbers of diverse trade-related NGOs to have a greater impact on WTO activities: "They have to find a middle ground" (Kuiten 2001).

The four brief case studies that follow were selected as broadly illustrative of the categories in the Scholte, O'Brien, and Williams typology. However, the organizations investigated also display elements of the Ostry functional categorization. They show not only the diversity in approach that exists among trade-related NGOs, but also the variance in use of ICT in their interaction with the WTO, member governments and civil society.

International Chamber of Commerce

The International Chamber of Commerce, established in 1919, represents thousands of corporations and business associations from more than 130 countries to both governments and international organizations. The ICC is a firm supporter of a liberal multilateral trading system operating on the "conviction that trade is a powerful force for peace and prosperity" (ICC 2001a, 1). Given its approach toward trade, the ICC may be considered a conformist-type NGO.

The ICC takes a proactive approach in representing the views of its members both directly and through ICT. In addition to being in regular contact with WTO member government representatives, the ICC effectively utilizes information technology. Its website (www.iccwbo.org) offers information on its membership, activities and services, position statements and commentary on current trade-related issues from a business perspective. The website also includes a members-only Global Intranet to encourage worldwide electronic collaboration. The only links available on ICC's site are to some of its corporate membership.

Regarding interaction with the WTO Secretariat, the ICC has submitted 13 proposals to the WTO Secretariat for availability to interested parties since 1998. Only the Union of Industrial and Employers' Confederations of Europe has submitted more. A key factor in ICC's successful interaction with the WTO is the high standard of its policy proposals. The following excerpt from its June 2001 Policy Statement on Trade Facilitation illustrates this point:

> Binding WTO rules that build on existing WTO Agreements and principles, recommendations in the revised Kyoto Convention, and other facilitation instruments, such as those of the UN and its specialized agencies, will secure many of the key elements of trade facilitation; simplify trade procedures; promote internationally agreed standards; and benefit government and business in all WTO member countries. To this end, it is critical that the WTO and organizations like the World Customs Organization and UN work together to establish the WTO framework and fulfill the objectives of time and cost savings for traders; cheaper goods for producers; lower prices for consumers; a more cost-effective recovery of revenue, and better surveillance of high risk consignments for customs (ICC 2001b, 3).

Through offering guidance and well-written commentary, ICC ensures that its interaction with the WTO is a two-way dialogue. Admittedly, the WTO-friendly position of ICC plays a role in its relationship with the WTO. However, more important is ICC's active contribution to the broader trade debate.

Third World Network

The Third World Network is a grouping of civil society organizations and citizens working on economic, social and environmental issues of importance to developing countries and the South. TWN is generally well-respected by both developing country delegations to the WTO as well as WTO staff members. Its reformist approach is illustrated in the following newspaper report: "From its base in Penang in Malaysia, the TWN acts as the intellectual nerve center of much of the global struggle against unrestrained economic liberalism, producing reports and journals which argue that the drive toward free trade as it is currently constituted is a fraud" (Beattie 2001b). TWN focuses on informing as well as educating the public and policy-makers of alternative approaches to the current neo-liberal trading system. Ostry (2000) places TWN among the 'virtual secretariats' that work to assist Southern NGOs in increasing their bargaining power within the trading system (Ostry 2000, 17). However, she later includes them as part of the core group of NGOs that serve as the "headquarters of dissent.com" (Ostry 2000, 5).

As part of its information campaign, TWN produces extensive, well-researched and sound publications, including position and briefing papers, newspaper articles and books. Many of its publications are written by its Cambridge-educated director, Martin Khor, and Bhagirath Lal Das, former Indian Ambassador to the GATT. Additionally, TWN frequently serves as a voice for Southern interests at international conferences. Khor and Das both have vast experience within the UN system that may explain TWN's willingness to interact with and offer guidance to the WTO as well as its member governments to bring about change.

The Third World Network has embraced the advantages of ICT. Its website (www.twnside.org.sg) is clear and informative, offering visitors a vast choice of documents related to trade, biosafety, biodiversity, the environment, human rights and more. WTO issues take up a considerable portion of the site. Immediately following the conclusion of the Doha Ministerial, held 9-14 November, the TWN website included several documents analysing the Ministerial Declaration and the agreed plans for a new round of multilateral trade negotiations from the perspective of the Third World. In general, the TWN site is a good source of information on WTO activities including reports of various committee and General Council meetings. However, the site has very few links, a relatively limited search engine and does not offer access to trade-related agreements.

Global Trade Watch

Global Trade Watch was established in 1993 as a division of Ralph Nader's US-based, multi-issue NGO, Public Citizen. GTW was one of the primary organizing NGOs of the Seattle demonstrations. Thus, Ostry (2000) groups both Public Citizen and GTW with similar 'headquarters executives' organizations such as TWN (2000, 5). The main line of GTW activity lies in pointing out the weaknesses in international trade agreements and bringing about a more just economic system. However, GTW also works on informing civil society on broader globalization issues such as the environment, health and safety and accountable governance. A goal of GTW is to ensure civil society and policy-makers are made aware that the current global economic model it describes as 'corporate-managed trade' is only one possible approach. GTW's activities aim to make the benefits of this model available to all citizens rather than a select few. If this model cannot produce equitable results, "then the model can and must be changed or replaced" (Public Citizen 2001a, 1).

This approach to the global economy places GTW in the reformist category similar to Third World Network. In fact, these two reformist trade-related NGOs share many aspects including an emphasis on information exchange and education, dynamic directors, and a willingness to work together in coalitions such as the 1999 WTO: No New Round, Turnaround and the more recent WTO: Shrink or Sink campaigns. However, regarding interaction with the WTO and approach to informing the public, the styles of these two reformist NGOs are significantly different. Unlike the amiable Khor, Wallach has been described as an "intelligent, well-informed and media-savvy political organizer [who is] also highly controversial" (Naím 2000, 30). She credits her style to her mother's advice: "Your friends should love you, and your enemies should think you're a major pain".[13] There are some within the WTO who most likely wish she would not have taken this particular bit of advice with some even going so far as to accuse GTW of manipulating the information provided to it by the WTO. The limited direct interaction between the WTO and GTW is currently characterized by mutual distrust and lack of respect.

GTW places great emphasis on providing its members, coalition partners and other members of civil society with information and its own analysis of trade agreements and other trade-related rules and uses ICT effectively. Its website (www.citizen.org/pctrade/tradehome.html) is highly organized, includes very well-documented material, and as noted earlier, acts rapidly with GTW being the first NGO to place a copy of the Multilateral Agreement on Investment on its website. In the run-up to the WTO Doha Ministerial, GTW's website contained a continuously updated chart of the various events throughout the world held to protest against the WTO and the launch of a new trade round.[14] So complete was the GTW chart that other organizations, including the radical organization Peoples' Global Action, referred to it on their own websites. The GTW website also provides links to many other websites, including the WTO and the Office of the US Trade Representative, as well as having the texts of some trade agreements available for downloading. However, the language of a considerable portion of GTW's on-line material is simplistic in content and adversarial in nature such as its description of the WTO as "a crazed pro-corporate, anti-environment, anti-worker octopus hiding under the name of 'free trade'" (Public Citizen 2001b, 2). It is obvious from this statement that, at least for the moment, GTW and the WTO do not share a common language for effective dialogue. Nevertheless, GTW is a voice to which many members of civil society are listening.

Peoples' Global Action

Growing from relatively small groups in the mid-1990s, by the time the second WTO Ministerial was held in Geneva in February 1998, some members of civil society opposed to the current global economic system had united under the loosely organized PGA. Due to PGA's loose organizational structure and its activity in the run-up to the WTO Seattle Ministerial, Ostry has identified the PGA as a 'mobilization network' (2000, 13). As stated in their documents, PGA is a "worldwide coordination of resistance against the global market" (PGA 2000b, 1). Among its principles, is the "very clear rejection of the WTO and other trade liberalization agreements (such as Asia Pacific Economic Co-operation, APEC; the European Union, EU; and North American Free Trade Agreement, NAFTA) as active promoters of a socially and environmentally destructive globalization" as well as adopting a "confrontational attitude" (PGA 2000a, 1). According to its manifesto, PGA's "means and inspiration will emanate from peoples' knowledge and technology, squatted houses and fields, a strong and lively cultural diversity and a very clear determination to actively disobey and disrespect all the treaties and institutions at the root of misery" (PGA 1998, 12). Notably, although an original hallmark of the PGA was a call for non-violent civil disobedience, at their Third Annual Conference in September 2001, the words 'non-violent' were deleted. Given its stated principles and means, PGA may be placed in the radical category of the Scholte, O'Brien, Williams typology.

During 2001, the PGA website (www.nadir.org/nadir/initiativ/agp/) broadened in scope to include not only highly-organized calls to action around the world and documents on its operational beliefs, but also a growing number of interesting, if not always well-documented, alternative viewpoints to the current global economic system. Although offering documents in many languages, the PGA website is weak in the number of links and search capacity. The following excerpt from a PGA Bulletin, explains the network's approach to ICT:

> While the internet was indeed useful (in organizing the 1999 Carnival against Capitalism in London), the mainstream media's devotion to exploring its use by radical groups reflects more current technological restructuring of the global economy then the reality of peoples' knowledge of and participation in the event ... for a more radical grassroots movement will require the real warmth of human togetherness and the raw 'shout on the street' to make a true social and ecological communication revolution and it probably won't be e-mailed (PGA 2000a).

Similar to other radical civil society networks, PGA does not interact with the WTO either directly or through ICT.

Admittedly, these four case studies provide only a glimpse into the particular trade-related NGOs highlighted and the possible typologies with which to categorize them and even less into the broader world of trade-related NGOs. However, they serve to illustrate the vast differences in the objectives and approaches of NGOs toward the global economic system as well as the more minor differences in use of information and ICT in their interaction with the WTO and civil society. The case studies also indicate that despite the increase in the volume of information and the rapidly developing technology with which to store and transmit this information, more must be done to facilitate communication between the WTO, member governments and all members of civil society.

Facilitating Communication between the WTO, Member Governments and Civil Society

Several measures are necessary in order for communication between the WTO and civil society to improve in qualitative and quantitative terms. But there are limitations to further interaction inherent in the WTO system.

Facilitating Communication

Increase transparency and legitimacy There have been frequent charges of the WTO's lack of transparency from civil society, specifically trade-related NGOs. Such accusations stem from a perceived lack of openness in decision-making, dispute settlement procedures and slow release of official documents. In turn, the

WTO and member governments claim that most trade-related NGOs are equally lacking in both transparency due to organizational opaqueness and democratic legitimacy. Scholte, O'Brien, Williams note: "... some of the organizations that have pressed hardest for a democratization of the WTO have done little to secure democracy in their own operations. This has allowed the WTO and states to take civil society less seriously than they might otherwise have done" (1999, 175).

It is clear that if interaction is to improve, all parties must acknowledge these criticisms and act to accommodate the others. As argued by Esty: "Improved decision-making, greater authority, and enhanced legitimacy would all help the WTO to quell the fear of 'globalization' growing around the world ... NGOs can also help to ensure that the public both feels connected to and actually is connected to these more distantly made decisions" (1998a, 729).

Increase knowledge of WTO/civil society through information exchange
Trade-related NGOs provide an extremely useful service by increasing the amount of information and knowledge on the activities of the WTO and the issues confronting the broader multilateral trading system. Due to their objectivity in gathering a broad spectrum of information as well as well-researched policy analysis, the Geneva-based International Centre for Trade and Sustainable Development (ICTSD) has become a widely respected provider of information and analysis of issues in trade and sustainable development. Established in 1996 as an umbrella organization representing a range of NGOs, ICTSD serves as a forum where trade policy-makers, business and NGOs may find common ground. ICTSD's standard of excellence in information exchange between all members of the trade debate is acknowledged by NGO representatives as well as WTO officials.

Such NGO activity is critical given the lack of information many WTO member governments supply their citizens. WTO Deputy Director General Andrew Stoler points out: "... it's quite clear that people in government and organizations and in business are not doing a good enough job right now explaining what the benefits are to people in the street, what the benefits to developing countries are, and how these concerns about the environment ... can be accommodated".[15]

An issue that trade-related NGOs and the WTO Secretariat agree on is that the first point of contact concerning the formulation of trade policy should be the national level. However, in order for informed dialogue to occur, WTO member governments must engage in transparent information exchanges with their citizens on trade-related issues. Keith Rockwell, WTO Director of Information and Media Relations explains that in order for the basis of WTO/NGO interactions to improve, "Member states must get the word out" (Rockwell 2001).

Guidance Although most trade-related NGOs are involved in some form of information exchange, only a small percentage provide the WTO Secretariat and member governments with regular, well-researched policy analysis, alternative policies and guidance. Since the WTO began offering NGOs the possibility of placing proposals on the WTO website in 1998, only slightly more than 100 of the thousands of active trade-related NGOs[16] have taken the opportunity to do so. Of those, only 18 have submitted three or more proposals in four years. In order to encourage NGOs to offer guidance to the WTO and its member countries, the WTO External Relations Division recently began to offer a podium to trade-related NGOs to present reports or studies to interested parties as well as continuously encouraging guidance during NGO briefings. However, the NGO response has been limited. As Bernard Kuiten, WTO Liaison Officer, notes: "There is not enough guidance from NGOs. However, it is a learning process" (Kuiten 2001).

If guidance from trade-related NGOs is to be relevant to WTO member governments, the information on which it is based must be sound and timely. While ICT is of considerable use in enabling NGOs to have access to such information, first-hand observation of WTO activity including meetings of the General Council and various committees would bring even more benefits. Opening these meetings to trade-related NGOs would result in a greater understanding of the frequently constrained environment in which member governments must work. Additionally, increasing NGO involvement in the formulation of WTO trade policy and monitoring of trade policy reviews as well as greater acceptance of NGO amicus briefs by Dispute Settlement Panels and the Appellate Body would go far in reducing claims of a democratic deficit. However, EU Trade Commissioner Pascal Lamy speaks for many WTO trade ministers in arguing that NGOs should "have a voice, but not a vote" (WTO 2001).

Limitations

Nature of trade negotiations Although most of the WTO's activities would benefit from increased NGO consultation, there are three primary reasons why NGO involvement in trade negotiations should remain at the national level rather than at the WTO. Firstly, the conduct of any type of negotiation requires a degree of confidentiality on the part of the individual negotiating parties. If a party's bottom-line is known in advance by other negotiating parties, it severely limits their ability to negotiate a better outcome. Secondly, during the WTO's multi-issue negotiations, much maneuvering occurs among the positions of member governments in order to obtain a better overall outcome. The involvement of many different single-issue trade-related NGOs during multilateral trade negotiations would severely restrict a country's flexibility. Thirdly, as stated earlier, it is generally acknowledged that NGOs should first approach their national government when attempting to influence trade policy. The possibility to again attempt to influence both their government and others at the WTO would result in NGOs having "two bites at the apple" (Esty 1998a, 725).

Lack of funds and staff The WTO Secretariat is extremely limited in taking further actions to facilitate interaction with trade-related NGOs due in part to a lack of funds. The total WTO budget for 2001, agreed among members, is approximately SF134,083,610 (US$80 million). From the total budget, technical co-operation activities were allocated approximately SF1,163,200 (US$694,000) while only SF260,000 ($155,000) was reserved for public information activities. In contrast, the total administrative budget for the World Bank in 2000 was approximately

US$1,469 million. Since 1999, an increasing number of member governments that support greater technical co-operation, training of trade officials from selected member governments, and increased interaction with trade-related NGOs have voluntarily provided trust funds that assist somewhat in overcoming the limitations of the WTO budget.

Another result of the relatively small WTO budget is the lack of sufficient numbers of staff to handle the increased demands placed on the Secretariat. The current number of Secretariat staff is approximately 500. However, there are only three members of staff within the External Relations Division, one of whom is the Director, another who deals primarily with relations with other intergovernmental organizations and parliamentarians, and only one who works full-time on outreach activities with civil society.

Lack of political will Despite the many benefits of increased WTO/NGO dialogue and pledges of agreement on a broadened mandate for the WTO Secretariat, only a very small percentage of the 144 member governments of the WTO currently have the political will to support increased interaction with NGOs. The member governments in favour, generally developed countries with a history of pluralism in their national political systems, include Canada, the 15 members of the European Union, Japan, New Zealand, the Nordic countries, Switzerland and the United States. However, due to the majority of member governments that are hesitant to engage in two-way dialogue with their own citizens or NGOs on issues related to trade policy, major progress is likely to remain limited. It is in such countries that trade-related NGOs need to take on the role of ambassadors of trade to inform the public of the issues at stake. In order to change the current situation, civil society will not only need to place continued pressure on their national governments to interact with them but also demonstrate by their actions that they have much to contribute to the trade debate.

Expanding the Trade Debate: Prospects and Recommendations

The WTO and the wider multilateral trading system have evolved to encompass many issues of great concern to civil society such as food safety, services, intellectual property rights, and the environment. Additionally, the actions taken by the WTO have direct impact on the lives of members of civil society. Thus, all members of civil society have a legitimate right to have their voices heard in the continuing debate over trade. Serving as representatives of segments of civil society, trade-related NGOs are the voice and ears of many members of civil society in this debate. As the WTO continues to evolve, this voice will increasingly demand to be listened to either from within the WTO and members' capitals or from without in massive demonstrations.

To date, pressure to make the WTO more transparent and open to members of civil society has been external – from civil society rather than member governments. In turn, the response has been for the most part unsatisfactory, ineffective, and haphazard. The following recommendations, involving actions on the part of the WTO, its member governments, and civil society would serve to expand the trade debate as well as make it more satisfactory, effective and systematic.

Incorporate civil society into the trade debate   Civil society needs to be incorporated in the WTO's trade debate. Failing this, there will be two separate debates on trade speaking at cross-purposes. Through increasing communication with their citizens and trade-related NGOs, WTO member governments will come to understand their citizens' concerns regarding the current global economic system, benefit from their expertise while having the opportunity to promote the government's vision of the multilateral trading system.

For the debate to be satisfactory to trade-related NGOs, their proposals and suggestions must be genuinely considered and not merely a public relations tool. Additionally, NGO participation should be balanced to include a representative number of NGOs from the North and South, developed and developing countries, as well as from various issues and perspectives.

To be effective, trade-related NGOs need to present well-informed and realistic proposals based on solid argument. Reliable information is thus critical. Trade-related NGO representatives require increased access to both documents and WTO meetings regardless of whether this is direct or through the use of ICT.

In order for civil society to be incorporated systematically into the WTO, a civil society policy committee should be established consisting of member government representatives, Secretariat staff, and a representative group of trade-related NGOs. Regular meetings would encourage dialogue, ensure implementation of organizational procedures concerning civil society, and increase legitimacy.

Establishment of an educative system   A greater awareness of both the functioning of the WTO and the various approaches to the multilateral trading system is needed among members of civil society. If the WTO is to respond effectively to those who are critical of it, increased efforts at explaining the WTO's activities, decision-making process, and benefits of free trade are necessary. The establishment of an educative system consisting of an ongoing series of lectures, conferences and symposia by respected trade experts, academics and NGO representatives in addition to the publication of a basic book on the operation of the WTO would serve to increase the public understanding of the issues at stake and thus raise the level of debate.

Expanded trade debate based on increased knowledge and information technology
The revolution in ICT offers the potential to expand the trade debate in terms of numbers and types of state and non-state actors involved and the variety of issues discussed. However, the choice to expand and transform the trade debate from diatribe to dialogue is one that both WTO member governments and civil society must make.

Notes

Note on internet addresses (URLs): Websites tend to appear, change or disappear, often without warning. Addresses cited in this bibliography were accurate and active at the time of writing (February 2002) unless otherwise noted.

1. See Peter Hajnal's discussion in the Introduction.
2. Robertson (2000) makes the distinction between operational NGOs that provide services and advocacy NGOs that aim to have influence on the policymaking process. Additionally, Ostry (2000) distinguishes between transformational NGOs that aim to have an impact on the policy-making process through influencing public opinion and distributional groups that wish to secure increased economic gains for their members.
3. 'NGO swarm' refers to large number of diverse NGOs focusing on an issue through the use of the internet. This term was coined by David Ronfeldt and John Arquilla in a recent RAND study (Arquilla and Ronfeldt, 1997).
4. See Chapter 5 for a detailed discussion of NGOs of the South.
5. However, certain activities of the WTO's Trade Policy Review and Dispute Settlement Procedure show elements of supranationalism.
6. See WTO 1996b.
7. According to WTO statistics, the types of NGOs attending the 1996 Singapore Ministerial consited of 48 business NGOs, 26 development, 11 other, 10 trade unions, 8 environment, 3 development/environment and 2 consumers. The 1998 Geneva Ministerial consisted of 46 business, 26 development, 22 environment, 21 trade unions, 6 consumers, 4 other and 3 farmer NGOs. See www.wto.org/english/forums_e/ngo_e/statsi_e.htm and www.wto.org/english/forums_e/ngo_e/statgen_e.htm
8. Telephone interview with a long-time, Geneva-based NGO representative, 26 June 2001.
9. For a current schedule, see www.wto.org/english/forums_e/ngo_e/briefs_e.htm
10. For an excellent summary of this symposium, see the report produced by the International Institute for Sustainable Development at www.iisd.ca/sd/wto-issues/
11. See www.gatt.org
12. As quoted in Naím 2000, 47.
13. As quoted in Naím 2000, 31.
14. See www.citizen.org/trade/
15. As quoted by Andrew Stoler, 13 September 2000. See transcript at www.abc.net.au/pm/s176169.htm (ABC 2000).
16. Robertson indicates that there are 29,000 'independent organizations' working to obtain representation with the WTO or OECD consultative groups (2000, 1123).

References

Arquilla, John and Ronfeldt, David (1997), *In Athena's Camp: Preparing for Conflict in the Information Age*, RAND, Santa Monica.

Australian Broadcasting Corporation. News Online (2000), *WTO Leader Undeterred by Globalisation Opposition*, Transcript of Broadcast with WTO Deputy Director-General Andrew Stoler, 13 September. www.abc.net.au/pm/s176169.htm

Bayne, Nicholas (2000b), 'Why Did Seattle Fail? Globalization and the Politics of Trade', *Government and Opposition*, Vol. 35(2), pp. 131-151.

Beattie, Alan (2001b), 'The Polite Face of Anti-globalisation', *The Financial Times*. 6 April, p. 8.

Carrier, Jean-Guy (2001), (Manager, WTO Internet Resources), Telephone conversation, 11 July.
Esty, Daniel C. (1998a), 'Linkages and Governance: NGOs at the World Trade Organization', *University of Pennsylvania Journal of International Economic Law*, Vol. 19(3), pp. 709-730.
Esty, Daniel C. (1998b), 'Non-Governmental Organizations at the World Trade Organization: Cooperation, Competition or Exclusion', *Journal of International Economic Law*, Vol. 1, pp. 123-147.
Esty, Daniel C. (1999a), 'Environmental Governance at the WTO: Outreach to Civil Society', in Gary P. Sampson and W. Bradnee Chambers (eds), *Trade, Environment, and the Millennium*, The United Nations University, Japan, pp. 97-117.
Esty, Daniel C. (1999b), 'Why the World Trade Organization Needs Environmental NGOS', *Transnational Associations*, Vol. 51(5), pp. 267-279.
GATT Secretariat (1994), *The Results of the Uruguay Round of Multilateral Trade Negotiations: The Legal Texts*, GATT Secretariat, Geneva.
Hajnal, Peter I. (2001), *Personal Assessment of the Role of Civil Society at the 2001 Genoa G8 Summit*, University of Toronto G8 Information Centre: Analytical Studies, 2001 Summit Assessment, 2 August,
www.g7.utoronto.ca/g7/evaluations/2001genoa/assess_summit_hajnal.html
Hocking, Brian and McGuire, Steven (eds) (1999), *Trade Politics: International, Domestic and Regional Perspectives*, Routledge, London.
International Chamber of Commerce (2001a), *ICC Actions and Achievements*, www.iccwbo.org/home/intro_icc/icc_actions_achievements.asp
International Chamber of Commerce (2001b), *ICC Recommendations to WTO Members on Trade Facilitation*, 6 June, Document No. 103-32/91.
www.iccwbo.org/home/statements_rules/statements/2001/wto_members_on_trade.asp
International Institute for Sustainable Development (2001), 'Summary of the WTO Symposium on Issues Confronting the World Trading System', *Sustainable Developments*, Vol. 55(1), www.iisd.ca/sd/wto-issues/
Keohane, Robert and Nye, Joseph (1998), 'Power and Interdependence in the Information Age', *Foreign Affairs*, Vol. 77(5), pp. 81-94.
Kuiten, Bernard (2001), Personal interview with author, 26 June, Geneva.
Marceau, Gabrielle, and Pedersen, Peter (1999), 'Is the WTO Open and Transparent?', *Journal of World Trade*, Vol. 33(1), pp. 5-49.
Naím, Moisés (2000), 'The FP Interview: Lori's War', *Foreign Policy*, No. 118, pp. 28-55.
'The Non-Governmental Order' (1999), *The Economist*, 11 December, pp. 20-21.
O'Brien, Robert et al. (2000), *Contesting Global Governance: Multilateral Economic Institutions and Global Social Movements*, Cambridge University Press, Cambridge, Cambridge Studies in International Relations, No. 71.
O'Neill, Kelly (2000), 'NGO Web Sites: Keeping Business in the Spotlight', *Transnational Associations*, Vol. 52(4), pp. 193-200.
Ostry, Sylvia (2000), *WTO: Institutional Design for Better Governance*, (Draft), Paper presented at J.F. Kennedy School of Government, Harvard University. 2-3 June, www.utoronto.ca/cis/WTOID.pdf
Pearsall, Judy (ed) (1999), *The Concise Oxford Dictionary*, 10th Ed, Oxford University Press, Oxford.
Peoples' Global Action (1998), 'Peoples' Global Action Manifesto', Geneva, February/March, www.nadir.org/nadir/initiativ/agp/en/
Peoples' Global Action (2000a), 'Bulletin 5', February, www.nadir.org/nadir/initiativ/agp/en/
Peoples' Global Action (2000b), 'People's Global Action against "Free" Trade and the World Trade Organization', 2 March, www.agp.org/agp/en/

Public Citizen for Global Trade Watch (2001a), 'About Global Trade Watch', www.citizen.org/trade/about/

Public Citizen for Global Trade Watch (2001b), 'Talking Points on 'WTO: Shrink or Sink Global NGO Campaign', www.citizen.org/pctrade/gattwto/ShrinkSink/talkingpts.htm

Robertson, David (2000), 'Civil Society and the WTO', *The World Economy*, Vol. 23(9), pp. 1119-1134.

Rockwell, Keith (2001), (WTO Director of Information and Media Relations), Telephone interview, 27 June.

Scholte, Jan Aart, O'Brien, Robert and Williams, Marc (1999), 'The World Trade Organization and Civil Society', in Brian Hocking and Steven McGuire (eds), *Trade Politics: International, Domestic and Regional Perspectives*, Routledge, London, pp. 162-179.

Simmons, P.J. (1998), 'Learning to live with NGOs', *Foreign Policy*, No. 112, pp. 82-96.

Wolfe, Robert (1999), 'The World Trade Organization', in Brian Hocking and Steven McGuire (eds), *Trade Politics: International, Domestic and Regional Perspectives*, Routledge, London, pp. 208-223.

World Trade Organization (n.d.), *WTO and NGOs Relations with Non-Governmental Organizations/Civil Society*, WTO, Geneva, www.wto.org/english/forums_e/ngo_e/intro_e.htm

World Trade Organization (1996a), 'Guidelines for Arrangements on Relations with Non-Governmental Organizations', WTO, Geneva, 23 July, WT/L/162.

World Trade Organization (1996b), 'Procedures for the Circulation and De-Restriction of WTO Documents', WTO, Geneva, 22 July, WT/L/160.

World Trade Organization (1998a), *Focus*, No. 32, July.

World Trade Organization (1998b), *Ruggerio Announces Enhanced WTO Plan for Cooperation with NGOs*, WTO, Geneva, Press 107, www.wto.org/english/news_e/pres98_e/pr107_e.htm

World Trade Organization (2000a), *Focus*, No. 51, January-February.

World Trade Organization (2000b), *WTO and World Bank Open Online Forum on Trade Issues*, WTO, Geneva, www.wto.org/english/news_e/news00_e/wto-wbforum_e.htm

World Trade Organization (2001), 'Opening Remarks', *Symposium on Issues Confronting the World Trading System*, WTO, Geneva, 6 July.

Chapter 12

Citizen Involvement in Canadian Foreign Policy: The Summit of the Americas Experience, Québec City, April 2001

Marc Lortie and Sylvie Bédard
Copyright © Marc Lortie and Sylvie Bédard

Globalization is not simply one option among many facing our societies. It is a reality that asserts itself daily in the lives of all citizens. It is neither the source of the world's ills nor their panacea. Nevertheless, globalization is a challenge with which every society must come to grips as they address their own particular problems.

The change that globalization wreaks finds expression in two dominant forces: the internationalization of the economy and the development of information and communication technologies, such as the internet. These forces affect us all, affording opportunities to some and visiting adversity on others. The impact of globalization on governance is profound.

For the countries of the Western Hemisphere, the Third Summit of the Americas, held in Québec City in April 2001, represented a collective effort to maximize the benefits of globalization and take up the challenges associated with it. The purpose of this chapter is to illustrate the extent to which the new global reality influenced the process of the Summit of the Americas and the undertakings made by the heads of state and government of the 34 democracies that inhabit the hemisphere. We in the Canadian government opted for a different way of doing things by introducing greater transparency, both in the process and in the substance of the Summit. This approach not only helped us to develop a more effective Plan of Action, but also raised the level of citizen involvement in hemispheric affairs.

Information and Communications Technologies

People today have access to an almost infinite range of information through the internet. By a mere click of the mouse, this medium enables them instantaneously to express and publish their feelings, opinions and concerns to thousands of people from all walks of life. The result is an unprecedented volume of information and ideas in circulation, most of it beyond the direct control of the state.

This has a definite impact on governance. It curtails the efforts of authoritarian regimes to restrict free speech. It enables citizens, especially young people and nongovernmental organizations (NGOs), to form direct ties across national boundaries, and to mobilize in large numbers and in record time.

The instantaneous availability of so much information makes people more sceptical when information is not accessible to them. With access to such a variety of sources of information, citizens are far less inclined to take the information provided by governments on faith. Critical of the information they do receive, they are outraged when information is denied them. In this age of skepticism, ensuring greater transparency serves to allay public apprehension of government intent by shedding light on how decisions are made, allowing citizens to judge for themselves. At the same time, the dissemination of relevant, current information opens the way for genuine participation by potential players who are interested and want to be more involved.

Internationalization of the Economy

The internationalization of the economy makes itself known through the growing presence of foreign companies, the availability of consumer products from all over the world, and the increased mobility of workers. Their daily lives affected, citizens take greater interest in international affairs and foreign policy.

This in turn stimulates them to travel more, to learn foreign languages, to study or work abroad. People also want to understand the challenges that face developing countries, and they are drawn to causes such as the elimination of anti-personnel mines, labour conditions for women working in 'maquiladoras', and child labour.

In addition, the hardships visited on have-not communities prompt concerns that the globalized economy and freer trade may in fact bring greater prosperity to no more than a select few. Threatened by globalization, these communities find it difficult to believe that the increased wealth enjoyed by some will eventually percolate down to them.

Many are affected directly by unemployment, uncertain working conditions and other problems. They understand that these are symptoms of a transitional period, but inevitably ask themselves how long they will have to suffer the dislocations of globalization before its benefits also touch their lives. They wonder whether they have what it takes to become part of an increasingly specialized labour force, and find it difficult to adapt to the fast pace of change in their working lives. They are sceptical about whether the state really intends to continue providing basic public services such as health care, education and welfare. As well, they are concerned about possible ecological imbalances, and they fear that globalization might undermine the cultural and linguistic diversity on which their identities are based.

Impact on Governance

Globalization has given rise to a multiplicity of social actors and has brought changes in their roles, influence and relationships. Among those who have acquired greater influence are the multinational corporations and a wide variety of NGOs, known collectively by the term 'civil society', representing all actors beyond the state.

The challenge to governance comes from all levels. To some, the size and influence of multinational corporations give them disproportionate power relative to the state. On the other hand, the ability of NGOs to mobilize people and to disseminate messages, through the internet and through their increased access to traditional media, provides an unprecedented level of influence.

Citizens, on their part, feel less and less control over the international decisions that affect them more directly than ever. Why is this?

Some feel that globalization has created a "democratic deficit" by transferring power to the top. They believe that more and more decisions are escaping the control of the parliamentarians and even the executive branch of national governments, because those decisions are being made by international organizations such as the World Trade Organization, the World Bank, and the International Monetary Fund.

Reports of governmental efforts to influence globalization are treated with suspicion. Surely the various summits being organized with great pomp around the world (Group of Eight industrialized countries, G8; Asia Pacific Economic Co-operation [forum], APEC; Summit of the Americas; and so on) will merely result in decisions of no relevance for the majority of citizens, or fine promises whose implications are not understood, which will not be respected or accompanied by resources needed to implement them?

The challenges of globalization will only be successfully met if the right balance is struck between the role and influence of the state, the market, and civil society. The increased influence of NGOs or of multinational corporations necessarily compels them to take greater measure of responsibility for their actions and statements.

For their part states must demonstrate greater transparency in the development and implementation of policies and ensure that citizens from all sectors, not merely the elites, are fully involved in decision-making. Our experience with the Québec Summit illustrates how the Canadian government has taken into account this reality and the lessons that were learned from this.

The Québec Summit

In the preparation of the Third Summit of the Americas, we took an approach that was both coherent and inclusive. We ensured that the Summit preparation process provided room for the new social actors and introduced greater transparency especially in trade negotiations and in the actual organization of the Summit. By taking into account the views and concerns of various citizens' groups, we developed a coherent, balanced programme of hemispheric co-operation and provided for the financing and mechanisms required to implement it.

A Coherent Approach

The main pillar of hemispheric co-operation is the firm commitment towards democracy. This shared conviction that democratic values and principles are fundamental to the continued development of all aspects of hemispheric co-operation was the *raison d'être* of the First Summit of the Americas, held in Miami, in 1994.

This deep conviction was also clear at the Québec Summit, for which the most significant outcome was the adoption of a "democratic clause" in the leaders' Declaration. This clause establishes respect for and the maintenance of democratic institutions as an essential condition for participation in the Summit process including the Free Trade Area of the Americas (FTAA). The Plan of Action of the Summit includes an array of provisions to strengthen the democratic institutions throughout the hemisphere. It also underlines the importance of involving the citizens of the hemisphere to a greater extent in public life.

One of the main tenets of hemispheric co-operation holds that maximum benefit can be derived from globalization through the development of a rules-based system to manage globalization at the regional level. Introducing the rule of law in international trade not only increases prosperity but also provides the conditions for advancement of social, cultural and political goals as well. The Canadian government firmly believes that the creation of a free trade area is the best way of promoting the economic growth and social development of the countries in the Hemisphere. The re-affirmation by leaders of their commitment to conclude the FTAA by 2005 was therefore a second major outcome of the Third Summit of the Americas.

The Plan of Action of the Summit also includes provisions to promote quality education for all, respect for workers' rights and for the environment, the enhancement and development of effective social policies and the promotion of cultural diversity. Recognizing the growing importance of information and communication technologies in daily life, the 34 countries also established a "connectivity agenda" designed to narrow the digital gap between the countries of the hemisphere and within their societies, in order to give citizens the choice of being more informed, of expressing their opinions and of being more involved in public life. This agenda is complementary to the main objectives of the Summit.

The challenge of hemispheric co-operation is to ensure that the benefits of globalization are distributed at all levels of society and lead to a better quality of life for all. It means putting a human face on globalization. In the Hemisphere, we must also take into account the various levels of development of the countries and plan our co-operation accordingly. This is a challenge that is difficult to surmount. This is why we have developed a coherent, balanced programme of hemispheric co-operation encompassing the political and social aspects of regional integration. This approach takes into account the concerns and expectations that had been voiced by the various groups of citizens and parliamentarians in the preparations for the Summit.

The Plan of Action endorsed by the heads of state and government in Québec City responds to another concern expressed by citizens; namely, that the tools and financing required to implement the decisions made are in place. States put their money where their mouths are: more than US$56 billion will be provided over the coming years through the Inter-American Development Bank and the World Bank to reinforce democratic institutions, economic infrastructures, education, health care and connectivity.

An Inclusive Approach

As mentioned earlier, the Canadian government developed a new approach in preparing for the Québec City Summit. It did this by placing greater emphasis on information and the involvement by parliamentarians and citizens' groups.

As host of the Summit of the Americas, Canada had the opportunity to showcase its democratic values and to establish a tradition of openness and transparency in the Summit process. It did so primarily by promoting hands-on participation by citizens' groups in the preparations for and holding of the Summit. Canada's leadership role in this area was already recognized in the Hemisphere, because we had initiated a number of resolutions of this kind within the Organization of American States (OAS) and had supported a number of parallel forums, conferences and consultative processes conducted by various groups from Canada and the Hemisphere. A number of Canadian ministers and senior officials had taken an interest in civil society events and views and encouraged their colleagues in the hemisphere to share this interest.

Preparing for the Summit: In the Hemisphere

In February 2000, Canada's Permanent Representative to the OAS took the initiative, as Chair of the Special Committee on Inter-American Summit Management, to open the Committee sessions to civil society and to broadcast them on the internet in real time. During the year leading up to the Summit, the Committee became the hemisphere's primary mechanism for civil society consultation.

In the course of the meetings, the apprehensions and skepticism of both the permanent representatives of OAS member states and of civil society representatives gave way to a constructive dialogue. The recommendations received were transmitted by Canada – as Chair of the Committee – to the national co-ordinators, 'sherpas', of the 34 member countries at the time of the preparatory meetings for the Summit (the Summit Implementation Review Group, or SIRG) following the Committee's meetings.

As for the questions pertaining specifically to the FTAA, Canada's leadership led to major advances in making the negotiation more transparent. In April 2001, in Buenos Aires, thanks to the persistent efforts of Canada's Minister for International Trade, trade ministers agreed to publish the draft negotiating text of the FTAA. The ministers recognized the importance of the Committee of Government Representatives on the Participation of Civil Society as a mechanism by which to fulfil their commitment to transparency, taking into consideration the views expressed by individuals and organizations in the hemisphere. The ministers also asked the Committee to work on a list of concrete options to encourage a more dynamic and sustainable communication process with civil society in order to shed light on the FTAA negotiating process.

Preparing for the Summit: In Canada

The involvement of Canadians in inter-American issues dates back before the 1998 Santiago Summit and has taken various forms as we have advanced in developing our hemispheric agenda. In 1997, the Department of Foreign Affairs and International Trade (DFAIT) asked the Canadian Foundation for the Americas/Fondation canadienne pour les Amériques (FOCAL) to conduct consultations across Canada. This served to increase the level of interest in the hemisphere. We have since introduced regular information exchange sessions to maintain this interest, to familiarize the Canadian expert community with the OAS and Summit processes and to receive their views.

In the same spirit, we invited representatives from the International Institute for Sustainable Development, Rights and Democracy, and from the Canadian Centre for International Cooperation to join the Canadian delegation to the SIRG in 1998. This gave these organizations a better grasp of the workings of the region's multilateral institutions and helped the government to familiarize itself with their concerns.

Next, in a more targeted fashion, from July 1999 to April 2000, the Canadian Centre for Foreign Policy Development (CCFPD) assembled NGOs, experts, academics, trade unionists, business people, parliamentarians and media representatives from across Canada to provide input into the development of Canada's foreign policy in the hemisphere. Nine round tables were organized by the CCFPD in various Canadian cities.

During the period of preparing and negotiating the Summit Plan of Action, we increased the frequency of the information exchange sessions. These provided a forum for government representatives and civil society organizations to exchange ideas and opinions. The sessions took place in Ottawa, two to three weeks before each meeting of the SIRG. Conference call connections were provided for those from outside the region. The minutes of these meetings were published on the Summit internet site (www.americascanada.org).

On the eve of the Summit, DFAIT organized a meeting with Minister of Foreign Affairs John Manley and Minister for International Trade Pierre Pettigrew, in which sixty or so Canadian organizations participated. This session was chaired by Member of Parliament (MP) Bill Graham [subsequently named Foreign Minister – Ed.], who was highly involved and interested in the Summit process. The discussions became more and more constructive from one session to another, since on the one hand, the organizations were better informed about the Summit themes and process, and on the other, the government representatives grew more and more familiar with civil society perspectives.

As an adjunct to these sessions, the various Canadian ministers, the Prime Minister's personal representative for the Summit, a number of Canadian ambassadors to the Americas, and the Summit team conducted an extensive public diplomacy campaign across Canada. The objective was twofold: to hear the views expressed in various sectors; and to raise awareness among the Canadian population concerning the issues before the Summit and the relevance of our hemispheric agenda to those issues.

This information campaign was supplemented through the traditional media and through a multimedia internet site devoted specifically to the Summit. This site proved to be an important tool, especially in reaching youth and civil society groups, since it uses their preferred means of communication. However, the fact that it is published in the four official languages (English, Spanish, French and Portuguese) of the Summit has slowed our efforts to update it regularly.

In Québec City itself, people were interested more directly in all aspects of the Summit but were especially concerned that things might get out of hand from a security point of view. Here we created a local internet site, published an information brochure, provided a dedicated telephone line, and financed or organized a series of cultural events and public and academic lectures on Americas-related themes. We also obtained the consent of all the participating heads of state and government to broadcast a part of the Summit live on national and international television, which not only strengthened our commitment to greater transparency but also enabled a number of citizens and groups from various sectors to better understand what a Summit is and what goes on "behind closed doors".

Parliamentarians also greatly contributed in involving citizens in the Summit process. During the period preceding the Summit, Parliament's (House of Commons) Standing Committee on Foreign Affairs and International Trade (SCFAIT) held a series of public hearings on the Summit process, in particular on the FTAA and the process of involving citizens and parliamentarians in the preparation for and follow-up to the Summit. The Committee published two reports containing a number of recommendations to which the government responded positively. The caucuses of all the political parties were informed of the evolution of the process through information sessions with the Prime Minister's personal representative for the Summit.

Parliamentarians from across the Americas decided to deepen their co-operation by establishing the Inter-Parliamentary Forum of the Americas, a parliamentary association at the national level, linked to the Organization of American States. The Canadian Parliament played a leadership role in the launching of this Forum by hosting its inaugural meeting from 7 to 9 March 2001. This meeting brought together more than 100 parliamentarians from 26 OAS member countries to discuss major hemispheric themes. Bill Graham, Chair of SCFAIT, was elected Chair of the Forum for 2001-2002.

During the runup to the Summit, the level of familiarity with, and interest in, the Americas among parliamentarians, citizens and civil society groups in Canada increased considerably, as did the diversity of the groups involved. Accordingly, our discussions with a number of the groups grew more and more constructive, helping to make our Plan of Action more relevant and better balanced. This showed that we stand to gain from building this relationship, increasing the opportunities for consultation and making our foreign policy more transparent.

Preparing for the Summit: Parallel Events

In the context of preparing for the Summit, the Canadian government also funded a wide variety of consultations carried out by civil society in Canada and the Americas. These events promoted closer ties between various groups in Canada and their hemispheric partners and produced concrete recommendations to improve the process of hemispheric integration.

Among the main events, there were the Second People's Summit; a consultation process with 900 hemispheric NGOs organized by Corporaciòn Participa (Chile), the Esquel Foundation (USA) and FOCAL (Canada); the Youth Forum of the Americas organized by the Canadian Students Commission; the Indigenous Peoples' Summit of the Americas; the Writers of the Americas' Meeting, organized by the Salon international du livre de Québec; the Montreal Conference on Free Trade in the Americas; the Symposium on Trade and Sustainability organized in collaboration with former Québec Premier Pierre-Marc Johnson; and the Conference on Hemispheric Integration organized by the Québec Institute of International Studies at Laval University.

The recommendations submitted by the various civil society groups were given to the Heads of State and Government by Prime Minister Chrétien and representatives of all these groups were invited to a programme arranged for civil society at the Summit itself. At the closing ceremony, then Argentine President Fernando de la Rúa, ended his speech with a quote from one of these events. This was elegant testimony to the importance he placed on civil society's contribution. Argentina will host the next Summit.

The Second People's Summit

The Second People's Summit, held in Québec City on the eve of the Summit of the Americas was the most visible demonstration of the high level of citizen interest and involvement in hemispheric affairs. It was organized by Common Frontiers and the Réseau québécois sur l'intégration continentale (RQIC), which bring together all the main Canadian trade unions and women's groups, as well as student associations and other Canadian NGOs espousing an alternate model for the FTAA. These networks fall under the umbrella of the Hemispheric Social Alliance, formed at the time of the first People's Summit on the fringe of the Santiago Summit in April 1998.

The Alliance is the network with the greatest power to mobilize support. Pressure tactics favoured by the network include organizing large-scale parallel events and staging massive, peaceful demonstrations. The Second People's Summit included about 1,500 people, one-third of them from outside Canada. It was financed by the Government of Canada and the Government of Québec and by contributions from various organizations, in particular Canadian and American trade unions. This event enjoyed wide coverage with the main media set up on the actual site of the People's Summit throughout the week, covering activities and conducting live interviews.

The Prime Minister's personal representative for the Summit met about ten times with the organizers of the People's Summit during the runup to the Summit to update them on the development of the hemispheric agenda and also to discuss the Canadian Government's financial contribution and various logistical details. The Ministers of Foreign Affairs and International Trade and the Secretary of State for Latin America and Africa also met with representatives of the People's Summit prior to the Summit.

At the actual time of the event, ministers were welcome to attend, but as observers, since this was an event organized primarily "by and for civil society". The Minister for International Cooperation, the Labour Minister and the Secretary of State for Latin America and Africa thus attended some thematic forums as well as the final plenary session. Their participation allowed them to further their contacts with a number of representatives from Canadian NGOs, to meeting with foreign representatives and gaining a better understanding of the dynamic of co-operation between the northern and southern NGOs and of the differences in their priorities and approaches.

We had lengthy discussions with the People's Summit organizers on the actual submission of the Declaration to the 'official Summit'. Canadian ministers were prepared to officially receive the People's Summit Declaration at the time of the final plenary for the event, which took place on the eve of the opening of the Summit of the Americas. However, this idea was not unanimously welcomed in the People's Summit Policy Committee, where some members insisted that the Declaration be handed over to heads of state and government or not at all.

This posed a crucial question for the government: should we recognize the People's Summit as the representative entity for the whole of civil society? The People's Summit itself agreed that it was not the case. Such a decision would have been counter to our objectives of increasing transparency, the involvement of all sectors of society and of favouring inclusion.

In consultation with different citizens' groups and networks, we opted instead to put in place a civil society programme at the Summit in which all the large organizations that had participated in the development of the Plan of Action would be represented. The organizers of the People's Summit chose to decline our invitation to take part in this programme even though a few of their representatives did attend, but only as representatives of their specific organizations. The absence of the union representatives lessened the degree of diversity in the civil society programme.

The Government nevertheless included the Declaration of the People's Summit in the civil society contribution book that was transmitted to the Heads of State and Government at the opening of the Summit. This experience proved to be a lesson learned both for the government and for the People's Summit.

The Indigenous People's Summit

Indigenous groups were particularly interested in the Québec Summit. They contributed to it by organizing an Indigenous People's Summit. This took place in

Ottawa, a few weeks prior to the Summit of the Americas. This was a precedent-setting and unique event, bringing together more than 300 leaders from Canada, the United States and many other countries of the Hemisphere.

The Indigenous Summit was organized by the Assembly of First Nations, the Métis National Council, the Inuit Tapirisat of Canada, the Native Women's Association of Canada, the Métis National Council of Women and the Pauktuutit Inuit Women's Association. The Canadian Government supported it both financially and logistically. The Personal Representative of the Prime Minister for the Summit received the recommendations of the indigenous peoples at the closing ceremony and transmitted them to the Prime Minister and to the hemispheric heads of states and government via the civil society contribution book. Many indigenous representatives participated in the civil society programme of the Summit of the Americas, which allowed them to express their opinions to hemispheric governmental representatives.

At the Summit: The Civil Society Programme

A large number of civil society groups and networks were involved in the development of the Plan of Action of the Summit. For the actual event, we felt that it was also important to invite the representatives of those groups and networks to participate in a programme of meetings. The objectives were to raise the profile of civil society among decision-makers, to familiarize civil society with the Summit of the Americas process, to receive their views and recommendations and to promote relations among the various groups invited. A complementary objective was to showcase the perspectives, commitment and contributions of constructive civil society groups by promoting contact between their membership and the media in attendance.

We had made a conscious effort over the year to involve the business community more extensively in the process of hemispheric integration beyond purely business issues. With this in mind, we invited the representatives of the Americas Business Forum from Argentina and Canada, along with the major business associations from Canada, the United States, Mexico and Brazil. The diversity of the participants in the Summit's civil society programme opened the way to promoting ties between groups that do not usually work together (for example, business people, indigenous representatives, religious groups, environmentalists and youth). The participants pointed to this positive aspect of the programme, indicating that it helped each party to better understand the other's viewpoint.

The Summit's civil society programme included three meetings along with protocol activities in which the various representatives met the delegates, ministers and heads of international and regional organizations, and in which the heads of state and government were present. The participants also took the opportunity to organize parallel activities among themselves as well as to participate in or organize a number of media activities, television interviews and media scrums.

The first meeting, on Friday afternoon, was co-chaired by Bill Graham and the Canadian Permanent Representative to the OAS. It was devoted to presenting the main recommendations emanating from the various conferences and consultative processes held prior to the Summit. The meeting proved to be very constructive, giving the participants an insight into the extent of the consultations conducted throughout the hemisphere and into the wide range of recommendations prepared. In particular, a number of people found it interesting and quite unusual to hear business people giving their opinions on matters well beyond the economic realm.

On the Saturday afternoon of the Summit, Canada's Foreign Affairs and International Trade Ministers invited their ministerial colleagues from the Hemisphere and the heads of the international and regional organizations involved in the Summit to join them, the Canadian Minister for International Cooperation and the Secretary of State for Latin America and Africa, in a round table discussion with the 60 civil society representatives. The meeting took place in the very same hall in which the heads of state and government had met that morning, and was covered by the host broadcaster, and in turn broadcast live by Radio Canada's Réseau de l'information (RDI) and Newsworld.

To ensure that the discussion was constructive and beneficial to all, we had developed the agenda in close co-operation with the participants and made all necessary arrangements so that they could meet on Saturday morning to prepare for the roundtable. The participants agreed on seven priority themes and formed working groups to prepare interventions on each of these themes.

Eduardo Gamarra of the Summit of the Americas Center of the University of Florida summarized for the hemispheric ministers the points to take into account on democracy and citizen participation in governance. Matthew Coon-Come, Chief of the Assembly of First Nations, underlined the challenges faced by indigenous peoples. Antonio Estrany y Gendre of the Inter-American Council for Trade and Production (organizer of the Buenos Aires Business Forum) exposed views on trade and investment. Pierre-Marc Johnson explained the links between trade and sustainable development. Sally Brown, of the Association of Universities and Colleges of Canada, underlined some imperatives of the social dimension of the hemispheric agenda. José Miguel Vivanco of Human Rights Watch outlined important issues relating to human rights in the Hemisphere. Finally Nobina Robinson of FOCAL and Robin Rosenberg of the Leadership Council for Inter-American Summitry highlighted the importance of civil society participation in the Summit of the Americas process.

This preparation not only allowed the various participants to get to know one another and to better understand one another's opinions, it opened the way for a constructive roundtable discussion with the ministers and heads of international organizations. In its editorial the day after the Summit, *The Globe and Mail* commented: "It was a strategic error on the part of those civil society groups who boycotted the session because it wasn't with the Heads of State" (The Globe and Mail 2001; A18).

Finally, the civil society programme included an evaluation meeting on Sunday afternoon. At that meeting, the representatives expressed their satisfaction with regards to the Declaration and Plan of Action of the Summit, while they underlined that it was important to make sure that the leaders clearly understood the scope of these two documents, complied with the undertakings made, and provided follow-up.

The participants congratulated Canada on the civil society programme, a precedent for a major international event of this kind. They emphasized the importance to themselves and to the governments of publicizing this experiment and the contribution made by constructive civil society, primarily by way of opinion pieces in the major newspapers, and they pledged to do the same. They stressed the importance of encouraging the host of the next Summit to build upon this experience. They left feeling that the relationships which they formed were no less important than the access provided to the ministers and heads of international and regional organizations.

They also suggested a number of areas for improvement, including: developing a strategy to increase participation of civil society groups from a wider selection of hemispheric countries, recognizing more fully the essential difference between indigenous groups and the rest of civil society, and allowing full media access to civil society discussions.

Conclusion

The credibility of the Summit of the Americas now rests on the follow-up to the commitments made by the heads of state and government. We have built a relationship with a significant portion of civil society in Canada and the Hemisphere. Sustaining this relationship and involving them in the process of hemispheric co-operation will be crucial.

For us, this was not simply an exercise in public relations, but a new approach, both coherent and inclusive, based on our firm commitment towards greater transparency in our approach to foreign policy development. We are in transition and we need to adjust.

Neither government nor civil society has found the perfect formula. Many players are acquiring a measure of influence that they did not have before. This places a great responsibility on them. They must ask themselves questions on their relation with parliamentarians, and to what extent they reflect the views and interests of citizens; and whether their methods of outreach are really getting their message across and influencing decisions for the general welfare. In government, and particularly in DFAIT, we must rethink our way of doing things and reorder our priorities and resources to reflect this new reality.

We all work with the same purpose in mind, that is, to strengthen the democratic basis that we share and value and deepen our co-operation in view of ensuring that we derive the maximum political, economic and social benefits out of globalization. Canada decided more than a decade ago that its future was closely linked to the development of the Americas in all its aspects. To truly be sustainable and beneficial for all sectors of society however, this commitment towards the region must also be shared with Canadians.

The Québec Summit allowed us to involve an array of groups from various sectors of society in the hemispheric agenda and, consequently, to promote the development of links among them. This greater enthusiasm for the region is particularly evident with Canadians. It is an important step in the construction of a better Hemisphere. We must continue to promote greater transparency in governance.

References

'Making it a Summit for All the Americas' (2001), *The Globe and Mail*, 23 April, p. A18.

Chapter 13
Civil Society Encounters the G7/G8

Peter I. Hajnal[*]

Introduction

As the leaders of the Group of Eight (the seven major democratic industrialized countries – Canada, France, Germany, Italy, Japan, the United Kingdom and the United States – plus Russia) gathered in the old northern Italian port city of Genoa for their annual summit meeting held from 20 to 22 July 2001, a huge mass protest was taking place outside. Demonstrators, estimated to number anywhere from 70,000 to 200,000, ranged from groups peacefully opposing what they saw as a world increasingly controlled by the most powerful states and by large multinational corporations, through those that sought dialogue with G8 governments, to anarchists of all shades including those bent on violence. Concerned with security, the local hosts of the summit had designated a red zone – maximum security zone – accessible 18 through 22 July only to local residents and those authorized to be in the immediate area of summit events; this red zone was surrounded by tall wire fences with massive police guard at each gate controlling access. In addition, a yellow zone, a larger area surrounding the central red zone, was designated in which all public demonstrations were prohibited. Other security measures included closing the area of the port of Genoa to navigation, and closing the city's airport and main railroad stations (Genoa Summit News 2001).

Some groups of protesters challenged the legality of these restricted zones on Italian constitutional grounds, but mainstream groups were willing to confine their demonstrations to officially approved areas. Only minor breaches of the security fence around the red zone occurred, and these were promptly repaired by police. Elsewhere, provocations and violent confrontations with Italian security personnel led to the tragic death of Carlo Giuliani, a 23-year-old Italian anarchist (the first death among Western protesters since violent demonstrations around high-level

---

[*] Earlier versions of parts of this chapter appear as Peter I. Hajnal (forthcoming 2002), 'Partners or Adversaries? The G7/G8 Encounters Civil Society', in *New Directions in Global Political Governance: Creating International Order for the Twenty-first Century*, John Kirton and Junichi Takase (eds), Ashgate, Aldershot; and Peter I. Hajnal (2001), 'Civil Society at the 2001 Genoa G8 Summit', *Behind the Headlines* 58(1). I wish to thank Dr Sylvia Ostry, Sir Nicholas Bayne and Professors John Kirton and Louis Pauly for their encouragement and the opportunity to exchange ideas; Liana Cisneros of Jubilee Plus and Jamie Drummond of Drop the Debt, and Dr James Orbinski and Ellen 't Hoen of Médecins Sans Frontières for sharing their insights; Diana Juricevic and Jennifer Acorn for their conscientious and enthusiastic research assistance; and Christine Lucyk and John King for their helpful comments.

meetings started in Seattle in late 1999 – there have, reportedly, been previous deaths of demonstrators in developing countries), some 230 injuries on both sides, 280 arrests, and property damage estimated at up to US$40 million. There were accusations that the police used excessive force, targeted peaceful demonstrators as well as journalists, and perhaps even provoked some of the violence.

This was but the latest stage in the progress of a significant phenomenon of international life: the proliferation and increased sophistication of nongovernmental organizations (NGOs) and other civil-society organizations and coalitions since World War II and especially since the end of the cold war.

NGOs have extended their concerns and activities into every area of human endeavour ranging from development, human rights, humanitarian action and the environment to peace and security, scientific and technical co-operation, and ethical and moral life. Their diversity, role and influence have seen a corresponding increase. Thanks to their efficient use of information technology and of the news media, the relevance, role and impact of civil-society movements and NGOs are now widely recognized.

This chapter focuses on the relationship of civil society with the G7/G8 system. It reviews the progress and highlights some of the milestones that mark the evolution of that relationship through three phases: mutual non-recognition; recognition of the G7 on the part of civil society; and recognition of civil society by the G7 (and later also by the G8). It continues with a case study of developing-country debt and the civil-society coalition Jubilee 2000 and its successors. Next, it discusses the G7/G8-civil society encounter at the summits of Okinawa in 2000 and Genoa in 2001. Finally, it presents some conclusions.

Phase 1 (1975-1983): Civil Society and the G7 Ignore Each Other

The G7/G8 saw itself from the very beginning of G7 summitry in 1975 as an informal, nonbureaucratic forum of the leaders of the most advanced market-economy countries with a democratic system of governance. Recognition of civil-society groups as interlocutors seems not to have entered the consciousness (at least the publicly expressed consciousness) of the G7 leaders and their support apparatus. On the other side, the power and importance of the G7 as a discrete entity does not appear to have been recognized during this phase by NGOs and broader civil society. This mutual ignoring can be taken not only in the English but also in the French sense of the word (*ignorer* meaning 'not to know').

Phase 2 (1984-1994): Civil Society Recognizes the G7

As the agenda of the summit expanded to embrace many issues beyond the early focus on macroeconomic policy co-ordination,[1] civil society began to see the G7 as a legitimate target both for lobbying and for opposing. This is not surprising because many of these new issues have been crucial to a wide variety of NGOs and civil-society coalitions. More generally, it was becoming common public knowledge that the G7 was indeed a powerful group that had evolved into a major global institution.[2]

In addition to pre-summit lobbying of individual G7 governments by business, labour and agricultural representatives, initial civil-society reaction to the G7 took rather an undifferentiated form. This was The Other Economic Summit or TOES (sometimes called the people's summit, the alternative summit, or *contre-sommet* (counter-summit) in French. The first TOES was organized by the London-based TOES/UK – later called New Economics Foundation – and took place simultaneously with the 1984 London G7 Summit. TOES describes itself as "an international non-governmental forum for the presentation, discussion, and advocacy of the economic ideas and practices upon which a more just and sustainable society can be built – 'an economics as if people mattered'".[3] In 1985, 1986 and 1987 TOES sent delegations to the G7 summits; starting with 1988, TOES has met in an event parallel with the summit, although after 1998 not always using the same collective name. Its prominence has declined in favour of more focused, issue-oriented civil-society approaches to the G7 (and, to a lesser extent, to the G8). Each year's TOES features a civil-society coalition, with varying NGO membership, meeting in the G7/G8 summit city. These counter-summits run workshops and demonstrations, and produce press releases and often a counter-communiqué critical of the official G7/G8 communiqué.[4] More recently, TOES has tended to create its own websites as its primary means of communication. It appears that in 2000 and 2001 TOES was inactive. Harriet Friedmann states that "[i]n the 1990s, TOES morphed into teach-ins and similar gatherings under the rubric of the International Forum on Globalization" (Friedmann 2001, 88).

Moving from generalized to issue-specific approaches – to take the important example of the environment – TOES began lobbying against the destruction of the rainforest as early as 1988, at the Toronto "Citizens' Summit" (TOES 1988). Without attempting to draw too many inferences concerning civil-society influence on the G7, one may note that the 1989 Paris Summit of the Arch, in its communiqué, welcomed the German initiative for the preservation of tropical forests (Summit of the Arch 1989, s.43). In 1990 the NGO Friends of the Earth was hosting lectures and conducting a campaign on this issue; in the same year the G7 affirmed the Tropical Forestry Action Plan and initiated the Pilot Program to Conserve the Brazilian Rainforest (Friends of the Earth 1990, s.66).

In 1991 an 'Enviro-summit' with a broader agenda met in London a few city blocks from the G7 summit site. This was during the lead-up to the 1992 Rio Earth Summit at which NGOs truly came into their own.

Phase 3 (1995-): The G7/G8 Recognizes Civil Society

The G7, on its part, was slower to acknowledge civil society. The terms 'civil society' and 'NGO' were not used in official G7 documents until the 1995 Halifax Summit. The Halifax communiqué refers to NGOs and civil society in the context of promoting sustainable development and the reform of international financial institutions, adding that the United Nations (UN) and the Bretton Woods institutions should "encourage countries to follow participatory development strategies and support governmental reforms that assure transparency and public accountability, a stable rule of law, and an active civil society" (Halifax Summit 1995a, s.26). In the same document, under the rubric "Reinforcing Coherence, Effectiveness and Efficiency of Institutions", the G7 undertakes that "[t]o increase overall coherence, cooperation and cost effectiveness we will work with others to encourage ... improved coordination among international organizations, bilateral donors and NGOs" (Halifax Summit 1995b, s.37).

The Halifax reference to civil society was only the beginning. The 1996 Lyon Summit, which began the fourth seven-year cycle of summitry, spoke out even more strongly about the positive role of civil society. In its economic communiqué, under "Implementing a New Global Partnership For Development", it refers to the need for "a strengthened civil society" in that partnership (Lyon Summit 1996, s.34). The communiqué of the 1997 Denver Summit of the Eight goes further, "reaffirm[ing] the vital contribution of civil society" to the environment, democratic governance and poverty eradication (Denver Summit 1997, s.13). In the 1998 Birmingham communiqué, under the rubric "Promoting sustainable growth in the global economy", the G8 "pledge ourselves to a shared international effort ... to provide effective support for the efforts of [poorer developing] countries to build democracy and good governance, stronger civil society and greater transparency" (Birmingham Summit 1998a, s.7).

The 1999 Cologne Summit communiqué refers to civil society three times, calling for governments, international governmental organizations, business, labour, civil society and the individual "to work together to ... realize the full potential of globalization for raising prosperity and promoting social progress while preserving the environment". It cites the productive role that civil society and the private sector can play in "national efforts towards economic and structural reform and good governance"; and it calls on the World Trade Organization (WTO) to be "more responsive to civil society while preserving its government-to-government nature" (Cologne Summit 1999, ss.3, 9, 27). Ironically, the Cologne Summit was followed six months later by the 'Battle of Seattle', and the rest is history. And not just history, for civil society, in all its complexity, is now a predictable presence at major international meetings.

Other levels of the G7/G8 system took up the civil society nexus. By 1996, when G7 environment ministers met in Cabourg, France (9-10 May), they chose as one of their main themes the mobilization of civil society; the Cabourg communiqué has several references to NGOs (G7 Environment Ministers 1996). In 1999, the G8 environment ministers (Schwerin, Germany, 26-28 March) stated: "transparency of the WTO and its openness to and effective engagement of the civil society are necessary for the continued public support for an open multilateral trading system" (G8 Environment Ministers 1999, s.6). Also in 1999, the Chair's statement of the Trade Ministers Quadrilateral (Tokyo, Japan, 11-12 May) added that on the issue of trade and environment "it [is] vital for us to pay due consideration to the concerns of civil society" (Quadrilateral Trade Ministers 1999, s. Environment). And the communiqué of the environment ministers' meeting in Otsu, Japan (7-9 April 2000) states that "sustainable development should be pursued with the full participation of all stakeholders". It also "welcome[s] the efforts of local governments, communities, private commercial enterprises and NGO's to promote sustainable development at the local level"; and expresses support for the "participation of stakeholders in developing, implementing and monitoring environmental policies locally, nationally, and internationally" (G8 Environment Ministers 2000, s.17).

The Communiqué issued by the G8 Environment Ministers' meeting at Trieste, Italy, 2-4 March 2001, builds on this. It records a pledge by the ministers to encourage and facilitate further voluntary actions by civil society to meet the challenges of climate change, sees an important place for civil society in environmental governance, and recognizes "that the engagement of civil society (citizens, non-governmental organizations, workers and business organizations, indigenous groups) will be critical to the success of [the 2002] Johannesburg Summit" on sustainable development and that these groups must participate in the preparatory process and in the implementation and monitoring of that summit's results (G8 Environment Ministers 2001, paras 13, 19, 25).

The trend is clear. The G7/G8 has expressed its increasing sense of the importance of civil society. This developing relationship reflects the evolution and maturing of both of these actors.

Case Study: Developing-Country Debt and the Jubilee 2000 Coalition

Third-world debt has been on the G7 agenda since 1982. It has, over the years, resulted in a number of attempts to deal with it, including the HIPC (Heavily Indebted Poor Countries) initiative in its various guises. Since G7 countries are the major lenders and they exert great influence over the IMF (International Monetary Fund), the World Bank and the Paris Club, it is natural that these countries (individually and as G7) have become a lighting rod for NGO campaigns for debt relief. The highest-profile NGO coalition concerned with debt has been Jubilee 2000, a single-issue group that has specifically targeted the G7.

Jubilee 2000, and its successor organizations to be discussed later in this chapter, are a well-organized group that use sophisticated analysis, communication and campaign strategies. It was launched (largely as a church-based effort) in the United Kingdom in April 1996, although the idea of debt relief for Africa by the year 2000 had first come up in 1990 under the aegis of the All African Council of Churches. Martin Dent and Bill Peters, the co-founders of Jubilee, describing the 1990 genesis of the idea of the campaign, recall the biblical paradigm of debt forgiveness: Leviticus Chapter 25 provides for debt remission and the freeing of slaves every 49 years; Deuteronomy 15, every 7 years; the New Testament also shows the need to forgive unpayable debt. Similarly, the Koran (Bakara, verse 279) calls for easy repayment or forgiveness of debts; and other religions and traditions mention debt cancellation (Dent and Peters 1999, 15-26). The campaign was launched in 1993. By 1997, the coalition broadened to include a number of secular and religious NGOs; for example, Oxfam International and Christian Aid, and many other environmental, social-justice and women's groups. At the end of 2000,

Jubilee had participating organizations in 69 countries spanning all continents.

The goal of Jubilee 2000 was the "cancellation of the unpayable debts of the world's poorest countries by the end of the year 2000, under a fair and transparent process" (Jubilee Plus n.d.). It was Jubilee 2000 that organized a spectacular human chain of some 70,000 participants who surrounded the site of the 1998 Birmingham Summit and presented a petition to the leaders, asking for debt cancellation. This prompted an unprecedented G7/G8 reaction: British Prime Minister Tony Blair, on behalf of the G8, responded to the petition in a separate document of the summit. (Birmingham Summit 1998b) In an additional statement, Blair said: "I pay tribute to the Jubilee 2000 campaign and its dignified breaking-the-chain demonstration in Birmingham. The most persuasive case for debt relief is that it is only when those countries can escape the burden of debt that they are able to benefit economically".[5]

A year later, in 1999, Jubilee 2000 welcomed the Cologne Debt Initiative (increasing debt forgiveness from $50 billion to $70 billion) (Dent and Peters 1999, 149) and the G7's new willingness to do something about seriously reducing the debt burden of developing countries (Kirton et al. 2001, 290-291). There were 50,000 demonstrators in Cologne, supported by a much larger worldwide constituency of the coalition. Also in 1999, Jubilee 2000 proposed the establishment of concordats on debt cancellation, calling for any heavily indebted country to apply to the UN for an independent review and cancellation of its debt, and for an independent Debt Review Body that would act as a binding arbitration panel[6] (Dent and Peters 1999, xi).

Post-Cologne progress has been disappointing; in contrast to the potential debt cancellation of $90 billion under the Initiative, only $12 billion was implemented by the end of 2000. Therefore, after Cologne, the campaign not only continued but picked up steam in preparation for the Okinawa Summit, to be described in the next section.

Jubilee 2000 and its successors understand the workings of the G7/G8 system very well. For example, during the year 2000 Jubilee followed and publicized the customary pre-summit host leader's visits of Japanese prime ministers Keizo Obuchi, then Yoshiro Mori, to the other summit countries. It staged demonstrations at G7/G8 ministerial meetings. It is familiar with the sherpa and sous-sherpa process.[7] It monitors and publicizes the performance of G7 governments and demands that those governments implement their past commitments.

Jubilee has reached for support to celebrities ranging from the Irish rock star Bono and former boxing champion Muhammad Ali to Pope John Paul II, the Dalai Lama and Archbishop Desmond Tutu (Jubilee 2000 Coalition 2000b). At the other end of the spectrum it used a letter from a ten-year old English girl who had written this to Prime Minister Tony Blair: "Please lower the debt to the bottom. Please keep your promise like you said at the meeting last year. Congratulations on your baby Leo. Please think about the babies in other countries too" (Jubilee 2000 Coalition 2000c). In various publications, Jubilee 2000 compared debt to the slave trade and to drug addiction.[8]

All this gives the whole debt issue a high public profile that governments and intergovernmental organizations (IGOs) would find difficult to match. The idiom could not be more different from that customarily used by governments, IGOs and the G7 itself. Although it is impossible to measure the precise impact of Jubilee 2000 on G7 governments, there is a strong perception that it is influential. A spokesperson for the World Bank stated: Jubilee 2000 "has managed to put a relatively arcane issue – that of international finance and development – on the negotiating table throughout the world. The pledges Clinton and [UK Chancellor of the Exchequer Gordon] Brown have made [to debt relief] would not have happened without Jubilee 2000. It's one of the most effective global lobbying campaigns I have ever seen".[9] And the *Financial Times* wrote in its 17 February 1999 issue: "When a plea for debt relief becomes the common cause of a coalition that embraces both the Pope and the pop world, creditors should take notice" (Hanlon and Garrett 1999, 6). In the weeks leading up to the Okinawa Summit, however, Jubilee 2000 went overboard in claiming that the G8 was retreating to Okinawa after being besieged by campaigners (Lovett 2000). And Jubilee 2000's final report, *The World Will Never Be the Same Again*, states rather grandly: "we have ... changed the world. ... Thanks to Jubilee 2000, the world will never be the same again" (Barrett 2000, 3-4). If nothing else, this shows that governments and IGOs have no monopoly on hyperbole.

Hyperbole, however, should not obscure results achieved. By the end of the year 2000, rich creditor countries promised to forgive $110 billion worth of debt (a 30 per cent cut in debt relief), twenty indebted developing countries expected to benefit from some relief, and third-world debt is now high on the global agenda. Jubilee has criticized both reckless lending and reckless borrowing, and corruption in developing and developed countries alike. Much, of course, remains to be done, and progress has lagged far behind what civil society would like to see.

In pursuit of their goals, Jubilee and its successors have used information technology with impressive effectiveness and sophistication. It developed a website rich in content, appealing to a broad audience ranging from those seeking practical information on getting involved in the campaign to those wishing to find detailed analytical studies. Jubilee's constant pressure on G7 and other world leaders, focusing on G7 summits and ministerial meetings as well as on top-level meetings of the Bretton Woods institutions, was aided vastly "by bold and innovative use of the internet's powers of communication. ... The internet has allowed cheap, rapid and efficient communication between debt campaigners worldwide, making up-to-date and incisive information available to millions of people". On the other hand, the majority of people in poor indebted countries have far more pressing immediate needs than information technology. Jubilee supporters staged a dramatic illustration of this by setting a laptop computer on fire on the beach at Okinawa. The message on the screen of the burning computer read: "This is worth nothing until you drop the debt" (Barrett 2000, 5, 24).

Jubilee 2000 and its successors have kept up the kind of popular pressure that governments in major democracies ignore at their peril. This pressure has likely contributed to the recognition by G7 governments of the need to work with civil society and other non-state actors.

Civil Society at the Okinawa Summit

In the lead-up to the Okinawa Summit the Japanese government made clear its determination, as G8 Chair for 2000, to reach out beyond the G8 to developing and other countries, IGOs, the private sector and civil society. This attitude of openness was in evidence before and during the summit in several ways:

Appointment of a Responsible Government Official

Ahead of the Okinawa Summit the Japanese government appointed, as part of its summit planning team, a director general for civil society participation (Kirton 2000). This official was in regular contact with a number of civil-society groups.

Pre-summit Events Involving NGOs

Japan sponsored or hosted several pre-summit events involving civil society. For example, an international symposium on the role of NGOs in conflict prevention, sponsored by the Japan Institute for International Affairs, was held on June 9-10, 2000 in Tokyo with the support of the Japanese Ministry of Foreign Affairs. And on the eve of the summit, on 20 July in Tokyo, five G8 leaders met for 2½ hours with four Southern leaders: President Olusegun Obasanjo of Nigeria, President Thabo Mbeki of South Africa, President Abdelaziz Bouteflika of Algeria, Prime Minister Chuan Leekpai of Thailand. They were joined later by representatives of the World Bank, World Health Organization (WHO), United Nations Development Programme (UNDP) – as well as by business people concerned with information technology. They discussed debt reduction, development issues, infectious diseases and information technology. Although NGO representatives were not present, these discussions covered issues of great concern to civil society.

NGO Centre

The Japanese government established an NGO centre for the duration of the summit. The centre, in what was an advance over previous G7/G8 practice, provided meeting and work facilities, including access to computers, telephones, photocopiers and other equipment, although NGOs had to pay rent to use the facilities, and at least one civil-society organization reports that its international telephone lines were cut on the last day and a half of the summit. In all, 43 Japanese and international NGOs were registered at the centre (Saito 2000, 5). The NGO Centre allowed civil-society proximity, though not necessarily adequate access, to the site of G8 meetings and the Summit Media Centre. Access was predominantly one way: government and media representatives were free to visit the NGO Centre but NGO representatives were not allowed to enter the Media Centre and thus could not have access to official briefings and to media personnel unless they were also accredited as journalists covering the summit. Distance between the two centres was temporal as well as spatial: accredited media personnel were briefed first, followed by spokespersons briefing NGOs, leading to the perception that NGOs were getting the information late and at second hand, making it difficult for them to express their reaction speedily.[10] In sum, the NGO Centre was a useful though imperfect resource, closely controlled by the Japanese government.

Host-government Dialogue with Civil Society

There was a dialogue between the Japanese government and civil-society leaders, both in Europe prior to the summit, and in Japan on the opening day of the summit. Prime Minister Mori's meeting with representatives of nine NGOs (these were selected on a first-come-first-served basis) on 21 July was presented by the Japanese government as a new initiative. In fact, it was at the 1998 Birmingham Summit that civil society had its first official dialogue with the G7/G8 as represented by British Prime Minister Tony Blair, and where Clare Short (Secretary of State for International Development), on behalf of Blair, accepted the 1.4 million signatures amassed by the Jubilee campaign (Dent and Peters 1999, 36). This was arguably the most successful of the four such successive dialogues (1999 Cologne, 2000 Okinawa and 2001 Genoa being the other three thus far). In contrast, speaking about the 2000 dialogue, an Okinawan academic and NGO supporter stated: "I would not call such a short encounter a real discussion. I really regret that because it was such an important chance for us to directly convey our viewpoints to [Prime Minister Mori]".[11] Moreover, G8 governments other than the Japanese host did not reach out to civil society sufficiently in Okinawa. Nonetheless, the Okinawa encounter has confirmed the consultation process as an established method of dialogue.

Civil Society Reflected in G7/G8 Documents

A number of references to civil-society participation appeared in the Okinawa G8 communiqué as well as in the documents of the meeting of the G8 Foreign Ministers that took place in Miyazaki, Japan, on 12-13 July 2000.

The Okinawa G8 communiqué refers to civil society in its preamble as well as under the first two of its three main headings – greater prosperity, greater peace of mind, and greater stability – thereby acknowledging the essential role of NGOs in various areas of world concern. Under the 'prosperity' rubric the G8 puts forward its view that co-operation of civil society, governments and the private sector is a must for achieving broad-based, equitable economic growth. Echoing the G7 statement of 21 July 2000 (issued before the start of the G8 summit), the G8 welcomes the participation of civil society in poverty-reduction strategies in HIPCs. It commits itself to working in partnership with civil society, governments, the WHO and other IGOs in the fight against infectious diseases – notably HIV/AIDS, tuberculosis and malaria. The Japanese government undertook to lead this effort by committing $3 billion over the next five years[12] (Kyushu-Okinawa Summit 2000b, paras 15, 24, 29, 30).

In the 'greater peace of mind' area, the Okinawa G8 communiqué reaffirms the need for civil-society co-operation in fighting crime and protecting the victims of crime. In its pursuit of 'active aging', the G8 undertakes to work with the private sector and civil society in promoting the participation of older people in community and volunteer activities. It notes with approval OECD's (Organisation for Economic Co-operation and Development) policy dialogue, including dialogue with civil society, to promote food safety (Kyushu-Okinawa Summit 2000c, paras 50, 52, 57, 59).

The communiqué's third section, on greater stability, does not mention civil society specifically, but the G8 foreign ministers, at their meeting held in Miyazaki prior to the Okinawa Summit, called on NGOs and other actors to commit themselves to conflict prevention, and emphasized the important role of NGOs and broader civil society in preventing the accumulation of small arms, in mitigating tensions, in helping the post-conflict transition from humanitarian emergency assistance to development, and in raising awareness of the problem of children in armed conflicts. The G8 foreign ministers further called for intensified co-operation between states, international and regional organizations and civil society in the area of human security. They also recognized the role of NGOs, along with other actors, in making free elections possible in Kosovo[13] (G8 Foreign Ministers 2000b).

In terms of substantive achievements, however, civil society groups gave the Okinawa Summit generally failing marks. Ann Pettifor, director of Jubilee 2000, responding to the G8 communiqué of 23 July stated: "This will be known as the Squandered Summit. While the G8 leaders have enjoyed Japan's $750 million hospitality, they have squandered an historic opportunity to cancel the unpayable debts of the poorest countries. ... Their failure to act on this issue was the defining moment of the summit" (Jubilee 2000 Coalition 2000d). Jubilee, having joined the human chain of Japanese and international NGOs and their supporters around the Kadena US Air Base in Okinawa, and having advocated in addition a 'virtual human chain' through the use of the internet, was clearly very disappointed with the summit. Alluding to divisions among G8 leaders on the debt issue, Pettifor adds that those G8 leaders who "feel they should have gone further" in debt relief "can show that now with a unilateral pledge to stop taking the money from the poorest countries" (Jubilee 2000 Coalition 2000a).

Médecins Sans Frontières (MSF) was more positive. It "welcomed the strong statement of the G8 leaders to ensure that life-saving medicines become accessible and affordable in the developing world" and acknowledged that the Okinawa Summit has signalled a change in attitudes concerning brand-name monopolies and patenting practices hindering the production of less-expensive generic drugs. To forestall empty promises, MSF "called for concrete action to ensure affordable treatment of patients" (MSF 2000). And Oxfam reacted favourably to the G8 commitment to work for universal primary education by the year 2015, calling this "one of the few bright spots of the Okinawa Summit" and claiming a victory for its Global Campaign for Education[14] (OI 2000).

Greenpeace, the environmental NGO that is not averse to using theatrical, headline-grabbing tactics, had its flagship, the Rainbow Warrior, enter the exclusion zone set up by the Japanese government around the summit site in Nago, Okinawa. To protest against illegal logging and the destruction of forests, the ship towed eight logs, hoping to deliver the logs, along with a letter, to the G8 leaders. On July 22, the second day of the summit, Japanese authorities impounded the ship and arrested four Greenpeace activists. The ship and the activists were not released until after the summit. At the same time, though, Greenpeace welcomed the G8's "endorsement of sustainable forest management, and particularly their commitment to examine how best they can combat illegal logging, including export and procurement practices" (Greenpeace International 2000).

Thus, on debt relief and several other substantive issues the NGO community's hopes were disappointed at Okinawa. In other areas civil society acknowledged some progress, not losing sight of the difference between G8 promises and the fulfilment of those promises. Eighteen NGOs at the NGO Centre "jointly urged the G-8 leaders to immediately honor all commitments they have made at international conventions and summits on poverty, health issues and primary education" and "call[ed] for the G-8 countries to set appropriate regulations concerning liberalization of trade, which leads to environmental destruction, invasion of human rights and monopoly of resources by the richest countries" ('Ties Strengthened 2000, 3). Although on specific issues civil-society expectations were insufficiently met, the fact that G8 dialogue with civil society is now a recognized, established process is a significant achievement of the Okinawa Summit, and one that gave impetus and endorsement to this important evolution in global governance.

From Okinawa to Genoa

There was a great deal of civil society activity following the Okinawa Summit and in preparation for the Genoa G8 Summit of 20-22 July 2001. Jubilee 2000 was succeeded by three new organizations (the various national Jubilee campaigns are continuing as well):

- Drop the Debt, a short-term organization whose goal was a 'New Deal on Debt' by the time of the Genoa Summit. It collaborated with the Italian debt campaign and with participants of the Jubilee 2000 Coalition. Drop the Debt called for "a major burst of campaigning pressure at and around the G8 Summit itself". It had a 'sunset' provision; it planned to follow up on debt-related decisions of the Genoa Summit, then cease operation. Drop the Debt had high expectations of the Italian presidency of the G8 in 2001, and it pointed to the presence in Italy of the Pope, a supporter of the Jubilee cause. The website of this group was an instrument of mobilization for the campaign but also a means to disseminate major reports, such as *Reality Check: The Need for Deeper Debt Cancellation and the Fight Against HIV/AIDS* (Drop the Debt 2001d). The website announced the group's belief that "there is an historic opportunity for a major leap forward on debt that would [r]elease significant new resources for fighting disease and reducing poverty; [c]reate greater confidence that the debt crisis will not build up again[; and g]ive a sense of resolution to the millennium-focused campaign for debt cancellation" (Drop the Debt, n.d.a.).

- Jubilee Plus, a programme of the London-based New Economics Foundation, is intended to continue for a longer period and act as a think tank providing analysis, data and news on debt and other financial issues, as well as a campaigning organization[15] (Jubilee 2000 Coalition n.d.). On the analysis side, Jubilee Plus is using the internet to publish reports, articles, book reviews and opinion pieces, and to develop a data bank of international debt and other key indicators. On the campaign side, it aims to post on the site news of events and actions. It has also begun an archive of daily press cuttings.
- Jubilee Movement International for Economic and Social Justice (JMI) is another new incarnation, intended to be an umbrella organization and continue the work of Drop the Debt as the latter phases itself out after the Genoa Summit. Jubilee Plus is itself a member of JMI. JMI's website is a page of the Jubilee Plus website (www.jubileeplus.org/jmi/main.htm).

Jubilee 2000's successor organizations have concentrated on dialogue with individual G7 governments (especially the government hosting the summit in any given year), in preference to targeting the G7 institution itself. Nonetheless, Drop the Debt called for mass mobilization in Genoa: "If you are able, come to Genoa to be part of history, or, if you can't get to Genoa, join the international week of action on debt beginning on July 15th (contact your national debt campaign). Wherever you are the week of July 15-21, make sure your voice, calling for a New Deal on Debt is heard loud and clear" (Drop the Debt, n.d.b.).

The Genoa Summit, 2001

Pre-Summit Events Involving NGOs

When Jubilee 2000 claimed that civil-society campaigners had forced the G8 leaders to retreat to the remote island of Okinawa for their 2000 summit meeting, the coalition could be criticized for indulging in hyperbole. A year later, however, when the G8 foreign ministers moved their pre-summit meeting of 7 July from Portofino – the previously announced venue – to Rome, reality caught up with rhetoric: concern with the presence of up to 200,000 demonstrators, a small but vocal percentage of whom were prepared to use disruptive or even violent tactics, was undoubtedly the main reason. At the Genoa Summit itself, venues and activities were severely restricted by the protests outside. It was out of concern for security that the local hosts of the G8 hired a luxury cruiser, the *Spirit of Europe*, to house all but one of the G8 leaders (George W. Bush stayed at the harbourfront Jolly Hotel Marina). The prefecture of Genoa took various security measures – setting up a red zone, a surrounding yellow zone, and closing most transportation access to the city – described in the opening paragraph of this chapter.

Security measures went as far as deploying anti-aircraft batteries along the runways of Genoa's Cristoforo Colombo airport. This seemed excessive at the time, but later, in the wake of the September 11 terrorist attacks against the World Trade Centre in New York and the Pentagon in Washington, President Hosni Mubarak of Egypt and Italian Deputy Prime Minister Gianfranco Fini reportedly said that Osama bin Laden's terrorist network had threatened to kill President Bush and other G8 leaders (Sanger 2001, B1).

Responsible civil-society groups had made clear before the summit their intention to demonstrate and protest peacefully against economic globalization and for more progress on debt relief. They expressed concern that anarchist and other potentially disruptive or violent groups would jeopardize peaceful, lawful, democratic protest. The Genoa Social Forum (GSF), an umbrella organization of some 700 international, Italian and local Genoa-based NGOs and civil-society coalitions included Drop the Debt but also *Ya Basta!*, an Italian anarchist organization (Beattie 2001c) (though essentially a nonviolent one). It was unclear from the start how this kind of contradiction could be resolved, especially in light of the announcement by the Social Forum that some of its member groups "would attempt peacefully to invade the red zone during the planned 'day of civil disobedience' on Friday July 20", the first day of the summit (Beattie 2001c).

GSF used its website (www.genoa-g8.org) to publicize its aims and participants; to disseminate news in English, French, Italian, Spanish, Portuguese and German; to announce planned events; and to solicit donations. It provided practical information to demonstrators on getting to Genoa; obtain accommodation as well as legal and medical assistance; and avoid possessing any object that could be considered an offensive weapon. It also asked doctors, lawyers, interpreters and journalists to help.

GSF planned three sets of demonstrations in the officially permitted area (that is, outside the red zone): a 'Migrants International March' on 19 July; 'Actions of Civil Disobedience' on 20 July; and an international mass demonstration on 21 July (Genoa Social Forum n.d.). Drop the Debt, on its part, met Italian national and local government representatives in June 2001 to negotiate plans for peaceful demonstrations. It asked its supporters to participate only in the 21 July march that was to take place outside of both the red and the yellow zones. Concerned about the safety of its supporters, Drop the Debt cautioned them to walk away and comply with the requests of the police and demonstration stewards should they encounter areas of conflict (Drop the Debt 2001c). Drop the Debt's website included, among many other features, an invitation to its supporters to e-mail a 'debt wish' to Italian Prime Minister Silvio Berlusconi. It was also reported that Drop the Debt and several other respected aid agencies had "drawn up contingency plans to avoid the Italian city during the summit on July 20-22 if a repeat of the violence that accompanied the recent European Union meeting in Gothenburg seem[ed] likely" (Beattie 2001a).

The violence exceeded everyone's expectations. G8 leaders and most NGO groups deplored the clashes. In a special statement issued on 21 July (the first official document of the Genoa G8 Summit), the leaders recognized and praised the role of peaceful protest and argument, but condemned unequivocally the violence and anarchy perpetrated by a small minority (Genoa Summit 2001f). And the final communiqué of 22 July reaffirmed the right of peaceful protesters to have their voices heard and again deplored the violence and vandalism of those who seek to disrupt discussion and dialogue (Genoa Summit 2001b, para 35).

Civil society groups, on their part, condemned the violence in equally strong terms. Tony Burdon, Senior Policy Advisor of Oxfam, said in a press release issued on 20 July that "violent disruption of international meetings doesn't help reach a solution, and it certainly doesn't help the poor. It drowns out the voice of many thousands of peaceful and serious people arguing for AIDS treatment and deeper debt relief" (OI 2001h). Adrian Lovett, director of the Drop the Debt campaign added: "Peaceful protest works, and it has made a hugely positive impact on recent G8 Summits. The violence we have seen in Genoa achieves nothing. Peaceful campaigners must reflect on how we make sure our concerns are addressed without the risk of hijack by violent extremists" (Drop the Debt 2001e). MSF put its condemnation in even stronger terms: "We take a sharp distance from every kind of violence and from those that in one way or another have chosen to manipulate these days in Genoa and created an atmosphere of violence and aggression – be it from the side of the radical demonstrators or the side of the police" (MSF 2001a).

Sadly but predictably, the media paid its closest attention to the violence. Several G8 leaders expressed their frustration at this disproportionate news coverage to the detriment of reporting the actual deliberations of the G7 and G8. What was more important, however, was the peaceful but vigorous action and productive networking by civil-society groups.

Civil Society Goals and Campaigns for Genoa

A whole spectrum of issues was represented in Genoa by a variety of NGO groups, ranging from the environment to women's rights. This assessment focuses on just three issues: debt, health, and education.

The dire consequences of unsustainable debt burdens on developing countries continued to be a major campaign objective for Drop the Debt, Jubilee Plus and JMI. But new linkages emerged as these groups added other issues to their long-standing concern with debt: education, and HIV/AIDS and other infectious diseases. *Reality Check*, cited earlier, documents this transition that has led to the formation of new alliances with organizations fighting against such diseases (for example, MSF) and with those promoting universal education (for example, Oxfam). Civil-society members of this new alliance stress the point that developing countries need deeper debt relief in order to fight the HIV/AIDS pandemic more successfully and to benefit from better educational opportunities.

Civil society received important support in this work from the UN General Assembly's special session on HIV/AIDS held 25-27 June 2001. The declaration of the session, entitled 'Global Crisis – Global Action', emphasizes the importance of partnership of state and non-state actors, including civil society, in the fight against HIV/AIDS (UN General Assembly 2001a, paras 27, 33, 35, 37, 46, 55, 67, 86, 94).

This was an interesting convergence of ideas, with some parallel developments on the part of the G8. A few weeks before the Genoa Summit, the Italian presidency of the G8 released a document entitled *Beyond Debt Relief*. This document sets forth the elements of an international strategy needed to stimulate growth and eradicate poverty in the poorest of the developing countries. The strategy rests on three pillars: ensuring greater export access for poor countries to the markets in industrial countries; facilitating foreign direct investment and technology transfer to the least developed countries; and channelling greater resources to the development of the social sector in the poorest countries in order to enable those countries to reduce the gap in poverty, health and education (Ministero degli Affari Esteri (Italy) 2001). The third pillar is particularly relevant to the concerns of civil society. The G8 presidency recognizes that although debt relief already given to countries eligible under the HIPC initiative presents a significant opportunity for those countries to use more of their own resources to enhance human capital, every country needs a healthy and well-educated population in order to achieve greater social and economic development. The G7 finance ministers, in their report to the leaders, *Debt Relief and Beyond*, revisited these themes. It is important to note, however, that civil-society goals in these areas far exceed G8 declarations and commitments.

In a confirmation of the poverty-health-education nexus, Jeffrey Sachs observes that "some impoverished countries are too poor to provide the basic public goods of minimally acceptable health and education, much less physical infrastructure. In these settings, the state cannot fulfil its basic tasks of helping to keep the population safe, healthy, and educated" (Sachs 2001, 189-190).

In health matters, it is the least developed countries that suffer from the greatest infant, child and maternal mortality, the lowest life expectancy, and the highest rates of HIV/AIDS and other infectious diseases. Overcoming these handicaps exceeds the capacity of these countries and demands concerted international action. Building on the Okinawa G8 commitment to fight HIV/AIDS, malaria and tuberculosis, *Beyond Debt Relief* presents specific proposals that include:

- intensified co-ordination among states, international governmental organizations, civil society, academic institutions, and industry;
- greater access to affordable essential medicines;
- monitoring HIPC to ensure that resources freed up by debt relief are used for investments in health and education;
- developing health indicators allowing measurement of progress;
- linking health to poverty reduction and development strategies;
- assistance by multilateral development banks; and
- establishment of a dedicated multilateral health facility and a trust fund.

Education is also closely related to poverty reduction. It is the poorest countries that suffer most from weak basic education systems and scarce resources. Specific proposals and objectives set out in *Beyond Debt Relief* include, *inter alia*:

- support for the principle of 'Education for All' – universal primary education by 2015 and gender equality in schools by 2005;

- reduction of barriers to access to education;
- greater involvement of civil society in the formulation, implementation and monitoring of national educational action plans;
- enhanced teacher training and training in information and communication technologies;
- enhancement of participatory learning methods developed by NGOs, linking literacy with empowerment and local development; and
- establishment of a trust fund to build up additional resources for education.

Here, too, there are signs of convergence of G7/G8 concerns with those of civil society. It was Oxfam International that was the moving force behind the 'Education Now' campaign. *The Oxfam Education Report*, published by Oxfam Great Britain for Oxfam International, documents the worldwide education crisis and proposes an agenda for reform (Watkins 2000). Moreover, Oxfam's agenda has expanded to embrace affordable medicines, conflict resolution, debt cancellation, and market access for developing countries – precisely the issues facing the G7/G8 as it prepared for the Genoa Summit.

Gathering Points for Civil Society

Although the Italian government did not set up an NGO centre similar to the one established by the Japanese government in Okinawa in 2000, GSF had several gathering points in the city: an operative centre cum press office on the Via Cesare Battisti; a 'convergence point' near the Piazzale Kennedy; a public forum site at the Punta Vagno; and a facility at the Armando Diaz elementary school near the Piazza Tommaseo. The many activities of the GSF included a public forum held 16 to 22 July entitled 'Another World Is Possible', an international demonstration of migrants on 19 July, actions of 'peaceful civil disobedience', and an international mass demonstration planned for 21 July. In the event, the migrant demonstration of 19 July took place more or less as planned but the demonstrations of 20 July were marred by anarchist violence (including instances of anarchists turning against peaceful demonstrators) and a similarly violent police response. The resulting death of Giuliani, the many injuries, and concern for the safety of their supporters led Drop the Debt and other groups, including the World Development Movement (WDM), to stage a vigil alongside the peaceful demonstrations still held on 21 July (WDM 2001).

The 'convergence point' was a staging area for marches and demonstrations, the place for tents for backpacking demonstrators from out-of-town. It was also the venue for various events including a dramatic exhibition (in a large van dubbed 'Fly Trap') organized by MSF to highlight the nature, consequences and needed solutions of HIV/AIDS, tuberculosis, malaria and other devastating infectious diseases that affect developing countries with special severity.

Other centres, too, served multiple functions: temporary lodging for demonstrators, internet and telephone access for NGOs, press conferences, and distribution of campaign literature. It was the school that Italian police stormed during the night of 21 July without a warrant, smashing computers, confiscating computer disks, arresting about 90 people including members of the violent anarchist 'Black Bloc' or 'Tute Nere' (Black Overalls, to be distinguished from the generally nonviolent and relatively transparent 'Tute Bianche' or White Overalls), and reportedly beating up protesters (many of whom were asleep) and some journalists.[16] Worse, there were eyewitness accounts of police complicity with the Black Bloc. Susan George tells of Don Vitaliano della Sala, a churchman, who reported seeing Black Bloc members leaving a van of the *carabinieri* (military police), and Arthur Neslen reports a film shown after the police raid at the Genoa Social Forum press conference "of muscular men in jeans and face-masks giving orders to 'activists' on motorbikes behind police lines"[17] (George 2001b, 6).

Italian Prime Minister Berlusconi and Interior Minister Claudio Scajola promised investigations into the violence. Berlusconi pledged that the investigations would not lead to a cover-up of alleged police brutality. It was subsequently announced that, in addition to the judicial investigations, there would be an Italian parliamentary inquiry. Amnesty International, the well-respected human-rights NGO, welcomed the criminal investigation to be undertaken by Italian authorities, but called also for an independent commission of inquiry into various allegations of human-rights violations before and during the summit (AI 2001). "Amnesty's call seems all the more justified in light of the result of the parliamentary inquiry, which absolved security forces of blame and termed the Genoa Summit a total success. In turn, opposition centre-left parties denounced the inquiry's findings as a 'whitewash' and came up with their own conclusions assigning most of the blame to poor performance of the law-and-order authorities" (Balmer 2001).

Civil Society Dialogue with G8 Governments

The tradition of host-government dialogue with civil society continued before and during the Genoa Summit. In the preparatory phase, the Italian government made a serious effort to communicate with NGOs, especially in the areas of development aid and poverty reduction. Four research institutes were tasked to consult NGOs and solicit their recommendations in what was termed the Genoa Nongovernmental Initiative (Zupi 2001, 59). The mayor of Genoa confirmed his intention, shared with Italian Prime Minister Berlusconi, "to open a dialogue with the movements that intend to demonstrate ... critically but peacefully during the summit". Italy's Interior Minister Scajola concurred (Genoa Summit 2001e). Media reports added, however, that, according to a statement of the Interior Ministry, "the right of peaceful demonstrations ... would be guaranteed but any form of violence would not be tolerated" (Zampano 2001). In its report on a 28 June meeting of Foreign Minister Renato Ruggiero and Interior Minister Scajola with protesters, Reuters noted Ruggiero's promise that the Genoa Summit would address some of their key concerns and would include representatives from poorer countries, adding that there would be special sessions during the summit that would be open to representatives from non-G8 countries. "Ruggiero called the meeting 'an open G8' and said the world's most industrialized nations would discuss hot topics championed by critics of globalization like reducing debt and fighting against poverty and AIDS" ('Italian Ministers ...' 2001).

Several NGO groups had met local authorities in Genoa ahead of the summit to discuss plans for peaceful protest. The Drop the Debt coalition's meeting, mentioned earlier, was an example of this.

Consultations with Italian and other G8 government leaders and ministers took place on several occasions during the summit. In a news conference on 20 July, Bono, Bob Geldof and Lorenzo Jovanotti, pop music stars and strong supporters of the Drop the Debt campaign, talked of a series of meetings they had with the British, German, Canadian, European Union and Russian leaders, as well as with George W. Bush's security advisor Condoleezza Rice, but they expressed frustration at the Italian host's refusal to facilitate meetings with leaders from the South. The three rock musicians found the Millennium Action Plan for Africa encouraging, and they welcomed the debt-forgiveness commitments of Canada and Italy as particularly praiseworthy. Nonetheless, they added that even some countries whose debt had been cancelled still had to continue to pay their rich creditors. The artists welcomed the opportunity that such meetings provided for asking the leaders hard questions such as "Is an African life not worth the same as a European life?" and they took advantage of being able to talk directly to the major shareholders of the IMF with the power to do something about debt. These widely popular musicians were articulate spokesmen and powerful symbols of the best aspirations and goals of civil society (Drop the Debt 2001a).

This kind of dialogue is no less important for the leaders of the G8 themselves. Equally significant were their outreach meetings with African leaders (the presidents of Algeria, Mali, Nigeria, Senegal and South Africa) and with UN Secretary-General Kofi Annan and administrative heads of the FAO (Food and Agriculture Organization of the United Nations), WHO, the World Bank and the WTO. But dialogue, to be meaningful, must not consist of empty words and promises, of which the world has heard too much. A representative of MSF expressed disappointment at what she saw as just that kind of inadequate dialogue at Genoa, in contrast with the more upbeat assessment of Bono, Geldof and Jovanotti.

Accountability and implementation of G8 promises will be the true test. And civil society is well placed to hold the leaders accountable.

NGOs and Civil Society Reflected in G7/G8 Documents

The *G7 Statement* of 20 July, in the section concerning the launching of a new round of trade negotiations, states that "[t]he WTO should continue to respond to the legitimate expectations of civil society, and ensure that the new Round supports sustainable development" (Genoa Summit 2001d, para 8). The final G8 *Communiqué* of 22 July makes several references to NGOs and civil society. It undertakes to "promote innovative solutions based on a broad partnership with civil society and the private sector". Under 'A Strategic Approach to Poverty Reduction', it promises to help (in unspecified ways) developing countries promote active involvement of civil society and NGOs. On the launching (with the UN) of the global fund to fight HIV/AIDS, malaria and tuberculosis, the *Communiqué* states that local partners, "including NGOs and international agencies, will be instrumental in the successful operation of the Fund". In welcoming Russia's proposal to convene a global conference on climate change in 2003, the *Communiqué* emphasizes the participation in the conference of "governments, business and science as well as representatives of civil society". Referring to another future conference, the 2001 Johannesburg World Summit on Sustainable Development, it commits the G8 to "work in partnership with developing countries for an inclusive preparatory process with civil society on a forward looking and substantial agenda with action-oriented results". On food security, the G8 promises to "support the crucial role international organizations and NGOs play in relief operations" in Sub-Saharan Africa and in Asia, and acknowledges civil society as an important stakeholder in food safety issues in general (Genoa Summit 2001a, paras 2, 6, 21, 26, 28).

Other official documents related to the Genoa Summit mention NGOs and civil society. The excellent report submitted to the G8 leaders by the Digital Opportunity Task Force (established by the 2000 Okinawa G8 Summit with membership drawn from governments, the private sector and civil society), and the Italian Presidency document *Beyond Debt Relief* (discussed earlier in more detail), include a number of such references (Genoa Summit 2001c). So do the *Conclusions* of the pre-summit meeting of the G8 foreign ministers (Rome, 18-19 July), and the report *Strengthening the International Financial System and the Multilateral Development Banks* issued by the pre-summit meeting of the G7 finance ministers (Rome, 7 July). The last-mentioned report addresses the issue of the reform of multilateral development banks (MDBs), and remark that they had "held informal consultations with the other MDB shareholders and NGOs/civil society in order to explain the objectives and the contents of the reform effort"[18] (G7 Finance Ministers 2001). Again, the actual implementation of these undertakings will need to be monitored carefully.

Civil Society Evaluation of the Genoa Summit

Civil society passed a rather negative verdict on the Genoa Summit. Drop the Debt welcomed the global health fund as a good beginning but asserted on 20 July that "the G8's failure to resolve the debt crisis means that they are giving [with] one hand and taking with the other. ... [In] six weeks ..., Africa will have paid back in debt repayments every penny of the $1.5 billion announced today for the health trust fund" (Drop the Debt 2001b). On 21 July, JMI expressed disappointment at "the failure of the richest nations to once again tackle the global debt crisis that is worsening the impoverishment of over 2 billion people in severely indebted countries". JMI acknowledged that the number of countries eligible for debt relief under the HIPC initiative had increased from 9 to 23 between the Okinawa and Genoa summits, but criticized the G7 for congratulating itself on progress when "most of these countries [were] approaching unsustainable levels of debt again" (Jubilee Plus 2001). JMI disputed the G7 claim of $53 billion in debt relief, contrasting this with the World Bank's June 2001 figure of $34 billion. Calculating the market value instead of the nominal value of the debt, Marco Zupi arrives at an even lower figure of $21 billion (Zupi 2001, 61).

MSF, in a statement issued on 21 July, criticized the global health fund, noting that pledges of $1.2 billion were "nowhere near what is required ..., [they] are shamefully low. Governments call upon multinationals and the private sector to contribute. Among these are the pharmaceutical companies whose pricing policies are a fundamental part of the problem". MSF pointed out that the health fund contained "no clear statement regarding who makes the decisions, on what the funds are to be spent, and no policy to ensure that the fund will be used to purchase medicines at the lowest possible cost". What is needed is "a flexible interpretation of the WTO agreements on intellectual property; promotion of the production and use of generic medicines; a tiered pricing system to ensure that medicines in developing countries are affordable; [and] public investment in research and development for neglected diseases" (MSF 2001b). The initial health fund pledges fell far short of the annual funding of 8 to 10 billion dollars Kofi Annan asked for, and it was unclear how much of the 1.2 billion was actually new money. And yet, the initiative itself and the fact that this is now of concern both to the UN and to the G8 are important, as Sir Nicholas Bayne observes, with the proviso that "[t]he main weakness in the G8 position is that their pledges look like one-time contributions, without any assurance of continuity of funding" (Bayne 2001).

Oxfam was equally critical of the Genoa Summit's record on debt and the health fund but had a slightly more positive reaction on education. It stated in its press release of 22 July: "The G8 did nothing meaningful on debt relief, and announced a global AIDS fund that still needs much more resources and does nothing about the cost of drugs in poor countries. It's unacceptable that these promises remain unmet. But the leaders laid groundwork for an ambitious agenda next year on Africa and education. The G8 agreed to work with poor countries on a detailed plan to get every child in every poor country into school, the kind of initiative that, if fulfilled, would restore a sense of legitimacy and purpose to these summits. Education breaks the cycle of poverty, and is essential in building democracy and fighting AIDS. Last year the G8 promised a global plan for education. In Genoa they said how to accomplish it. By this time next year, we'll know if they will pay their share. The world can't afford another unmet promise" (OI 2001c).

On energy, a joint statement issued on 22 July by WWF (World Wide Fund for Nature, formerly World Wildlife Fund), Greenpeace and ECA (Export Credit Agencies) Watch condemned the G8 leaders for refusing to adopt the action plan proposed by the Renewable Energy Task Force that the G8 itself had set up in Okinawa a year earlier. The statement added: "By rejecting its own findings, the G8 are actively denying people in the developing world access to clean reliable energy" (WWF 2001).

WDM, assessing the Genoa G8 final communiqué of 22 July, commented on the wide gap "that remains between the leaders and the rest of us". It gave an almost point-by-point response to the language of the G8, welcoming certain initiatives but giving the G8 a poor mark overall. Jessica Woodroffe, head of policy at the WDM, said: "Ultimately these summits must be judged by the benefits they deliver to the world's poor. The result this year has been an anti-poor trade plan, nothing on debt and a feeble [global health] fund" (WDM 2001).

A significant concern was expressed by Drop the Debt about the shifting priorities of the G8: "This year the G8's big idea is to fight disease in the poorest countries. But most people are sick to death of G8 initiatives that never quite get delivered. In 1999, it was debt. Last year, it was computers. This year it is health. Next year, we know it will be education. Every unfinished initiative is another blow to the credibility of the G8. They were half way there with debt – this summit is on its way to being a tragic missed opportunity" (Drop the Debt 2001b). The G8 would do well to reflect on this perception of shifting attention to and away from crucial issues and policy initiatives. Civil society, for its part, could temper its criticism by recognising that the G7/G8 has been able to deal with several issues simultaneously and has at times achieved results by an iterative process, a case in point being the conclusion of the Uruguay Round of multilateral trade negotiations – it took several years of G7 deliberation to achieve success (Bayne 2000a, 200-201). There may thus be some hope for an increase of G8 commitment followed by real, even if not immediate, release of more substantial funding to combat the scourge of AIDS and other infectious diseases. Of course, civil society must (and undoubtedly will) continue to exert pressure to bring this about.

In an early sign of serious post-Genoa questioning of tactics and strategies by civil society, Susan George wrote that "this movement for a different kind of globalization is in danger. Either we'll be capable of exposing what the police are actually up to and manage to contain and prevent the violent methods of the few, or we risk shattering the greatest political hope in the last several decades. ... If we can't guarantee peaceful, creative demonstrations, workers and official trade unions won't join us; our base will slip away, the present unity – both trans-sectoral and trans-generational – will crumble. We, the immense majority with serious proposals to make; we who believe that another world is possible, have got to act responsibly" (George 2001a).

Conclusions

Several lessons can be drawn from this analysis of G7/G8-civil society interaction. First, civil society is an increasingly important and powerful actor in both national and international settings, including the G7/G8 system. At its best, civil society gives voice to the plight and aspirations of those marginalized or left behind by globalization, and it fights for the universal extension of the benefits of globalization. It is here to stay and cannot be ignored. It is not sufficient to group all protesters under the 'anti-globalization' umbrella; a more nuanced approach is necessary.

Second, distinguishing various segments of protesters is not merely an academic or journalistic exercise. Serious civil-society organizations realize that in order to pursue their goals and protect their members and supporters they must isolate and prevent violent groups from sabotaging democratic rights, peaceful demonstrations and legitimate programmes. Ideally, responsible civil-society groups should find ways to police the demonstrations in which they participate, in order to prevent destructive elements from infiltrating and hijacking peaceful protest. Such self-examination has already begun, for example by the environmental coalition Friends of the Earth (Peterson 2001, A21).

Third, a crucial factor in the growing influence of civil society has been information technology. Civil society has learned fast and has used this relatively inexpensive and powerful tool purposefully and efficiently. As well, civil society has developed and employed impressive expertise in using the mass media to disseminate its message and exert its influence.

Fourth, unlike the regular, often formal arrangements with civil society found in the UN system, the OECD, and other structured, traditional IGOs, civil-society relations with the G7/G8 – a flexible institution by and large unhampered by bureaucratic machinery – are characterized by informal practice. There is increasing mutual recognition of the desirability of dialogue and partnership among these actors, along with the inevitable tensions resulting from differing and sometimes conflicting perceptions, objectives and tactics. How can the G7/G8 bring major, responsible NGOs and civil-society coalitions into some sort of association? Some possible ways that may help achieve this objective are:

- Since the G7/G8, lacking a secretariat, cannot itself conduct an effort to inform the world public about its goals and concerns, it is analysts and supporters of the G7/G8 (as well as individual G8 governments and the EU) who can engage in this sort of public information activity. The G8 Research Group and the G8 Information Centre website (www.g7.utoronto.ca) have been playing a part in this.
- The G8-civil society dialogue initiated in Birmingham in 1998 and continued at the 1999 Cologne, 2000 Okinawa and 2001 Genoa summits should be institutionalized and made more meaningful.[19] The G7/G8 could work with responsible, constructive civil-society groups in partnership rather than confronting those groups as adversaries (although constructive, peaceful confrontation is sometimes necessary). The challenge is to muster the political will and then to find ways to develop such partnerships in a meaningful and mutually beneficial manner. A certain convergence of views and programmes of the G8 and responsible civil society groups evident at the 2001 Genoa Summit is cause for some optimism.
- The Japanese government's initiative of establishing an NGO Centre at the 2000 Okinawa Summit site is worth repeating and improving at future summits, although in Genoa NGO groups proved themselves perfectly capable of organising their own centres and convergence points at or near summit sites. Should that route be taken at future summits, the lesson to be learned from Genoa is that here, too, what is needed is co-operation rather than confrontation with national and local authorities.

Fifth, civil society and the G8 (and individual G8 governments) need each other. The injustices of indebtedness of the poorest countries, environmental degradation, lack of access to affordable essential medicines to fight against devastating diseases, educational deficits – these are some of the major concerns of civil society, and it is civil society that plays a crucial role in campaigning for solutions, mobilizing people for support of these causes, and lobbying the most powerful governments and international institutions. But, in the end, it is the governments of rich countries, powerful institutions such as the G7/G8, the IMF, the World Bank and the WTO, as well as large pharmaceutical companies, respectively, that must implement debt forgiveness, large-scale health and education measures, and access to essential medicines at affordable prices.

And a sixth and final point: in the wake of the turbulent Genoa G8 Summit, many questions have been raised about the future of the G8 and the way its business is conducted, as well as about civil society and other protester groups and their methods of operation (for the latter, see above, under point two). For many years, the G7/G8 leaders have voiced their wish to stage smaller, more intimate and more focused meetings, with fewer officials in attendance and perhaps fewer media personnel around. Although some advances have been made – notably with the 1998 Birmingham Summit when leaders began to meet without their foreign and finance ministers – much remains to be done. The *Financial Times*, in a post-Genoa leader, questions whether "G8 summits should exist and, if so, in what form"; notes that "summits have worked best when the leaders have had a chance to be separate from their national entourages ... and when there has been a crisis to try to sort out"; and concludes that there "should have been ... a commitment to hold the next G8 only when there is a burning topic to discuss" ('For Slimmer ...' 2001, 10). Will the G8 leaders have the wisdom to recognize this and act on it? Although there were indications in Genoa that at least the Italian Prime Minister had lost some of his ardour for these summits, it is far from clear that the leaders can reach consensus on reducing the frequency of these get-togethers.

Civil society's dialogue with the G8 is set to continue. Canadian Prime Minister Jean Chrétien, host of the 2002 G8 summit to be held 26-28 June in Kananaskis in the province of Alberta, has already confirmed his intention to engage in dialogue with NGO groups. John Kirton writes that in the post-September 11 era "[f]inding better and more innovative ways to connect with civil society, at the summit itself, and ... through the media, throughout the G8, and around the world, has become a critical and compelling task". To aid that task, he offers a ten-point programme for the Canadian host government in the preparation and holding of the Kananaskis Summit. Among his recommendations are: better public information about the G7/G8 (this would include an important role for parliamentarians); the establishment of government-supported G8 study centres; sponsorship of G8 scholarships (perhaps through the G8 education ministers); better work with the news media; drafting the communiqué in clearer, more accessible language; and bringing civil society closer to the Summit through such means as establishing a multi-stakeholder civil society forum, building on the patterns of the Okinawa G8 Summit and the Québec City Summit of the Americas (Kirton 2002).

G8 governments and civil society share the responsibility to see that their interaction is meaningful and productive. Meeting this difficult challenge will be a true test of the viability both of the G7/G8 and of responsible civil-society movements.

Notes

Note on internet addresses (URLs): Websites tend to appear, change or disappear, often without warning. Addresses cited in this source list were accurate and active at the time of writing (February 2002) unless otherwise noted.

1   For a recent account of the evolution of G7/G8 agenda, see Hajnal and Kirton 2000.
2   John Kirton has termed the G7/G8 "a centre of global governance". Some disagree with this characterization. See, for example, Baker 2000a.
3   TOES USA (n.d.), 'Brief Introduction to TOES', pender.ee.upenn.edu/~rabii/toes/ToesIntro.html. An account of the first two TOES can be found in (Ekins 1986), a compendium of thirty-nine essays. Two more recent works are Mander and Goldsmith 1996 and Schroyer 1997.
4   See, for example, People's Summit 1995.
5   Quoted in Dent and Peters 1999, 188.
6   See also Jubilee Plus, www.jubileeplus.org/analysis/reports/concordats.htm.
7   The term 'sherpa' originates from the name (or, rather, nationality) of the mountain guides in the Himalayas and denotes the senior official who is the personal representative of the leader of each summit country and the European Union (EU). Sherpas meet several times a year as part of their function to prepare for each summit, and sometimes to follow up on the past summit. National sherpa teams generally include, in addition to the sherpa, two sous-sherpas (one for finance, the other for foreign affairs) and a political director from each foreign ministry.
8   See Jubilee 2000 Coalition 1999a; Hanlon and Petifor 2000; and Dent and Peters 1999, 15.
9   Cited in Jubilee 2000 Coalition 1999b.
10 This assessment is based on interviews with NGO representatives at Okinawa.
11 Sadao Ikehara of the University of the Ryukyus, quoted in Saito 2000.
12 See also Kyushu-Okinawa Summit 2000a, para 20.
13 See also G8 Foreign Ministers 2000a.
14 See also Oxfam's website at www.oxfam.org/what_does/advocacy/papers/g8feedback1.html
15 See also Jubilee Plus n.d.
16 See, for example, 'Picking Up the Pieces' 2001.
17 See also *La Republica*, 22 July 2001 and *Le Monde*, 24 July 2001; and Neslen, Arthur (2001), 'Mean Streets: On Location, Genoa Summit', *Now* (Toronto), Vol. 20(47), 26 July-1 August, p. 20. Susan George is vice-president of ATTAC France (ATTAC stands for Association pour une Taxation des Transactions financières pour l'Aide aux Citoyens, or Association for the Taxation of financial Transactions for the Aid of Citizens) and associate of the Transnational Institute (an Amsterdam-based group of scholar-activists).
18 See also G8 Foreign Ministers 2001.
19 Andrew Baker comments briefly on a potential fifth dimension of G7 diplomacy, involving dialogue with transnational social movements. Baker 2000b, pp. 186-187 endnote 11.

References

Amnesty International (2001), *Italy/G8 Summit: Amnesty International Calls for Commission of Inquiry*, Press Release, 31 July,
www.web.amnesty.org/web/news.nsf/WebAll/20BF49CBA0C2F82580256A9A004DEFC3?OpenDocument

Baker, Andrew (2000), 'The G-7 As a Global 'Ginger Group': Plurilateralism and Four-Dimensional Diplomacy', *Global Governance: A Review of Multilateralism and International Organizations*, Vol. 6(2), pp. 165-89.

Baker, Andrew (2000), 'The G-7 As a Global 'Ginger Group': Plurilateralism and Four-Dimensional Diplomacy', *Global Governance: A Review of Multilateralism and International Organizations*, Vol. 6(2), pp. 186-187, endnote 11.

Balmer, Crispian (2001), 'G8 Violence Report Splits Italian Parties', *Reuters Newswire*, 20 September.

Barrett, Marlene (ed) (2000), *The World Will Never Be the Same Again*, Jubilee 2000 Coalition, London.

Bayne, Nicholas (2000a), *Hanging in There: The G7 and G8 Summit in Maturity and Renewal*, Ashgate, Aldershot. The G8 and Global Governance Series.

Bayne, Nicholas (2001), *Impressions of the Genoa Summit, 20-22 July 2001*, G8 Information Centre, Analytical Studies,
www.g7.utoronto.ca/g7/evaluations/2001genoa/assess_summit_bayne.html

Beattie, Alan (2001a), 'Aid Groups Could Miss G8 Talks', *Financial Times*, 2 July.

Beattie, Alan (2001c), 'Protests Aim to Breach G8 Cordon', *Financial Times*, 6 July.

Birmingham Summit (1998a), *Communiqué*, 17 May, Section 7,
www.library.utoronto.ca/g7/summit/1998birmingham/finalcom.htm

Birmingham Summit (1998b), *Response By the Presidency on Behalf of the G8 to the Jubilee 2000 Petition*, 16 May, www.library.utoronto.ca/g7/summit/1998birmingham/2000.htm

Cologne Summit (1999), *Communiqué*, 20 June,
www.library.utoronto.ca/g7/summit/1999koln/finalcom.htm

Dent, Martin and Peters, Bill (1999), *The Crisis of Poverty and Debt in the Third World*, Ashgate, Aldershot.

Denver Summit of the Eight (1997), *Communiqué*, 22 June, Section 13, www.library.utoronto.ca/g7/summit/1997denver/g8final.htm

Drop the Debt (n.d.a), *Background to Drop the Debt*, www.dropthedebt.org

Drop the Debt (n.d.b), *The G8 Genoa Summit: Time for a New Deal on Debt*, www.dropthedebt.org

Drop the Debt (2001a), *Bono, Bob Geldof and Lorenzo Jovanotti Meet G8 Leaders in Genoa*, Press Release, 27 July, www.dropthedebt.org/news/genoastars2707.shtml

Drop the Debt (2001b), *Drop the Debt Response to the G7 Communiqué, Genoa*, 20 July, www.dropthedebt.org.

Drop the Debt (2001c), *Genoa Update*, 21 June, www.dropthedebt.org <8 July 2001>.

Drop the Debt (2001d), *Reality Check: The Need for Deeper Debt Cancellation and the Fight Against HIV/AIDS*, London.

Drop the Debt (2001e), *Verdict on Genoa Summit*, Press Release, 22 July.

Ekins, Paul (1986), *The Living Economy: A New Economics in the Making*, Routledge & Kegan Paul, London.

'For Slimmer and Sporadic Summits' (2001), *Financial Times*, 23 July, p. 10.

Friedmann, Harriet (2001), 'Forum: Considering the Québec Summit, the World Social Forum at Porto Alegre and the People's Summit at Québec City: A View from the Ground,' *Studies in Political Economy: A Socialist Review*, Vol. 66 (Autumn), pp. 85-106.

Friends of the Earth and the EnviroSummit (1990), 'Tropical Forest Destruction', *Economic Declaration*, 11 July, Section 66, Houston,
www.library.utoronto.ca/g7/summit/1990houston/communique/environment.html

G7 Environment Ministers (1996), *Chairman's Summary*, Cabourg, France, 9-10 May, www.library.utoronto.ca/g7/environment/1996cabourg/summary_index.html

G7 Finance Ministers (2001), *Strengthening the International Financial System and the Multilateral Development Banks: Report of G7 Finance Ministers and Central Bank Governors*, Rome, 7 July www.g7.utoronto.ca/g7/finance/fm010707.htm

G8 Environment Ministers (1999), *Communiqué*, Schwerin, Germany, 26-28 March, Section 6 www.library.utoronto.ca/g7/environment/1999schwerin/communique.html

G8 Environment Ministers (2000), *Communiqué*, Otsu, Japan, 7-9 April, Section 17, www.library.utoronto.ca/g7/environment/2000otsu/communique.html

G8 Environment Ministers (2001), *Communiqué*, Trieste, Italy, 2-4 March, paras. 13, 19, 25, www.esteri.it/g8/documentazione/docum02e.htm and www.g7.utoronto.ca/g7/environment/2001trieste/communique.html

G8 Foreign Ministers (2000a), *Conclusions*, Miyazaki, Japan, 13 July, www.library.utoronto.ca/g7/foreign/fm000713.htm.

G8 Foreign Ministers (2000b), *G8 Miyazaki Initiatives for Conflict Prevention*, Miyazaki, Japan, 13 July, www.library.utoronto.ca/g7/foreign/fm000713-in.htm

G8 Foreign Ministers (2001), *Conclusions*, Rome, 18-19 July, www.g7.utoronto.ca/g7/foreign/fm091901_conclusion.html

Genoa Social Forum (n.d.), 'Next Stop: Genoa', www.genoa-g8.org/faq-eng.htm

Genoa Summit (2001a), *Communiqué*, 22 July, paras. 2, 6. 21, 26 and 28 www.genoa-g8.it/eng/attualita/primo_piano/primo_piano_13.html and www.g7.utoronto.ca/g7/summit/2001genoa/finalcommunique.html

Genoa Summit (2001b), *Communiqué*, 22 July, para. 35, www.genoa-g8.it/eng/attualita/primo_piano/primo_piano_13.html and www.g7.utoronto.ca/g7/summit/2001genoa/finalcommunique.html

Genoa Summit (2001c), *Digital Opportunities for All: Meeting the Challenge: Report of the Digital Opportunity Task Force (DOT Force), Including a Proposal for a Genoa Plan of Action*, 11 May, www.g7.utoronto.ca/g7/summit/2001genoa/dotforce1.html;

Genoa Summit (2001d), *G7 Statement*, Genoa, 20 July, para. 8 www.g7.utoronto.ca/g7/summit/2001genoa/g7statement.html

Genoa Summit (2001e), *Genoa, City of Dialogue*, www.genoa-g8.it/eng/attualita/primo_piano/primo_piano_2.html

Genoa Summit (2001f), *Statement by the G8 Leaders*, 21 July, www.g7.utoronto.ca/g7/summit/2001genoa/g8statement1.html

Genoa Summit. News. (2001), *Genoa and G8: Directions for Use*, www.genoa-g8.it/eng/attualita/primo_piano/primo_piano_1.html

George, Susan (2001a), 'G8: Are You Happy?', 24 July, www.tni.org/george/misc/genoa.htm.

George, Susan (2001b), 'L'ordre libéral et ses basses oeuvres', *Le Monde Diplomatique*, Vol. 48(569), pp. 1, 5-6.

Greenpeace International (2000a), *G-8 Adopts Greenpeace Demand to Fight Illegal Logging by Tackling Export Practices And Procurement Policies*, Press Release, Okinawa, 23 July, www.greenpeace.org/pressreleases/

Greenpeace International (2000b), *Greenpeace Activists Released from Okinawa Jail After Carrying Out Peaceful Protests*, Press Release, Amsterdam and Okinawa, 24 July.

Hajnal, Peter I. and Kirton, John J. (2000), 'The Evolving Role and Agenda of the G7/G8: A North American Perspective', *NIRA Review*, Vol. 7(2), pp. 5-10.

Halifax Summit (1995a), *Communiqué: Promoting Sustainable Development*, 16 June, Section 26, www.library.utoronto.ca/g7/summit/1995halifax/communique/development.html

Halifax Summit (1995b), *Communiqué: Reinforcing Coherence, Effectiveness, and Efficiency of Institutions*, 16 June, Section 37, www.library.utoronto.ca/g7/summit/1995halifax/communique/institution.html

Hanlon, Joseph and Garrett, John (1999), *Crumbs of Comfort: The Cologne G8 Summit and the Chains of Debt*, Jubilee 2000 Coalition, London.

Hanlon, Joseph and Petifor, Ann (2000), *Kicking the Habit: Finding a Lasting Solution to Addictive Lending and Borrowing – and Its Corrupting Side-effects*, Jubilee 2000 Coalition, London.
'Italian Ministers Meet Protesters Before G8 Summit', Reuters newswire, 28 June.
Jubilee 2000 Coalition (n.d.), *What Happens Next: Campaigning on Debt Beyond the Millennium Year*, www.jubilee2000uk.org/jubilee2000/whatnext/debt.html
Jubilee 2000 Coalition (1999a), *Breaking the Chains*, Jubilee 2000 Coalition, London.
Jubilee 2000 Coalition (1999b), 'IMF/World Bank Spring Meetings 1999', www.jubilee2000uk.org/jubilee2000/news/meetings1905.html <16 August 2000>.
Jubilee 2000 Coalition (2000a), 'Betraying the Poor: The Squandered Summit and the G7 Leaders' Broken Promises', policy briefing, August, www.jubilee2000uk.org/reports/droppedfull.html <22 August 2000>.
Jubilee 2000 Coalition (2000b), *Cannes Stars Sign Up To Drop The Debt*, Press Release, 12 May, www.jubileeplus.org/media/jubilee2000_archive/cannes120500.htm <15 August 2000>.
Jubilee 2000 Coalition (2000c), *London Red Letter Day on Third World Debt*, Press Release, 3 June, www.jubileeplus.org/media/jubilee2000_archive/london030600.htm <15 August 2000>.
Jubilee 2000 Coalition (2000d), *The Squandered Summit*, Press Release, Okinawa, 23 July.
Jubilee Plus (n.d.), 'About Us', www.jubilee2000uk.org/about/about.htm
Jubilee Plus (2001), *Jubilee Movement International For Economic and Social Justice: Statement on G7 Final Communiqué*, Press Release, Genoa, 21 July, www.jubileeplus.org/jmi/jmi-news/pressrelease_210701.htm
Kirton, John J. (2000), 'Broadening Participation in Twenty-First Century Governance: The Prospective and Potential Contribution of the Okinawa Summit', paper presented at The Kyushu-Okinawa Summit: The Challenges and Opportunities for the Developing World in the 21st Century conference, co-sponsored by the United Nations University, the Foundation for Advanced Studies in Development, and the G8 Research Group, Tokyo, 17 July, www.library.utoronto.ca/g7/scholar/kirton20000717/
Kirton, John J. (2002 forthcoming), 'Guess Who's Coming to Kananaskis? Civil Society and the G8 in Canada's Year as Host', *International Journal*.
Kirton, John J., Daniels, Joseph P. and Freytag, Andreas (2001), 'The G8's Contributions to Twenty-first Century Governance, in John J. Kirton, Joseph P. Daniels, and Andreas Freytag (eds), *Guiding Global Order: G8 Governance in the Twenty-first Century*, Ashgate, Aldershot, pp. 283-304.
Kyushu-Okinawa Summit (2000a), *G7 Statement*, July 21, 2000, para. 20 www.g8kyushu-okinawa.go.jp/e/documents/g7state.html
Kyushu-Okinawa Summit (2000b), *G8 Communiqué*, paras. 15, 24, 29 and 30 www.library.utoronto.ca/g7/summit/2000okinawa/finalcom.htm
Kyushu-Okinawa Summit (2000c), *G8 Communiqué*, paras. 50, 52, 57 and 59 www.library.utoronto.ca/g7/summit/2000okinawa/finalcom.htm
Lovett, Adrian (2000), *Island Mentality: The Okinawa G8 Summit and the Failure of Leadership*, Jubilee 2000 Coalition, London.
Lyon Summit (1996), *Economic Communiqué*, 28 June, Section 34, www.library.utoronto.ca/g7/summit/1996lyon/communique/eco4.htm
Mander, Jerry and Goldsmith, Edward (eds) (1996), *The Case Against the Global Economy and for a Turn Toward the Local*, Sierra Club Books, San Francisco.
Médecins Sans Frontières (2000), *MSF Welcomes Ambitious Targets to Fight Infectious Diseases but Calls on G8 for Equally Strong Action, Not Empty Promises*, Press Release, Okinawa, 23 July, www.accessmed-msf.org/index.asp
Médecins Sans Frontières (2001a), *G8 Window Dresses While Poor Die from Lack of Medicines*, Press release, Genoa, 21 July, www.msf.org/content/page.cfm?articleid=5A05508A-AAD9-474E-AEDA9C6F6A3D5AAA.

Médecins Sans Frontières (2001b), *Violence Grants No Perspectives*, Press Release, Genoa, 20 July.
Ministero degli Affari Esteri (Italy) (2001), *2001 Presidency: Beyond Debt Relief*, www.esteri.it/g8/ and
www.library.utoronto.ca/g7/summit/2001genoa/pres_docs/pres1.html
Neslen, Arthur (2001), 'Mean Streets: On Location, Genoa Summit', *Now* (Toronto), Vol. 20(47), p. 20.
Oxfam International (2000), *Oxfam and Education Campaigners: Education One of Few Bright Spots in Okinawa*, Press Release, Okinawa, July.
Oxfam International (2001c), *Genoa Fails: Big Promise for Next Year*, Press Release, Genoa, 22 July, www.oxfam.org/news/pressreleases.htm
Oxfam International (2001h), *Violence Doesn't Help*, Press Release, 20 July, www.oxfaminternational.org/what_does/advocacy/papers/010720_Violence%20doesn'thelp%20G80720.doc
People's Summit (1995), *Communiqué from the People's Summit*, 16 June, Halifax, www.igc.org/habitat/p-7/p7-comm.html
Peterson, Luke (2001), 'Civil Society Groups Begin To Question Tactics Used at Trade Talks', *The Toronto Star*, 3 August, p. A21.
'Picking Up the Pieces: After the Genoa Summit' (2001), *The Economist*, Vol. 360(8232), 28 July, pp. 49-50.
Quadrilateral Trade Ministers (1999), *Chair's Statement*, 33rd Meeting, Tokyo, Japan, 11-12 May, [section on environment] www.library.utoronto.ca/g7/trade/quad33.html
Sachs, Jeffrey D. (2001), 'The Strategic Significance of Global Inequality', *The Washington Quarterly*, Vol. 24(3), pp. 187-198.
Saito, Jun (2000), 'NGOs Shunned by G-8 Attendees', *Asahi Evening News*, 23 July.
Sanger, David (2001), '2 Leaders Tell of Plot to Kill Bush in Genoa', *The New York Times*, 26 September, p. B1.
Schroyer, Trent (ed) (1997), *A World That Works: Building Blocks for a Just and Sustainable Society*, The Bootstrap Press, New York.
Summit of the Arch (1989), *Economic Declaration*, 16 July, Section 43, Paris, www.library.utoronto.ca/g7/summit/1989paris/communique/environment.html
'Ties Strengthened: Future Cooperation Key to NGO Goals' (2000), *The Japan Times*, 25 July 25.
TOES (1988), *Summit Echo: A Newspaper of the Summit Citizens Conference*, 19 June, Toronto.
TOES USA (n.d.), 'Brief Introduction to TOES',
pender.ee.upenn.edu/~rabii/toes/ToesIntro.html
United Nations. General Assembly (2001a), *Declaration of Commitment on HIV/AIDS: Global Crisis – Global Action*, paras. 27, 33, 35, 37, 46, 55, 67, 86 and 94, Special Session on HIV/AIDS, New York, 25-27 June, A/RES/S-26/2,
www.un.org/ga/aids/coverage/FinalDeclarationHIVAIDS.html
Watkins, Kevin (2000), *The Oxfam Education Report*, Oxfam GB for Oxfam International, Oxford.
World Development Movement (2001), *WDM Report Back from the G8 Summit in Genoa*, 23 July; www.wdm.org.uk/campaign/Genoa.htm
World Wide Fund for Nature (2001), *G8 Plan for Africa Pointless without Renewable Energy Support*, Press Release, Genoa, 22 July, World Wide Fund for Nature, Greenpeace, and Export Credit Agencies International NGO Campaign.
Zampano, Giada (2001), 'Italy Confirms Genoa as Venue of G8', Reuters newswire, 19 June.
Zupi, Marco (2001), 'The Genoa G-8 Summit: Great Expectations, Disappointing Results,' *The International Spectator*, Vol. 36(3), pp. 57-68.

Chapter 14

Conclusion

Peter I. Hajnal

Nongovernmental organizations (NGOs) and other civil society organizations and coalitions are proliferating and increasing in complexity, in the scope of their programmes, and in their interactions with one another and with governmental and intergovernmental actors. Their ability to fill new or newly opened political space has resulted in their increasing influence on processes, decisions and policies of governments and international governmental institutions. The chapters comprising this volume, written by academics, civil society activists, and United Nations (UN) and Canadian government officials, reflect a spectrum of interpretations of NGOs and civil society, and mirror our complex world that does not lend itself to neat classifications.

Several lessons can be drawn from this examination of goals, activities, governance structures and working methods of major international NGOs and civil society coalitions, as well as NGOs of the South. Analysis of the relationship of NGOs and civil society groups with one another and with state and intergovernmental actors strengthens these conclusions.

Based on the contributions to this book, the answer to the question 'How has information and communications technology (ICT) helped civil society in advocacy, service delivery and networking?' is this: technology has greatly enhanced civil society's ability to engage in all three facets of their work cheaply and efficiently. In her chapter, Joanne Lebert notes that ICT has greatly increased the speed with which Amnesty International (AI) can collect and circulate data both internally and publicly. She asserts that technology has facilitated the co-ordination of action and the mobilization and delivery of organizational support to AI activists. Writing about the internet Network of the Global Security Program of the Union of Concerned Scientists, John Spykerman concludes that ICT will play an increasingly important role in the process whereby scientists continue to expose the technical vulnerabilities of the proposed missile defence systems. Peter Hajnal, tracing the work of Oxfam International (OI), finds that the organization has made considerable advances in co-ordinating its multifaceted work in the areas of development, emergency response and advocacy. ICT has played a major role both in OI's internal work and public outreach and has enabled the organization to respond to challenges in a speedy and flexible manner. In his chapter about NGOs of the South, Juris Dilevko states that for those NGOs ICT is the tool of choice to aid fundraising, advocacy and networking activities. William R. Pace and Rik Panganiban, writing about the NGO coalition for an International Criminal Court, note that the wide availability of ICT has allowed both the scope and the speed of civil society activity in that campaign to increase greatly. And James Orbinski asserts that the internet, e-mail, mobile telephones and fax machines have had a great impact on the speed and scope of the Access to Essential Medicines campaign led by Médecins Sans Frontières (MSF).

How has ICT shaped and altered NGOs and civil society coalitions? All chapters in this book, in their diverse ways, affirm that ICT has played a crucial role in transforming and empowering civil society. These technologies extend beyond the internet to include videoconferencing, e-mail, mobile telephones, satellite hookups and other advances. Dilevko notes that Southern NGOs, by enthusiastically embracing ICT, have improved their decision-making processes and contributed to the emergence of local networks of expertise. Kenneth Rutherford asserts that civil society, by using ICT in its campaign to ban landmines, was able to reduce the cost of coalition-building and of communication. Pace and Panganiban conclude that the evolution of the NGO coalition for an International Criminal Court (ICC) has shown that ICT is an increasingly integral aspect of the functioning and effectiveness of civil society in international decision-making.[1] Orbinski notes that e-mail, mobile telephones and other ICTs have been critical in that they have enabled participants and supporters of the Access to Essential Medicines campaign to reach one another instantaneously and worldwide, in order to clarify a point, receive immediate information, or clear up contentious issues.

How has ICT furthered civil society's aims and influenced government and IGO policy and behaviour? Rutherford remarks that the International Campaign To Ban Landmines (ICBL) and the Landmine Survivors Network (LSN) have used information technologies in new and creative ways to influence the making of foreign policy. He adds that the rapid development of ICT and the fact that the state no longer has a monopoly on information have contributed to the transformation of NGOs into important international actors able to influence international politics in issue areas that used to be the exclusive domain of states. On a more cautious note, Benjamin Rivlin (who comments extensively on the use of ICT by religious NGO groups) leaves open the question of whether such groups are effective players within the 'new diplomacy'. Although many such NGOs have distinguished themselves in humanitarian relief work, they have rarely been at the forefront of major global undertakings such as the drafting of the statute of the International Criminal Court, or the Mine Ban Treaty. He concludes that the effectiveness of the role that religious NGOs play in international society in dealing with the adverse consequences of globalization depend on how those religions live up to their theology and how well they can overcome their complicity in conflicts around the world. Heidi Ullrich concludes her investigation of the role of information in the relationship between the World Trade Organization (WTO) and trade-related NGOs with a series of recommendations aimed at making that interaction more effective, leading to a knowledgeable two-way dialogue. She calls for increased transparency and legitimacy on the part of the WTO, more effective information exchange using ICT, and enhanced civil society guidance for the WTO. In his study of the G7/G8-civil society nexus, Hajnal states that civil society gives voice to the plight and aspirations of the marginalized, and fights for the universal extension of the benefits of globalization. ICT, a relatively inexpensive and powerful tool – when used purposefully and efficiently – has been a crucial factor in increasing the influence of civil society.

What role has ICT played in enhancing the legitimacy of civil society groups? NGOs and civil society movements gather information strategically, and use information technology with increasing efficiency in order to influence international policies, programs and treaties and thereby enhance their own legitimacy. Dilevko suggests that, aided by ICT, a broad-based alliance of Southern NGOs could enhance the capacity and influence of those NGOs and could thus bring about more meaningful collaboration with international civil society. Orbinski concludes that, by allowing the posting on the web an NGO coalition's position on a given issue together with the rationale and evidence for that position, ICT facilitates the evaluation and endorsement of that position by visitors to the website; if the recipients of that information verify and accept the credibility and integrity of the information, they will accept the legitimacy of the work of the originating organization. Barbara Adams asserts that NGO involvement was a significant factor in the achievement of international consensus and government commitment on difficult policy challenges – for example on issues of women's rights and reproductive health – at major UN conferences. She concludes that the participation of civil society has provided the UN not only with technical expertise but has increased public awareness of global issues, and contributed to greater democracy, transparency and accountability on the part of UN member governments. Skilful use of ICT has assisted NGOs in achieving these results. Marc Lortie and Sylvie Bédard argue that the complexity of our globalized world has made the input of diverse actors – government, business, civil society and others – necessary because each actor brings a different expertise and perspective to decision-making. They conclude that a concerted, integrated approach on the part of government leads to increased understanding and cooperation among different sectors of society, leading to an expanded social consensus. They point out that the greater influence that the new actors have acquired – with the significant aid of ICT – places commensurately greater responsibility on them.

Under what circumstances is the use of modern technologies inappropriate? ICT is not always the preferred method of operation; face-to-face and other traditional communication, or massive street demonstrations, can produce better results in certain situations. As Dilevko points out, many NGOs of the South suffer from the digital gap or lack access to ICT altogether. As well, technology can be used or misused. Lebert maintains that her organization faces the dilemma of remaining accessible while protecting itself against technological abuse such as misinformation, misinterpretation and manipulation. AI's answer is to use technology in conjunction with more traditional forms of interaction. Pace and Panganiban remark that traditional means of communication, including print publications, will remain necessary components of campaigning. And it is useful to remember that effective global civil society campaigns were mounted well before the advent of the information age. Orbinski asserts that technology is not an end in itself but a means to an end; he states that people must meet face-to-face to share ideas, develop mutual trust and articulate a shared vision and shared goals. In a postscript dealing with the September 11, 2001 terrorist attacks, Pace and

Panganiban warn that apparently benign technologies can be used by criminal and terrorist organizations for their own ends. Ullrich cautions that although information is a most important power resource, it must be transformed into shared knowledge to realize its potential to generate power.

One of the most important conclusions of this book is that results of civil society activity – whether positive as exemplified by bringing about the landmine ban treaty or negative as in defeating the Multilateral Agreement on Investment (MAI) – cannot be achieved by NGOs and civil society groups alone or even by any combination of these actors.[2] Civil society advocacy and mobilization are crucial in prodding, shaming, persuading or speeding the action of governments or business enterprises, but it is governments that must sign and ratify the landmine treaty or the treaty establishing the International Criminal Court; and it is the pharmaceutical companies that must lower the price of antiretrovirals and other essential medicines in the poorest countries. Governments and international governmental organizations may not have the political will or may be paralysed by inertia; business corporations are often motivated solely by profit rather than profit accompanied by social conscience. Governments and corporations often cannot or will not move without the impetus of civil society. In a similar vein, Michael Edwards, an analyst of civil society, observes that "[a]lthough non-governmental actors cannot replace the functions of elected governments, they do provide ideas, information, pressure for results, and the leverage required to implement solutions on the ground – all of which are necessary to solve global problems. ... Acting alone, governments cannot confer legitimacy on global decisions ... [;] further engagement with ... non-state actors is inevitable" (Edwards 2002, A17). And Kamal Malhotra asserts that "civil society's main role is in holding both the state and the market accountable, to be ... a societal watchdog [vis-à-vis both the state and the market" but cautions that civil society cannot be a substitute for the state (CBC 2001, 23).

Public goods can be produced by partnership, by patient advocacy, or sometimes by confrontation – which can be, but is not always, counterproductive. Whether by willing co-operation or by intentional or unintended complementarity, civil society, government and business need one another to achieve social, economic and political goals. Synergy can and does occur, whether there are formal structures of interaction, well-functioning practical arrangements, or convergences of views and programmes among state and non-state actors. In this context, the 'new diplomacy' that has seen NGOs and civil society coalitions working with governments and IGOs is a significant development. Non-state actors – NGOs, business groups, nongovernmental funding agencies and others – familiar with the situation on the ground, can tap into grassroots movements and can achieve better results than governmental entities, working alone, could. At its best, civil society works in partnership with IGOs and governments for the benefit of the greatest number of people; at its worst, it acts to undermine IGOs and governments; and there are many shades of interaction along this continuum.

But governments, IGOs and the business sector cannot take it for granted that civil society will act on their terms. On 7 December 2001, in conjunction with the 100th anniversary of the Nobel prize, 100 laureates warned in their statement that "[t]he most profound danger to world peace in the coming years will stem not from the irrational acts of states or individuals but from the legitimate demands of the world's dispossessed. ... It cannot be expected ... that in all cases they will be content to await the beneficence of the rich" ('Our Best Point the Way' 2001, A21). The international community must find ways to address such legitimate demands and to remedy inequalities. Responsible civil society groups will continue to push for those goals.

Notes

1   See also Ottaway 2001, 271. She observes that improvements in ICT "have made it easier and cheaper to disseminate information and to maintain contacts among groups ... around the world" and have been a major factor in the "exponential growth in the number of NGOs and in the variety of causes they espouse".
2   Although the civil society community often cites its victory in bringing about the defeat of MAI, there were multiple factors at play. But the defeat illustrates the possible consequences of political processes where civil society is excluded from participation. For background information, see Dymond 1999, 30-31; and Smith and Smythe 2000.

References

Canadian Broadcasting Corporation (2001), 'Civil Society', *Ideas*, 18, 25 June, ID 2395, CBC Ideas Transcripts, Toronto.

Dymond, William A. (1999), 'The MAI: A Sad and Melancholy Tale', in Fen Osler Hampson, Martin Rudner and Michael Hart (eds), *Canada Among Nations 1999: A Big League Player?*, pp. 25-53, Oxford University Press, Toronto.

Edwards, Michael (2002), 'The Mouse That Roared', *The Globe and Mail* (Toronto), 3 January, p. A17.

Ottaway, Marina (2001), 'Corporatism Goes Global: International Organizations, Nongovernmental Organization Networks, and Transnational Business', *Global Governance: A Review of Multilateralism and International Organizations*, Vol. 7(3), pp. 265-292.

'Our Best Point the Way' (2001), *The Globe and Mail* (Toronto), 7 December, p. A21.

Smith, Peter (Jay) and Smythe, Elizabeth (2000), 'Globalization, Citizenship and Technology: The MAI Meets the Internet', paper presented at the annual meeting of the International Studies Association, Los Angeles, 17 March.

Electronic Sources

Compiled by Peter I. Hajnal and Gillian R. Clinton

Note on internet addresses (URLs): Websites tend to appear, change or disappear, often without warning. Addresses cited in this source list were accurate and active at the time of writing (February 2002) unless otherwise noted.

Adventist Press Service (2000), 'World Religious Summit Brings Mixed Responses', Adventist Press Service, 2 September, Basel, www.stanet.ch/APD

American Physical Society (APS). National Policy Statement (2000), 'National Missile Defense System Technical Feasibility and Deployment', 29 April, www.aps.org/statements/00.2.html

Amnesty International, www.amnesty.org

Amnesty International (2001), *Italy/G8 Summit: Amnesty International Calls for Commission of Inquiry*, Press Release, 31 July, www.web.amnesty.org/web/news.nsf/WebAll/20BF49CBA0C2F82580256A9A004DEFC3?OpenDocument

Annan, Kofi (1998), *'Act on Your Ideals', Secretary-General Urges Young People at World Youth Forum*, UN Press Release, SG/Youth/1, 7 August, World Youth Forum, Braga, Portugal, www.un.org/events/Youth98/pressrel/sgyouth.htm

The Appeal of Conscience Foundation, www.appealofconscience.org

Australian Broadcasting Corporation. News Online (2000), *WTO Leader Undeterred by Globalisation Opposition*, Transcript of broadcast with WTO Deputy Director-General Andrew Stoler, 13 September. www.abc.net.au/pm/s176169.htm

Ballantyne, P., Labelle, R. and Rudgard, S. (2000), *Information and Knowledge Management: Challenges for Capacity Builders*, www.oneworld.org/ecdpm/pmb/b11_gb.htm

Bayne, Nicholas (2001), *Impressions of the Genoa Summit, 20-22 July 2001*, G8 Information Centre, Analytical Studies, www.g7.utoronto.ca/g7/evaluations/2001genoa/assess_summit_bayne.html

Birmingham Summit (1998a), *Communiqué*, 17 May, Section 7, www.library.utoronto.ca/g7/summit/1998birmingham/finalcom.htm

Birmingham Summit (1998b), *Response By the Presidency on Behalf of the G8 to the Jubilee 2000 Petition*, 16 May, www.library.utoronto.ca/g7/summit/1998birmingham/2000.htm

Castells, M. (1998), *Information Technology, Globalization and Social Development*. Paper presented at the UNRISD Conference on Information Technologies and Social Development, Palais des Nations, Geneva, June 22-24, 1998 www.unrisd.org/infotech/conferen/castelp1.htm

Churchill, Winston (1946), *Sinews of Peace*, speech delivered at Westminster College, Fulton, Missouri, March 5. www.winstonchurchill.org/sinews.htm

Cirincione, Joseph (1997), 'Why the Right Lost the Missile Defense Debate', *Foreign Policy*, No. 106, Spring 1997. www.stimson.org/rd-table/fornpol.html

Coalition for an International Criminal Court, www.igc.org/icc/

Coalition to Reduce Dangers, www.crnd.org

Cologne Summit (1999), *Communiqué*, 20 June, www.library.utoronto.ca/g7/summit/1999koln/finalcom.htm

The Committee of Religious NGOs at the United Nations (2000), *Survey of Activities of Religious NGOs at the UN, 1989-1999*, New York www.rngo.org

Council for a Liveable World, www.clw.org/ef/nmddelay.html

Coyle, Philip E. (2001), *FY2000 Annual Report of the Office of the Director, Operational Test & Evaluation*, www.dote.osd.mil/reports/FY00/index.html

Denver Summit of the Eight (1997), *Communiqué*, 22 June, Section 13, www.library.utoronto.ca/g7/summit/1997denver/g8final.htm

Drop the Debt, *Background to Drop the Debt*, www.dropthedebt.org

Drop the Debt, *The G8 Genoa Summit: Time for a New Deal on Debt*, www.dropthedebt.org

Drop the Debt (2001a), *Bono, Bob Geldof and Lorenzo Jovanotti Meet G8 Leaders in Genoa*, Press Release, 27 July, www.dropthedebt.org/news/genoastars2707.shtml

Drop the Debt (2001b), *Drop the Debt Response to the G7 Communiqué, Genoa*, 20 July, www.dropthedebt.org

Drop the Debt (2001c), *Genoa Update*, 21 June, www.dropthedebt.org <8 July 2001>.

Engh, Gabrielle. (2000), 'Conservative Religious Groups Complain of Prejudice by UN, NGOs', *Ecumenical Women 2000+*, www.ew2000plus.org/OTRPanelArticlePrint.htm

Federation of American Scientists (2000), 'Increased Missile Defense Secrecy Proposed', *Secrecy News*, 15 November, www.fas.org/sgp/news/secrecy/

Friends of the Earth and the EnviroSummit (1990), 'Tropical Forest Destruction', *Economic Declaration*, 11 July, Section 66, Houston, www.library.utoronto.ca/g7/summit/1990houston/communique/environment.html

G7 Environment Ministers (1996), *Chairman's Summary*, Cabourg, France, 9-10 May, www.library.utoronto.ca/g7/environment/1996cabourg/summary_index.html

G7 Finance Ministers (2001), *Strengthening the International Financial System and the Multilateral Development Banks: Report of G7 Finance Ministers and Central Bank Governors*, Rome, 7 July www.g7.utoronto.ca/g7/finance/fm010707.htm

G8 Environment Ministers (1999), *Communiqué*, Schwerin, Germany, 26-28 March, Section 6, www.library.utoronto.ca/g7/environment/1999schwerin/communique.html

G8 Environment Ministers (2000), *Communiqué*, Otsu, Japan, 7-9 April, Section 17, www.library.utoronto.ca/g7/environment/2000otsu/communique.html

G8 Environment Ministers (2001), *Communiqué*, Trieste, Italy, 2-4 March, paras. 13, 19, 25, www.esteri.it/g8/documentazione/docum02e.htm; www.g7.utoronto.ca/g7/environment/2001trieste/communique.html
G8 Foreign Ministers (2000a), *Conclusions*, Miyazaki, Japan, 13 July, www.library.utoronto.ca/g7/foreign/fm000713.htm
G8 Foreign Ministers (2000b), *G8 Miyazaki Initiatives for Conflict Prevention*, Miyazaki, Japan, 13 July, www.library.utoronto.ca/g7/foreign/fm000713-in.htm
G8 Foreign Ministers (2001), *Conclusions*, Rome, 18-19 July, www.g7.utoronto.ca/g7/foreign/fm091901_conclusion.html
G8 Information Centre, www.g7.utoronto.ca
Genoa Social Forum, www.genoa-g8.org
Genoa Summit (2001a), *Communiqué*, 22 July, paras. 2, 6, 21, 26 and 28 www.genoa-g8.it/eng/attualita/primo_piano/primo_piano_13.html and www.g7.utoronto.ca/g7/summit/2001genoa/finalcommunique.html
Genoa Summit (2001b), *Communiqué*, 22 July, para. 35, www.genoa-g8.it/eng/attualita/primo_piano/primo_piano_13.html and www.g7.utoronto.ca/g7/summit/2001genoa/finalcommunique.html
Genoa Summit (2001c), *Digital Opportunities for All: Meeting the Challenge: Report of the Digital Opportunity Task Force (DOT Force), Including a Proposal for a Genoa Plan of Action*, 11 May, www.g7.utoronto.ca/g7/summit/2001genoa/dotforce1.html
Genoa Summit (2001d), *G7 Statement*, Genoa, 20 July, para. 8 www.g7.utoronto.ca/g7/summit/2001genoa/g7statement.html
Genoa Summit (2001e), *Genoa, City of Dialogue*, www.genoa-g8.it/eng/attualita/primo_piano/primo_piano_2.html
Genoa Summit (2001f), *Statement by the G8 Leaders*, 21 July, www.g7.utoronto.ca/g7/summit/2001genoa/g8statement1.html
Genoa Summit. News (2001), *Genoa and G8: Directions for Use*, www.genoa-g8.it/eng/attualita/primo_piano/primo_piano_1.html
George, Susan (2001a), 'G8: Are You Happy?', 24 July, www.tni.org/george/misc/genoa.htm
Global Trade Watch, www.citizen.org/pctrade/tradehome.html
Greenpeace International (2000a), *G-8 Adopts Greenpeace Demand to Fight Illegal Logging by Tackling Export Practices And Procurement Policies*, Press Release, Okinawa, 23 July, www.greenpeace.org/pressreleases/
Group of 77, www.g77.org
Hajnal, Peter I. (2001), *Personal Assessment of the Role of Civil Society at the 2001 Genoa G8 Summit*, University of Toronto G8 Information Centre: Analytical Studies, 2001 Summit Assessment, 2 August, www.g7.utoronto.ca/g7/evaluations/2001genoa/assess_summit_hajnal.html
Halifax Summit (1995a), *Communiqué: Promoting Sustainable Development*, 16 June, Section 26, www.library.utoronto.ca/g7/summit/1995halifax/communique/development.html

Halifax Summit (1995b), *Communiqué: Reinforcing Coherence, Effectiveness, and Efficiency of Institutions*, 16 June, Section 37, www.library.utoronto.ca/g7/summit/1995halifax/communique/institution.html

Hamelink, C.J. (1997), *New Information and Communication Technologies, Social Development and Cultural Change*,
www.unrisd.org/engindex/publ/list/dp/dp86/dp86.htm

Hidden Killers: The Global Problem with Uncleared Landmines (United States Department of State, Washington, DC, July 1993), p. 2. www.state.gov/www/global/arms/rpt_9809_demine_toc.html

ICC Monitor, www.igc.org/icc/html/monitor.htm

International Campaign to Ban Landmines, www.icbl.org

International Campaign to Ban Landmines (1999b), *Landmine Monitor Report 1999: Toward a Mine-Free World*, Human Rights Watch, New York www.icbl.org/lm/1999/

International Chamber of Commerce, www.iccwbo.org

International Chamber of Commerce (2001a), *ICC Actions and Achievements*, www.iccwbo.org/home/intro_icc/icc_actions_achievements.asp

International Chamber of Commerce (2001b), *ICC Recommendations to WTO Members on Trade Facilitation*, 6 June, Document No. 103-32/91. www.iccwbo.org/home/statements_rules/statements/2001/wto_members_on_trade.asp

International Criminal Court: Resources in Print and Electronic Format, www.lib.uchicago.edu/~llou/icc.html

International Institute for Sustainable Development, *World Trade Organization Symposium on Issues Confronting the World Trade System*, www.iisd.ca/sd.wto-issues/

Isaacs, John (2000), *Anatomy of a Victory: Clinton Decides Against a Missile Defense*, 5 September, Council for a Livable World, www.clw.org/nmd/nmddelay.html

Johnson, Martin (1999), 'Non-Profit Organisations and the Internet', *First Monday: Peer-Reviewed Journal on the Internet* 4(2) www.firstmonday.dk

Joint United Nations Programme on HIV/AIDS (UNAIDS) (2001), *AIDS Epidemic Update*, December,
www.unaids.org/epidemic_update/report_dec01/index.html#full

Jubilee 2000 Coalition, *What Happens Next: Campaigning on Debt Beyond the Millennium Year*, www.jubilee2000uk.org/jubilee2000/whatnext/debt.html

Jubilee 2000 Coalition (1999b), 'IMF/World Bank Spring Meetings 1999', www.jubilee2000uk.org/jubilee2000/news/meetings1905.html <16 August 2000>.

Jubilee 2000 Coalition (2000a), 'Betraying the Poor: The Squandered Summit and the G7 Leaders' Broken Promises', policy briefing, August, www.jubilee2000uk.org/reports/droppedfull.html <22 August 2000>.

Jubilee 2000 Coalition (2000b), *Cannes Stars Sign Up To Drop The Debt*, Press Release, 12 May,
www.jubileeplus.org/media/jubilee2000_archive/cannes120500.htm <15 August 2000>.

Jubilee 2000 Coalition (2000c), *London Red Letter Day on Third World Debt*, Press Release, 3 June, www.jubileeplus.org/media/jubilee2000_archive/london030600.htm <15 August 2000>.

Jubilee Movement International for Economic and Social Justice, www.jubileeplus.org/jmi/main.htm

Jubilee Plus, 'About Us', www.jubilee2000uk.org/about/about.htm

Jubilee Plus (2001), *Jubilee Movement International For Economic and Social Justice: Statement on G7 Final Communiqué*, Press Release, Genoa, 21 July, www.jubileeplus.org/jmi/jmi-news/pressrelease_210701.htm

Jubilee Plus, www.jubileeplus.org/analysis/reports/concordats.htm

Judge, Anthony, *Types of International Organizations*, Section 2.2, Union of International Associations, www.uia.org/uiadocs/orgtypec.htm

Kirton, John J. (2000), 'Broadening Participation in Twenty-First Century Governance: The Prospective and Potential Contribution of the Okinawa Summit', paper presented at The Kyushu-Okinawa Summit: The Challenges and Opportunities for the Developing World in the 21st Century conference, co-sponsored by the United Nations University, the Foundation for Advanced Studies in Development, and the G8 Research Group, Tokyo, 17 July, www.library.utoronto.ca/g7/scholar/kirton20000717/

Kyushu-Okinawa Summit (2000a), *G7 Statement*, July 21, 2000, para. 20 www.g8kyushu-okinawa.go.jp/e/documents/g7state.html

Kyushu-Okinawa Summit (2000b), *G8 Communiqué*, paras. 15, 24, 29 and 30 www.library.utoronto.ca/g7/summit/2000okinawa/finalcom.htm

Kyushu-Okinawa Summit (2000c), *G8 Communiqué*, paras. 50, 52, 57 and 59 www.library.utoronto.ca/g7/summit/2000okinawa/finalcom.htm

Lal, B. (1999), *Information and Communication Technologies for Improved Governance*, www.abtassociates.com/reports/governance/ict.pdf

Landmines Survivors Network, www.landminesurvivors.org

Lyon Summit (1996), *Economic Communiqué*, 28 June, Section 34, www.library.utoronto.ca/g7/summit/1996lyon/communique/eco4.htm

Madison, James (1787), 'The Same Subject Continued: The Union as a Safeguard Against Domestic Faction and Insurrection', *Federalist Papers*, No. 10, memory.loc.gov/const/fed/fed_10.html

Mathews, Jessica Tuchman (1999), Statement to the 75th Anniversary Symposium, Harvard School of Public Health, Boston, 25 September, www.hsph.harvard.edu/digest/mathews.html

Médecins Sans Frontières (2000), *MSF Welcomes Ambitious Targets to Fight Infectious Diseases but Calls on G8 for Equally Strong Action, Not Empty Promises*, Press Release, Okinawa, 23 July, www.accessmed-msf.org/index.asp

Médecins Sans Frontières (2001a), *G8 Window Dresses While Poor Die from Lack of Medicines*, Press release, Genoa, 21 July, www.msf.org/content/page.cfm?articleid=5A05508A-AAD9-474E-AEDA9C6F6A3D5AAA

Ministero degli Affari Esteri (Italy) (2001), *2001 Presidency: Beyond Debt Relief*, www.esteri.it/g8/ and
www.library.utoronto.ca/g7/summit/2001genoa/pres_docs/pres1.html
Monthly NGO bulletin from the WTO. Contact: ngobulletin@wto.org
NGO Coalition for an International Criminal Court (1998a), *The Numbers: NGO Coalition Special Report on Country Positions*, 10 July, www.igc.apc.org/icc/rome/html/rome_other.html
NGO Coalition for an International Criminal Court (1998b), *The Virtual Vote: NGO Coalition Special Report on Country Positions on L.59*, 15 July, www.igc.apc.org/icc/rome/html/rome_other.html
Orbinski, James (1999), *The Nobel Lecture*, Oslo, 10 December. Speech by James Orbinski, Médecins Sans Frontières, accepting the Nobel Peace Prize. www.nobel.no/eng_lect_99m.html
Ostry, Sylvia (2000), *WTO: Institutional Design for Better Governance*, (Draft), Paper presented at J.F. Kennedy School of Government, Harvard University. 2-3 June, www.utoronto.ca/cis/WTOID.pdf
Oxfam, www.oxfam.org or www.oxfaminternational.org
Oxfam Canada, *Fair Trade in Coffee*, www.oxfam.ca/what/campaigns/coffee/index.htm
Oxfam Community Aid Abroad, *East Timor*, www.caa.org.au/world/asia/east_timor/index.html
Oxfam Community Aid Abroad, *Oxfam International Policy Papers*, www.caa.org.au/oxfam/advocacy/index.html
Oxfam Great Britain, *About Oxfam Fair Trade*, www.oxfam.org.uk/fairtrad/aboutft1.htm
Oxfam International, *Afghanistan*, www.oxfam.org/news/afghan.htm
Oxfam International, *Annual Report, 1999*, www.oxfam.org/what_is_OI/a_report/default.htm
Oxfam International, *Campaigns: Change the World*, www.oxfam.org/what_does/advocacy/default.htm
Oxfam International (2001c), *Genoa Fails: Big Promise for Next Year*, Press Release, Genoa, 22 July, www.oxfam.org/news/pressreleases.htm
Oxfam International, *How are Oxfam's Funds Used?*, www.oxfam.org/involve/donations.htm
Oxfam International, *Mission Statement*, www.oxfaminternational.org/strategic_plan/intro2.htm
Oxfam International, *Policy Papers*, www.oxfam.org/what_does/advocacy/papers.htm
Oxfam International, *Towards Global Equity: Strategic Plan, 2001-2004*, www.oxfam.org/strategic_plan/index.htm
Oxfam International (2001h), *Violence Doesn't Help*, Press Release, 20 July, www.oxfaminternational.org/what_does/advocacy/papers/010720_Violence%20doesn'thelp%20G80720.doc
Peoples' Global Action, www.nadir.org/nadir/initiative/agp/
People's Summit (1995), *Communiqué from the People's Summit*, 16 June, Halifax, www.igc.org/habitat/p-7/p7-comm.html

Public Citizen for Global Trade Watch, www.citizen.org/trade/
Public Citizen for Global Trade Watch (2001b), 'Talking Points on 'WTO: Shrink or Sink' Global NGO Campaign',
www.citizen.org/pctrade/gattwto/ShrinkSink/talkingpts.htm
Quadrilateral Trade Ministers (1999), *Chair's Statement*, 33rd Meeting, Tokyo, Japan, 11-12 May, [section on environment]
www.library.utoronto.ca/g7/trade/quad33.html
Secretariat of the Millennium World Peace Summit of Religious and Spiritual Leaders (2000), *Commitment to Global Peace*,
www.millenniumpeacesummit.org/declaration.html
Smillie, Ian (1999), *Narrowing the Digital Divide: Notes on a Global Netcorps*,
www.unites.org/reference/smillie0.html
Spencer, Jack and Scardaville, Michael (2000), *Missile Defense and the Arms Race*, 13 October, Heritage Foundation,
http://heritage.org/views/2000/ed101300.html
Summit of the Arch (1989), *Economic Declaration*, 16 July, Section 43, Paris,
www.library.utoronto.ca/g7/summit/1989paris/communique/environment.html
Third Summit of the Americas - Canada: The Cyber Hemisphere, www.americascanada.org
Third World Network, www.twnside.org.sg
TOES USA, 'Brief Introduction to TOES',
pender.ee.upenn.edu/~rabii/toes/ToesIntro.html
Union of Concerned Scientists, www.ucsusa.org
Union of Concerned Scientists (2001), *Countermeasures: The Achilles Heel of Missile Defenses*, www.ucsusa.org/security/countermeasures.html
United Nations, Department of Public Information, *Directory of NGOs Associated with DPI*, UN, www.un.org/MoreInfo/ngolink/ngodir.htm
United Nations. Department of Public Information (1989), *Charter of the United Nations and Statute of the International Court of Justice*, UN, New York, DPI/511 www.un.org/Overview/Charter/chapte10.html
United Nations. Department of Public Information (1948), *Universal Declaration of Human Rights*, DPI, New York. www.un.org/Overview/rights.html.
United Nations. Economic and Social Council (1996a), *Consultative Relations Between the United Nations and Non-governmental Organizations*, UN, New York, 25 July, E/RES/1996/31 www.hri.ca/uninfo/resolutn/res31.shtml
United Nations, Economic and Social Council (2001), *NGOs in Consultative Status with ECOSOC*, UN, 29 November,
www.un.org/esa/coordination/ngo/pdf/INF_List.pdf
United Nations. General Assembly (2001a), *Declaration of Commitment on HIV/AIDS: Global Crisis – Global Action*, paras. 27, 33, 35, 37, 46, 55, 67, 86 and 94, Special Session on HIV/AIDS, New York, 25-27 June, A/RES/S-26/2, www.un.org/ga/aids/coverage/FinalDeclarationHIVAIDS.html
United Nations. Sustainable Development (1992), 'Agenda 21: Programme of Action for Sustainable Development, Rio Declaration on Environment and Development, Statement of Forest Principles : the Final Text of Agreements Negotiated by Governments at the United Nations Conference on Environment

256 *Civil Society in the Information Age*

and Development (UNCED), Rio de Janeiro, 3-14 June, ST/DPI/1344, www.un.org/esa/sustdev/agenda21text.htm

United States. Department of State. Office of International Security and Peacekeeping Operations (1994), *Hidden Killers: The Global Landmine Crisis, 1994 Report to the U.S. Congress on the Problem with Uncleared Landmines and the United States Strategy for Demining and Landmine Control*, Washington, DC, Department of State Publication 10225, January, www.state.gov/www/global/arms/rpt_9401_demine_toc.html

United States. Department of State. Bureau of Political-Military Affairs. Office of Humanitarian Demining Programs (1998), *Hidden Killers: The Global Landmine Crisis*, Washington, DC, Department of State Publication 10575, September, www.state.gov/www/global/arms/rpt_9809_demine_toc.html

Williams, Jody (1997), *The International Campaign to Ban Landmines: A Model for Disarmament Initiatives?* Oslo, Speech by Jody Williams, International Campaign to Ban Landmines, accepting the Nobel Peace Prize, www.nobel.se/peace/articles/williams/index.html

World Council of Churches, Office of Communication, (2000), *Press Update 30 August, 2000*, www.wcc-coe.org/wcc/news/press/00/27pu.html

World Development Movement (2001), *WDM Report Back from the G8 Summit in Genoa*, 23 July; www.wdm.org.uk/campaign/Genoa.htm

World Federalist Movement, www.wfm.org

'World Religious Summit Brings Mixed Responses' (2000), *Adventist Press Service*, 2 September, Basel, www.stanet.ch/APD

World Trade Organization, www.wto.org

World Trade Organization, *Final Statistics of the 1st WTO Ministerial Conference in Singapore*, www.wto.org/english/forums_e/ngo_e/statsi_e.htm

World Trade Organization, *Final Statistics of the 2nd WTO Ministerial Conference in Geneva*, www.wto.org/english/forums_e/ngo_e/statgen_e.htm

World Trade Organization, *WTO and NGOs Relations with Non-Governmental Organizations/Civil Society*, WTO, Geneva, www.wto.org/english/forums_e/ngo_e/intro_e.htm

World Trade Organization (1998b), *Ruggerio Announces Enhanced WTO Plan for Cooperation with NGOs*, WTO, Geneva, Press 107, www.wto.org/english/news_e/pres98_e/pr107_e.htm

World Trade Organization, *WTO Briefings for Non-governmental Organizations* www.wto.org/english/forums_e/ngo_e/briefs_e.htm

World Trade Organization (2000b), *WTO and World Bank Open Online Forum on Trade Issues*, WTO, Geneva, www.wto.org/english/news_e/news00_e/wto-wbforum_e.htm

World Trade Organization. *Community: Forum*, www.wto.org/english/forums_e/chat_e/chat_e.htm

World Trade Organization, Ministerial (2001), *Declaration on the Trips Agreement and Public Health*, 14 November, WTO, Doha, Qatar, WT/MIN(01)/DEC/2, www.wto.org/english/thewto_e/minist_e/min01_e/mindecl_trips_e.htm

Bibliography

Compiled by Peter I. Hajnal and Gillian R. Clinton

Note on internet addresses (URLs): Websites tend to appear, change or disappear, often without warning. Addresses cited in this bibliography were accurate and active at the time of writing (February 2002) unless otherwise noted.

Adventist Press Service (2000), 'World Religious Summit Brings Mixed Responses', Adventist Press Service, 2 September, Basel, www.stanet.ch/APD
AI-USA. (2000), Unpublished Internal Memorandum. 17 November.
Allen, Robert (ed) (2000), 'Information', *The New Penguin English Dictionary*, Penguin Books, London, p. 720.
American Physical Society (APS). National Policy Statement. (2000), 'National Missile Defense System Technical Feasibility and Deployment', 29 April, www.aps.org/statements/00.2.html
Amnesty International. Computer Communications Working Group (2001), *Meeting Notes*, June.
Amnesty International (2001), *Italy/G8 Summit: Amnesty International Calls for Commission of Inquiry*, Press Release, 31 July, www.web.amnesty.org/web/news.nsf/WebAll/20BF49CBA0C2F82580256A9A004DEFC3?OpenDocument
Annan, Kofi (1998), *'Act on Your Ideals', Secretary-General Urges Young People at World Youth Forum*, UN Press Release, SG/Youth/1, 7 August, World Youth Forum, Braga, Portugal, www.un.org/events/Youth98/pressrel/sgyouth.htm
Annan, Kofi (2000), *Partnership With Civil Society Necessity in Addressing Global Agenda*, UN Press Release, SG/SM/7318, 29 February, Wellington, New Zealand.
Annan, Kofi (2001), *Opening Remarks at Press Conference*, (UN General Assembly Special Session on HIV/AIDS) UN, New York, 27 June.
Arquilla, John and Ronfeldt, David (1997), *In Athena's Camp: Preparing for Conflict in the Information Age*, RAND, Santa Monica.
Ashman, Darcy (2001), 'Strengthening North-South Partnerships for Sustainable Development', *Nonprofit and Voluntary Sector Quarterly*, Vol. 30(1), pp. 74-98.
Australian Broadcasting Corporation. News Online (2000), *WTO Leader Undeterred by Globalisation Opposition*, Transcript of broadcast with WTO Deputy Director-General Andrew Stoler, 13 September. www.abc.net.au/pm/s176169.htm

Aviel, JoAnn Fagot (1999), 'NGOs and International Affairs: A New Dimension of Diplomacy', in James P. Muldoon, Jr., JoAnn Fagot Aviel, Richard Retiano, and Earl Sullivan (eds), *Multilateral Diplomacy and the United Nations Today*, Westview Press, Boulder, pp. 156-166.

Axworthy, Lloyd (1997), Statement by the Canadian Foreign Minister to the NGO Forum on Banning Anti-Personnel Landmines, Oslo, 7 November.

Baker, Andrew (2000a), 'The G-7 As a Global 'Ginger Group': Plurilateralism and Four-Dimensional Diplomacy', *Global Governance: A Review of Multilateralism and International Organizations*, Vol. 6(2), pp. 165-89.

Baker, Andrew (2000b), 'The G-7 As a Global 'Ginger Group': Plurilateralism and Four-Dimensional Diplomacy', *Global Governance: A Review of Multilateralism and International Organizations*, Vol. 6(2), pp. 186-187, endnote 11.

Ballantyne, Peter, Labelle, Richard and Rudgard, Stephen (2000), *Information and Knowledge Management: Challenges for Capacity Builders*, www.oneworld.org/ecdpm/pmb/b11_gb.htm

Balmer, Crispian (2001), 'G8 Violence Report Splits Italian Parties', *Reuters Newswire*, 20 September.

Barrett, Marlene (ed) (2000), *The World Will Never Be the Same Again*, Jubilee 2000 Coalition, London.

Bayne, Nicholas (2000a), *Hanging in There: The G7 and G8 Summit in Maturity and Renewal*, Ashgate, Aldershot, The G8 and Global Governance Series.

Bayne, Nicholas (2000b), 'Why Did Seattle Fail? Globalization and the Politics of Trade', *Government and Opposition*, Vol. 35(2), pp. 131-151.

Bayne, Nicholas (2001), *Impressions of the Genoa Summit, 20-22 July 2001*, G8 Information Centre, Analytical Studies,
www.g7.utoronto.ca/g7/evaluations/2001genoa/assess_summit_bayne.html

Beattie, Alan (2001a), 'Aid Groups Could Miss G8 Talks', *Financial Times*, 2 July.

Beattie, Alan (2001b), 'The Polite Face of Anti-globalisation', *The Financial Times*, 6 April, p. 8.

Beattie, Alan (2001c), 'Protests Aim to Breach G8 Cordon', *Financial Times*, 6 July.

Becker, Elizabeth (2000), 'Citing Flaws in Concept, Experts Ask Delay in Missile Defense Plan', *The New York Times*, 12 April, p. A12.

Bhattacharyya, G. (1997), 'Information: Its Definition for its Service Professionals', *Library Science with a Slant to Documentation and Information Studies*, Vol. 34(2), pp. 69-83, Paper C.

Binyon, Michael (1998), 'Britain Opposes War Crime Status for Landmines', *The Times* (London), 6 July, p. 11.

Birmingham Summit (1998a), *Communiqué*, 17 May, Section 7, www.library.utoronto.ca/g7/summit/1998birmingham/finalcom.htm

Birmingham Summit (1998b), *Response By the Presidency on Behalf of the G8 to the Jubilee 2000 Petition*, 16 May,
www.library.utoronto.ca/g7/summit/1998birmingham/2000.htm

Black, Maggie (1992), *A Cause for Our Times: Oxfam, the First 50 Years*, Oxfam and Oxford University Press, Oxford.

Bornstein, David (1999), A Force Now in the World, Citizens Flex Social Muscle. *The New York Times*, 10 July, pp. A15, A17.

Boutros-Ghali, Boutros (1994), *Speech to the DPI Annual Conference*, UN, New York, 19 September.

Brasher, Brenda E. (2001), *Give Me That Online Religion*, Jossey-Bass, San Francisco.

Bray, Hiawatha. (2001a), 'The Wiring of a Continent: Africa Goes Online', *The Boston Globe*, 22 July, p. A25.

Bray, Hiawatha. (2001b), 'The Wiring of a Continent: Entering the Queue', *The Boston Globe*, 23 July, p. A8.

Brem, Stefan and Rutherford, Ken (2001), 'Walking Together or Divided Agenda? Comparing Landmines and Small-Arms Campaigns', *Security Dialogue*, vol 32(2), June, pp. 169-186.

Brown, Bernard E. (2001), 'What is the New Diplomacy?', *American Foreign Policy Interests*, Vol. 23, pp. 3-21.

Butler, Jennifer (2000a), 'The Christian Right Coalition and the UN Special Session on Children: Prospects and Strategies', *The International Journal of Children's Rights*, Vol. 8(4), pp. 351-371.

Butler, Jennifer (2000b), 'For Faith and Family: Christian Right Advocacy at the UN', *The Public Eye*, Vol. 9(2/3), pp. 1, 3-17.

Cameron, Maxwell A., Lawson, Robert J. and Tomlin, Brian W. (1998), 'To Walk Without Fear', in Maxwell A. Cameron, Robert J. Lawson, and Brian W. Tomlin (eds), *To Walk Without Fear: The Global Movement to Ban Landmines*, Oxford University Press, Toronto, pp. 1-17.

Canadian Broadcasting Corporation (2001), 'Civil Society', *Ideas*, 18, 25 June, ID 2395, CBC Ideas Transcripts, Toronto.

Carrier, Jean-Guy (2001), (Manager, WT Internet Resources), Telephone conversation with Heidi Ullrich, 11 July.

Carstairs, Tim (2000), Mines Advisory Group, e-mail interview with Ken Rutherford, 31 January.

Castells, Manuel (1998), *Information Technology, Globalization and Social Development*, Paper presented at the UNRISD Conference on Information Technologies and Social Development, Palais des Nations, Geneva, June 22-24, 1998 www.unrisd.org/infotech/conferen/castelp1.htm

Catholics for a Free Choice (2001), 'Bad Faith at the UN: Drawing Back the Curtain on the Catholic Family and Human Rights Institute', CFFC, Washington DC.

Chambat, Pierre (2000), 'Computer-Aided Democracy: The Effects of Information and Communication Technologies on Democracy', in Ken Ducatel, Juliet Webster and Werner Herrmann (eds), *The Information Society in Europe*, Rowman & Littlefield, Oxford, pp. 259-278.

Chrétien, Jean (1997), Statement by the Canadian Prime Minister at the Signing Conference for the Ottawa Convention, Ottawa, 3 December.

Churchill, Winston (1946), *Sinews of Peace*, speech delivered at Westminster College, Fulton, Missouri, March 5. www.winstonchurchill.org/sinews.htm

Cirincione, Joseph (1997), 'Why the Right Lost the Missile Defense Debate', *Foreign Policy*, No. 106, Spring, www.stimson.org/rd-table/fornpol.html

Clark, Ann Marie, Friedman, Elisabeth J. and Hochstettler, Karen (1998), 'The Sovereign Limits of Global Society: A Comparison of NGO Participation in UN World Conferences on the Environment, Human Rights, and Women', *World Politics*, Vol. 51(1), pp. 1-35.

Coalition for an International Criminal Court www.igc.org/icc/

Cole, Patrick (2000), 'UN World Peace Summit Draws Colorful Array of Religious Leaders', *Chicago Tribune*, 30 August, p. 14.

Cologne Summit (1999), *Communiqué*, 20 June, www.library.utoronto.ca/g7/summit/1999koln/finalcom.htm

Commission on Global Governance (1995), *Our Global Neighbourhood: The Report of the Commission on Global Governance*, Oxford University Press, Oxford.

Commission on Global Governance (1999), *The Millennium Year and the Reform Process: A Contribution from the Commission on Global Governance*, Commission on Global Governance, London.

Commission to Study the Organization of Peace (1957), *Strengthening the United Nations*, Harper & Brothers Publishers, New York.

The Committee of Religious NGOs at the United Nations (2000), *Survey of Activities of Religious NGOs at the UN, 1989-1999*, New York www.rngo.org

Cox, Robert W. (1999), 'Civil Society at the Turn of the Millennium: Prospects for an Alternative World Order', *Review of International Studies*, Vol. 25(1), pp. 3-28.

Coyle, Philip E. (2001), *FY2000 Annual Report of the Office of the Director, Operational Test & Evaluation*, www.dote.osd.mil/reports/FY00/index.html

Dent, Martin and Peters, Bill (1999), *The Crisis of Poverty and Debt in the Third World*, Ashgate, Aldershot.

Denver Summit of the Eight (1997), *Communiqué*, 22 June, Section 13, www.library.utoronto.ca/g7/summit/1997denver/g8final.htm

Dichter, Thomas W. (1999), Globalization and its Effects on NGOs: Efflorescence or a Blurring of Roles and Relevance?, *Nonprofit and Voluntary Sector Quarterly*, Vol. 28(4), pp. 38-58.

Drop the Debt (n.d.a), *Background to Drop the Debt*, www.dropthedebt.org

Drop the Debt (n.d.b), *The G8 Genoa Summit: Time for a New Deal on Debt*, www.dropthedebt.org

Drop the Debt (2001a), *Bono, Bob Geldof and Lorenzo Jovanotti Meet G8 Leaders in Genoa*, Press Release, 27 July, www.dropthedebt.org/news/genoastars2707.shtml

Drop the Debt (2001b), *Drop the Debt Response to the G7 Communiqué*, Genoa, 20 July, www.dropthedebt.org

Drop the Debt (2001c), *Genoa Update*, 21 June, www.dropthedebt.org <8 July 2001>

Drop the Debt (2001d), *Reality Check: The Need for Deeper Debt Cancellation and the Fight Against HIV/AIDS*, London.

Drop the Debt (2001e), *Verdict on Genoa Summit*, Press Release, 22 July.

Dymond, William A. (1999), 'The MAI: A Sad and Melancholy Tale', in Fen Osler Hampson, Martin Rudner and Michael Hart (eds), *Canada Among Nations 1999: A Big League Player?*, Oxford University Press, Toronto, pp. 25-53.

'Editorial Preface' (2000), *The Public Eye*, Vol. 9(2/3), p.1.

Edwards, Michael (1999), International Development NGOs: Agents of Foreign Aid or Vehicles for International Cooperation?, *Nonprofit and Voluntary Sector Quarterly*, Vol. 28(4), pp. 25-37.

Edwards, Michael (2002), 'The Mouse That Roared', *The Globe and Mail* (Toronto), 3 January, p. A17.

Edwards, Michael and Sen, Gita (2000), NGOs, Social Change and the Transformation of Human Relationships: A 21st-century Civic Agenda', *Third World Quarterly*, Vol. 21(4), pp. 605-616.

Ekins, Paul (1986), *The Living Economy: A New Economics in the Making*, Routledge & Kegan Paul, London.

Engardio, Pete (1999), 'Activists Without Borders', *Business Week*, 4 October, no. 3649, pp. 144-150.

Engh, Gabrielle (2000), *Conservative Religious Groups Complain of Prejudice by UN, NGOs*, Ecumenical Women 2000+, www.ew2000plus.org/OTRPanelArticlePrint.htm

Esty, Daniel C. (1998a), 'Linkages and Governance: NGOs at the World Trade Organization', *University of Pennsylvania Journal of International Economic Law*, Vol. 19(3), pp. 709-730.

Esty, Daniel C. (1998b), 'Non-Governmental Organizations at the World Trade Organization: Cooperation, Competition or Exclusion', *Journal of International Economic Law*, Vol. 1, pp. 123-147.

Esty, Daniel C. (1999a), 'Environmental Governance at the WTO: Outreach to Civil Society', in Gary P. Sampson and W. Bradnee Chambers (eds), *Trade, Environment, and the Millennium*, The United Nations University, Japan, pp. 97-117.

Esty, Daniel C. (1999b), 'Why the World Trade Organization Needs Environmental NGOS', *Transnational Associations*, Vol. 51(5), pp. 267-279.

Feather, John and Sturges, Paul (eds) (1997), 'Information', *International Encyclopedia of Information and Library Science*, Routledge, London, p. 184.

Federation of American Scientists (2000), 'Increased Missile Defense Secrecy Proposed', *Secrecy News*, 15 November, www.fas.org/sgp/news/secrecy/

Fernandez, Sylvia (1998), Argentinian delegation to the Rome Conference, correspondence with William R. Pace and Rik Panganiban.

FitzGerald, Frances (2000), *Way Out There in the Blue: Ronald Reagan, Star Wars and the End of the Cold War*, Simon & Schuster, New York.

Florini, Ann M. (2000), *The Third Force: The Rise of Transnational Civil Society*, Japan Center for International Exchange, Tokyo; Carnegie Endowment for International Peace, Washington, DC.

'For Slimmer and Sporadic Summits' (2001), *Financial Times*, 23 July, p. 10.

Foreman, Karen (1999), Evolving Global Structures and the Challenges Facing International Relief and Development Organizations, *Nonprofit and Voluntary Sector Quarterly*, Vol. 28(4), pp. 178-97.

Foster, John W. And Anand, Anita (eds) (1999), *Whose World Is It Anyway? Civil Society, the United Nations and the Multilateral Future*, United Nations Association in Canada, Ottawa, quoting Wapner, Paul (1996), *Environmental Activism and World Civic Politic*, State University of New York Press, Albany, p. 158.

Fox, Jonathan (2001), 'Religion as an Overlooked Element of International Relations', *International Studies Review*, Vol. 3(3), pp. 52-73.

Friedmann, Harriet (2001), 'Forum: Considering the Quebec Summit, the World Social Forum at Porto Alegre and the People's Summit at Quebec City: A View from the Ground', *Studies in Political Economy: A Socialist Review*, Vol. 66 (Autumn), pp. 85-105.

Friends of the Earth and the EnviroSummit (1990), 'Tropical Forest Destruction', *Economic Declaration*, 11 July, Section 66, Houston, www.library.utoronto.ca/g7/summit/1990houston/communique/environment.html

G7 Environment Ministers (1996), *Chairman's Summary* Cabourg, France, 9-10 May, www.library.utoronto.ca/g7/environment/1996cabourg/summary_index.html

G7 Finance Ministers (2001), *Strengthening the International Financial System and the Multilateral Development Banks: Report of G7 Finance Ministers and Central Bank Governors*, Rome, 7 July, www.g7.utoronto.ca/g7/finance/fm010707.htm

G8 Environment Ministers (1999), *Communiqué*, Schwerin, Germany, 26-28 March, Section 6, www.library.utoronto.ca/g7/environment/1999schwerin/communique.html

G8 Environment Ministers (2000), *Communiqué*, Otsu, Japan, 7-9 April, Section 17, www.library.utoronto.ca/g7/environment/2000otsu/communique.html

G8 Environment Ministers (2001), *Communiqué*, Trieste, Italy, 2-4 March, paras. 13, 19, 25, www.esteri.it/g8/documentazione/docum02e.htm; www.g7.utoronto.ca/g7/environment/2001trieste/communique.html

G8 Foreign Ministers (2000a), *Conclusions*, Miyazaki, Japan, 13 July, www.library.utoronto.ca/g7/foreign/fm000713.htm

G8 Foreign Ministers (2000b), *G8 Miyazaki Initiatives for Conflict Prevention*, Miyazaki, Japan, 13 July, www.library.utoronto.ca/g7/foreign/fm000713-in.htm

G8 Foreign Ministers (2001), *Conclusions*, Rome, 18-19 July, www.g7.utoronto.ca/g7/foreign/fm091901_conclusion.html

Garwin, Richard and Bethe, Hans (1968), 'Anti-Ballistic Missile Systems', *Scientific American*, Vol. 218(3), pp. 21-31.

GATT Secretariat (1994), *The Results of the Uruguay Round of Multilateral Trade Negotiations: The Legal Texts*, GATT Secretariat, Geneva.

Gelernter, Judith (2001), 'The Internet: Yesterday, Today, and Tomorrow', *Information Outlook*, Vol. 5(6), pp. 67-68.

Genoa Social Forum (n.d.), 'Next Stop: Genoa', www.genoa-g8.org/faq-eng.htm

Genoa Summit (2001a), *Communiqué*, 22 July, paras. 2, 6, 21, 26 and 28 www.genoa-g8.it/eng/attualita/primo_piano/primo_piano_13.html and www.g7.utoronto.ca/g7/summit/2001genoa/finalcommunique.html

Genoa Summit (2001b), *Communiqué*, 22 July, para. 35, www.genoa-g8.it/eng/attualita/primo_piano/primo_piano_13.html and www.g7.utoronto.ca/g7/summit/2001genoa/finalcommunique.html

Genoa Summit (2001c), *Digital Opportunities for All: Meeting the Challenge: Report of the Digital Opportunity Task Force (DOT Force), Including a Proposal for a Genoa Plan of Action*, 11 May, www.g7.utoronto.ca/g7/summit/2001genoa/dotforce1.html

Genoa Summit (2001d), *G7 Statement*, Genoa, 20 July, para. 8 www.g7.utoronto.ca/g7/summit/2001genoa/g7statement.html

Genoa Summit (2001e), *Genoa, City of Dialogue*, www.genoa-g8.it/eng/attualita/primo_piano/primo_piano_2.html

Genoa Summit (2001f), *Statement by the G8 Leaders*, 21 July, www.g7.utoronto.ca/g7/summit/2001genoa/g8statement1.html

Genoa Summit. News. (2001), *Genoa and G8: Directions for Use*, www.genoa-g8.it/eng/attualita/primo_piano/primo_piano_1.html

George, Susan (2001a), 'G8: Are You Happy?', 24 July, www.tni.org/george/misc/genoa.htm

George, Susan (2001b), 'L'ordre libéral et ses basses oeuvres', *Le Monde Diplomatique*, Vol. 48(569), pp. 1, 5-6.

Gilpin, Robert and Wright, Christopher (eds) (1964), *Scientists and National Policy-Making*, Columbia University Press, New York, pp. 281-282.

Gordenker, Leon (1995), 'NGOs and the United Nations in the Twenty-First Century', in *Envisioning the United Nations in the Twenty-First Century*, The United Nations University, Tokyo pp. 124-134. Proceedings of the Inaugural Symposium on the United Nations System in the Twenty-first Century, 21-22 November.

Gordenker, Leon and Weiss, Thomas G. (1996), 'Pluralizing Global Governance: Analytical Approaches and Dimensions', in Thomas G. Weiss and Leon Gordenker (eds), *NGOs, the UN, and Global Governance*, Lynne Rienner Publishers, Boulder, pp. 17-47.

Gottfried, Kurt (1999), 'Physicists in Politics', *Physics Today*, Vol. 52(3), pp. 42-48.

Greenpeace International (2000a), *G-8 Adopts Greenpeace Demand to Fight Illegal Logging by Tackling Export Practices And Procurement Policies*, Press Release, Okinawa, 23 July, www.greenpeace.org/pressreleases/

Greenpeace International (2000b), *Greenpeace Activists Released from Okinawa Jail After Carrying Out Peaceful Protests*, Press Release, Amsterdam and Okinawa, 24 July.

Hajnal, Peter I. (2001), 'International Nongovernmental Organizations and Civil Society', in Peter I. Hajnal (ed), *International Information: Documents, Publications and Electronic Information of International Organizations*, Vol. 2, Libraries Unlimited, Englewood, CO.

Hajnal, Peter I. (2001), *Personal Assessment of the Role of Civil Society at the 2001 Genoa G8 Summit*, University of Toronto G8 Information Centre: Analytical Studies, 2001 Summit Assessment, 2 August www.g7.utoronto.ca/g7/evaluations/2001genoa/assess_summit_hajnal.html

Hajnal, Peter I. and Kirton, John J. (2000), 'The Evolving Role and Agenda of the G7/G8: A North American Perspective', *NIRA Review*, Vol. 7(2), pp. 5-10.

Halifax Summit (1995a), *Communiqué: Promoting Sustainable Development*, 16 June, Section 26,
www.library.utoronto.ca/g7/summit/1995halifax/communique/development.html

Halifax Summit (1995b), *Communiqué: Reinforcing Coherence, Effectiveness, and Efficiency of Institutions*, 16 June, Section 37,
www.library.utoronto.ca/g7/summit/1995halifax/communique/institution.html

Hamelink, Cees J. (1997), *New Information and Communication Technologies, Social Development and Cultural Change*,
www.unrisd.org/engindex/publ/list/dp/dp86/dp86.htm

Hanlon, Joseph and Garrett, John (1999), *Crumbs of Comfort: The Cologne G8 Summit and the Chains of Debt*, Jubilee 2000 Coalition, London.

Hanlon, Joseph and Petifor, Ann (2000), *Kicking the Habit: Finding a Lasting Solution to Addictive Lending and Borrowing – and Its Corrupting Side-effects*, Jubilee 2000 Coalition, London.

Hasenclever, Andreas and Rittberger, Volker (2000), 'Does Religion Make a Difference? Theoretical Approaches to the Impact of Faith on Political Conflict', *Millennium: Journal of International Studies*, Vol. 29(3), pp. 641-674.

Heeks, Richard (1999), *Information and Communication Technologies, Poverty and Development*, Working Paper 5 of the Development Informatics Working Paper Series. Manchester, England: University of Manchester.

Hocking, Brian and McGuire, Steven (eds) (1999), *Trade Politics: International, Domestic and Regional Perspectives*, Routledge, London.

Hooper, John and Black, Ian (1998), 'Self-interest Brings Court into Contempt', *The Guardian* (London), 15 July, p. 17.

Human Rights Watch and Physicians for Human Rights (1993), *Landmines: A Deadly Legacy*, The Arms Project of Human Rights Watch and Physicians for Human Rights, New York.

Institute for Democracy Studies (2000), *The Global Assault on Reproductive Rights: A Crucial Turning Point*, IDS, New York, May.

International Campaign to Ban Landmines (1997), Recorded notes from workshop discussion on "Using the Campaign as a Model for Other Issues", in *ICBL Report: NGO Forum on Landmines*, Oslo, 7-10 September.

International Campaign to Ban Landmines (1999a), 'Islamic Extremists in Dagestan are Also Using Landmines' Press Release, Geneva, 13 September; (from 'Russian Troops Clearing Dagestan Rebel-Planted Mines', Foreign Broadcast Information Service, Transcribed Text, Moscow *Interfax*, Report #LD2508105399, 25 August 1999).

International Campaign to Ban Landmines (1999b), *Landmine Monitor Report 1999: Toward a Mine-Free World*, Human Rights Watch, New York www.icbl.org/lm/1999/

International Chamber of Commerce (2001a), *ICC Actions and Achievements*, www.iccwbo.org/home/intro_icc/icc_actions_achievements.asp

International Chamber of Commerce (2001b), *ICC Recommendations to WTO Members on Trade Facilitation*, 6 June, Document No. 103-32/91. www.iccwbo.org/home/statements_rules/statements/2001/wto_members_on_trade.asp

International Committee of the Red Cross (1999), *Overview 1999: Landmines Must Be Stopped*, ICRC 1 March.

International Forum on Capacity Building (1998), *Southern NGO Capacity-building: Issues and Priorities*, New Delhi, India: International Working Group on Capacity-Building of Southern NGOs.

International Institute for Sustainable Development (2001), 'Summary of the WTO Symposium on Issues Confronting the World Trading System', *Sustainable Developments*, Vol. 55(1), www.iisd.ca/sd/wto-issues/

Isaacs, John (2000), *Anatomy of a Victory: Clinton Decides Against a Missile Defense*, 5 September, Council for a Liveable World www.clw.org/em/nmddelay.html

'Italian Ministers Meet Protesters Before G8 Summit', Reuters newswire, 28 June.

Jack, Homer A. (1993), *WCRP: A History of the World Conference on Religion and Peace*, World Conference on Religion and Peace, New York.

Johnson, Martin. (1999), 'Non-Profit Organisations and the Internet', *First Monday: Peer-Reviewed Journal on the Internet*, Vol. 4(2). www.firstmonday.dk

Joint United Nations Programme on HIV/AIDS (UNAIDS) (2001), *AIDS Epidemic Update*, December, www.unaids.org/epidemic_update/report_dec01/index.html#full

Jubilee 2000 Coalition (n.d.), *What Happens Next: Campaigning on Debt Beyond the Millennium Year*, www.jubilee2000uk.org/jubilee2000/whatnext/debt.html

Jubilee 2000 Coalition (1999a), *Breaking the Chains*, Jubilee 2000 Coalition, London.

Jubilee 2000 Coalition (1999b), 'IMF/World Bank Spring Meetings 1999', www.jubilee2000uk.org/jubilee2000/news/meetings1905.html <16 August 2000>.

Jubilee 2000 Coalition (2000a), 'Betraying the Poor: The Squandered Summit and the G7 Leaders' Broken Promises', policy briefing, August, www.jubilee2000uk.org/reports/droppedfull.html <22 August 2000>.

Jubilee 2000 Coalition (2000b), *Cannes Stars Sign Up To Drop The Debt*, Press Release, 12 May, www.jubileeplus.org/media/jubilee2000_archive/cannes120500.htm <15 August 2000>.

Jubilee 2000 Coalition (2000c), *London Red Letter Day on Third World Debt*, Press Release, 3 June, www.jubileeplus.org/media/jubilee2000_archive/london030600.htm <15 August 2000>.

Jubilee 2000 Coalition (2000d), *The Squandered Summit*, Press Release, Okinawa, 23 July.

Jubilee Plus (n.d.), 'About Us', www.jubilee2000uk.org/about/about.htm

Jubilee Plus (2001), *Jubilee Movement International For Economic and Social Justice: Statement on G7 Final Communiqué*, Press Release, Genoa, 21 July, www.jubileeplus.org/jmi/jmi-news/pressrelease_210701.htm

Judge, Anthony (n.d.), *Types of International Organizations*, Section 2.2, Union of International Associations, www.uia.org/uiadocs/orgtypec.htm

Kaul, Inge, Grunberg, Isabelle and Stern, Marc A. (1999), *Global Public Goods: International Cooperation in the 21st Century*, Oxford University Press for the United Nations Development Programme, New York, pp. 450-507.

Keenan, Stella and Johnston, Colin (eds) (2000a), 'Information', *Concise Dictionary of Library and Information Science*, 2nd ed, Bowker Saur, London, p. 133.

Keenan, Stella and Johnston, Colin (eds) (2000b), 'Information Age', *Concise Dictionary of Library and Information Science*, 2nd ed, Bowker Saur, London, p. 133.

Keohane, Robert and Nye, Joseph (1998), 'Power and Interdependence in the Information Age', *Foreign Affairs*, Vol. 77(5), pp. 81-94.

Bibliography 267

Kirton, John J. (2000), 'Broadening Participation in Twenty-First Century Governance: The Prospective and Potential Contribution of the Okinawa Summit', paper presented at The Kyushu-Okinawa Summit: The Challenges and Opportunities for the Developing World in the 21st Century conference, co-sponsored by the United Nations University, the Foundation for Advanced Studies in Development, and the G8 Research Group, Tokyo, 17 July, www.library.utoronto.ca/g7/scholar/kirton20000717/

Kirton, John J. (2002 forthcoming), 'Guess Who's Coming to Kananaskis? Civil Society and the G8 in Canada's Year as Host', *International Journal*.

Kirton, John J., Daniels, Joseph P. and Freytag, Andreas (2001), 'The G8's Contributions to Twenty-first Century Governance, in John J. Kirton, Joseph P. Daniels, and Andreas Freytag (eds), *Guiding Global Order: G8 Governance in the Twenty-first Century*, Ashgate, Aldershot, pp. 283-304.

Korey, William (1998), *NGOs and the Universal Declaration of Human Rights*, St. Martin's Press, New York.

Kuiten, Bernard (2001), Personal interview with Heidi Ullrich, 26 June, Geneva.

Kyushu-Okinawa Summit (2000a), *G7 Statement*, July 21, 2000, para. 20 www.g8kyushu-okinawa.go.jp/e/documents/g7state.html

Kyushu-Okinawa Summit (2000b), *G8 Communiqué*, paras. 15, 24, 29 and 30 www.library.utoronto.ca/g7/summit/2000okinawa/finalcom.htm

Kyushu-Okinawa Summit (2000c), *G8 Communiqué*, paras. 50, 52, 57 and 59 www.library.utoronto.ca/g7/summit/2000okinawa/finalcom.htm

Lal, Bhavya (1999), *Information and Communication Technologies for Improved Governance*, www.abtassociates. com/reports/governance/ict.pdf

Lee, Roy S. (1999), 'The Rome Conference and its Contribution to International Law', in Roy S. Lee, (ed), *The International Criminal Court: The Making of the Rome Statute*, Kluwer Law International, Boston, pp. 1-39.

Ligteringen, Ernst (1999), (former Executive Director of Oxfam International), interview with Peter Hajnal, 29 July.

Lindenberg, Marc and Dobel, J.Patrick (1999), The Challenges of Globalization for Northern International Relief and Development NGOs, *Nonprofit and Voluntary Sector Quarterly*, Vol. 28(4), pp. 4-19.

Losee, Robert M. (1997), 'A Discipline Independent Definition of Information', *Journal of the American Society for Information Science*, Vol. 48(3), pp. 254-269.

Love, Janice (2001), 'Religion in Politics: Reflections on the UN's Millennium World Peace Summit of Religious and Spiritual Leaders', *International Studies Perspectives*, Vol. 2(1), inside back cover.

Lovett, Adrian (2000), *Island Mentality: The Okinawa G8 Summit and the Failure of Leadership*, Jubilee 2000 Coalition, London.

Lumpe, Lora and Donarski, Jeff (1998), *The Arms Trade Revealed: A Guide for Investigators and Activists*, Federation of American Scientists, Washington, DC.

Lutheran Office for World Community (1990), *Lutheran Work With the United Nations*, New York.

Lyon Summit (1996), *Economic Communiqué*, 28 June, Section 34, www.library.utoronto.ca/g7/summit/1996lyon/communique/eco4.htm

Madison, James (1787), 'The Same Subject Continued: The Union as a Safeguard Against Domestic Faction and Insurrection', *Federalist Papers*, No. 10, memory.loc.gov/const/fed/fed_10.html

'Making it a Summit for All the Americas' (2001), *The Globe and Mail*, 23 April, p. A18.

Mander, Jerry and Goldsmith, Edward (eds) (1996), *The Case Against the Global Economy and for a Turn Toward the Local*, Sierra Club Books, San Francisco.

Marceau, Gabrielle, and Pedersen, Peter (1999), 'Is the WTO Open and Transparent?', *Journal of World Trade*, Vol. 33(1), pp. 5-49.

Mathews, Jessica Tuchman (1999), Statement to the 75th Anniversary Symposium, Harvard School of Public Health, Boston, 25 September, www.hsph.harvard.edu/digest/mathews.html

Meadow, Charles T. (2000), 'Data, Information, and Knowledge', in Charles T. Meadow, Bert R. Boyce and Donald H. Kraft (eds), *Text Information Retrieval Systems*, 2nd ed, Academic Press, San Diego, pp. 34-48.

Meadow, Charles T. and Yuan, Weijing (1997), 'Measuring the Impact of Information: Defining the Concepts', *Information Processing & Management*, Vol. 33(6), pp. 697-714.

Médecins Sans Frontières (2000), *MSF Welcomes Ambitious Targets to Fight Infectious Diseases but Calls on G8 for Equally Strong Action, Not Empty Promises*, Press Release, Okinawa, 23 July, www.accessmed-msf.org/index.asp

Médecins Sans Frontières (2001a), *G8 Window Dresses While Poor Die from Lack of Medicines*, Press release, Genoa, 21 July, www.msf.org/content/page.cfm?articleid=5A05508A-AAD9-474E-AEDA9C 6F6A3D5AAA

Médecins Sans Frontières (2001b), *Violence Grants No Perspectives*, Press Release, Genoa, 20 July.

Ministero degli Affari Esteri (Italy) (2001), *2001 Presidency: Beyond Debt Relief*, www.esteri.it/g8/ and
www.library.utoronto.ca/g7/summit/2001genoa/pres_docs/pres1.html

Murphy, Caryle (1998), 'The Nobel Prize Fight', *Washington Post*, 22 March, p. F4.

Naím, Moisés (2000), 'The FP Interview: Lori's War', *Foreign Policy*, No. 118, pp. 28-55.

Nelson, Paul J. (1997), 'Deliberation, Leverage or Coercion? The World Bank, NGOs, and Global Environmental Politics', *Journal of Peace Research*, vol 34(4), pp. 467-472.

Neslen, Arthur (2001), 'Mean Streets: On Location, Genoa Summit', *Now* (Toronto), Vol. 20(47), p. 20.

NGO Coalition for an International Criminal Court. (1998a), *The Numbers: NGO Coalition Special Report on Country Positions*, 10 July, www.igc.apc.org/icc/rome/html/rome_other.html

NGO Coalition for an International Criminal Court. (1998b), *The Virtual Vote: NGO Coalition Special Report on Country Positions on L.59*, 15 July, www.igc.apc.org/icc/rome/html/rome_other.html

'The Non-Governmental Order' (1999), *The Economist*, 11 December, pp. 20-21.

Numrich, Paul D. (2000), *Religion Counts Looks at the Summit: One Observer's View of the Millennium World Peace Summit of Religious and Spiritual Leaders*, The Park Ridge Center for the Study of Health, Faith and Ethics, Chicago.

Numrich, Paul D. (2001), 'United Religions at the United Nations', *Second Opinion*, Vol. 8, pp. 53-68.

O'Brien, Robert, Goetz, Anne Marie, Scholte, Jan Aart and Williams, Marc (2000), *Contesting Global Governance: Multilateral Economic Institutions and Global Social Movements*, Cambridge University Press, Cambridge, Cambridge Studies in International Relations, No. 71.

Offenheiser, Raymond, Holcombe, Susan and Hopkins, Nancy (1999), Grappling with Globalization, Partnership, and Learning: a Look Inside Oxfam America, *Nonprofit and Voluntary Sector Quarterly*, Vol. 28(4), pp. 121-140.

O'Neill, Kelly (2000), 'NGO Web Sites: Keeping Business in the Spotlight', *Transnational Associations*, Vol. 52(4), pp. 193-200.

Orbinski, James (1999), *The Nobel Lecture*, Oslo, 10 December. Speech by James Orbinski, Médecins Sans Frontières, accepting the Nobel Peace Prize. www.nobel.no/eng_lect_99m.html

Ostry, Sylvia (2000), *WTO: Institutional Design for Better Governance*, (Draft), paper presented at the conference *Efficiency, Equity and Legitimacy: The Multilateral Trading System at the Millennium*, Kennedy School of Government, Harvard University, 2-3 June, www.utoronto.ca/cis/WTOID.pdf

Ottaway, Marina (2001), 'Corporatism Goes Global: International Organizations, Nongovernmental Organization Networks, and Transnational Business', *Global Governance: A Review of Multilateralism and International Organizations*, Vol. 7(3), pp. 265-292.

'Our Best Point the Way' (2001), *The Globe and Mail* (Toronto), 7 December, p. A21.

Oxfam Canada (2001), *Fair Trade in Coffee*, www.oxfam.ca/campaigns/fairTrade.htm

Oxfam Community Aid Abroad, *Oxfam International Policy Papers*, OCAA, www.caa.org.au/oxfam/advocacy/index.html

Oxfam Great Britain, *About Oxfam Fair Trade*, www.oxfam.org.uk/fairtrad/aboutft1.htm

Oxfam International (a), *Campaigns: Change the World*, OI, Oxford www.oxfam.org/what_does/advocacy/default.htm

270 *Civil Society in the Information Age*

Oxfam International (b), *How Are Oxfam's Funds Used?*, OI, Oxford, www.oxfam.org/involve/donations.htm

Oxfam International (c), *Policy Papers*, OI, Oxford, www.oxfam.org/what_does/advocacy/papers.htm

Oxfam International (d), *The Timor Crisis and the OI Response*, OI, Oxford.

Oxfam International (1998), *Annual Report, 1998*, OI, Oxford.

Oxfam International (1999), *Annual Report, 1999*, OI, Oxford, www.oxfam.org/what_is_OI/a_report/default.htm

Oxfam International (2000), *Oxfam and Education Campaigners: Education One of Few Bright Spots in Okinawa*, Press Release, Okinawa, July.

Oxfam International (2001a), *Afghanistan*, OI, Oxford, www.oxfam.org/news/afghan.htm

Oxfam International (2001b), 'Foreward', *Towards Global Equity: Strategic Plan, 2001-2004*, OI, Oxford, www.oxfam.org/strategic_plan/intro3.htm

Oxfam International (2001c), *Genoa Fails: Big Promise for Next Year*, Press Release, Genoa, 22 July, www.oxfam.org/news/pressreleases.htm

Oxfam International (2001d), 'Introduction', *Towards Global Equity: Strategic Plan, 2001-2004*, OI, Oxford, www.oxfam.org/strategic_plan/index.htm

Oxfam International (2001e), 'Marketing and Communications', *Towards Global Equity: Strategic Plan, 2001-2004*, OI, Oxford, www.oxfam.org/strategic_plan/business3.htm

Oxfam International (2001f), 'Mission Statement', *Towards Global Equity: Strategic Plan, 2001-2004*, OI, Oxford, www.oxfam.org/strategic_plan/intro2.htm

Oxfam International (2001g), 'Our Three Promises', *Towards Global Equity: Strategic Plan, 2001-2004*, OI, Oxford, www.oxfam.org/strategic_plan/humane6.htm

Oxfam International (2001h), *Violence Doesn't Help*, Press Release, 20 July, www.oxfaminternational.org/what_does/advocacy/papers/010720_Violence%20doesn'thelp%20G80720.doc

Park Ridge Center for the Study of Health, Faith and Ethics (2002), *We the Religions: The Role of Religion in the United Nations System*, Park Ridge Center, Chicago.

Pearsall, Judy (ed) (1999), *The Concise Oxford Dictionary*, 10th Ed, Oxford University Press, Oxford.

Peoples' Global Action (1998), 'Peoples' Global Action Manifesto', Geneva, February/March, www.nadir.org/nadir/initiativ/agp/en/

Peoples' Global Action (2000a), 'Bulletin 5', February, www.nadir.org/nadir/initiativ/agp/en/

Peoples' Global Action (2000b), 'People's Global Action against "Free" Trade and the World Trade Organization', 2 March, www.agp.org/agp/en/

People's Summit (1995), *Communiqué from the People's Summit*, 16 June, Halifax, www.igc.org/habitat/p-7/p7-comm.html

Peterson, Luke (2001), 'Civil Society Groups Begin To Question Tactics Used at Trade Talks', *The Toronto Star*, 3 August, p. A21.

'Picking Up the Pieces: After the Genoa Summit' (2001), *The Economist*, Vol. 360(8232), 28 July, pp. 49-50.

Price, Richard (1998), 'Reversing the Gun Sights: Transnational Civil Society Targets Land Mines', *International Organization*, Vol. 52 (Summer), 613-644.

Public Citizen for Global Trade Watch (2001a), 'About Global Trade Watch', www.citizen.org/trade/about/

Public Citizen for Global Trade Watch (2001b), 'Talking Points on 'WTO: Shrink or Sink' Global NGO Campaign', www.citizen.org/pctrade/gattwto/ShrinkSink/talkingpts.htm

Quadrilateral Trade Ministers (1999), *Chair's Statement*, 33rd Meeting, Tokyo, Japan, 11-12 May, [section on environment] www.library.utoronto.ca/g7/trade/quad33.html

Rebello, Joseph (2000), 'International Economists Fear the Free-Trade Chill', *The Globe and Mail*, 28 August, p. B5, quote by Stanley Fischer at Federal Reserve Bank of Kansas City Symposium on *Global Opportunities and Challenges*, Jackson Hole, Wyoming, 24-26 August 2000.

Reinalda, Bob (2001), 'Private in Form, Public in Purpose: NGOs in International Relations Theory', in Bas Arts, Math Noortmann and Bob Reinalda (eds), *Non-State Actors in International Relations*, Ashgate, Aldershot, pp. 11-40. Non-State Actors in International Law, Politics and Governance Series.

Reitano, Richard and Elfenbein, Caleb (1999), 'Diplomacy in the Twenty-First Century: Civil Society Versus the State', in James P. Muldoon, Jr., JoAnn Fagot Aviel, Richard Retiano, and Earl Sullivan (eds), *Multilateral Diplomacy and the United Nations Today*, Westview Press, Boulder, pp. 234-244.

Risse-Kappen, Thomas (1995), *Bringing Transnational Relations Back In: Non-State Actors, Domestic Structures and International Institutions*, Cambridge University Press, Cambridge.

Roberts, Adam (2000), International NGOs: New Gods Overseas, *The Economist*, 49, 79-81.

Robertson, David (2000), 'Civil Society and the WTO', *The World Economy*, Vol. 23(9), pp. 1119-1134.

Rockwell, Keith (2001), (WTO Director of Information and Media Relations), Telephone interview with Heidi Ullrich, 27 June.

Ruse, Austin (2000), President, Catholic Family and Human Rights Institute, Speech to the Cardinal Mindszenty Foundation, St. Louis, March.

Ruse, Austin (2001), Personal interview with Benjamin Rivlin, 29 May; and memorandum, 'The Ways of UN Pro-Life Lobbying'.

'Russians Drop Mines in Georgia' (1999), *Washington Post*, 18 November, p. A36.

Rutherford, Ken (1999), 'The Hague and Ottawa Conventions: A Model for Future Weapon Ban Regimes?', *Nonproliferation Review*, Spring-Summer 1999, vol 6(3), pp. 36-50.

Sachs, Jeffrey D. (2001), 'The Strategic Significance of Global Inequality', *The Washington Quarterly*, Vol. 24(3), pp. 187-198.

Saito, Jun (2000), 'NGOs Shunned by G-8 Attendees', *Asahi Evening News*, 23 July.

Sand-Trigo, Ariane (1997), International Committee of the Red Cross Delegation to the United Nations, letter to Ken Rutherford, 3 March.

Sanger, David (2001), '2 Leaders Tell of Plot to Kill Bush in Genoa', *The New York Times*, 26 September, p. B1.

Scholte, Jan Aart (1998), 'The IMF Meets Civil Society', *Finance and Development*, Vol. 35(3), pp. 42-45.

Scholte, Jan Aart (2001), *Civil Society and Democracy in Global Governance*, Department of Politics and International Studies, University of Warwick, CSGR Working Paper No. 65/01; also (forthcoming), 'Civil Society and Democracy in Global Governance' *Global Governance*, Vol. 8(3).

Scholte, Jan Aart, O'Brien, Robert and Williams, Marc (1999), 'The World Trade Organization and Civil Society', in Brian Hocking and Steven McGuire (eds), *Trade Politics: International, Domestic and Regional Perspectives*, Routledge, London, pp. 162-179.

Scholte, Jan Aart, O'Brien, Robert and Williams, Marc (1999), 'The WTO and Civil Society', *Journal of World Trade*, Vol. 33(1), pp. 107-23; cited in Ullrich, Heidi (2000), 'Stimulating Trade Liberalization After Seattle: G7/8 Leadership in Global Governance', paper presented at the Academic Symposium *G8 2000: New Directions in Global Governance? G8's Okinawa Summit*, University of the Ryukyus, Okinawa, 19-20 July.

Schroyer, Trent (ed) (1997), *A World That Works: Building Blocks for a Just and Sustainable Society*, The Bootstrap Press, New York.

Schwartz, Stephen I. (ed) (1998), *Atomic Audit: The Costs and Consequences of U.S. Nuclear Weapons Since 1940*, Brookings Institution Press, Washington, DC.

Shannon, Claude E. and Weaver, Warren (1949), *The Mathematical Theory of Communication*, University of Illinois Press, Chicago.

Simmons, P.J. (1998), 'Learning to live with NGOs', *Foreign Policy*, No. 112, pp. 82-96.

Smillie, Ian (1999), *Narrowing the Digital Divide: Notes on a Global Netcorps*, www.unites.org/reference/smillie0.html

Smith, Jackie, Chatfield, Charles and Pagnucco, Ron (eds) (1997), *Transnational Social Movements and Global Politics: Solidarity Beyond the State*, Syracuse University Press, Syracuse, New York.

Smith, Peter (Jay) and Smythe, Elizabeth (2000), 'Globalization, Citizenship and Technology: The MAI Meets the Internet', paper presented at the annual meeting of the International Studies Association, Los Angeles, 17 March.

Smock, David (2001), *Faith-Based NGOs and International Peacebuilding*, United States Institute of Peace, Washington DC, 22 October.

Spencer, Jack and Scardaville, Michael (2000), *Missile Defense and Arms Control*, 13 October, Heritage Foundation. http://heritage.org/views/2000/ed101300.html

St. Clair, Guy (2001), 'Knowledge Services: Your Company's Key to Performance Excellence', *Information Outlook*, Vol. 5(6), pp. 6-12.

Summit of the Arch (1989), *Economic Declaration*, 16 July, Section 43, Paris, www.library.utoronto.ca/g7/summit/1989paris/communique/environment.html

Thomas, Scott M. (2000), 'Taking Religious and Cultural Pluralism Seriously: The Global Resurgence of Religion and the Transformation of International Society', *Millennium: Journal of International Studies*, Vol. 29(3). Special Issue, 'Religions and International Relations' pp. 815-841.

'Ties Strengthened: Future Cooperation Key to NGO Goals' (2000), *The Japan Times*, 25 July 25.

TOES (1988), *Summit Echo: A Newspaper of the Summit Citizens Conference*, 19 June, Toronto.

TOES USA (n.d.), 'Brief Introduction to TOES', pender.ee.upenn.edu/~rabii/toes/ToesIntro.html

Ullrich, Heidi (2000), 'Stimulating Trade Liberalization After Seattle: G7/8 Leadership in Global Governance', paper presented at the Academic Symposium *G8 2000: New Directions in Global Governance? G8's Okinawa Summit*, University of the Ryukyus, Okinawa, Japan, 19-20 July 2000.

Union of Concerned Scientists (2001), *Countermeasures: The Achilles Heel of Missile Defenses*, www.ucsusa.org/security/countermeasures.html

Union of International Associations (1998/99), *Yearbook of International Organizations*, 35th ed, UIA, Brussels.

Union of International Associations (2001/2002), *Yearbook of International Organizations: Guide to Global and Civil Society Networks*, 38th ed, Vol. 1B, UIA, Brussels.

United Nations, Department of Humanitarian Affairs (1997), Robert Eaton, Chris Horwood, and Norah Niland (eds), *Cambodia: The Development of Indigenous Mine Action Capabilities*, UN DHA.

United Nations, Department of Public Information, *Directory of NGOs Associated with DPI*, UN, www.un.org/MoreInfo/ngolink/ngodir.htm

United Nations, Department of Public Information (1948), *Universal Declaration of Human Rights*, DPI, New York. www.un.org/Overview/rights.html

United Nations, Department of Public Information (1989), *Charter of the United Nations and Statute of the International Court of Justice*, UN, New York, DPI/511 www.un.org/Overview/Charter/chapte10.html

United Nations, Economic and Social Council (1950), *Review of Consultative Arrangements with Non-governmental Organizations*, UN, New York, 27 February, E/RES/288(X).

United Nations, Economic and Social Council (1968), *Arrangements for Consultations with Non-governmental Organizations*, UN, New York, 27 May, E/RES/1296 (XLIV).

United Nations, Economic and Social Council (1993), *Review of the Arrangements for Consultation with Non-governmental Organizations*, UN, New York, 12 February E/1993/214.

United Nations, Economic and Social Council (1996a), *Consultative Relations between the United Nations and Non-governmental Organizations*, UN, New York, 25 July, E/RES/1996/31 www.hri.ca/uninfo/resolutn/res31.shtml

United Nations, Economic and Social Council (1996b), *Non-governmental Organizations*, UN, New York, 25 July, E/DEC/1996/297.

United Nations, Economic and Social Council (2001), *NGOs in Consultative Status with ECOSOC*, UN, 29 November, www.un.org/esa/coordination/ngo/pdf/INF_List.pdf

United Nations, General Assembly (1946), *Establishment of the Department of Public Information of the Secretariat*, UN, New York, 13 February, A/RES/13 (I).

United Nations, General Assembly (1981), *Declaration on the Elimination of All Forms of Intolerance and of Discrimination Based on Religion or Belief*, UN, New York, A/RES/36/55, 25 November.

United Nations, General Assembly (1998), *United Nations Year of Dialogue Among Civilizations*, UN, New York, A/RES/53/22, 16 November.

United Nations, General Assembly (2000a), *United Nations Year of Dialogue Among Civilizations*, UN, New York, A/RES/54/113, 7 February.

United Nations, General Assembly (2000b), *We the Peoples: The Role of the United Nations in the 21st Century*, Secretary-General's Report to the Millennium Summit, Press Release GA/9704, 3 April.

United Nations, General Assembly (2001a), *Declaration of Commitment on HIV/AIDS: Global Crisis – Global Action*, paras. 27, 33, 35, 37, 46, 55, 67, 86 and 94, Special Session on HIV/AIDS, New York, 25-27 June, A/RES/S-26/2, www.un.org/ga/aids/coverage/FinalDeclarationHIVAIDS.html

United Nations, General Assembly (2001b), *Protection of Religious Sites*, UN, New York, A/RES/55/254, 11 June.

United Nations, General Assembly (2001c), *United Nations Year of Dialogue Among Civilizations*, UN, New York, A/RES/55/23, 11 January.

United Nations, Office for the Coordination of Humanitarian Assistance (1999), *Mine Action Programme: Afghanistan*, UNOCHA.

United Nations, Secretariat (1992), *An Agenda for Peace: Preventive Diplomacy, Peacemaking and Peace-keeping*, Secretary-General's Report Pursuant to the Statement Adopted by the Summit Meeting of the Security Council, UN, New York, ST/DPI/1247, 31 January.

United Nations, Secretary-General (1997), *Renewing the United Nations: A Programme for Reform*, UN, New York, 14 July, A/51/950.

United Nations, Secretary-General (1998), *Arrangements and Practices for the Interaction of Non-governmental Organizations in All Activities of the United Nations System*, UN, New York, 10 July, A/53/170.

United Nations, Secretary-General (1999), *Views of Member States, Members of the Specialized Agencies, Observers, Intergovernmental and Non-governmental Organizations from All Regions on the Report of the Secretary-General on Arrangements and Practices for the Interaction of Non-governmental Organizations in All Activities of the United Nations System*, UN, New York, 8 September, A/54/329.

United Nations, Secretary-General (2000), *Secretary-General Addresses Millennium Summit of Religious, Spiritual Leaders, Urges Participants to Set Example of Interfaith Cooperation*, UN, New York, UN Press Release SG/SM/7520, 29 August.

United Nations, Security Council (1992), *Provisional Verbatim Record of the 3046th Meeting: Security Council Summit*, UN, New York, S/PV.3046, 31 January.

United Nations, Sustainable Development (1992), 'Agenda 21: Programme of Action for Sustainable Development, Rio Declaration on Environment and Development, Statement of Forest Principles : the Final Text of Agreements Negotiated by Governments at the United Nations Conference on Environment and Development (UNCED)', Rio de Janeiro, 3-14 June, ST/DPI/1344, www.un.org/esa/sustdev/agenda21text.htm

United States, Department of State. Political-Military Affairs Bureau. Office of International Security Operations (1993), *Hidden Killers: The Global Problem with Uncleared Landmines*, Washington, DC.

United States, Department of State. Office of International Security and Peacekeeping Operations (1994), *Hidden Killers: The Global Landmine Crisis*, 1994 Report to the U.S. Congress on the Problem with Uncleared Landmines and the United States Strategy for Demining and Landmine Control, Washington, DC, Department of State Publication 10225, January, www.state.gov/www/global/arms/rpt_9401_demine_toc.html

United States, Department of State. Bureau of Political-Military Affairs. Office of Humanitarian Demining Programs (1998), *Hidden Killers: The Global Landmine Crisis*, Washington, DC, Department of State Publication 10575, September, www.state.gov/www/global/arms/rpt_9809_demine_toc.html

Van Tongeren, Paul (1998), 'Exploring the Local Capacity for Peace: The Role of NGOs', *The Courier ACP-EU*, 168 (March-April), 70-72.

Vitagliano, Marissa (1999), U.S. Campaign to Ban Landmines, telephone conversation with Ken Rutherford, 19 October.

Von Hippel, Frank (1991), *Citizen Scientist*, American Institute of Physics, New York.

Wapner, Paul (1995), 'Politics Beyond the State: Environmental Activism and World Civic Politics', *World Politics*, Vol. 47(3), pp. 391-425.

Wareham, Mary (1999), Senior Researcher, Human Rights Watch and former Coordinator, U.S. Campaign to Ban Landmines, telephone conversation with Ken Rutherford, 19 October.

Watkins, Kevin (2000), *The Oxfam Education Report*, Oxfam GB, Oxford.

Weiss, Thomas G. and Gordenker, Leon (eds) (1996), *NGOs, the UN and Global Governance*, Lynne Rienner Publishers, Boulder.

Weschler, Lawrence (2000), 'Exceptional Cases in Rome: The United States and the Struggle for an ICC', in Sarah B. Sewall and Carl Kaysen, (eds), *The United States and the International Criminal Court: National Security and International Law*, Rowman & Littlefield, Lanham, MD, pp. 85-111.

Whaley, Patti. (2000), 'Human Rights NGOs: Our Love-Hate Relationship with the Internet', in Steven Hick, Edward F. Halpin and Eric Hoskins (eds), *Human Rights and the Internet*, Macmillan Press, London, pp. 30-40.

Willetts, Peter (ed) (1996), *The Conscience of the World: The Influence of Non-Governmental Organizations in the UN System*, Hurst, London.

Williams, Jody (1997), *The International Campaign to Ban Landmines: A Model for Disarmament Initiatives?* Oslo, Speech by Jody Williams, International Campaign to Ban Landmines, accepting the Nobel Peace Prize. www.nobel.se/peace/articles/williams/index.html

Williams, Jody and Goose, Steve (1998), 'The International Campaign to Ban Landmines', in Maxwell A. Cameron, Robert J. Lawson, and Brian W. Tomlin (eds), *To Walk Without Fear: The Global Movement to Ban Landmines*, Oxford University Press, Toronto, pp. 20-47.

Wolfe, Robert (1999), 'The World Trade Organization', in Brian Hocking and Steven McGuire (eds), *Trade Politics: International, Domestic and Regional Perspectives*, Routledge, London, pp. 208-223.

Wood, Ellen Meikins (1991), 'The Uses and Abuses of "Civil Society"', in Ralph Miliband (ed), *The Socialist Register, 1990*, Monthly Review Press, New York, pp. 60-84.

Woodard, Joe (2001), 'The UN Quietly Wages War on Religion: Does This Respected Body Suppress Monothesism in Order to Regulate Global Values?', *Calgary Herald*, 11 August, p. OSO8.

World Council of Churches (1999), *The Role of the World Council of Churches in International Affairs*, WCC, Geneva.

World Council of Churches, Office of Communication (2000), *Press Update*, Geneva, 30 August, PR-00-27,
www.wcc-coe.org/wcc/news/press/00/27pu.html

World Development Movement (2001), *WDM Report Back from the G8 Summit in Genoa*, 23 July; www.wdm.org.uk/campaign/Genoa.htm

World Trade Organization (n.d.), *WTO and NGOs Relations with Non-Governmental Organizations/Civil Society*, WTO, Geneva, www.wto.org/english/forums_e/ngo_e/intro_e.htm

World Trade Organization (1996a), 'Guidelines for Arrangements on Relations with Non-Governmental Organizations', WTO, Geneva, 23 July, WT/L/162.
World Trade Organization (1996b), 'Procedures for the Circulation and De-Restriction of WTO Documents', WTO, Geneva, 22 July, WT/L/160.
World Trade Organization (1998a), *Focus*, No. 32, July.
World Trade Organization (1998b), *Ruggerio Announces Enhanced WTO Plan for Cooperation with NGOs*, WTO, Geneva, Press 107, www.wto.org/english/news_e/pres98_e/pr107_e.htm
World Trade Organization (2000a), *Focus*, No. 51, January-February.
World Trade Organization (2000b), *WTO and World Bank Open Online Forum on Trade Issues*, WTO, Geneva, www.wto.org/english/news_e/news00_e/wto-wbforum_e.htm
World Trade Organization (2001), 'Opening Remarks', *Symposium on Issues Confronting the World Trading System*, WTO, Geneva, 6 July.
World Trade Organization. Ministerial (2001), *Declaration on the Trips Agreement and Public Health*, 14 November, WTO, Doha, Qatar, WT/MIN(01)/DEC/2, www.wto.org/english/thewto_e/minist_e/min01_e/mindecl_trips_e.htm
World Wide Fund for Nature (2001), *G8 Plan for Africa Pointless without Renewable Energy Support*, Press Release, Genoa, 22 July, World Wide Fund for Nature, Greenpeace, and Export Credit Agencies International NGO Campaign.
Wren, Christopher S. (1995), 'U.N.-Backed Drive to Restrict Land Mines Fails at Talks', *New York Times*, 13 October, p. A6.
Zampano, Giada (2001), 'Italy Confirms Genoa as Venue of G8', Reuters newswire, 19 June.
Zupi, Marco (2001), 'The Genoa G-8 Summit: Great Expectations, Disappointing Results,' *The International Spectator*, Vol. 36(3), pp. 57-68.

Index

20/20 Vision 45

ABM (Anti-ballistic Missile) Treaty 38-39, 43-44, 53
Abortion 164-65, 169
ACCESS (NGO in Thailand) 127, 133
Access to Essential Medicines campaign *See* MSF, Campaign for Essential Medicines
Accountability 86, 92, 141, 150, 190, 219, 232, 245-46
ACT UP 127, 133
Activism 7-8, 20-23, 25, 28-32, 34, 38, 40, 44-45, 50, 52, 103, 117, 123, 131, 151
Adams, Barbara 10-11, 141-53, 245
Adjustment With a Human Face 151
Afghanistan 60, 97, 101-102, 160
Africa 1, 9, 31, 62, 69, 71, 81, 102, 115, 127, 132, 160, 209, 211, 232-33
 See also South Africa; Southern Africa; United Nations, Economic Commission for Africa
  debt 219
  traditional religions 166
African sleeping sickness 130, 135
An Agenda for Peace 157
Aging 77, 224
Agriculture 148, 164, 175, 188
 See also FAO
AIDS *See* HIV/AIDS
Algeria 222, 232
All-African Council of Churches 219
American Chamber of Commerce 177
American Farm Bureau 177
American Jewish Committee 159
American Physical Society 44, 48-49
Americas *See also* Central America; FTAA; Hemispheric Social Alliance; Inter-Parliamentary Forum of the Americas; Latin America, OAS; South America; Summit of the Americas; Western hemisphere; Youth Forum of the Americas
  traditional religions 166
Americas Business Forum 210
Amnesty International 7-8, 19-35, 110, 231, 243
  fundraising 30
  information production and dissemination 20-23
  internal access to information 21, 28, 34
  internal web use 25-27
  International Secretariat 20-21, 26-28, 30, 32
  letter-writing actions 21-24, 28
  public access to information 21-23, 28-30
  Urgent Action Networks 20-21, 23-25, 28, 32
  use of ICT 7-8, 19-35, 243, 245
Anglican/Episcopal churches 160
Angola 98, 101-102
Annan, Kofi 109, 150, 157, 165-66, 232
Anti-ballistic Missile Treaty *See* ABM Treaty
Anti-globalization movement 1, 6, 175, 185-86, 191, 232, 235
Antiretroviral (ARV) therapy 127, 129-30, 135
Apartheid 160
APEC (Asia-Pacific Economic Co-operation) 191, 203
Appeal of Conscience Foundation 160, 162
Arab-Israeli conflict 158
Arabic language 31, 121
Argentina 119, 208, 210
Arinze, Francis (Cardinal) 166

Armenia 158
Armenian churches 160, 166
Arms control 37, 39, 41-42, 46-47, 50, 52-54, 59, 61, 96, 100, 141, 153, 155-56, 224
Ashman, Darcy 69-70, 92
Ashoka 68
Asia 9, 62, 68, 71, 121, 127, 132, 160, 164, 233
Asia-Pacific Economic Co-operation *See* APEC
Assembly of First Nations 210-11
Association of Universities and Colleges of Canada 211
Asylum 23
Atheism 159
Australia 115
Axworthy, Lloyd 95, 98
Azerbaijan 158

Bahá'í religion 163-64
Balkans 160
Ballantyne, Peter 69-70, 91
Ballistic missile defence *See* BMD
Bangladesh Rural Advancement Committee 92
Baptist World Alliance 164
Bayne, Nicholas 6, 178, 234
Bédard, Sylvie 12, 201-13, 245
Berlusconi, Silvio 227, 231, 237
Bethe, Hans 45
Beyond Debt Relief 229, 233
Bible 219
Bin Laden, Osama 4, 158, 227
BINGOs (business international NGOs) 3
Black Bloc 177, 231
Blair, Tony 220, 223
Blaustein, Jacob 159
BMD (ballistic missile defence) 37-43, 52, 243 *See also* NMD
Bono (Irish rock star) 220, 232
Bornstein, David 67

Bosnia 97, 101-103
Boston Globe 48
Bouteflika, Abdelaziz 222
Boutros-Ghali, Boutros 150, 157
Brazil 210, 217
Bretton Woods institutions 147, 150-51, 217-18, 221 *See also* IMF; World Bank
Brown, Gordon 221
Brown, Sally 211
Buddhist religion 158, 163, 166
Bumblebee federation 91
Burdon, Tony 228
Bush, George 43
Bush, George W. 39, 43, 52-54, 226-27, 232
Business (profit-oriented) international NGOs *See* BINGOs
Business sector 68, 129, 131-32, 151, 157, 175, 177, 180, 188-89, 193, 203, 206, 210-11, 213, 217-19, 222-23, 232-34, 245-46 *See also* Multinational corporations

Cambodia 97-98, 101-102
Campaigns *See* ICBL; ICC, NGO campaign; Jubilee 2000 coalition, debt-relief campaigns; MSF, Campaign for Essential Medicines; MSF, MSF, neglected diseases campaign; NMD, Union of Concerned Scientists campaign against; Oxfam International, Education Now campaign; Treatment Access Campaign
Canada 12, 20, 25, 32, 98, 147, 195, 201-13, 215, 232, 237, 243
Canadian Centre for Foreign Policy Development 206
Canadian Centre for International Cooperation 206

Capacity building 69-70, 83, 87-88, 91-92
    See also International Forum on Capacity Building
Caribbean area 9, 71
Carnegie Endowment for Peace 104
Carrier, Jean-Guy 183-84
Castells, Manuel 69
Catholic church and organizations 157-58, 160, 164-65
Catholic Family and Human Rights Institute 164-65
Catholics for a Free Choice 165
Central America 58, 60
Centro de Acción Legal en Derechos Humanos 21
Chechnya 97, 158
Cheney, Richard B. 53
Child soldiers 100, 123
Children 127, 202, 224, 229
    street children 129
Chile 23
China 21, 46, 52, 119, 158, 166
Chinese language 78
Chrétien, Jean 208, 237
Christian Aid 219
Christian churches 158, 162, 164-66
Chuan Leekpai 222
Church Center for the United Nations 160, 164
Churchill, Winston 159
Civil society 1-2, 39, 44, 67-68, 120, 150, 155-69, 175, 203, 216, 218, 223-24, 229, 243-47 *See also* NGOs; Nongovernmental social movements; Non-state actors; Uncivil society
    advocacy 6-9, 60, 64-65, 89-91, 116-17, 132-33, 141-42, 150, 156, 168, 175, 185-86, 217, 243, 246
    and developing countries 178-79, 232-33
    and G7/G8 12-13, 215-38, 244-45
    and global governance 149-51, 175
    and IGOs 6, 10-13, 102, 150, 221, 223, 226, 236, 243-44, 246
    and landmines 95-104
    and OECD 224
    and Quebec City Summit of the Americas 201-13
    and Union of Concerned Scientists 43-45, 243
    and United Nations 10-11, 112, 116, 141-53, 155-69, 236, 245
    and WTO 11, 175-96
    classification 3, 6-7, 91, 142, 146, 151-52, 161, 176-79, 188, 192
    definition 2-4, 142, 156, 175
    financing 109, 185-87
    functional types 178-79, 188
    interaction with governments 6, 98-99, 102, 115-18, 128-29, 132-33, 141-42, 144-45, 150, 175, 178, 181, 192-96, 212, 221, 223, 226, 243-46
    internet use 7, 10, 34, 47, 63, 71, 76, 95, 100-103, 109, 111, 131, 134, 176, 243-44
    legitimacy 7, 20, 134-35, 193, 196, 245-46
    Millennium NGO Forum, New York (2000) 151
    networking 6-7, 25, 35, 72, 76, 90, 92, 102, 109-110, 115, 123, 155, 167, 178, 184, 186, 188, 191, 210, 243-44
    operational groups 6, 142, 175, 185
    religious groups 1, 114, 155-69, 210, 219
        use of ICT 167-68

282 *Civil Society in the Information Age*

Southern 7, 9, 67-92, 101, 114, 145-46, 177-79, 186, 189, 196, 209, 243-45
    and international NGOs 9, 67-71, 80-92
    technical networks 178
        use of ICT 9, 67-80, 90-92, 116, 178, 186, 216, 243-45
    use of ICT 5, 7-13, 38, 47, 54, 95-96, 104, 109, 111-12, 116, 122-23, 131, 155, 175-76, 181, 185, 196, 201-203, 216, 224, 236, 243-45
        social and cultural consequences 73-80
    use of media technologies 98
Climate change 156-57, 168, 233
Clinton, Bill 8, 37-39, 43, 45-53, 101, 180, 221
Coalition for International Justice 111-12
Coalition To Reduce Nuclear Dangers 38, 45-46
Cold War 40-43, 46, 104, 128, 149, 155, 216
Comic Relief 102
Commission on Global Governance 3-4, 150
Commission on a Just and Durable Peace 159
Commission To Study the Organization of Peace 159, 161
Committee of Religious NGOs at the United Nations 163-64
Common Frontiers 208
Community of Sant'Egidio 157
Comprehensive Test Ban Treaty *See* CTBT
Computers 5, 71-72, 76, 88-90, 111-12, 114, 155, 182, 185, 235 *See also* ICT
Concise Dictionary of Library and Information Science 5
Conflict diamonds 29

Conflicts 61, 63, 96, 98, 156-58, 163, 167, 169, 222, 224, 230, 244
Confucianism 163, 166
The Conscience of the World 169
Consumer organizations 175, 180
Consumer Project on Technology 127, 133
Convention on Conventional Weapons, Landmines Protocol 97
Cook, Robin 119
Coon-Come, Matthew 211
Corporacion Participa 207
Corruption 221
Council for a Livable World 45
Countermeasures Report 38, 47-52
Cox, Robert W. 4
Coyle, Philip 49
Crime 4, 224, 246
CTBT (Comprehensive Test Ban Treaty) 46-47
Cultural diversity 89, 202, 204

Dagestan 97
Dalai Lama 166, 220
Das, Bhagirath lal 190
Data, definition of 4-5
Death penalty 28
Debt *See under* Developing countries
Debt Relief and Beyond 229
Democracy 141, 150, 158-59, 193-94, 203-205, 211-12, 218, 234-35, 245
Democratic Party (US) 39, 47, 51-52
Demonstrations 6, 25, 133, 175, 178, 180-81, 186, 188, 190, 195, 208, 215-16, 220, 224, 226-28, 230, 235-36, 245-46
    media coverage 6, 178, 208, 216, 228
Dent, Martin 219
Developing countries 6, 68-69, 72, 91-92, 112, 127, 132, 136, 146, 178, 181, 184, 186-87, 189, 193, 196, 202, 222, 229, 232, 234 *See also* North-South
    and civil society 178-79, 232-33

debt 12-13, 60-61, 63, 145, 219-22, 224, 226-27, 229-30, 232-37
Development 7-8, 10, 58-60, 64, 69, 75, 78, 80, 88, 90, 92, 102, 141-43, 155-56, 160, 163, 180, 204, 216-18, 221-22, 224, 229-31, 243 *See also* Sustainable development
Dichter, Thomas W. 70
Digital cameras 77
Digital divide 8, 31, 34, 76-77, 112, 187, 204, 245
Dilevko, Juris 9, 67-92, 243-45
Disarmament *See* Arms control
Disaster relief 58, 61, 64, 83-84, 87-88, 91, 163
Dobel, J. Patrick 91
Dole, Robert 43
DONGOs (donor-organized NGOs) 3
Drayton, William 68
Drop the Debt *See* Jubilee 2000 coalition
Drugs 153, 220
Dulles, John Foster 159

Earth Summit, Rio de Janeiro (1992) 144, 151, 156, 217
  Agenda 21 148
  Rio+10 conference 148, 150, 233
East Timor 61
East Timor Action Network 114
Eastern Europe 1, 62
ECA (Export Credit Agencies) Watch 234
Economy, internationalization of 201-202
Education 40, 60-61, 63-64, 72, 76-79, 89, 142-43, 164-65, 185-87, 189-90, 196, 202, 204-205, 224, 228-30, 234-35, 237
Education Now: Break the Cycle of Poverty 60, 63
Edwards, Michael 70, 246
Egypt 227
Eliot, T. S. 5

E-mail 19-25, 28-30, 32, 38, 42, 47-48, 50-52, 63, 70, 72, 76-77, 79-81, 90, 98-99, 101-103, 109-115, 117-18, 121-24, 155, 168, 182, 184-86, 227, 244
Emergency response 8, 60, 62-64, 141, 224, 243
Energy 148, 234
English language 70, 74, 77-79, 86, 90-91, 121-22, 182, 187, 207
Environment 50, 70, 77, 81, 86, 98, 104, 131, 144, 155-56, 175-76, 178, 180, 188-91, 193, 195, 202, 204, 216-19, 228, 236-37 *See also* Climate change; Earth Summit
Enviro-summit (1991) 217
Eritrea 97, 101-103
Esquel Foundation 207
Estrany y Gendre, Antonio 211
Esty, Daniel C. 193
Ethics 128, 158, 168, 216, 244
Ethiopia 97, 101-102
Ethnic groups 114
Europe 54, 115, 121, 132 *See also* Eastern Europe
European Union 59, 147, 177, 191, 194-95, 227, 232, 236
Evangelical Covenant Church 164

FAO (Food and Agriculture Organization of the UN) 232
FAS (Federation of American Scientists) 44-45, 52
Fax machines 10, 20, 23, 25, 72, 80-81, 99-100, 102, 110-13, 117, 120, 122, 134, 168, 184, 244
Federal Council of Churches 159
Federation of American Scientists *See* FAS
Fernandez, Sylvia 119
Filters and firewalls 21-22, 31
Financial Times 221, 237
Fini, Gianfranco 227
Fischer, Stanley 6

Fitzgerald, Frances 42
FOCAL 208, 211
Food and Agriculture Organization *See* FAO
Food safety 195, 224, 233
Ford, Gerald R. 41
Foreman, Karen 91
Forests 217, 225
Foster, John W. 3
France 119, 215
Free Trade Area of the Americas *See* FTAA
French language 31, 78, 121-22, 182, 187, 207
Friedmann, Harriet 217
Friends of the Earth 236
FTAA (Free Trade Area of the Americas) 204-208
FTP (file transfer protocol) 5
Fundraising 9, 30, 76, 90, 243

G7/G8 (Group of 7/Group of 8) 203, 215, 221, 228, 237 *See also* Envirosummit; Genoa Nongovernmental Initiative; Genoa Social Forum; TOES
   agenda 216, 219, 235
   and civil society 12-13, 215-38, 244-45
   Birmingham summit (1998) 217-18, 220, 223, 236-37
   Bonn summit (1985) 217
   Cologne summit (1999) 218, 220, 223, 236
   communiqués and other documents 217-18, 220, 223-25, 227-29, 232-34, 237
   compliance with commitments 220, 232-35
   Denver summit (1997) 218
   Digital Opportunity Task Force 233
   education ministers 237
   environment ministers 218
   finance ministers 229, 237
   foreign ministers 223-24, 226, 233, 237
   Genoa summit (2001) 12, 133, 175, 215-16, 217, 223, 225-37
   security measures 215-16, 226-27
   Halifax summit (1995) 217-18
   Kananaskis summit (2002) 237
   leaders 226-27, 232
   legitimacy 234
   London summit (1984) 217
   London summit (1991) 217
   Lyon summit (1996) 218
   ministerial meetings 221
   Okinawa summit (2000) 12, 217, 220-25, 229-30, 233, 237
   Paris summit (of the Arch) 217
   Renewable Energy Task Force 234
   sherpas 220
   Tokyo summit (1986) 217
   Toronto summit (1988) 217
   Trade ministers quadrilateral 218
   Venice summit (1987) 217
   Versailles summit (1982) 219
G8 Information Centre 236
G8 Research Group 236
Gamarra, Eduardo 211
Garwin, Richard 45, 50
GATT (General Agreement on Tariffs and Trade) 176, 179, 190
Geldof, Bob 232
General Agreement on Tariffs and Trade *See* GATT
Genoa Nongovernmental Initiative 231
Genoa Social Forum 227, 231
George, Susan 231, 235
Georgia 97
German language 78, 121

Germany 39, 101, 215, 217, 232
Giuliani, Carlo 215
Global Conference on Small Island Developing States SIDS+5 149
Global warming *See* Climate change
Globalization 2, 5, 7, 11-12, 31, 58, 61, 69, 91, 128, 151, 156, 164, 169, 175, 190-91, 193, 201-204, 212, 218, 227, 232, 235, 244-45 *See also* Anti-globalization movement
Globe and Mail (Toronto) 211
Goetz, Anne Marie 2
GONGOs (government-organized NGOs) 3
Gopher 111-13
Gordenker, Leon 2, 4
Gore, Albert 43, 46
Gottfried, Kurt 50
Governance 2, 11, 58-60, 91-92, 149-51, 175, 190, 202-203, 211, 213, 218, 243
Government-organized NGOs *See* GONGOs
Governments 12-13, 24-25, 31, 48, 64-65, 67-68, 98-100, 102-104, 112-13, 115, 122, 129-32, 156-57, 159, 188, 196, 201, 203, 213, 215, 217-19, 220-23, 226, 233, 237, 243-46
    and civil society 6, 98-99, 102, 115-18, 128-29, 132-33, 141-42, 144-45, 150, 175, 178, 181, 192-96, 212, 221, 223, 226, 243-46
    documents 113-14
Graham, Bill 206-207, 211
Graham, Billy 166
Graham Lotz, Anne 166
Grameen Bank 92
Gramsci, Antonio 3
Grassroots organizations 3, 7, 25-26, 31, 38, 44-45, 52, 246
Greenpeace 177, 185, 224-25, 234
Group of 7/Group of 8 *See* G7/G8
Group of 77 70, 147
Gronlund, Lisbeth 48

Grunberg, Isabelle 2
Guatemala 21
Gulf War 40, 43

Hajnal, Peter I. 1-13, 57-65, 177, 215-38, 243-47
Hamelink, Cees J. 69, 90
Hammarskjöld, Dag 159
Handicap International 102
Health 11, 13, 127, 131, 135-37, 190, 202, 205, 228-29, 232-35, 237, 245 *See also* Infectious diseases; MSF; WHO
Health Action International 127, 133
Heavily-indebted poor countries *See* HIPC
Heeks, Richard 69, 90
Hegel, Georg Wilhelm Friedrich 3
Helms, Jesse 47
Hemispheric Social Alliance 208
Hindu religion 163, 166
HIPC (heavily-indebted poor countries) initiative 219, 223, 229, 233
HIV/AIDS 10, 61, 127, 129-30, 136, 149-50, 223, 228-30, 232-35
Holcombe, Susan 91
Holy See 165-66
Homosexuals 25-26
Hopkins, Nancy 91
Human rights 7, 10, 19, 33-34, 59, 98, 104, 117, 131, 135, 141, 143, 150, 155-56, 158-59, 163-65, 175, 177, 188, 190, 211, 216 *See also* Women; World Conference on Human Rights
    Universal Declaration 19, 160
    violations 23, 28, 114-15, 231
Human Rights Watch 34, 110, 211
Humanitarian action 7, 10, 60, 128-29, 156, 162-64, 168, 216, 224, 244
Hurricane Mitch 58, 60
Hussein, Saddam 40
Hynes, Ross 147

286 *Civil Society in the Information Age*

ICBL (International Campaign To Ban Landmines) 9, 95-100, 102 *See also* Mine Ban Treaty
    internal communications 99
    membership 99
    Nobel Peace Prize 96
    use of ICT 9, 96, 98-101, 104, 244
    use of media technologies 98
ICBM (intercontinental ballistic missile) 37, 40 *See also* NMD
ICC (International Criminal Court) 9-11, 100, 109-24, 156-57, 243-44, 246
    NGO campaign 109-24
        access to UN and government documents 113-14
        Global Information Network 111-12
        information dissemination 114-17, 119-20
        regional and thematic networks 115
        use of ICT 9-10, 109-118, 120-24, 243-44
        use of media 110, 117, 120
        website 121
    Rome Treaty 110, 119-20, 122, 124, 145, 156, 168
        conference 9, 110, 115-20, 123
        entry into force 124
ICC Monitor 113, 117, 122-23
ICRC (International Committee of the Red Cross) 97, 102
ICT (information and communication technology) 2, 5, 31, 69, 155, 201-202, 204-205, 207, 222, 230, 235 *See also* Computers; E-mail; Electronic FreeNets; FTP; Gopher; Internet; Media technologies; Mobile telephones; Radio; Satellite communications; Telephones; Text messaging; Videoconferencing; World Wide Web
    limitations 23
    misuse 8, 10, 22, 27-29, 34, 79, 124, 167, 177, 183, 185, 245-46
    use by Amnesty International 7-8, 19-35, 243
    use by civil society 5, 7-13, 38, 47, 95-96, 104, 111-12, 116, 122-23, 155, 175, 178, 181, 185, 196, 202-203, 216, 224, 236, 243-45
    use by Global Trade Watch 191
    use by ICBL 9, 96, 98-101, 104, 244
    use by International Chamber of Commerce 189
    use by Jubilee 2000 12, 221, 225
    use by Landmine Survivors Network 9, 96, 101-104, 244
    use by MSF 10, 131, 134-35, 244
    use by NGO Coalition for an International Criminal Court 9-10, 109-118, 120-24, 243-44
    use by NGOs 5, 7-13, 38, 47, 95-96, 104, 111-12, 155, 175, 202-203, 216, 224, 236, 243-45
    use by non-state actors 12, 104
    use by Oxfam International 8, 62-64, 243
    use by Peoples' Global Action 192
    use by religious groups 167-68
    use by Southern NGOs 9, 67-80, 90-92, 178, 186, 243-45
        social and cultural consequences 73-80
    use by trade-related NGOs 11, 176, 185-92, 196, 244
    use by Union of Concerned Scientists 8, 38, 42-45, 47, 50-51, 54, 243

use by WTO 11, 180, 182-85
versus traditional communication 8, 10, 19-20, 24-25, 35, 69, 74-75, 80-81, 90, 100, 103, 123, 134, 176, 184-87, 203, 207, 245-46
IFIs (international financial institutions) 217 *See also* IMF; Inter-American Development Bank; Multilateral development banks; World Bank
IGOs (international governmental organizations) 3, 102, 123, 157, 221, 222-23, 246 *See also* International organizations
    and civil society 10, 13, 129, 150, 178, 236, 243-44, 246
    legitimacy 150
IMF (International Monetary Fund) 6, 13, 59-60, 65, 203, 219, 232, 237
    Prague meeting (2000) 175
India 57, 68, 115, 127, 133, 158, 190
Indigenous peoples 21, 69, 74-75, 77-79, 92, 166, 210-12
Indigenous Peoples Summit of the Americas 208-10
Indonesia 158
Infectious diseases 129, 223, 225, 228-30, 235, 237 *See also* HIV/AIDS; malaria; MSF; tuberculosis
Informal communication *See* Traditional communication
Information 79, 141-42, 182 *See also* Knowledge
    definition 4-6
    government control 100, 104, 201
    volume 187
Information age 5, 155, 168
Information and communication technology *See* ICT
INGOs (international NGOs) 3, 67-70, 80-92, 161-62

governance 92, 150
Institute for Agriculture and Trade Policy 178, 188
Institute for Global Communications 112
Intellectual property 176, 195, 234
Inter-American Council for Trade and Production 211
Inter-American Development Bank 205
Intercontinental ballistic missile *See* ICBM
Interfaith Center (New York) 165
International Campaign To Ban Landmines *See* ICBL
International Centre for Human Rights 177
International Centre for Trade and Sustainable Development 178, 193
International Chamber of Commerce 177, 187-89
    and WTO 189
    use of ICT 189
International Civil Society Opposing a Millennium Round 178
International Committee of the Red Cross *See* ICRC
International Confederation of Free Trade Unions 177
International Conference on Financing for Development, Monterrey (2002) 149
International Conference on Population and Development, Cairo (1994) 144, 155-56, 164-65
    ICPD+5 149, 165
International Council of Religious and Spiritual Leaders (proposed) 167
International Criminal Court *See* ICC
International Criminal Tribunal for the Former Yugoslavia 111-12
International finance 221
International financial institutions *See* IFIs
International Forum on Capacity Building 69
International governmental organizations *See* IGOs

International Institute for Sustainable Development 296
International Labor Rights Fund 177
International law 7, 96-97, 133, 150, 218
International Mahawir Jain Mission 165
International Monetary Fund *See* IMF
International NGOs *See* INGOs; NGOs, international
International organizations 41, 64-65, 188, 218, 232, 237
International Policy Council on Agriculture, Food and Trade 177
International South Group Network 177
International trade 63, 131, 175-96, 189-90, 193, 195-96, 202, 204-205, 211, 218, 229-30, 232, 235 *See also* GATT; WTO, Millennium Round; NGOs, trade-related; Oxfam International, fair trade initiative; UNCTAD, Uruguay Round of trade negotiations, WTO
    negotiations 194, 203
    trade in services 176, 195
International Women's Decade (1976-85) 144
International Women's Year (1975) 144
Internet 5, 7, 10, 20-22, 30-31, 34, 38, 47, 62-64, 71-72, 76, 81, 95, 100-103, 109, 111-13, 117, 122-23, 131, 134, 147, 164, 168, 176, 182-87, 192, 201-203, 205-207, 221, 224, 226, 243-44
    languages 31, 63, 74, 78, 90, 121, 187, 207, 227
Inter-Parliamentary Forum of the Americas 207
Inter-Press Service 117
Inuit Tapirisat of Canada 210
Investment 63, 176, 211, 229, 246 *See also* MAI
Iran 43
Iraq 40, 43
Islam 158, 160, 163-66

Ismail, Razali 146-47
Israel 158, 166 *See also* Arab-Israeli conflict
Italy 54, 157, 215, 225, 227-33, 237
    police actions at Genoa summit 133, 230-31

Jain, Bawa 165
Jainism 163, 165-66
Jamaica 32
Japan 44, 47, 115, 195, 215, 220, 222-25, 236
Japan Institute for International Affairs 222
Jensen, Jane 4
Jewish religion 158, 160, 163-66
John Paul II (Pope) 220-21
Johnson, Lyndon B. 41
Johnson, Martin 30
Johnson, Pierre-Marc 208, 211
Jordan 101-103
Jovanotti, Lorenzo 232
Jubilee 2000 coalition 12, 145, 219-21, 224-28, 233, 235
    analytical studies 221
    debt-relief campaigns 219-21, 223, 226, 228, 232
    use of ICT 12, 221, 224-27
    website 225-27
Judge, Anthony 2

Kadena US Air Base (Okinawa) 224
Karekin II (Patriarch) 166
Kashmir 158
Kaul, Inge 2
Kennedy, John F. 41
Keohane, Robert 182
Khmer Rouge 97
Khor, Martin 190
Kirsch, Philippe 120
Kirton, John 237
Knowledge 11, 78, 182
    definition 4-5

indigenous 69, 74-75, 77-79, 92, 191
   medical 130-31
Knudsen, Kjell 99
Koran 219
Korea 57, 118 *See also* North Korea
Kosovo 60, 97, 224
Küng, Hans 168
Kuftato, Ahmad 166
Kuiten, Bernard 181, 188, 194
Kuwait 40

Labelle, Richard 69-70, 91
Labour 1, 131, 166, 175-78, 202, 204
Labour unions 1, 175, 177, 180, 188, 206, 208-209
Lal, Bhavya 69
Lamy, Pascal 194
Land use 96, 98
Landmine Survivors Network 9, 95-96, 100-103
   financing 100
   use of ICT 9, 96, 101-104, 244
Landmines 9, 95-104, 119, 133, 145, 156-57, 202, 244 *See also* Convention on Conventional Weapons, Landmines Protocol; ICBL; Middle East Conference on Landmine Injury and Rehabilitation; Mine Ban Treaty; Mines Advisory Group; Open Society Institute, Landmines Project; United States Campaign To Ban Landmines
   victims 95-98, 100, 102-103
Laser technology 42
Latin America 1, 115, 118, 160, 209, 211
   See also Central America; South America
Lau, Isaac Meir 166
Laval University 208
Lawrence Berkeley National Laboratory 48
Lawyers Committee on Nuclear Policy 114
Leadership Council for Inter-American Summitry 211

League of Nations 165
Lebanon 102, 158
Lebert, Joanne 7-8, 19-35, 243
Leishmaniasis 130
Lewis, George 48
Lindenberg, Marc 91
Literacy 72, 79
Lortie, Marc 12, 201-13, 245
Los Angeles Times 52
Lovett, Adrian 228

Macroeconomic policy 216
MAD (mutually assured destruction) 40-41
MAI (Multilateral Agreement on Investment) 176, 191, 246
Malaria 136, 223, 229-30, 233
Malaysia 189
Malhotra, Kamal 246
Mali 232
Manhattan Project 44
Manley, John 206
Marable, Manning 4
Marty, Martin 169
Mathews, Jessica 104
Mbeki, Thabo 222
Mchumo, Ali 181
Meadow, Charles T. 5
Médecins Sans Frontières *See* MSF
Media 22, 40-41, 45, 60, 62, 77, 102, 109, 117, 120, 157, 176, 206, 210, 212, 216
   coverage of demonstrations 9, 178, 208, 216, 228
   coverage of G7/G8 summits 222-23
   coverage of NMD 51-52
   technologies 9, 49, 98
Medical relief 128-29
MEDICO 97
Mennonites 162
Métis National Council of Women 210
Mexico 118, 210
Middle East 57, 62, 101

290 *Civil Society in the Information Age*

Middle East Conference on Landmine Injury and Rehabilitation (Jordan, 1998) 101, 103
Millennium World Peace Summit of Religious and Spiritual Leaders (2000) 165-68
Mine Ban Treaty 9-11, 95-96, 101-102, 133, 145, 156, 168, 244, 246 *See also* Landmines
Mines Advisory Group 102
Minorities 114
MIT (Massachusetts Institute of Technology) 38, 48, 52
Mobile telephones 10, 123-24, 131, 134, 182, 185-86, 244
Mobilization 6-7, 12, 23-30, 34, 131, 178, 191, 237, 243, 246
Moravian church 157
Mori, Yoshiro 220, 223
Mormons 165-66
Mozambique 101-103, 157
MSF (Médecins Sans Frontières) 7, 127-35, 224, 228, 230, 232, 234
    Campaign for Essential Medicines 7, 10, 61, 127-35, 224, 229-30, 234, 237, 244, 246
    financing 129
    humanitarian work 10, 128-29
    interaction with governments 129, 132-33
    neglected diseases campaign 130, 132, 234
    Nobel Peace Prize 10, 128
    position papers 135
    use of ICT 10, 131, 134-35, 244
    witnessing 10, 128-29, 133
Mubarak, Hosni 227
Muhammad Ali 220
Multilateral Agreement on Investment *See* MAI
Multinational corporations 3, 131, 203, 215, 234
Multilateral development banks 233
Multilateral economic institutions 2
Mutually assured destruction *See* MAD

Nader, Ralph 190
NAFTA (North American Free Trade Agreement) 191
National Academy of Sciences (US) 44
National Missile Defence *See* NMD
Native Women's Association of Canada 210
Ndugane, Njongonkulu 166
Netherlands 57
New diplomacy 1, 11, 96, 104, 109, 115-17, 119, 141, 144-45, 148-50, 156-57, 168, 194, 196, 206, 244, 246
New Economics Foundation 217, 226
New York Times 48, 52
New Zealand 115, 195
NGO Forum on Banning Anti-personnel Landmines 95
NGOs (nongovernmental organizations) 1-2, 39, 46, 67-68, 102, 104, 150, 157, 175, 216, 218-19, 203, 223-24, 230, 243-47 *See also* BINGOs; Civil society; DONGOs; GONGOs; GROs; INGOs; PINGOs; QUANGOs
    advocacy 6-9, 60, 64-65, 89-91, 116-17, 132-33, 141-42, 150, 156, 168, 175, 185-86, 217, 243, 246
    African 115
    and developing countries 178-79, 232-33
    and G7/G8 12-13, 215-38, 244-45
    and global governance 149-51, 175
    and IGOs 6, 10-13, 102, 150, 221, 223, 226, 236, 243-44, 246
    and landmines 95-104

and Quebec City Summit of the Americas 201-13
and Union of Concerned Scientists 43-45, 243
and United Nations 10-11, 112, 116, 141-53, 155-69, 236, 245
and WTO 11, 175-96
Asian 115
campaign against NMD 38-54, 243
classification 3, 6-7, 91, 142, 146, 151-52, 161, 176-79, 188, 192
Coalition for an International Criminal Court 9-10, 109-24, 244
    access to UN and government documents 113-14
    information dissemination 114-17, 119-20, 185-87
    regional and thematic networks 115
    secretariat 109-11
    use of ICT 9-10, 109-18, 120-24, 243-44
    use of media 109, 117, 120
    website 121
conformists 6, 177-78, 188
definition 2-3, 142, 156, 175
European 115
financing 109, 185-87
functional types 178-79, 188
interaction with governments 6, 98-99, 102, 115-18, 128-29, 133, 141-42, 144-45, 150, 175, 178, 181, 192-96, 212, 221, 223, 226, 243-46
international 1, 3, 9, 67-68, 80-92
internet use 7, 10, 34, 47, 63, 71, 76, 95, 100-103, 109, 131, 134, 176, 243-44
Latin American 115, 118
legitimacy 7, 20, 134-35, 193, 196, 245-46
Millennium NGO Forum, New York (2000) 151
networking 6-7, 25, 35, 72, 76, 90, 92, 102, 109-110, 115, 123, 155, 167, 178, 184, 186, 188, 191, 210, 243-44
radicals 6, 177-78, 185, 191-92
reformists 6, 177-78, 189-90
religious 1, 114, 155-69, 210, 219
    activities 162-67
    use of ICT 167-68
    witnessing 163
science-based 45
service-delivery 6-7, 60, 87, 102, 168, 243
Southern 7, 9, 67-92, 101, 114, 145-46, 177-79, 189, 196, 209, 243-45
    and international NGOs 9, 67-71, 80-92
    financing 70, 74, 76, 81-85, 87-92
    use of ICT 9, 67-80, 90-92, 116, 178, 186, 216, 243-45
technical networks 178
trade-related 6, 175-96, 175, 178-79, 244
    information dissemination 193
    transparency and legitimacy 193, 196
    use of ICT 11, 176, 178, 185-92, 196, 244
use of ICT 5, 7-13, 38, 47, 54, 95-96, 104, 109, 111-12, 116, 131, 155, 175-76, 181, 185, 196, 202-203, 216, 224, 236, 243-45

social and cultural
consequences 73-80
use of media technologies 98
Nicaragua 157
Nigeria 158, 222, 232
Nixon, Richard M. 41
NMD (National Missile Defence) 8, 37-54, 243
media coverage 51-52
Union of Concerned Scientists campaign against 38-54, 243
No Peace Without Justice International 110
Nobel prizes 52, 246-47
Nobel Peace Prize 10, 96, 128
Nolde, Frederick 159
Non-Aligned Movement 147
Nongovernmental organizations *See* NGOs
Nongovernmental social movements 2, 4, 67-68 *See also* Civil society; NGOs
Non-state actors 2-3, 12-13, 19, 24, 128, 131, 156-57, 221, 246 *See also* Civil society; NGOs
use of ICT 12, 104
Noor (Queen of Jordan) 101
Nordic countries 195
Norris, Pascale 115
North American Free Trade Agreement *See* NAFTA
North Korea 40, 43, 46-47
North-South 7, 9, 101, 103, 114, 127, 130, 132, 145-46, 155, 177-79, 186-87, 189, 196, 209, 222, 232
Northern Ireland 158
Norway 99
Nuclear weapons 37, 39-42, 44, 53
Nye, Joseph 182

OAS (Organization of American States) 205-207, 211
OAU (Organization of African Unity) 59
Al-Obaid, Abdullah Salaih 166
Obasanjo, Olusegun 222

O'Brien, Robert 2, 177-78, 188, 192-93
Obuchi, Keizo 220
OECD (Organisation for Economic Co-operation and Development) 151, 176, 224, 236
Offenheiser, Raymond 91
On the Record 117
Online activism *See* Activism
Open Society Institute
Landmines Project 102
Orbinski, James 7, 10, 127-37, 243-45
Organization of African Unity *See* OAU
Organization of American States *See* OAS
Orthodox churches 160 *See also* Russian Orthodox church
Ostry, Sylvia 6, 176, 178, 188-91
Ottaway, Marina 6
Our Global Neighbourhood 150
Oxfam America 57, 59
Oxfam Canada 58
Oxfam Education Report 63, 230
Oxfam Germany 57
Oxfam Great Britain 57-59, 63-64
Oxfam in Australia 61, 63
Oxfam International 6-8, 57-65, 127, 133, 177, 179, 219, 224, 228, 230, 234, 243
activities 58, 60-61-63-65
annual reports 58, 61-64
Education Now campaign 60-61, 224
fair trade initiative 60-61
financing and budget 59, 61-63
intranet 63
mandate, governance and structure 58-60, 62, 64
mission statement 58-59
policy papers 63, 65
public information 65
publications 63-64
strategic plans 58, 61-62, 64
use of ICT 8, 62-64, 243
Washington Advocacy Office 57, 59, 63, 65

website 62-65

Pace, William 9-10, 109-24, 243-46
Pakistan 158
Palestine 158
Panganiban, Rik 9-10, 109-24, 243-46
Paris Club 219
Park Ridge Center for the Study of Health, Faith, and Ethics 161, 169
Parliamentarians 120, 157, 203-207, 237
    See also Inter-Parliamentary Forum of the Americas
Parliamentarians for Global Action 110
Patents 130-31
Pauktuutit Inuit Women's Association 210
Pax Christi International 164
Peace 59, 114, 141, 155-56, 158-59, 161-67, 188, 216
Peace Action 45
Peoples' Global Action 177-78, 187, 191-92
    and WTO 191-92
    use of ICT 192
People's Summit [of the Americas], 2nd 208-209
Peters, Bill 219
Pettifor, Ann 224
Pharmaceutical corporations 13, 128-29, 131, 133, 136, 234, 237, 246
Philippines 67, 115, 158
PINGOs (public-interest-oriented NGOs) 3
Poland 121
Polish language 121
Population 1, 60, 77, 97, 128, 144-45, 149, 155-56, 164-65 See also International Conference on Population and Development
Portuguese language 121, 207
Poverty 59-60, 64, 70, 79, 141, 156, 163, 165, 218, 223, 225, 229, 231-32, 234-35
Private sector See Business sector

Presbyterian church 159
Proskauer, Joseph 159
Protestant denominations and organizations 157, 162, 164, 166
Protests See Anti-globalization movement; Demonstrations
Public Citizen's Global Trade Watch 176, 186-87, 190-91
    information dissemination 190
    use of ICT 191
Public goods 246
Public-interest-oriented NGOs See PINGOs

Qatar 181
Quakers 110, 162
QUANGOs (quasi NGOs) 3
Québec City Summit of the Americas See Summit of the Americas, Québec City (2001)

Racism 123
Radio 95, 176
Rainbow Warrior 224-25
Rainforest Action Network 81
Raiser, Konrad 166, 168
Reagan, Ronald 37, 42-43, 50
Reality Check 225
Redress 114
Refugees 10, 97, 128, 141 *See also* United Nations, High Commissioner for Refugees
Reinalda, Bob 3
Religion Counts 169
Religious conservatism and fundamentalism 158, 164-66
Religious freedom and tolerance 158, 160, 164, 166
Religious NGOs 1, 11, 114, 121, 155-69, 210, 244
    activities 162-67
    use of ICT 11, 155, 244

Renewing the United Nations 150
Republican Party (US) 39, 42-43, 47
Réseau québécois sur l'intégration continentale 208
Rice, Condoleezza 232
Ríos Montt, General 21
Rivlin, Benjamin 1, 4, 11, 155-69, 244
Roberts, Adam 67
Robertson, David 188
Robey, Duane 101
Robinson, Nobina 211
Rockwell, Keith 193
Rogue states 43, 47, 54
Rome Treaty, 1998 *See under* ICC
Roosevelt, Franklin D. 159
Rosenberg, Robin 211
Rúa, Fernando de la 208
Ruckus Society 177, 186
Rudgard, Stephen 69-70, 91
Ruggiero, Renato 180, 231
Rumsfeld, Donald 53
Ruse, Austin 165
Russia 37, 43, 46, 52-53, 97, 101, 127, 215, 232-33
Russian language 121
Russian Orthodox church 158
Rutherford, Kenneth 9, 95-104, 244
Rwanda 60, 88, 97

Sachs, Jeffrey 229
Satellite communications 19, 21, 42, 88, 244
Scajola, Claudio 231
Scholte, Jan Aart 2-4, 6, 177-78, 188, 192-93
Science and Scientists 37-54, 216, 243 *See also* Union of Concerned Scientists
SDI (Strategic Defense Initiative) 37-38, 42-44, 50
Security 7, 39, 42, 46, 50, 53-54, 100, 149, 155, 216, 224
Senegal 232

September 11, 2001 terrorist attacks 8, 10, 37-38, 54, 60, 124, 135, 181, 227, 245-46
Serbia 97
Sessler, Andrew M. 48
Seventh-Day Adventists 166
Shannon, C. E. 4
Shintoism 163, 166
Short, Clare 223
Sierra Leone 29
Sikhism 163, 166
Slavery 220
Smillie, Ian 69
Social justice 34, 59, 134-35, 156, 158, 161, 163-64, 169, 189, 218-19
Somalia 95, 97
South *See* North-South; Civil society, Southern; NGOs, Southern
South Africa 31, 121, 127, 133, 135, 222, 232
South America 9, 62, 68, 71, 115, 118, 132-33 *See also* Latin America
Southern Africa 61, 79, 233
Soviet Union 1, 41-43, 70, 127, 158, 160
Spanish language 121-22, 182, 187, 207
Spirit of Europe 226
Spykerman, John 8, 37-54, 243
Star Wars *See* SDI
Stern, Marc A. 2
Stoler, Andrew 193
Strategic Defense Initiative *See* SDI
Strengthening the International Financial System 233
Sudan 129, 158
Summit of the Americas *See also* Indigenous Peoples Summit; People's Summit [of the Americas]
    Miami (1994) 204
    Québec City (2001) 12, 201-13, 237
        and civil society 201-13

connectivity agenda 204-205
democratic clause 204
information campaign 206-207
Plan of Action 204-207, 209-11
preparations 205-208
security 207
use of ICT 205-207
Santiago (1998) 206, 208
Summit Implementation Review Group 205
Survey of Activities of Religious NGOs at the United Nations 164
Sustainable development 70, 123, 141, 148-49, 175, 177, 183, 206, 211, 217-19, 232-33
Switzerland 195

Taliban 101, 160
Tanzania 180-81
Taoism 166
Telecommunications 5, 32, 104
Telephones 80-81, 99, 123, 134, 187, 207
See also Mobile telephones
Teller, Edward 42
Terrorism 4, 54
September 11, 2001 attacks 8, 10, 37-38, 54, 60, 124, 135, 181, 227, 245-46
Text messaging 19
Thailand 222
Third World Network 177, 179, 187, 189-90
information dissemination 190
website 190
Tibet 166
TNCs (transnational corporations) *See* Multinational corporations
TOES (The Other Economic Summit) 217
Toronto Citizens' Summit (1988) 217
use of ICT 217

Tourism 148
Towards an Ever Closer Union 62
Towards Global Equity 58
Trade-related NGOs *See* NGOs: Trade-related
Trade unions *See* Labour unions
Traditional communication 8, 10, 19-20, 24-25, 35, 69, 74-75, 80-81, 90, 100, 103, 123, 134, 176, 184-87, 203, 207, 245-46
Transcaucasian area 9, 71
Transnational corporations *See* Multinational corporations
Transparency 30, 64, 141, 150, 176, 192-93, 195, 201-203, 205, 207, 209, 212-13, 217, 219, 244-45
Transportation 104
Treatment Access Campaign 127, 133
Tropical diseases 130
Tuberculosis 223, 229-30, 233
Tunisia 21, 27-28
Turner, Ted 165
Tute Bianche 231
Tutu, Desmond 220

Uganda 97
Ullrich, Heidi 4, 6, 11, 175-96, 244, 246
Uncivil society 4, 27, 177
UNCTAD (UN Conference on Trade and Development) 59
UNDP (UN Development Programme) 132, 162, 222
Unemployment 202
Union of Concerned Scientists 8, 37-54
ArmsNet e-mail network 47, 49-54
campaign against NMD 37-54
Sound Science Initiative 50
use of ICT 8, 38, 42-45, 50-51, 54, 243
Union of Industrial and Employers' Confederations of Europe 189
Unitarian Universalist Association 164

United Kingdom 39, 118-119, 215, 219, 232
United Methodist Church 160
United Nations 31, 59, 70, 95, 101, 109, 112-13, 115, 122-24, 163, 233, 243, 245
   accountability and transparency 141, 150
   agenda 156, 164
      and religion 157-61
   and civil society 10-11, 112, 116, 141-53, 155-69, 236, 245
   and NGOs 10-11, 112, 116, 141-53, 155-69, 236, 245
      formal and informal practices 10, 141-49
      review of arrangements 145-48
   and Oxfam International 59
   and religious NGOs 1, 11, 155-69
   Charter 158-59, 162
   Commission on Human Rights 160
   Commission on Social Development 147
   Commission on the Status of Women 147
   Department of Public Information 59
      NGOs in association with 143, 153, 161-62, 168
      website 153
   documents 113-14, 121, 123, 152-53
   Economic and Social Council 2, 59, 142-43, 146-49
      NGOs in consultative status with 142-43, 145-46, 148, 151-53, 159, 161-63, 168
   Economic Commission for Africa 151
   election monitoring 141
   General Assembly 114, 143, 146-50, 160, 162, 165, 228
      NGO participation 147-48, 150, 153
      Sixth Committee (Legal) 110-11, 116
   Global Compact 151
   High Commissioner for Refugees 162
   information activities 141-43
   membership 155
   Millennium Summit 151, 157
   Optical Disk System 10, 113, 147
   reform 146-47, 150, 217-18
   San Francisco Conference (1945) 159
   Secretariat 113, 141-42, 148
   Secretary-General 147-52, 165, 167
   Security Council 111, 146, 155, 161
      NGO participation 147
   world conferences 10, 123, 141, 143-46, 148, 155-56, 164
United Nations Conference on Environment and Development *See* Earth Summit
United Nations Conference on Human Settlements, 2nd, Istanbul (1996) 145, 156
   Habitat II+5 149
United Nations system 141, 146-47, 149, 155, 163, 169, 190
United States 8, 28-29, 37-43, 46-48, 50, 52-54, 60, 96, 119, 146-47, 159, 162, 191, 195, 210, 215
United States Campaign To Ban Landmines 99
United States Institute of Peace 163
Universal Declaration of Human Rights 19
University of Florida 211
Uruguay Round of trade negotiations 235

Vatican *See* Holy See
Videoconferencing 123, 244
Vietnam 21, 101
Vietnam Veterans of America Foundation 97, 102
Vietnam War 41-42, 44, 96
Virtual communities 5, 25, 35
Vivanco, José Miguel 211

Wack, John 101
Wallach, Lori 186, 190-91
War crimes 119-20
Wareham, Mary 99
Washington Post 48, 52
Weaver, W. 4
Web *See* World Wide Web
Weiss, Thomas G. 2, 4
Western hemisphere 12, 201, 203-207, 210-13 *See also* Hemispheric Social Alliance; Summit of the Americas
White, Jerry 100
WHO (World Health Organization) 132, 222-23, 232
Williams, Jody 100
  Nobel Peace Prize 96
Williams, Marc 2, 177-78, 188, 192-93
Willkie, Wendel 159
Wilson, Woodrow 159
Witnessing *See under* MSF; Religious NGOs
Women 11, 114-15, 127, 141, 144-45, 155, 159, 164-65, 168, 202, 208, 219, 228, 245 *See also* International Women's Decade; International Women's Year; United Nations, Commission on the Status of Women; World Conference on Women
Women's Caucus for Gender Justice 115
Women's Environment and Development Organization 114
Won Buddhism International 164
Woodroffe, Jessica 234-35
World Bank 13, 59, 65, 183, 194-95, 203-205, 219, 221-22, 232, 234, 237
  Prague meeting (2000) 175
World Civil Society Conference, Montreal, 1999 3
World Confederation of Labour 177
World Conference on Human Rights, Vienna (1993) 145, 156

World Conference on Religion and Peace 162-64
World Conference on Women, 2nd, Copenhagen (1980) 144
World Conference on Women, 3rd, Nairobi (1985) 144
World Conference on Women, 4th, Beijing (1995) 144, 156, 164-65
  Beijing+5 149, 165
World Council of Churches 114, 159, 166, 168
World Development Movement 230, 234
World Economic Forum 177
World Federalist Movement 9, 110-12
World Health Organization *See* WHO
World Summit for Social Development, Copenhagen (1995) 144, 156, 164
  WSSD+5 149
World Summit for Sustainable Development (2002) *See* Earth Summit, Rio+10 conference
World Trade Organization *See* WTO
World Union of Progressive Judaism 164
World War II 39, 44, 101, 216
World Wide Fund for Nature *See* WWF
World Wide Web 5, 21-22, 25-30, 33-34, 38, 42, 62-64, 71-72, 75-77, 88, 90, 99, 109, 111-15, 117, 121, 123, 134-35, 153, 155, 168, 180, 182, 185, 187, 190-94, 206-207, 217, 221, 225-27, 245
  misuse 27-29, 34, 79, 124, 167, 177, 183, 185
The World Will Never Be the Same Again 221
World's Parliament of Religions, Chicago (1893) 165-67
Wright, David 48
WTO (World Trade Organization) 13, 59, 130, 176, 193, 196, 203, 232, 234, 237
  and civil society 11, 175-96, 218, 244
  Guidelines for Arrangements 180

institutional aspects 179-81
   limitations of interaction 194-95
 and Global Trade Watch 190-91
 and International Chamber of
   Commerce 189
 and Peoples' Global Action 191-92
 dispute settlement procedures 176,
   192, 194
 documents 180, 182, 192, 196
 financing 194
 legitimacy 11, 192-93, 196, 244
 Millennium Round 178, 190-91
 ministerial meetings 180
   Doha (2001) 131-32, 134-37,
     181, 183, 188, 190-91
   Geneva (1998) 180
   Marrakesh (1994) 179
   NGO participation 180-81
   Seattle (1999) 6-7, 132, 175,
     178, 180-81, 188, 190-91, 216,
     218
   Singapore (1996) 180
 online forum 183
 public information 194
 reference centres 184
 reform 176, 181
 Secretariat 177, 179-81, 185, 189,
   193-95
 Trade and Development Centre 183
 transparency 11, 176, 192-93, 195,
   244
 TRIPS agreement 131-33, 135-37
 use of ICT 11, 180, 182-85
   limitations 183-85
 website 180, 182-83, 185, 187, 193-
   94
WWF (World Wide Fund for Nature) 177,
 185, 234

Ya Basta! 227
Yearbook of International Organizations 1-
 2, 70
Youth Forum of the Americas 207
Yuan, Weijing 5
Yugoslavia 111 *See also* International
 Criminal Tribunal for the Former
 Yugoslavia

Zoroastrians 163, 166
Zupi, Marco 234